Defeating Depression

Roslyn Law

ROBINSON

ROBINSON

First published in the UK by Robinson,
an imprint of Constable & Robinson Ltd., 2013

Reprinted in 2016 by Robinson

3 5 7 9 10 8 6 4

Important Note
This book is not intended as a substitute for medical advice or treatment.
Any person with a condition requiring medical attention should consult a
qualified medical practitioner or suitable therapist.

A CIP catalogue record for this book
is available from the British Library.

ISBN 978-1-84901-712-1

Printed and bound in Great Britain by
CPI Group (UK) Ltd, Croydon CR0 4YY

Papers used by Robinson are from well-managed forests
and other responsible sources

MIX
Paper from
responsible sources
FSC
www.fsc.org FSC® C104740

Robinson
An imprint of
Little, Brown Book Group
Carmelite House
50 Victoria Embankment
London EC4Y 0DZ

An Hachette UK Company
www.hachette.co.uk

www.littlebrown.co.uk

To Mum and Dad,
with love and thanks for their story.

Contents

Acknowledgements   ix

How to use this book   xi

1   Introduction: what can IPT do for you?   1

2   How IPT developed   15

3   Why stories are so important   29

4   Practising storytelling   51

5   What is your story about?   65

6   Understanding your depression   82

7   Your role in your recovery   111

8   Understanding the story of your depression   122

9   Your interpersonal inventory   148

10   Finding your story and selecting a focus   170

11   Setting achievable goals   187

12   The process of communication   197

13   Understanding emotions   230

14   Theme one: changing roles   251

15	Paul's story		287
16	Theme two: interpersonal role conflict		300
17	Suzanna's story		345
18	Theme three: grief and loss		359
19	Jean's story		394
20	Theme four: isolation		409
21	Miranda's story		449
22	Reviewing your progress and planning for the future		466
	References		487
	Appendix 1	Symptoms of depression: your weekly rating form	491
	Appendix 2	Interpersonal inventory diagrams	493
	Appendix 3	Monitoring links between symptoms and relationships	495
	Appendix 4	Information for family and friends	497
	Appendix 5	Early warning signs and response plan	505
	Appendix 6	What the research says	509
	Appendix 7	Useful links and contact details	517
	Index		521

Acknowledgements

I continue to owe thanks to the people who taught me about IPT in the first place, Edward McAnanama and Laurie Gillies, and to Ellen Frank for her unstinting support and warmth. Thanks are also due to Anthony Bateman and Alessandra Lemma for their generosity and encouragement during my time in London. I am very grateful to the friends and colleagues who generously gave their time in reading and commenting on earlier drafts of this book and listened to many, many versions of the story: Mark Matheson, Liz Robinson, Helen Birchall, Gwynn Binyon and Kate Halliday. Andrew Flynn helped enormously during our many discussions on the role of narrative and has been invaluable in helping me to develop my thoughts in this area. Many others have directly and indirectly contributed to this book by inspiring me and demonstrating its core principles in their friendship, and in particular I would like to thank Adrienne, Jo, M, Gilly and PD, who continually reminds me just what language can do. This book would not have come about were it not for Fritha Saunders and Constable & Robinson Publishers inviting me to write it, and I am grateful for the opportunity and challenge. I would also like to offer very grateful thanks to Gillian Somerscales, who was the embodiment of a good communicator in her encouraging, insightful and very helpful copy-editing. And most especially I am very grateful to all the people with whom I have worked and who have had the courage to share their stories. I am deeply and fortunately indebted.

How to use this book

One of the ironies of writing a self-help book on Interpersonal Psychotherapy (IPT) is that IPT, at its core, is – well, interpersonal: that is, it's about you *and other people*. That means it's not a private therapy, an approach to treating depression you can use on your own, because it is all about the interactions *between* people. The work of IPT happens in the space between people – how we relate to, communicate with and understand each other. And so there is a proviso in trying to use IPT as a self-help approach: in order for it to work, you have to involve other people. Approaching this treatment as a solo venture runs at odds with the social ideas about depression that we will use in this book – ideas that will be helpful when you are working towards recovery. The instinct to go it alone, however, tells us a lot about how easy it is to become isolated in depression, and why that makes it so difficult to ask for the help we need in order to recover.

I am going to suggest therefore that you are better placed to use IPT as a self-help approach if you think about how you *and the team you will recruit* are going to use this book. You might know your team already. They are the people you already talk to and spend time with – partners, friends, family, maybe your IPT therapist. The size of your team will be up to you, and you might involve people for different reasons. There might be a relatively small number of people with whom you feel comfortable sharing the detail of what you are doing, and another group you might want to tap into for different kinds of support and company. The people on your team are the people who are interested in your recovery and would like to help you to get there. You might have lost sight of who these people are while you have been depressed; or maybe you have yet to find them, and will need to go on a recruitment drive. Either way, IPT has some useful ideas about how a collective effort can help you to tackle depression.

By now you will probably have reacted in one of two ways. You may be relieved that you're not going to have to take this on alone; or you may be thinking perhaps this isn't the right approach for you, because you want to protect yourself and hide away from everyone else. Whichever reaction is uppermost for you, stick with me for a little longer, and we will consider how reducing depression and improving the quality of your relationships can be achieved from many different starting points. This book will show you many routes out of depression. It won't dictate the route you must take, but it will serve as a guide along the way, and will encourage and help you to consider who your most useful companions might be and when they should be invited along.

Chapter 1

Introduction:
what can IPT do for you?

The greatest challenge to any thinker is stating the problem in a way that will allow a solution.

BERTRAND RUSSELL, PHILOSOPHER

Interpersonal Therapy – IPT – focuses on the difficulties in relationships with other people that are often important in depression, recognizing that depression is likely both to spark relationship problems and to be the result of them. IPT isn't burdened by complicated explanations about why these problems happen. Instead, it looks at the day-to-day difficulties you may be experiencing in keeping relationships going or in sorting out the inevitable problems with other people that develop when you are depressed, and helps you to disentangle the two strands.

IPT is a well-researched and well-practised approach that has been used effectively for over forty years in lifting people out of depression and helping them to stay well for longer. It has helped people of all ages from teenagers to women and men well into their retirement. IPT has also helped people with eating disorders, bipolar disorder (a mix of very high and low moods) and some anxiety problems. This book will focus on IPT as a treatment for depression, although the basic ideas and themes are similar for everyone who uses it, no matter what the problem they are experiencing. A summary of the research findings on IPT is provided in appendix 6.

IPT doesn't use much jargon but works through refreshingly simple and pragmatic ideas. It deliberately focuses on what will be realistic for you and useful to you now. The basic aim is to help you to learn to track the links between your symptoms of depression and what is going on in your relationships, and to recognize that by tackling the relationship problems you can improve your relationships and your depression at the same time.

John

John finds it very difficult to sleep. As a result, he often lacks energy and motivation. Feeling physically washed out and having little interest in things, he tends to back out of plans, because it feels like too much effort to be around other people. Over time his friends begin to feel neglected because their invitations are repeatedly turned down. Gradually the unexplained change in his routine creates problems in a number of John's relationships, and he feels more and more isolated. Trying to tackle this problem when he is already struggling to get through the day feels just too much, and John withdraws further into himself and into depression.

Now imagine that John started to pinpoint some reasons why his sleep had become disrupted, e.g. drinking too many cups of coffee as a stimulant to get him through the day and falling into the habit of a daytime nap to boost his energy. By tackling these unhelpful routines and changing them to more *anti-depressant routines,* such as cutting down on the amount of coffee he drinks and taking a short walk with a colleague at lunchtime instead of having a nap, he can re-establish a more restful sleep routine. Waking refreshed can give a remarkably different look to the day, and it helps him to find the energy and motivation to explain more clearly to his friends why he does not currently feel up to all of his normal activities – and, importantly, he now feels able to work out alternative plans with his friends for what he *does* feel up to doing. In this way the relationship problems that came tumbling around his disrupted sleep pattern are minimized or averted, in turn making it easier for him to relax and enjoy his friends' company.

The above example is very simple and, of course, not all difficulties can be sorted out in such a straightforward way. In IPT you will gradually build up a picture of your own depression and how it overlaps with your current interpersonal circumstances – that is, what is going on between you and the people around you – to help you to work out a personal plan that will help you to break out of your repeating, unhelpful cycle.

As you work with this book you will come across exercises in many of the chapters. These will ask you to think about your depression and your relationships in more detail. It's a good idea to keep a notebook in which you can write down the questions and the thoughts you come up with in answering them. Remember to add the date each time you do an exercise: that way, you can refer back to what you've written, discuss it with your IPT team and update your thoughts as you go along. Also, many of the exercises will be referred back to later in the book, so it will be helpful to be able to go back to them whenever you need to.

The diagram below illustrates how depressive symptoms and relationships can become intertwined in a self-perpetuating sequence.

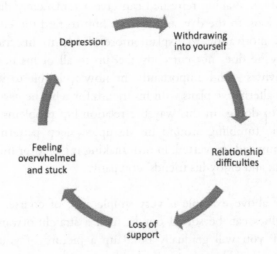

Exercise 1.1: Identifying the cycle of depression and relationship difficulties

- Can you see yourself in this cycle or one that is similar?
- How could you change the repeating pattern?
- Who would be involved in making those changes?

IPT in outline: three phases, four themes

IPT has a relatively flexible structure that continues over three interconnected phases. Each phase has its own tasks and goals, and these will inform the phases to come, and pick up on the work already completed.

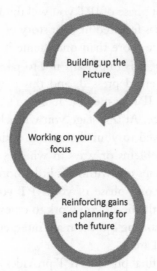

During the first phase you set the scene. Depression does not exist in a vacuum, and so you will be encouraged to see it in context. You will look at your depression very closely and work out which relationships provide the most important backdrop to your story. This is at the heart of IPT – linking depression to your relationships. Relationship problems don't directly cause depression, or vice versa, but each can each keep the other going. The points at which symptoms and relationship difficulties overlap will become the focus for the rest of your IPT.

IPT suggests four main themes, which are common problem areas for many people with depression. These are sometimes called 'focal areas', that is, common difficulties on which it is useful to focus attention. The four themes are:

- change
- conflict
- loss
- isolation

During the first phase of IPT you will think about how each of these themes has featured in your story of depression. Often you will recognize more than one theme in your life, maybe three or four; but it is important not to take on too much at once when you are depressed, and this is where one of the main benefits of IPT comes in. It doesn't ask you to tackle everything at once. At this stage you will select just one main theme that is linked to your depression. Often this will relate to unresolved problems or ways in which you feel stuck and unable to sort things out without a little more help.

During the second phase of your IPT you will repeatedly refer back to this theme, as you work to relieve your symptoms of depression by sorting out the main interpersonal difficulty in your chosen focal area.

The third and final phase of IPT provides an opportunity to review what you have done, reinforce what you have achieved and plan how to keep that going in the future.

So IPT is a clearly focused therapy. It is also a time-limited therapy, typically completed over twelve to sixteen weekly sessions when used with a therapist. This time limit is used for a number of reasons:

- Untreated episodes of depression often last for around six months, sometimes longer. Actively sorting out current relationship problems increases the likelihood of a quicker recovery.
- IPT takes advantage of the fact that many of us respond to a deadline, even if it is one that we set for ourselves. We marshal our energy and attention in anticipation of the psychological finishing line.
- Focusing our energy over a short period feels more manageable than having to keep going until everything is 'fixed'. When we are depressed, we often find that

energy and motivation are in short supply, so it is best not to use them up at the prospect of getting started.

The time limit can also help you and the people around you to focus your minds on what has to be done. One way to get stuck in depression is getting distracted by side issues. We can end up circling around problems, changing bits and pieces here and there but never quite getting down to the real changes that are necessary. This might happen for a number of reasons, including feeling unclear about what the problem actually is, not knowing how or where to start, or lacking the confidence to make big changes. Research has shown that if you set realistic goals to work towards on a clear and manageable timescale, you are more likely to make a start and to keep going. When everything feels bad it is natural to wish that everything would feel better. However, 'feeling better' and 'everything' can be difficult to define and therefore difficult to achieve. IPT will help you to focus more carefully on what 'feeling better' will involve and how that can be achieved.

So:

- Set yourself a realistic timescale to work through this book – around ten to twelve weeks is usually about right – and pace your efforts accordingly. Some people will work through the chapters more quickly, and others will prefer to take their time, perhaps going over a chapter more than once. Don't feel under pressure to rush through to the end – you can pause and come back to the place where you left off any time you feel you need to. It may feel too much to work through the whole book in one go, so think about setting yourself smaller goals to help you along the way. You might, for instance, find it helpful to read the case examples first to get a feel for IPT; or you might find it helpful to read through a chapter and then go back and try the exercises when you have a better sense of what each section is about. Whichever approach you take, write the date you are working towards for each goal you set in your notebook. This will help you to stay focused and to see the benefits of the work you are doing.

Using support from the people around you

Recovery is a team process in IPT. Now is the time to start thinking about who might be useful to have on your team. Exercise 1.2 sets out some questions that will help you in considering whom to recruit.

Exercise 1.2: Thinking about putting your team together

- Who is interested in your recovery and could help you to achieve it?
- Who knows you bought this book and that you are using it to help with your depression?
- Who do you think it would be useful to tell?
- How well do those people understand the nature of depressive illness and, importantly, how well do they understand your experience of depression?
- If they do not understand well, what could you tell them to help them to understand better? (Appendix 4, which you can copy as a handout for family and friends, can help here.)
- If they do understand, do you think you are making the most of the support they can offer you?
- How could you make better use of the support that is available to you?

You will be asked to discuss many of the ideas and exercises set out in this book with your IPT team. Starting to think about who can support you and how letting them know what you are trying to do will help you to make the most of the suggestions in this book. Don't worry if you are still unsure who your team members will be. The exercises in the chapters to come will help you to identify the people who will be in the best position to support you and will help you to ask for this support.

A closer look: ITP step by step

This section of the chapter outlines the important steps in IPT and gives you an idea of how they are covered in the chapters that follow.

UNDERSTANDING YOUR DEPRESSION

So far I have referred to 'depression' as a catch-all term. The first thing you will be asked to do is to think about your own experience of depression in more detail, to recognize the different symptoms and their effects, so that you become an expert in your own depression. Many people experience depression more than once in their lifetime, and while the IPT approach will focus most attention on current concerns, it will be useful to understand how your recent difficulties may fit into a longer history of depression over your lifetime and to link your personal experience to what research has revealed about being depressed. We will look at this in chapter 6.

YOUR ROLE IN RECOVERY AND THE PART OTHER PEOPLE WILL PLAY

Recovering from depression is an active process and a team effort in IPT. What you will learn about depression and its personal impact on your life will help you decide what you have to do to make the changes you want to see. It will be your responsibility to make anti-depressant choices – that is, choices that reduce depression – in your behaviour and relationships, and the people you are close to will play a crucial role in supporting you to do this. We will look at how you can do this in chapter 7.

UNDERSTANDING THE STORY OF YOUR DEPRESSION

IPT makes use of your own stories to help you understand the events that contributed to your current difficulties. You will create a timeline, which will highlight the main events around the time you became depressed, especially those that involved other people. This will help you to pinpoint when depression started, what was going on at the time and what continues to trouble you now. We will look at the value of stories in chapter 3 and how to create your own timeline in chapter 8.

YOUR INTERPERSONAL WORLD

As IPT focuses very carefully on the links between depression and your current interpersonal problems it is important to look closely at the people around you and think about how they will feature in your recovery plan. 'Interpersonal' refers to interactions between people, and the problems you experience might relate not only to people you have close relationships with but also people you interact with on a more casual or occasional basis, perhaps not even thinking of yourself as having a relationship with them. You will map out an inventory of your current relationships, both the close and the more distant, which will help you to see where you can find support and which relationships are most closely tied to your depression right now. We will look at this in chapter 9.

FINDING THE LINKS AND FOCUS

In helping you to focus on an area you can work on, IPT draws on the four interpersonal themes listed above that are common in many people's experience of depression, and in our relationships with other people: change, conflict, loss and isolation. You might recognize more than one theme in your own experience. The IPT process will help you to identify which themes are important in your life, and to select a manageable chunk of the big picture to focus on, so that you can begin to make change. We will look at these themes in chapter 5, and then at how you can select the most useful one for yourself and set relevant and realistic goals in chapters 10 and 11.

WHAT ARE YOU SAYING OR NOT SAYING?

IPT operates in the space between people, and so the more the people around you, such as your family and friends, understand about how difficult it is to live with depression and to make the changes you are trying to make, the more they will be able to help you. This does not mean everyone needs to know all of your business, but the IPT process will help you to consider who needs to know what and how they can help. We will look at how you can communicate more effectively in chapter 12.

WHAT ARE YOU FEELING?

Acknowledging, naming and talking about your feelings features at every step of IPT. Feelings are used to help you to understand your own situation and responses and to talk more effectively with the people around you. We will look at this in chapter 13.

STAYING ON TRACK

When we face a complex situation, it can be tempting to try to tackle all our difficulties at once. This can lead to feeling overwhelmed and giving up on any attempts to make change. This is why IPT suggests that you focus on only one, or possibly two, central themes at a time, even if you feel all four apply to your own depression. To help keep you focused on your chosen theme, it is useful to start with a general overview of how it features in your experience, followed by more detailed attention to your feelings and expectations and ways of talking about the problem with other people. This will help you to consider and plan alternative ways to approach the problem. Specific ideas related to the focus you choose will be suggested and you will be guided to use them in making helpful changes. The boundaries are not rigidly set between the interpersonal themes, but for clarity's sake the main goals and strategies for each of the IPT focal areas are described in turn over chapters 14–21, with detailed examples provided for each area to help you to think about how the individual themes relate to your personal story.

KEEPING IT GOING

IPT focuses on current difficulties, but we know that for many people depression is an illness that recurs. In concluding this process you will think about what skills and which relationships will be important for you to take with you to sustain the changes you have made into the future. We will look at this in chapter 22.

The IPT approach fully appreciates the complexity of the lives we live. It is exactly because of this complexity that you are encouraged to simplify your goals. Trying to cope with too many things at once rarely leads to progress. Many people with depression try over and over again to make changes, only to feel overwhelmed by the prospect of all that needs to be done and so sink back into the despondency they felt at the start. Tackling one thing at a time, and tolerating some other things being temporarily set aside, creates much more scope for change. Imagine trying to disentangle the knot of cables behind your television. If you plunge in with both hands and pull in all directions the cables are likely to become even more tangled and knotted. If, on the other hand, you take one cable and follow it through the loops and spirals it forms around the others, progress may be slow but the knots will loosen and the cable will eventually come free. What is more, some of the cables you were *not* trying to disentangle will have found their way out of the knot as well, as an indirect result. This is how IPT tries to tackle the problems of living – one at a time.

Knowing something about the ideas and principles that guided the development of IPT will be helpful as you consider what it can offer you – so this is where we will start with the next chapter.

Summary

- IPT is not a private therapy that will only involve you. It works in the 'interpersonal' space between people.
- The basic aim is to help you to learn to track the links between your symptoms of depression and what is happening in your relationships with other people – relationships of all sorts, distant or close, fleeting or permanent. By constructively tackling problems in

relationships, you can ease your depression and improve your relationships with other people at the same time.

- IPT has three phases which will help you to build up a detailed picture, work on a current interpersonal difficulty and plan for the future.
- IPT focuses on four interpersonal themes: change, conflict, loss and isolation.

Chapter 2

How IPT developed

*In approaching the subject of mental disorder, I must empha-
size that, in my view, persons showing mental disorder do
not manifest anything specifically different in kind from what
is manifest by practically all human beings.*

HARRY STACK SULLIVAN, PSYCHIATRIST

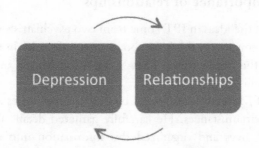

The origins of IPT are clear in the way it works. It was developed
in the 1970s by Gerry Klerman and his colleagues – a group of
psychiatrists, psychotherapists, social workers and researchers
who were interested in how the social, biological and psychological parts of depression overlap, and how they could be used
together in treatment. They did not try to develop another
novel approach to treating depression, when so many already
existed. Instead, they learned from ideas that had already been

developed and thoroughly researched, believing a collaborative approach would be more robust than any individual strand of thinking alone. And so they drew together a range of ideas from well-researched good practice, somewhat like a jigsaw puzzle in which a number of pieces are arranged to make a more coherent bigger picture.

Clinical experience and research evidence at the time led them to use relationships as a backdrop for understanding depression. Many academics had written about depression and the importance of relationships in understanding and managing its impact, but current relationships did not yet figure as a main focus of the major treatment approaches. This was something new in IPT.

The importance of relationships

Many of the ideas in IPT come from two psychiatrists who had a major impact on thinking about mental disorder in the early part of the last century. They were Adolf Meyer and Harry Stack Sullivan.

Adolf Meyer was fascinated by people's life stories and day-to-day circumstances. He carefully gathered details about his patients' lives and organized this information into comprehensive timelines, which set out the step-by-step sequence of events over the course of each person's life. In gathering the detail of events and ordering them like this he was trying to capture the many overlapping stories that characterize all of our lives. This type of detailed attention to many forms of personal story is a significant feature of IPT.

In the case examples in this book you will read about:

- Paul, whose life was thrown into disarray when he lost his job and he was faced with trying to develop better relationships with his family, who had been ignored when his life had revolved around work (see chapter 15);

- Suzanna, who became depressed when the on–off pattern in her relationship with her long-term partner became so uncertain that she was not sure from week to week whether they were still together and whether they had a future together (see chapter 17);
- Jean, who struggled to come to terms with the death of her husband some years earlier and became increasingly exhausted as attempt after attempt to fill her time and occupy her mind wore her down (see chapter 19);
- Miranda, who found it very difficult to make relationships and had little to fall back on when her one friend moved away and once again she felt on the outside of the world around her (see chapter 21).

Meyer was greatly influenced by a philosophical tradition called 'pragmatism', which believes in the importance of logical reasoning behind what we think and what we do. Pragmatists would argue that if an idea works in practice it should be used, and if it doesn't, it should be given up. For example, when you are unwell, it is reasonable to believe that taking a break from some of the demanding or draining things you do day to day will help you recover more quickly. The truth of the idea is seen in your speedy recovery. It would not be pragmatic to think that you could continue to do everything you normally do and still recover just as quickly. The flaw in that idea would be evident when you took longer to recover. By taking a pragmatic approach, we can avoid getting stuck with ideas that we may treasure but which are of little practical use to us and may actually be unhelpful.

One example of a treasured idea that Meyer focused on was *diagnosis*. He warned against using diagnosis as a convenient shorthand, that is, a simple label that is familiar and easy, but may suggest more understanding than is actually the case. 'Depression' as an idea is only useful if it describes our actual experience. Meyer insisted that a person's attempts to adapt to their specific circumstances should not to be overlooked in preference for a simple label. For example, dismissing someone as 'just depressed' fails to appreciate all the difficulties the person might have in coping with the pressures and demands of life. He argued that we are best understood in the context of our day-to-day lives, and saw the symptoms of depression as our attempts to cope with our life situations. When 'depression' is used in IPT it is always seen through what is happening in our relationships: that is, it is the interaction, rather than the label, that is the main focus of our attention. We are encouraged to examine the impact of depression in our lives with care, so that we become experts in our own depression.

In this way Meyer redirected attention from the unconscious and invisible – the focus of psychoanalysis – to the observable and known. In other words, he focused on the practical realities in the lives people live and the challenges they grapple with. So in the example of John in the previous chapter (see page 2), the focus would be not on John's unconscious mind or suppressed emotions, but on how his difficulty in sleeping was affecting his friendships, what he could do to help himself sleep better, and how he could communicate better with his friends about how he was feeling.

Meyer was curious about the shifting interplay between what happens in our bodies, minds and relationships. He recognized that different interactions could make a person vulnerable or could protect them against depression. If you are physically healthy, with an even temperament, good coping skills and secure and stable relationships, this all offers protection against depression. If any of these features change, for example if you become physically unwell or an important relationship breaks down, you become more vulnerable to depression. Our physical and mental make-up is not rigidly set, but will change over time and in response to circumstances. With these changes comes a corresponding change in our vulnerability to depression. Understanding this interplay and its implications for life right now is at the heart of IPT.

Harry Stack Sullivan was a psychiatrist who studied with Meyer. He stressed the importance of the *interpersonal* over the *intrapersonal* – that is, what happens *between people* rather than what happens *inside a person*. Sullivan particularly focused on how people manage the difficulties and opportunities thrown up by their relationships, which he described as the 'problems of living'. He was the first to coin the now well-used term 'significant others' and stressed the developmental significance of having a 'chum'. He used this term to refer to a child's first close friendship motivated by mutual interest, which marks the progression from relationships simply being a means to an end. Sullivan considered the lack of connection with other people, in other words loneliness, to be the most painful of all human experiences. In contrast, he argued, 'when the satisfaction or the security of another person becomes as significant to one as one's own satisfaction or security, then the state of love exists.' In other words, our well-being comes from our relationships; we all need someone to care for – and, by implication, to care for us.

Sullivan believed that our personality is formed *in* our relationships, as we adjust and adapt to the demands and opportunities they present. Our way of being with other people is, effectively, who we are. He believed that good mental health reflected good relationships and poor mental health occurred when relationships did not lead to feelings of satisfaction or security. For example, if someone's relationships were too rigid or too complicated, they might well have problems, especially if those patterns appeared across their relationships. This view of mental disorder as a struggle to cope with the demands of relating to other people in our lives influenced IPT, where depression is treated by focusing on key themes and difficulties in relationships This is where the four key themes introduced earlier come in: change, conflict, loss and isolation.

Repeating patterns

Sullivan was interested in how repeating patterns occur in relationships, setting up a cycle of habitual responses that block genuine connection and communication. If we repeatedly behave in the same way, we can unintentionally prompt other people to make the same unhelpful responses that have been upsetting in the past. In relationships, one size does not fit all, and this unhelpful inflexibility can be the basis for poor mental health.

It's because human relationships tend to be repetitive, going through the same patterns over time, that IPT focuses on relationships in the here and now. When a relationship gets into difficulty there is often a heart-sinking moment when the picture starts to look all too familiar, and we wonder, 'How did I end up here again?' IPT looks at the pattern as it plays out now, rather than where it came from. Looking at relationships in the here and now, rather than in the past, opens up the possibility of directly working on change now and into the future.

Julie

Julie became depressed when she broke up with her boyfriend. They had been together for two months and she had hoped they would have a future together. Julie had met her boyfriend through internet dating and had been delighted when the relationship progressed quickly. Her boyfriend told her he loved her on their second date and she said she felt the same way. But the relationship had not developed in the way she had hoped and she soon felt taken for granted. Julie was disappointed, but felt unable to talk about this with her boyfriend, as she feared complaining would push him away. While she was in the relationship she didn't see much of her friends, nor did she tell them about her growing dissatisfaction with it. When the break-up happened, she turned to them for support but they couldn't help her to understand why the relationship had ended because Julie had concealed her doubts and difficulties. Julie felt hopeless and confused when she saw how closely the pattern matched each of her past intimate relationships. Each of them had started rapidly and intensely, but none had lasted more than a few months, every one coming to an end when her partners lost interest and drifted away.

The British psychologist John Bowlby was also interested in the idea of repeating patterns. He described long-term relationships as 'attachments', and wrote eloquently about the relationship 'dance' that each of us learns in childhood. Infants must develop a relationship with a caregiver, usually a parent, in order to develop mentally, socially and emotionally. The interaction between the caregiver and child in these early relationships shapes the quality of the attachment, creating feelings of security, insecurity or perhaps ambivalence in the growing child. These early experiences become a working template that will guide our experience in later relationships. If we learn to follow the music and adapt as the tempo changes, we are well placed to dance with many different people throughout our lives. However, if we only learn one set of steps, to one rhythm, we hit difficulties when the people we meet are dancing to a different tune. These early experiences can give us confidence that our needs will be met by other people, and so the dance flows, or they can lead us to fear that other people will be unreliable and may even cause us harm, and so we bump and clash and stand on each other's toes.

We tend to be reasonably consistent as individuals in the way we approach and respond in our relationships, even if that means being consistently inconsistent, and the expectations and relationship skills we develop at an early age are evident in all of the relationships that follow. They might lead to a relaxed, give-and-take approach, if we feel secure that our needs will be met, or to an anxious search for attention, if we feel uncertain that other people will be there when we need them. In the first scenario, relationships are likely to form and continue without much difficulty, confirming the positive expectation. In the second scenario, problems might develop when other people resist our anxious demands or fail to meet our needs, thus confirming our negative expectation and so repeating the pattern.

The American psychologists Cindy Havan and Phil Shaver suggested that many adult relationships fall into one of four patterns, as set out in the chart below, revealing attachment patterns established in childhood and repeated as adults.

Secure attachment	Dismissing attachment
Key features: a sense of worth and confidence, an ability to ask for help and to cope independently when necessary. *Relationships are often stable and long lasting*	Key features: distrust of others and a surface appearance of independence, while being more fragile underneath. Others might be treated coldly if they get close. *Relationships are often distant and vulnerable to breaking down*
Preoccupied attachment	Disorganized attachment
Key features: uncertainty about being able to cope, focus on others helping and a greater than average fearfulness if support is lost. *Relationships are often intense and difficult to sustain*	Key features: suspicion and confusion around others, sometimes approaching and sometimes avoiding, with other people provoking and soothing fear at the same time. *Relationships are often unstable and difficult to sustain*

Bowlby's work was very important in understanding our social foundations as human beings and reinforces the interpersonal perspective used in IPT. Bowlby, like Meyer and Sullivan, stressed the significance of personal relationships in how we develop as people, and emphasized that when close ties are broken, or inflexible relationship patterns are repeated, we become more vulnerable to depression. This link between depression and the quality of our relationships is at the heart of IPT.

Finding a new pattern

Bowlby's important work was developed by Michael Rutter, who was the first consultant in child psychiatry in the UK.

His research demonstrated that we are not absolutely bound to repeat early relationship patterns. Our experience of later relationships can help us to develop new skills and understanding. These new experiences compensate to some extent for poor experiences earlier in life and begin to heal the wounds that remain. This is very encouraging because it means that, while you may be vulnerable to depression, it is possible to manage that vulnerability by developing more helpful and positive ways to interact with other people.

This adaptive capacity, which promotes well-being and protects against depression, is called resilience. It is often thought that this capacity must be part of our make up, but just like all of the other patterns described so far, it can be learned. Many things contribute to resilience, the most important of which are having caring and supportive relationships and using them when we face difficulties. Alongside this openness to being helped by others, resilience requires a readiness to take care of oneself and to persevere when faced with the challenges of living. If we can accept that life is sometimes difficult and inevitably changes over time, we are more likely to be able to see beyond our immediate circumstances and stay optimistic about the future. Talking about what troubles us, temporarily tolerating strong emotions and setting achievable goals that take us in the direction we want to go, all of which are targeted directly in IPT, contribute to our resilience. This is more than simply being 'tough', and relies on a combination of personal resourcefulness and looking outside yourself and to others to help you to manage the inevitable 'problems of living'.

The American Psychological Association describes 'Ten Ways to Build Resilience', and a link to a full description is available in appendix 7.

Margaret

Margaret faced an enormous challenge when she was diagnosed with cancer. Immediately she surrounded herself with friends and family, who accompanied her on each step of her journey through treatment. She identified who could offer practical help and who could support her emotionally, and used the support people were best able to provide. She recognized that she had a number of important decisions to make and gave herself a realistic timescale in which to plan the changes she had to make in her life, marking the way with smaller milestones. She involved people who could provide relevant information, and balanced the difficult and challenging times with enjoyable and relaxed times with friends and family, who could boost her energy and help her to continue when her motivation and positive approach faded at times. She distinguished between the difficulties and issues that were related to her health and those that were the natural consequences of living, such as disappointment over missed opportunities, financial worries and not having enough time to balance competing demands. With this resilience, she was able to accept that some difficulties were more likely to come into sharp focus during a crisis but could be expected to fade back into the background in the future.

Biology and symptoms

The development of IPT was influenced by increasing medical and biological understanding of depression. It is now understood that depression is not just a passing low mood or 'the blues', but is an illness with recognizable symptoms. These symptoms are used to make a diagnosis, and the illness can then be treated appropriately and effectively.

Knowing about the symptoms of depression can help you to track the ways in which it interferes with your life and to target your efforts to recover. These symptoms occur in various combinations and can be physical, emotional and cognitive (mental). The main ones include the following:

- feeling sad;
- having difficulty motivating yourself and enjoying things;
- trouble sleeping;
- feeling tired;
- losing your appetite or overeating;
- feeling guilty and to blame for everything;
- having difficulty concentrating;
- having difficulty making decisions;
- thinking that life is not worth living.

Individual experiences of depression vary, and not everyone will experience all of these symptoms all of the time. Several other symptoms might also be added to the list, such as low self-confidence and self-esteem, less interest in sex than usual, and feeling irritable and intolerant of other people. Whatever particular symptoms cluster you experience, managing or recovering from the illness involves identifying that depression is the underlying problem and then understanding your own personal experience of depression in the context of your own life in order to treat or manage it effectively.

IPT combines expertise from more than one source, and importantly, this includes you as the expert on your own experience. Drawing on what is known about depression, it will provide you with reliable information about the disorder to help you to become an expert in depression *as it affects you*. In IPT, the person with depression is not secondary to the diagnosis: we understand and treat depression in context, that is, we look at how it is affecting *your* relationships and *your* life. The symptoms of depression are used to confirm the disorder, to track how it develops over time and to identify the relationships in your life that are most directly affected. As the symptoms lift, your relationships are under less pressure and, as relationship problems are sorted out, the symptoms of depression are triggered less often.

Coming back to the pragmatic origins of IPT, all these interesting ideas are only really of use if they actually work in practice. This challenge has been taken very seriously by IPT and it is now one of the best-researched therapies for the treatment of depression, with hundreds of published studies reporting on how it has helped people with this illness. As a result, it is one of the few talking therapies that is included in guidelines recommending the treatments most likely to be helpful for depression in the UK, the USA, Australia and across Europe (see appendix 6).

Now you know a bit about where IPT came from, and why it is so firmly rooted in our relationships with other people, it is time to turn to some of the key ideas in how you can use the therapy. We begin in the next chapter with one of the most basic ways of understanding our lives: telling stories.

Summary

- In IPT, timelines are used to set out the step-by-step sequence of events and to capture the many overlapping stories in our lives.
- Each of us is best understood in the context of our day-to-day life.

- At the heart of IPT is curiosity about the interaction between body, mind and relationships.
- IPT is about change and building resilience.
- IPT combines expertise in depression with expertise about your life.

Chapter 3

Why stories are so important

We dream in narrative, daydream in narrative, remember, anticipate, hope, despair, believe, doubt, plan, revise, criticize, construct, gossip, learn, hate, and love by narrative.

BARBARA HARDY, LITERARY CRITIC,
BIOGRAPHER AND POET

Read the list above and it seems only reasonable to ask: can we also recover from depression by narrative?

Using narrative or stories has been part of human experience for as long as we have been able to communicate. Storytelling has been used to inform, entertain and educate from one generation to the next and the next. This is the case across all cultures and periods of history. It is the dominant form of interaction in our lives. People have found many ways to tell stories, from cave drawings depicting the journey of a community, and the oral tradition of sharing ideas and values through song and poetry and over the garden fence, to the written stories that fill our bookshops. Many forms of story will have featured in your own life, including fairy tales told in childhood, legends portrayed in books and on film, biographies of significant people and commentaries in daily newspapers. Some stories aim to communicate universal truths or ideas, while others will be delivered on a much more personal and day-to-day level.

Stories provide a vehicle to communicate ideas and messages that makes them more easily accessible than lists of facts or random, scattered details. When you enter into the world created by a story it can provoke feelings that give you insights that the raw facts would never have achieved alone – a felt sense of what it is about. This is true for both the person telling the story and the person listening to it. You may have noticed that you often understand what you think about something more clearly when you have to explain it to someone else. The very act of organizing the information in order to share it adds to our understanding. As the writer E. M. Forster put it, 'How can I know what I think until I see what I say?' It's clear from the very persistence of storytelling across human history how valuable and important this process is, both for the person who understands, through creating the story or passing it on, and those whose understanding is enhanced by hearing it.

We have all experienced the subtle and sometimes dramatic differences that are revealed when several people tell the same story from their own points of view or when they try to tell the story together, each pitching in with the moments that were significant for them. The individual stories capture different fragments of the big picture, and it can sometimes be difficult to piece them together. A story that communicates a personal perspective, but also includes feelings and ideas from other points of view, is richer and more revealing than one confined to the one perspective alone. Keeping your own voice at the centre while drawing on several sources can be a real challenge when you are depressed. Simply remembering the different parts of your own experience, let alone taking into account someone else's perspective, is really difficult when your thinking narrows down and becomes inflexible. However, re-establishing your ability to step back and look afresh at perplexing and painful experiences is central to stepping out of the prison depression can create. By developing your storytelling skills you will find a vehicle to do this.

Why do I need a story at all?

Storytelling is something we are asked to do all the time, even if we are not aware of it. When someone asks how your day has been, this demands a kind of story – the story of your day. In return, you might offer a story vivid with detail and characters and events, or you might brush aside the request in a single word, 'fine' or 'terrible'.

When you become unwell you can't avoid the need to tell a story. Family or friends ask for an explanation when they see a change in you. Employers ask for an explanation when your work performance suffers or you have to take time off. Healthcare professionals ask you over and over to tell your story to guide their attempts to help. Perhaps you are using IPT with a therapist, and you are trying to understand your story together. These stories will serve different functions and will take different forms. Providing these stories is all the more difficult if you are not quite sure what is going on yourself.

Frank's stories

When Frank spoke to his boss about his time off work, he was organized and specific in his explanation and focused on the facts he had learned about depression, which could help them both to understand the difficulties he had been having at work and the adjustments that would help his recovery.

When he spoke to his IPT therapist, he brought fragments of feelings and reactions, and they worked together
to create a story that helped him to make sense of experiences that had confused and distressed him.

At work, the story was the tool Frank used to help his
own and his boss's understanding; in therapy, it was the
product he and his therapist created together. The natures
of these stories were quite different, but each could be
used to serve Frank in settings where he and another person needed to understand to help him to move forward.

The reason we tell stories in IPT is in order to make sense
of our current experiences. The story of a period of depression
is a story within a story. That bigger story is the story of your
life. An episode of depression can feel like a poorly understood
diversion, taking you away from the track you expected to follow. This has been called the 'anti-plot' – a narrative that takes
off in a direction completely different from the main story.
With depression the main direction of your life story is interrupted and redirected by a force that is not entirely under your
control. In IPT the basic themes of change, conflict, loss and
isolation offer you some initial structures around which you
can think about building your story, and the ideas presented in
the chapters to come offer signposts through uncharted terri-
tory and around the anti-plot.

The story you will focus on will be your own story of
depression, and the process we follow in IPT will help you to
capture some of the different voices and layers to your story.
The layers will be built up one after the other, perhaps starting
with the simple sequence of events, then a layer that describes
the physical setting, another that adds detail on the feelings and
symptoms that were triggered and another that populates the
story with the characters involved and their different points

of view. Each layer will be gradually gathered during the first phase of IPT to create a richer and more rounded overall picture. It will still be your story, but informed and enriched to reflect the context and characters of the story you are telling.

In creating your own story and sharing it with the people around you, you are beginning to put the vehicle of the story to work for you. Creating the story will help you understand what is happening to you and re-establish a sense of direction. It both builds a bridge back to the people who have become distant and confused while you've been depressed, and helps you to plan a way forward to the changed but continuing story of your life.

Storytelling and the brain: a dance for two

Neuroscientists examining how we interact when we tell and hear stories looked at brain activity in people telling and listening to an everyday story of 'what happened to me today'.

The brain activity they recorded revealed a kind of dance between the two brains, with the listener mirroring the speaker after a slight delay – following the steps, as it were. However, they also noticed that some of the listener's brain activity happened *before* the storyteller spoke: the listener appeared to be imagining where the story might go and using this information to prepare for what was coming next. The researchers also found that this 'dance' of brain activity was liveliest when the listener understood the story. If the story was told in a language the listener did not understand, there was no match, suggesting the person who engaged in the 'dance' wasn't simply hearing and reacting to sound, but was listening and understanding a story.

What this tells us is that communication is more successful when it involves speaking in a way the listener can understand and listening actively to what is being said. The speaker must take into account what the listener is *able to hear* and the listener must take into account what the speaker is *trying to say*. Effective communication is teamwork.

How do stories help us to remember and understand?

Illness, and in particular depression, can rob you of your sense of direction and purpose. You lose your way on a journey that previously had a relatively clear destination, and the map showing the next step has been lost. As Arthur Frank wrote in his book *The Wounded Storyteller:*

> The conventional expectation of any narrative, held alike by listeners and storytellers, is for a past that leads into a present that sets in place a foreseeable future. The illness story is wrecked because its present is not what the past was supposed to lead up to, and the future is scarcely thinkable . . . the way out of the narrative wreck is telling stories.

Depression is like a disorientating interruption in the story of your life. You lose not just your place but also, temporarily, your ability to find your way back on track. Perhaps you had imagined a future with a partner before an unexpected split, or a career path before the need for redundancies was announced. Then the anticipated story is interrupted and your ability to plan a way ahead is undermined by the fog of depression. Narrative or stories can be used to repair the damage and the disorientating effect of depression, repositioning you in your life journey and re-establishing a sense of direction. They can help you to reclaim authorship of your own life and reconnect you with the players in that life story.

The way we understand and remember stories is in part to do with the structure of the story and the language used to tell it. The structure of most stories carries the detail along broadly familiar lines, with a beginning, a middle and an end, and the language we use can reinforce the way this works. So we begin, for example, with 'Once upon a time . . .' and signal the approach of the end with 'And finally . . .' Knowing where we are in the story helps our understanding of it.

While there are many individual stories, there isn't an unlimited number of *types* of story. Fans of detective novels enjoy the suspense created before the connections between partially revealed details are finally explained in the end, while travel writing shines a detailed light on each scene as it is encountered. We rarely confuse the two. You know roughly what to expect before you know the detail because you recognize the type of story it is, and these expectations help you to make sense of information provided.

The language we use to tell a story plays a big part in how successful we are in getting the intended message across. It must, at a basic level, be a language the listener understands. The problems are obvious if the languages are literally different – just think about the confusion you may have felt during your first French lesson – but they can equally apply when people speak the same language. You need only imagine teenagers telling their parents about life lived through social media, or a young woman trying to explain why she's upset to a boyfriend who does not talk about feelings, and you can see the force of the phrase 'divided by a common language'. 'Depression' itself is a highly relevant example of how a single word can be used, and understood, in several different ways, as we shall see in chapter 6.

So in telling a story we need to choose words that will not only get across what we want to say, but will also help the listener understand what we are trying to express, thereby creating the basic teamwork of communication. The purpose is not only to *express* but also to *be heard*. To put it another way, the question is really: *how do you tell a story so that the people around you can hear it?*

Good stories also repeat central themes. Key points are highlighted and revisited to make sure we hold these details in mind to assist our understanding later in the tale. Repeating key words or ideas is the verbal equivalent of a familiar cinema technique in which the camera momentarily closes in on a vital detail, signalling its importance in understanding what comes next.

In other words, the story structure does some of the work for both the storyteller and the listener. Having a clear and coherent structure for a story organizes the details to make them easier to tell and to hear. In IPT you will develop your own story to help you understand your current experience, and you will be encouraged to find the most effective ways to share your story, so that the people who hear it can understand and will be better placed to help your recovery. Chapters 15, 17, 19 and 21 tell familiar stories of learning to live with a loss, overcoming an apparently insurmountable obstacle, getting a second chance and making a new beginning. Even without knowing the details, it is likely that you can start to imagine versions of each of these stories now, because you are familiar with the types of story they represent. This is the story structure doing some of the work for you.

Drawing others into your story

IPT regularly uses familiar themes. The broad theme is one of recovery and managing your depression through your current relationships. Within this broad theme, as we saw in chapter 1, IPT suggests four more specific themes that capture many of the types of stories that are common for people with depression: stories about change, conflict, loss and isolation. It is likely you will recognize more than one of these themes in your own recent life experiences. Most people do – and that's the key point here. Crucially, IPT uses the familiarity of these themes to get other people on board in supporting your journey through the challenges you face. Having a story is helpful, but it's not enough in itself. It is in *telling* your story, and in someone else *hearing* your story, that recovery begins to happen. When someone recognizes your story, they have a better chance of understanding what you are going through and perhaps seeing their own role in the part of the story that is still to come. In Paul's story (chapter 15), when work colleagues heard how he was made redundant they recognized the opportunity in a story of change and started to make plans for a new business together; in Jean's story (chapter 19), her sister-in-law understood the loss she felt after her husband died and suggested ways that they could salvage some of the plans Jean thought she would have to abandon. The process outlined in this book will help you to decide which of these stories will be most useful for you to focus on in helping you to recover from this period of depression. We'll discuss the themes in more detail in chapter 5.

Difficulties in telling your story

In IPT you will develop your story of depression in the context of your relationships, to aid your recovery and to engage the people close to you who can help. You will be telling a particular kind of story, quite possibly one that confuses and confounds you at the moment. Because it is a real story of real

life, not a fanciful drama to entertain and amuse, it is likely
to be untidy and incomplete. This doesn't matter. The aim is
not to create the perfect story, or the right story: it is to create
one that does its job – to make something out of reach more
accessible, to you, to the people who are involved in your life
and to the people who can help.

Talking about depression and about relationships requires a
certain kind of language, and finding ways to talk about your
personal story of depression can be a challenge. Let's consider
some of the difficulties you might face.

YOU DO NOT WANT TO TELL YOUR STORY

Depression often makes you feel both alone and that you don't
want to be around other people. It may make you want to shy
away from storytelling because you have lost faith that you
have anything worth saying. It can be difficult to tolerate being
with yourself when you are depressed, and so even more difficult to imagine that someone else will want to be with you and
listen to you telling them a story.

YOU DO NOT KNOW HOW TO TELL YOUR STORY

The confusion and concentration difficulties that are common
in depression can also make it difficult to form your ideas
clearly, especially when the feelings and experiences you want
to describe are sometimes difficult to put into words. Even if
you want to tell your story, doing so may require a language
and style that you do not feel confident using.

YOU CANNOT REMEMBER YOUR STORY

Memory difficulties are common in depression, as is the

tendency to focus on the negative. So you might feel that you don't have a full grasp of the whole story because you can't quite remember how it unfolded or the sequence of events, so it becomes jumbled and confused.

YOU CANNOT IMAGINE ANYONE WOULD WANT TO HEAR YOUR STORY

You might feel concerned that you will not be able to find anyone to listen to your story. When you are tired and bored with the same critical and undermining thoughts circling around your head, you may fear the effect of exposing someone else to the same, imagining that they won't be interested. Many depressed people say they cannot imagine that other people would want to hear about them when they themselves have already lost interest.

You might even worry that telling your story will provoke an angry or dismissive response in other people. Perhaps you have already tried and been told to be quiet, to stop moaning or that your difficulties are no worse than anyone else's. It is very difficult to keep trying with such a hostile or dismissive audience.

IPT can help you overcome these difficulties in telling your story. The process of creating your story will be broken down into a series of small and manageable steps. We will look at the different components that make up a story and work through a series of exercises that will help you to see how each of them fits into *your* story. You will gradually build up your expertise in depression and the relationship difficulties that are commonly associated with it; this will give you confidence to talk to others about how you have been affected and how they can help.

The basics of storytelling

So let's start by working it out together. What is a story? How are the layers of a story built up? What makes it something you want to tell, and something others want to listen to?

Jack Hart, a newspaper editor and writing coach, examines ways of telling true-life stories in his book *Storycraft*. Hart says that 'at its most basic, a story begins with a character who wants something, struggles to overcome barriers that stand in the way of achieving it, and moves through a series of actions – the actual story structure – to overcome them'. He argues that all stories have basic parts that can be arranged in a variety of ways. Understanding the basic components, and how to use them, helps us to tell our stories more effectively. IPT will help you to create your own story, using these building blocks, and to share it with the people in your life in a way that will lead towards recovery from depression.

THEME

This is the bigger picture: what the story is *about*. Stories play out over a number of events, but the central theme of the story remains relatively constant. For example, in chapter 15, Paul's story involves several events including preparing for an interview, leaving his job, talking openly with his wife, going cycling with friends and planning with new colleagues. The main theme of managing unwanted change is apparent across this potentially random list of events and is the thread that ties them together.

The significance of any individual event in your story will be determined by how closely it relates to the main theme, and by the response it provokes in you. When events *occur around the same time* and are *closely related to the main theme of the story,* especially if they *trigger strong feelings or symptoms*, they are significant and worth looking at more closely. If any or all of these features are missing, the event is less likely to be significant in this story, and might simply distract from the main theme. We are all in the midst of several stories at any given time, because life is complicated, and having a central theme helps to clarify which story you are telling.

Let's see how this works in relation to Jean.

Jean's story (which we will look at in more detail in chapter 19) had been one of hard work and struggling to make ends meet. She was looking forward to a happy ending in her retirement, when she planned to travel with her husband and to enjoy the time they never had when the children were growing up. This story was cut short when her husband died suddenly. Jean looked around her and, seeing other people cope with similar losses, expected to do the same. She tried to restart her story several times, taking new jobs and making new friends, each time hoping to turn things around. But each time her story ground to a halt when her enthusiasm dwindled and she couldn't see the point. She lost track of the theme of her story, and as a result used up her energy on things that had little realistic chance of helping her to move on. Her life gradually closed in around her, until the only thing that motivated her to get out of bed was her granddaughter. When she thought that even this was under threat, after a falling-out with her daughter, she felt hopeless and lost.

When she started to tell this story of plans for the future, bereavement, false starts and arguments, she realized that the difficulties began with her husband's death. She had set that theme (loss) aside some time earlier, because she had not expected it to have such a far-reaching impact. When it became clear to her that this theme was still central in her life, she could make more sense of the subsequent false starts and why an apparently trivial falling-out had felt so devastating. The theme gave her a context in which to understand the various events and relationships in her recent life. It also gave her the basis of the story she could start to share with her children and friends, who had fallen into silent confusion about the change they had witnessed in her. Having a sense of what the story was about helped them to plan what to do about it.

Exercise 3.1: Thinking about your own story

- Which themes (change, conflict, loss, isolation) can you find in your own story of becoming depressed?
- What barriers are you facing as you try to recover?
- What impact is depression having on your story?

STRUCTURE

Having a structure for your story means you have an idea of the end point before you begin. That is not to say you have to know how the story will turn out, but you have an idea of the shape of the story you are trying to tell. All stories, however elaborate, have a beginning, a middle and an end, although they might not be told in that order. It is common for the stories we tell to start in the middle, especially if something happens to stir up emotions at that point, but missing the beginning of the story, which gives it context, can create a lot of confusion. You might feel stuck in the middle of your own story, with the end as yet unknown. That the story is unfinished doesn't mean that you do not have a story, simply that you are telling the story so far.

The IPT process will help you to become author of your own story, however complete or incomplete it feels. In IPT we begin by assessing the features of the story in order to work out the main theme. Is it about unwanted change or conflict, loss or isolation, or perhaps a mixture? During the second phase we examine the main theme in more detail and our efforts are channelled into making constructive changes in a story that has stalled and is struggling to find its ending. In the final phase of IPT we review the story in order to look at how it has moved on, and we start to make preparations for the next phase of the unfolding story of your life.

In particular, IPT will help you to chart out the story of your most recent period of depression to reveal your own timeline (see chapter 8). This might be part of a bigger story of living with depression, and understanding the role depression has played in your life story will be one of our first objectives.

If you sketch the outline of your story – its beginning, middle and end – this can help you to visualize where you are in the story at the moment. You might find this easiest to do by starting at the end, or at least where you are now, and working backwards. This way you can first set out what your main difficulties and relationship problems are *right now*, and then add details of the twists and turns that got you here. Be prepared to set some of these details aside as you refine your story. You will gradually sharpen the focus on only those events and people that most closely and meaningfully relate to the main story you are trying to tell.

One of the things you will develop in IPT is your own timeline or *storyboard* of the most recent period of depression. This involves adding your personal details to the basic story arc shown in the diagram below. Your storyboard, or timeline, will also include many additional features, such as where you were, who was involved, what happened, the main current problems and the key background issues, and will be a way of understanding your own experiences in a more coherent way.

It will also give you a structure for telling other people about it more effectively and clearly. The storyboard or timeline will allow you to look back and forth across this episode of depression, discovering what made you vulnerable at the time, what protected you then and can do so again, and who and what will enable you to move out of the 'stuckness' that has stalled the story at the point you have reached. The storyboard can be a verbal description or a picture or a mixture of both. We will look at this in detail in chapter 8.

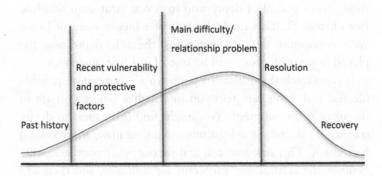

So how might Suzanna, whose story is told in full in chapter 17, go about constructing her storyboard? The basic sketch would highlight difficulties in her relationship with her partner. Her depression became clear when she gave her partner an ultimatum on their relationship and he did not agree to do what she wanted. As a result they were caught in an unstable relationship, not quite knowing if the relationship was over or not.

Looking back, Suzanna appeared vulnerable to depression because she had been depressed before: once when she and the same partner had split up earlier in the relationship, and further back in her life, as a teenager. The relationship was also vulnerable because the couple had not been able to talk about the arguments they had and so disagreements were never fully resolved. Suzanna had friends who could have provided support, but she rarely talked to them about her difficulties, thus creating a further vulnerability. Further back still, Suzanna had had an unhappy childhood and had experienced a breakdown in family relationships early in her life. This meant she had not had the chance to develop skills to manage disagreements in relationships in a constructive ways, making her vulnerable to the impact of conflict in her adult relationships.

Here is how Suzanna might have sketched out her timeline:

Past history	Protective/ vulnerability	Main relationship difficulties	Resolution
Unhappy childhood; left home and didn't return; depressed as a teen.	Break up and depression earlier in relationship; pattern of not discussing arguments.	Ultimatum on relationship; uncertain status in relationship.	? IPT

Exercise 3.2: Sketching out the timeline of your story

• Draw out your own initial storyboard of your recent period of depression in your notebook. Add all the details that seem relevant to you, as you understand it so far.

POINT OF VIEW

A story can be told from many points of view. When we look at it from different angles, the story opens up, and this can be really helpful in breaking out of the tunnel vision that is created in depression. Changing your point of view might involve seeing a situation from another person's perspective, or from closer or further away. As you move closer, more detail is revealed; as you move further away, patterns and wider context become clearer. Both can be useful when overcoming depression, and the trick is to be flexible in gathering the information you need.

In depression, our ability to change our point of view temporarily diminishes as we become more inward-looking and our perspective narrows. We see things the way we see things, and it is difficult to imagine seeing them any other way. It becomes more difficult to imagine others' points of view and even to adjust our own viewpoint, for example to see things closer up or in a wider context. We often miss the way in which details of a situation influence each other: how a conversation, for instance, is influenced by its timing, the tone of voice used, shifts in feelings while talking or listening, and the opportunities to change course that lie in each detail. There is some logic to having a fixed focus when we're under threat and struggling for survival – in those circumstances it makes sense to focus all our attention on finding the source of the threat in order to deal with it. But this instinctive tunnel vision is less useful in the normal course of life, when far from helping us to deal with a problem, it can immobilize us for a long period of time, as often happens in depression.

As you build up your story you will be asked to consider it from different points of view. You can do some of this alone e.g. moving closer in or further away from the detail. Other parts of the story will involve getting a clearer idea about others' perspective, in order to cast light on your own. You might be able to imagine this, or you could ask the other person how the situation looked to them. Changing your point of view in this context doesn't mean changing your opinion. Seeing someone else's point of view doesn't mean you have to agree with them; only that you look at things as they do. You can return to your point of view again if you wish, but it will be better informed now that you have looked at the situation in another way.

CHARACTERS

The characters are the life-blood of a story, whether they are central to it or appearing in someone else's. The events that happen in the story happen to the characters or are caused by them. The story unfolds through the actions, reactions and interactions of the people involved. Knowing who the relevant characters are is one of the basic building blocks of a story.

It seems safe to imagine that as you have chosen a self-help book on Interpersonal Psychotherapy you have some interest in the people who populate your story. IPT, as I have said before, happens in the space between people. Knowing who the other people are gives that space shape. IPT can only work if we know about the interpersonal context – that is, who is in your life and how they influence your depression. We will discuss this in more detail in chapter 9, which will look at ways of describing your relationships with the people in your life.

In your own story, one character is certain: you. However, you may feel that you have been changed by your experience of depression. So you will be discovering (or rediscovering) yourself in your own story, coming out of the shadow cast by depression, which so often seems to reduce you to only a pale imitation of your healthy self.

The other characters in your story are less fixed. They will
vary in number and feature in a variety of ways: some will be
supportive and resourceful, others challenging and problematic. An early task in IPT is to look carefully at the people in
your story and how interacting with them, or not interacting
with them, affects your symptoms of depression.

SCENE

A story moves through a series of events or scenes, in which
people act on and react to their current circumstances. Some
events are more important than others because of the way they
influence the course of the story. Less important scenes could
be dropped without affecting the sense of the story. If important
scenes are dropped the story begins to feel less coherent and it
is less clear how one 'scene' leads to the next. It might feel as
if the story has stalled or lost its way. Struggling to distinguish
between the more and less important scenes of the story is not
uncommon in depression. You might wonder how you got
here and how you will get out.

Over the next few weeks you will become more skilled
at identifying the key scenes in your story that deserve closer
attention. These scenes will be marked by how they made you
feel, how they relate to your symptoms of depression and how
they are linked to the main theme of your story. In particular,
you will learn to pay attention to the main events involving
other people that happen every day and contribute to the ebb
and flow of your depression. Once again, the central themes of
IPT – change, conflict, loss and isolation – will be used to help
you to give shape to your story. You will consider how these
themes are revealed in the events in your story and across the
period when you have been depressed.

Some of the events in your story will have only a temporary

impact, perhaps because the issues they threw up were resolved or didn't have a lasting effect on you, for example the day-to-day frustrations of the regular commute to work. Other events will have more lasting impact, and you will start to notice times when your story stalls and doesn't start up again because of their impact. It is more difficult to move on from some events, such as losing an important relationship or being forced out of a role that was important to you. In this way you will start to distinguish between individual one-off events that are not particularly significant and those that reflect the recurring themes that will be useful as a focus for your efforts to recover.

As I have mentioned before, IPT is a therapy of repetition. This makes sense for a treatment of depression – a disorder in which remembering things and making plans and decisions are often difficult. But it also takes into account the fact that repetition is the way in which we learn best. So there will be a fair bit of repetition in this book, and it's intentional. New information can be hard to take in at first, and you might become anxious if you think you have not remembered all of the information provided. Don't worry: there is no need to remember lots of new ideas and jargon in IPT. You will be reminded of the key ideas over and over again. Each time an idea is introduced in IPT it becomes part of a repeating loop. Ideas are not used once and left behind. They are revisited again and again to help you to understand your story and recovery.

And so, having examined why storytelling is so important, we now move on in the next chapter to see how you can practise this crucial skill.

Summary

- Storytelling is the dominant form of communication in our lives.

- Stories can make ideas and messages more accessible.
- Effective communication is teamwork.
- The purpose of storytelling is not only to express but also to be heard.
- The need to tell stories is unavoidable when you are unwell.
- Creating your story assists your understanding and re-establishes a sense of direction.
- A good story has structure, character, different points of view, key scenes, and a central theme which holds all the elements together.

Chapter 4

Practising storytelling

The real difference between telling what happened and telling a story about what happened is that instead of being victim to our past, we become a master of it. We cannot change our past, but we can change where we stand when we look at it.

DONALD DAVIS, STORYTELLER

The whole of this chapter is devoted to an exercise to help you think about the value of storytelling. I first came across this exercise in a workshop run by 'The Whole Story', which was designed to help colleagues share information more effectively in the workplace – but it was easy to see how it would apply to personal stories too. It works best if you do this exercise with someone else – one of you will be the storyteller, the other the listener. This way you can experience the process from both sides. If you do not have anyone who could help you with this exercise at the moment, you can still go through it on your own to develop your own storytelling. Simply follow the steps to build up your story, writing it down in your notebook and notice what each layer adds to the picture. You can always come back to it and try again when your IPT team develops.

The basic idea is to help you to communicate what you need to more effectively, and to involve the people you speak to more fully. Depression can make it difficult to tell an engaging story for a number of reasons. You might not understand the story yourself; you might find it difficult to remember the whole story; or you might feel reluctant to go over the same story again and again, and imagine no one wants to listen. Each of these problems produces a story that is hard to tell and difficult to follow, leading to the risk that the listener (and sometimes the storyteller) may switch off. Organized and layered stories, on the other hand, keep people hanging in there, wondering what is going to happen next and how it will work out. This is just as true of simple, everyday stories as it is for more complicated or involved stories. The aim isn't to make you into a sparkling raconteur who can hold any audience enthralled, but rather to give you some basic ideas that will help you to organize what you want to say in a way that will get your point across and help the person listening to follow the thread.

The first step is to think of a brief story about yourself. This does not need to be a very personal story, and for the moment you should try to avoid stories that you find upsetting or that are closely linked to your depression. We will come back to this exercise later and use it again to develop your story of depression, but for now keep it simple and reasonably neutral. The main point to hold in mind is that the story will tell the listener something about you. It is the kind of story that someone who knows you would recognize as being just like you.

By way of illustration, I would tell a story about riding my motorbike. It is something I enjoy and it often produces unexpected stories. The twist in most of these stories is that I have a dreadful sense of direction. So, I have something I want to do and an obstacle to doing it. An example would be a story about a charity motorbike ride I take part in each year. One year, on the longest day of the year, a number of bikers gathered together and rode for most of the day between set start and end points. The day started early with the prospect of a grand journey. However, our progress was interrupted when it soon became clear that the lead riders, myself among them, did not actually know our way through the local one-way system close to the starting point. So we spent the early part of the ride looping back around and passing the riders behind us before ending up just where we had started! We reorganized, someone read a map, and the ride started out again, this time with more success and a much longer road ahead of us.

In my description you will see that I have given you little more than the sketch of a story. I told you something about why I chose that particular story. I chose it because it is about something I enjoy doing – riding my motorbike – and a routine complication for me in doing this – a tendency to get lost. Implicit in my story is a message: obstacles are inevitable, but worth overcoming. However, this is not very clear yet. At the moment it is a pretty basic story and it will need to be developed to hold your interest. I will add to my story as you develop your story and we will watch our stories grow together.

Step one: choosing your story

You and your storytelling partner should each think of a story that will reveal something about the person telling the story: so your story will be about you and your partner's story will be about them. Don't worry about what story you choose. *Any story can be used* – in this exercise, the process of building up the layers is much more important than the subject of the story. Someone who tried this exercise once told the story of not being able to think of a story, and still managed to use it successfully!

When you have chosen your stories, you and your storytelling partner should think about why you chose the particular stories you did. Take a few minutes to think and prepare your ideas before you tell each other the stories you have chosen. Ask yourself:

- What are the main things about you that are captured in the story?
- What do you hope that your listener will know about you after they have heard the story?

(*In my story:*

- *I like riding motorbikes, I have no sense of direction and I enjoy being part of a charity event.*
- *I persevere in doing things, even when I come up against difficulties.*)

We rarely plan our stories in a deliberate way like this, thinking in detail about our purpose in telling them and our intended message. This kind of planning might seem like hard work at first, but it can greatly improve the effectiveness of your communication and transform the way other people listen to you.

Step two: putting the pieces together

There are components to a story and ways to put them together that will make it more interesting and compelling, and these can be learned to make your own stories better.

We identified some of the components that make up a story in the last chapter. We will go through each in turn again here, and briefly note how they feature in the stories you are about to tell.

(1) Characters. These are the people who feature in the story. You will be one of the characters because it is a story about you, but most stories will also involve other people as a more or less central feature of the story.

- Make a list of ALL the people involved in your story, noting who they are.

(In my story: Almost 100 riders in a group; some were friends I had gone riding with before, some were people I had just met and some I had never met. And there was a bemused local bystander.)

(2) Subject or theme. What is the story about? On one level the story is about you, so you could say you are the subject of the story. However, depending what story you have chosen it might also be about something else too.

- What is your story about?

(In my story: It is about a charity motorbike ride; the unexpected problems that routinely crop up during a ride; not having a sense of direction; keeping going regardless.)

(3) Plot points or scenes. The plot points capture the main events or actions in your story that keep it moving forward. Without plot points the story does not go anywhere, so for example my story would have been reduced to a statement that I ride motorbikes. The plot point took this fact and fitted it into an unfolding narrative.

- What are the main events in your story, i.e. what happened?
- What was the order of events?
- Does it go from beginning to end or does the sequence move back and forth?

- Who does what to move the story forward (how do characters and plot interact)?

(In my story: Starting on the ride; hitting the one-way system; being one of the riders in front looping back around and passing the riders behind; seeing the bystander's face; ending up where we started; working out a plan together and trying again. The story progresses from beginning to end. The lead rider and the person with a map moved the story on.)

(4) Timing. When did your story take place? We live stories now, as they are happening, but we also carry stories with us from the past. Understanding when the story is happening is important to help your listener to make sense of your story.

- When did your story happen?

(In my story: Two years ago, starting at 2 a.m.)

(5) Setting. As well as being set in time, a story will have a physical setting. Where did it happen? Inside or outside? In a familiar or unknown setting? Across a series of different settings?

- Where did your story happen?

(In my story: In an unfamiliar seaside town, covering about one mile – twice.)

The story in this exercise does not need a lot of elaborate detail on each of these points. You are not trying to write a script for your story, simply becoming familiar with the different parts that make up your story.

One of the things that good storytellers do is to map out their story in advance. Without such a plan the story will be at risk of meandering off track, perhaps never getting to the end.

So when you and your storytelling partner have both decided on the stories you want to tell and have considered the jigsaw pieces of your stories, map out the sequence of the story – the beginning, the middle and the end – in your notebook. Not all stories will be told in this sequence. Sometimes they move between these points, often starting in the middle, looking back for context and forward for resolution. For now, keep it simple and work from beginning to end. You will be deliberately keeping your story brief, so there will be little scope for mystery or surprise revelations. We will think about the advantages and disadvantages of changing the sequence of the story in later chapters.

(6) Beginning. What do you need to explain and describe at the start of the story to help your listener to follow and understand what you are going to tell them, e.g. the timing and setting? In summary, what it is about, what do you think this story reveals about you?

(In my story: This was a story about a charity ride I was taking part in for the second time; it is something I looked forward to across the year; I had already ridden a long way to get to the start; I was with the lead riders because I wanted to have someone I could follow; it is an example of the unexpected little adventures and mishaps that make me enjoy riding my bike so much.)

(7) Middle. What are the main plot points or scenes you want to include? What sequence do they follow? Who is involved in moving the story on at each of these points? Is there a complication in your story? If there is, how did this get resolved and were you involved?

(In my story: The initial roar as the bikes edged out of the car park at the start of the journey; the pleasure of setting out on a beautiful

morning before most people are awake; the dawning realization that we had almost instantly got lost and were going to meet ourselves on the way back; the delight that not everyone was asleep and there was someone to witness the peculiar sight; the mix of reactions, including my own, to what had happened; working out plan B and starting again.)

(8) End. How did the story end? And importantly, remembering the point of the story in the first place, why do you think this represents you so well?

(In my story: Starting off again; delighted there was an episode worth recounting so early in the day; finding the right road and setting off for a day when, with any luck, there would be a few more incidents just like it; the story captures one of my biggest pleasures and weaknesses and illustrates that if you keep trying and ask for a bit of help you can get there in the end.)

Step three: telling your story

FIRST ROUND: TRYING IT OUT

This is the first time you and your storytelling partner are going to tell your stories to each other. You will tell your stories in turn, with one telling and one listening and then swapping roles. The listener should not interrupt at any point during the story, simply listen attentively. The listener should take note of what they like about the story and the way it is told, but should not say anything until the story is over.

The storyteller will have two minutes to tell their story, so it might help to use an alarm so that you can both give your full attention to what you are doing. The storyteller should aim to *finish* the story *at two minutes*, not finishing early and not running over time – this way you have to make sure you prioritize the main points in the story and move through them at a pace that matches the time you have. Making sure you get to your point while you have the listener's attention is a useful skill when telling a story.

When the first story has been completed the listener should tell the storyteller what they *liked* about the way the story was told, what worked and caught their interest, what should be kept in next time the story is told. This is not a time for criticism, so keep it positive. The storyteller should take note of the feedback to use when they repeat the story later.

Now swap roles and do the same thing again, this time with the other person's story.

SECOND ROUND: SETTING THE SCENE

In the second round the listener has an opportunity to ask for more detail while the story is being told, but *only about the physical setting*, e.g. what it looked like, where the person was in the scene being described, etc. The storyteller should provide the descriptions in as much detail as they can, and use these details to help the listener picture the scene more clearly. So in this round the listener will interrupt the story to ask for the extra information they need. When sufficient detail has been offered, the listener should ask the storyteller to pick up the story from where they left off. Try not to get into a chat at this point: simply ask and answer specific questions and then get back to the story.

After you have told the story again, this time the listener should tell you what they think the extra detail adds to the story and comment on any area they found difficult to follow or which did not help the story to progress. The storyteller should think about how this part of the story could be improved next time.

Now swap roles and do the same for the other person's story.

(In my story: It was 4 a.m. when we left; we had watched sunrise as we were preparing to leave and there was a beautiful early light; it was fresh but not cold; there was lots of excited chatter and laughing and the bikes made a great roar as everyone set off together.)

THIRD ROUND: THE INTERNAL STORY

During the third round, the listener can ask for more details again, this time about *feelings* related to the scenes being described. The questions should be about feelings at the time the events described were happening, not the feelings of the storyteller now. The listener can ask about the storyteller's feelings or the feelings of any of the other characters who feature in the story. Again, when the listener is satisfied that they have enough detail to fully appreciate the story they should point out what they think this adds to or takes away from the story. Then swap roles and do the same for the other story.

(In my story: I was very excited to be starting on the ride, I was initially confused when I saw the riders doubling back but was then very amused and laughed all the way back to the start; the bystander looked surprised and interested in the unexpected long line of bikes and then completely confused as we all looped around a figure of eight; some of the other bikers were less amused than me and seemed a little exasperated, having been all geared up to get going, and so quickly got into organizing mode to sort out the bunch of directionless stragglers; the lead rider was undeniably embarrassed.)

FOURTH ROUND: ANOTHER PERSPECTIVE

This is the final practice round.

This time the listener is going to give a voice to the other characters in the story. So far the story will have been told entirely from the storyteller's point of view. This is important, but it is not the only perspective on the story; so this time the listener should ask for someone else's point of view as a way of expanding the story. This could be the perspective of any other character or characters in the story. The point is to find out not whether the other person agrees with the storyteller but rather how they would tell the story at any given point. What would they be focusing on? What would be important from another point of view? The storyteller should switch perspective to give the other point of view and then return to their own point of view to carry on with the story. After the story the listener should comment on what contribution this new perspective made. Then swap roles and do the same for the second story.

(In my story: The front rider had no intention of leading the ride and just ended up there by accident when we left the car park. He knew very quickly that he had no idea where he was going and was suitably embarrassed when he faced almost every other rider as his efforts took him (and everyone else) back down the road he had just come along. He knew he would not be allowed to forget it any time soon. The last rider in the group had not left the car park by the time the first group returned and could not quite believe what he was seeing. The administrator, who monitors the ride from home and updates the charity website throughout the day, was delighted to have a story within five minutes of the event starting.)

FIFTH ROUND: REVISING THE STORY

This is your opportunity to tell your revised stories. This time you will each have five minutes to tell your story. You should keep talking for the full five minutes but should not run over time, aiming to *finish* your story *at five minutes*, so again think about pacing and what detail you should include. You should take note of all of the feedback you have been given, including the extra detail that has been added to your story in each previous discussion and avoiding the features that did not engage the listener.

When you have finished your story this time, your listener should tell you how they see your story having changed, what has improved since the first telling, and what they enjoyed about your story this time. If there are parts of the story that do not work so well, the listener should highlight these as features of your storytelling to continue to work on.

For the last time, swap roles and repeat the exercise.

(In my story: A charity event I had been looking forward to all year started at 4 a.m. on a fresh and bright morning in a sleepy seaside town. The plan was to ride from the east coast of one county to the west coast of another, so we had a beautiful sunrise as our backdrop. The early morning silence was broken when almost a hundred bikes started up and made their way into the centre of town. I could not keep the smile off my face and I deliberately worked my way close to the lead group because I know how easily I get lost and I wanted to be able to follow someone else. Within a few minutes we entered a one-way system that looped around a series of twists and turns. As we passed a curious bystander several bikers waved and the gentleman waved back. Then . . . the loops kept going, we missed the exit and ended up heading back along a parallel road in the opposite direction to the one we had just travelled. The front rider shook his head as he rode past all of his fellow riders who waved and cheered as they realized what had happened. I glanced up at the clock tower and laughed out loud when I realized it had only taken us five minutes to get lost and to start clocking up the stories of the day. Getting lost did not seem such a bad thing after all. After a bit of huffing and puffing, backslapping and sending messages to be posted on the website, someone looked at a map

and worked out the correct route and a now slightly longer day started all over again. And I was just as excited.)

Step four: reviewing the exercise

When you have completed the exercise, take note of how your story changed. Consider how it felt to tell your story for the first time, compared to the final telling.

- What did you notice about how purposeful your story-telling felt?
- How did your ideas of what your story was about and what you wanted to communicate change?
- What ideas did you develop about how to engage a listener?
- What did you learn from your listener's feedback or from your own experience as a listener?
- How will this exercise change the way you will tell stories of yourself in the future?

This is obviously a more detailed process than you could go through when spontaneously talking to someone, but it introduces you to some of the ideas that will be used in IPT:

- Thinking about what you want to achieve when you speak to someone.
- Using feedback to improve your communication.
- Making your main points and not being distracted.
- Thinking about what makes it easier for the other person to listen and understand you.
- Including details about your feelings as well as the facts.

In the following chapters we will look at ways you can use these ideas to develop your story of depression and communicate more clearly with the people around you. This will help to make the most of the support that is available to you and help you to find ways to sort out the problems that have developed in some of your relationships and which are keeping your depression going.

Summary

- Practising storytelling with a partner gives you the chance to see stories from both sides, as teller and as listener.
- All stories involve several parts – characters, subject, plot, timing, setting – and have a beginning, a middle and an end.
- Building up a story in 'layers' enables you to see what additional elements help get the story across to the listener.

Chapter 5

What is your story about?

*. . . do not start at the beginning. Write about the period
that interests you, then go back – gradually pick up the rest.*

ALAN BENNETT, PLAYWRIGHT

The four focal areas in IPT – change, conflict, loss, isolation
– capture common difficulties in relationships. They are *interpersonal* themes because they home in on what happens *between
people*. They are called focal areas because we use them as the
focus of our attention: each one of them can serve as an anchor
point to which we return. Although originally developed in
North America with adults, the focal areas have been useful
in many countries and across continents with many different
age groups. This suggests that the themes are universal in our
human experience of relationships.

IPT uses focal areas to help to focus our attention on individual strands of our life stories. This doesn't suggest that there
is only one thread or story happening. Inevitably we are all
living through many overlapping narratives at any one time.
Sometimes we are the central figure in the story and at other
times we are taking part in stories in which someone else is
the central figure. What the focal areas do is help to break a
complex picture into more manageable sections, each one of

which can be the target for making constructive changes over a relatively brief period of time.

Let's revisit the four themes that serve as focal areas in IPT, filling them out just a little:

- *Change* **focuses on changes in our important roles, such as being a partner or a parent, an employee or a friend, and the difficulties surrounding losing one of these significant roles.**
- *Conflict* **focuses on a repeating pattern of disagreement and dispute within an important relationship when the dispute persists over time and shows little indication of being sorted out.**
- *Loss* **focuses on the painful aftermath of losing someone important to you when they die.**
- *Isolation* **focuses on long-term difficulties in making or holding on to satisfying relationships.**

These focal areas capture common difficulties in relationships that make us vulnerable to depression. Depression can also make the challenges associated with each area more difficult and undermine your ability to cope as you usually would. Managing change is something we all face at times, whether in our working life, for example with redundancy or retirement, in our personal lives, such as a partnership ending or becoming a parent, or in our involvement in other people's lives, such as parents becoming ill and needing more care. Relationships fluctuate in how well they work: we might retreat and feel very alone in a once close relationship, or find ourselves having the same arguments, that don't seem to resolve anything, again and again. One of the inevitable experiences of life is that at some point people we care about will die, and this can have a significant ripple effect across many people's lives. Feeling that your network of relationships does not have enough, or the right mix, of people to meet your needs, can create terrible loneliness and frustration.

Although a list of just four themes may seem too simple to capture all of our possible relationship troubles, it soon becomes clear how many common difficulties, and especially those that are troublesome when you are depressed, are covered by this brief list. Of course, you will often manage these difficulties successfully, but it is not uncommon to lose your way, especially if you are faced with several demands at once, and to feel over-whelmed and hopeless about finding a way forward. That is why it is useful to consider these themes when you are thinking about your own relationships. Are you perhaps grappling with some of these issues, but having difficulty putting your finger on quite what it is that you are struggling with? This is an opportunity to pinpoint the difficulties that are tripping you up and keeping you depressed, and – most importantly – to plan what to do about it.

It is not unusual to find more than one of these themes in your story. After all, they were chosen because they capture so many of the experiences common to people with depression. Sometimes the difficulty lies in choosing a single theme, because two or more seem to be equally relevant. There might have been a big change for your or your partner in one of your roles, which has led to more arguments between you (change and conflict); you might have found it very hard to adjust after a bereavement and struggled to cope with the new demands that now face you (loss and change).

It can be very difficult to decide which direction to go in, but for now simply start to consider the possibilities. Do not feel under pressure to choose between them at the moment; simply note how they feature in your own story. Next we will go on to explain briefly how each area is addressed in IPT and consider how this might help you to resolve your depression and break down the links with interpersonal difficulties.

Objectives and strategies

MANAGING ROLE CHANGE

This focal area is about managing unwelcome change in a significant role, for example when a close relationship has ended or you have lost your job. This is also called *role transition*, which captures the change from old into new. This area is inevitably far-reaching because each of us performs many roles in the different areas of our lives, e.g. we may be a mother in our family, a confidante to some of our friends and a boss at work. We often have to manage change within these roles, but sometimes the magnitude or permanent nature of the change makes it difficult to come to terms with. In particular, the process of making the transition from one role to a new, different role might be difficult for us if we:

- find it hard to let go of what has been lost;
- find it hard to accept the way the change happened; and/or
- find it hard to adapt to new demands.

The strategies in this area will enable you to get an overview of the change and to identify where you are getting stuck, so that you can move ahead again, as summarized in the diagram below.

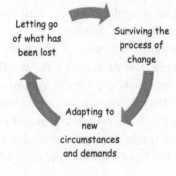

Letting go of what has been lost

Surviving the process of change

Adapting to new circumstances and demands

You will then examine each part of the change to clarify what is being given up, how the manner of the change is affecting your ability to adjust, and what resources you have and will need to meet the demands of your new situation (see diagram below).

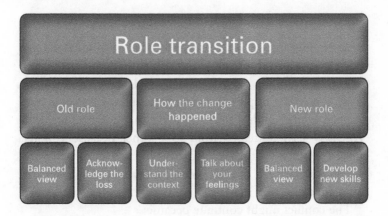

An example: Paul

Paul became depressed when he was made redundant. It had come as a great shock to him, as he had worked for his company for fifteen years and had been hoping for a promotion. He felt let down and betrayed by the colleagues who succeeded in his place. He had been very dedicated to his job and had worked very hard to be a success. He had often had to work long hours and in recent years had neglected other areas of his life in order to keep up with the demands of the job. This had created a distance between Paul and his family and he had had little time to devote to his friends or hobbies, so when

the biggest part of his life disappeared he felt completely
at a loss. He felt ashamed to face people because he saw
himself as a failure and struggled to motivate himself to
build a new routine. Days turned into weeks and he felt
trapped and hopeless in his new situation.

MANAGING ROLE CONFLICT

Role conflict focuses on a current dispute with someone significant in your life which is difficult to resolve. It might be
an obvious dispute, with arguments and open disagreement,
or a more silent dispute, where efforts to make change have
stopped even though the difficulty itself has not been resolved.
You may have retreated from each other because you feel
unsure about how to make changes, or feel unable to leave
the issue alone even though you are repeatedly going over the
same ground.

The conflict might continue because:

- one or both of you have given up actively trying to
  resolve the dispute;
- one or both of you have problems in communicating
  clearly and in a way that can be heard;
- you have different expectations of the relationship;
- the issues that are difficult in this relationship are also
  difficult in other relationships you have.

The strategies here, as summarized in the diagram below, will
look at how you have been communicating in the relationship,
including any unexpressed or mismatched expectations, and at
how communication can be improved, especially in relation to
the main issues at the centre of the conflict.

An example: Suzanna

Suzanna had been with her partner for six years. She wanted the relationship to work but believed that she and her partner had different ideas about a number of important issues. She found it very difficult to talk directly to her partner about how she felt and relied on dropping hints and withdrawing in the hope that he would realize how unhappy she was. Suzanna's partner was very practical and tended not to pick up on hints, which left Suzanna feeling ignored and helpless. Increasingly regularly, when either one became exasperated with the other's behaviour, they would have angry arguments followed by long silences that left Suzanna feeling very insecure about the future of the relationship. Neither Suzanna nor her partner clearly understood what the other wanted and they both felt stuck in the constant on/off pattern of their relationship.

DEALING WITH GRIEF AND LOSS

In IPT, the grief and loss theme focuses specifically on the difficulties that follow bereavement. That is, this focal area tackles the distinct challenges of learning to live with the death of someone close. This is something we all have to face at some point, but the painful process of learning to live with this kind of loss can be interrupted in a number of ways and can make it very difficult to connect with the people who remain in your life.

Feelings of grief and loss that are *not* related to an actual bereavement are of course common in all of the focal areas, and we will also look at them in those contexts.

Mourning can be complicated, and you may feel you are unable to adjust after your loss because of:

- unfinished business with the person who died;
- the way in which the person died;
- lack of or difficulty using social support after the death;
- difficulties with remaining relationships after the death.

Strategies here will involve first looking back to the time before the person died to construct a balanced view of the relationship you have lost. Then you will look at the time around the death itself to examine both the support you received and the range of your feelings at the time of the loss, before moving on to work at current relationships and how they can help you into the future (see diagram below).

An example: Jean

Jean had dipped in and out of depression over the three years following her husband's death. She did not feel she had been able to prepare for the loss, partly because his death had been very sudden, and partly because her husband had not wanted to speak about dying, and she felt

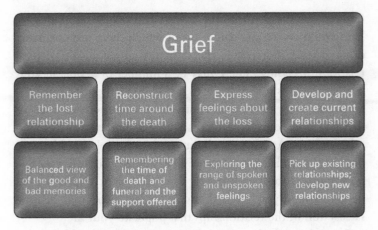

they had not said goodbye properly. Jean struggled with a sense of panic as other people appeared to move on with their lives; she felt that her husband was being forgotten and that no one would be able to understand the pain she still felt. She did not want to burden her children with how she felt but struggled on her own to cope with mixed feelings about the difficult relationship she and her husband had had over the thirty years of their marriage. Jean had lost any sense of having ever felt differently from how she did now, and thought she would have to live with these feelings and a shrunken life from now on.

DEALING WITH ISOLATION

The final area in IPT relates to a persistent difficulty in making relationships and keeping them going over time. The difficulties that people experience in this area vary and can create quite different interpersonal pictures. For some people starting relationships can feel daunting and unsettling. This might be because of shyness or anxiety in social situations or simply

finding it difficult to connect with the people around you.
This could create a social world in which there are not many
other people. For others the difficulty might be in keeping
relationships going. There may be a number of people in your
life but perhaps it is difficult to feel close to them or to maintain contact for more than relatively short periods of time, so
that you find yourself regularly having to start again with new
relationships. Another possibility is that the relationships you
have feel unsatisfying in some way, perhaps because you feel
poorly understood or regularly find yourself at odds with the
people around you. Even though they last, there may be little
satisfaction in the relationships that populate your life.

In each example considered here, strategies will involve
looking at significant past relationships to identify any recurring
patterns, and then homing in on how styles of communication
with other people contribute to these unhelpful patterns. The
information will help you to change these patterns and make
the most of opportunities to meet more people and develop
new relationships (see diagram below).

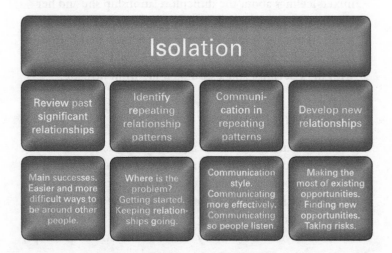

An example: Miranda

Miranda had always found it difficult to make friends. She had been a loner at school and found being around lots of people at college too difficult, so had given up her place before completing her course. She lived and worked alone. She had one friend who tried to encourage her, and would include Miranda in plans with her friends. When her friend moved to another country, Miranda's social life stopped abruptly and Miranda quickly became depressed. She had tried to introduce herself to new people but often found that it went badly, sometimes leading to other people getting angry with her and misunderstanding her. She decided that having a social life was too difficult and retreated to her bedroom where she would eat, play music and follow other people's lives on Facebook. She felt sure she would not be able to have the same kind of life for herself.

Questions and concerns about focal areas

WHY CHOOSE JUST ONE FOCUS WHEN THERE IS SO MUCH GOING ON?

By suggesting that you choose a single focus in IPT, we are acknowledging how depression can limit our energy, our ability to solve problems and make plans, and our motivation. These limitations are temporary and typically resolve themselves as the depression lifts, but while you are depressed you do not have all of the resources you would typically be able to call on. Consequently it makes sense to set your goals according to the resources you have available right now.

It is understandable when you are faced with several difficulties that you would want them all to be sorted out. It is hard living with uncertainty, conflict and loneliness. However, trying to tackle everything at once can place overwhelming demands on you, and even the prospect of starting on such an enormous task can stop you in your tracks. Making changes often involves trial and error, persevering through setbacks and, at least at first, tolerating slow progress. This is made all the more difficult if your already limited resources are stretched too far. If you break down the task into more manageable steps, all focused on the same area, so that you can monitor your progress and gain a real sense of achievement, it is much more likely that change will happen.

Working in a focused way:

- gives you a clear idea of what you are trying to do;
- helps you to set clear and relevant goals and monitor progress;
- breaks a more complex picture into manageable chunks;
- helps you to target your efforts to make changes;
- makes it easier to tell other people what you are trying to do and to be specific about how they can help;
- helps you to understand an area of difficulty in more depth;
- helps to fit what you are trying to do to a limited period of time so that you do not become overwhelmed or exhausted;
- helps to clarify confusing problems to help with decision-making;
- helps you to distinguish between things you are managing or have managed and those that need more attention.

Complex difficulties have a number of common features and the focused approach of IPT offers a means of coping with them, as set out in the table below.

Common difficulties	Problem	IPT response
The problem is unclear	The problem is not understood or recognized so cannot be effectively targeted	Name the specific interpersonal problem area clearly and identify how it is linked to current depression
Multiple competing goals	Resources are pulled in many competing directions, undermining progress within and across goals	Set simple goals: • to reduce depression • to improve relationships related to the focal area
Large numbers of interrelated factors and decisions	Confusion is compounded rather than resolved and the process stalls	Examine and understand the links between two main factors: depression and the chosen focal area
Time considerations	Without an end point in mind it feels too difficult to start, or momentum is lost when time runs on endlessly	Decide on a time period in which to complete the work, pace yourself accordingly, and review progress when the specified time period is over

Despite all this, you might still have some worries about working on your depression in this way; so in the next few sections we will discuss some of the most common concerns.

WHAT IF I CHOOSE THE WRONG FOCAL AREA?

It might be more helpful to think about the focal areas being more or less 'useful' rather than 'right' or 'wrong'. It is quite likely that you will see things in your life right now that relate to more than one of the focal areas. Chapters 14–21 will help you to think about how relevant each of the areas is to your current depression. It is a good idea to read through each of the case examples in those chapters (Paul, Suzanna, Jean and Miranda) before making your decision. This will give you a clearer idea of the options available to you before you decide which focus to take.

Making a choice about which focal area to work on is a positive part of IPT. It helps to reduce the distraction and exhaustion that tend to intrude when you try to tackle too many things at once. However, you do not have to stick rigidly to one area, and it will sometimes be very useful to dip into some of the other areas for ideas. For example, if you notice that you are having more arguments after going through a big change, you can use some of the ideas about role change and some of the ideas about dealing with conflict.

Having said that, it is helpful to try to stick with one main theme, even if you do dip into other areas for ideas. If you find that you are not making the progress you had hoped for after a few weeks, you can revisit your story of depression (chapter 8) and consider how taking a different direction might serve you. Do give yourself a few weeks before switching direction, though, because change in relationships is normally a very gradual process.

It can also be tempting to switch direction if you come up against a difficult part of the process. By all means pace it gently and ask for help, but do try to persevere, even when it is painful, as this is often what will lead to the greatest progress.

There are many common themes across the focal areas, such as understanding the link to depression and involving the people around you, so the work you have done on one theme will not be lost even if you do decide to change direction.

ONE FOCAL AREA CANNOT CAPTURE THE COMPLEXITY OF MY SITUATION

IPT assumes that we all live complex lives. The fact that you are working on one type of interpersonal difficulty, that is, one kind of difficulty between you and other people, does not mean there *is* only one difficulty. It is just that by being focused and persisting with this one area, in order to work through setbacks and difficulties, it is likely that you will make more progress than if you repeatedly redirect your energy to different problems and keep finding yourself back at square one. This can be demoralizing and frustrating and might make it more likely that you will give up on making any changes and feel even more stuck in depression. So in fact it is exactly *because* our lives are complex that a simple approach is suggested. It's not denying complexity, just helping you to cope with it rather than allowing it to become overwhelming.

WHAT IF SOMETHING IMPORTANT HAPPENS THAT IS NOT RELATED TO THE FOCAL AREA I HAVE CHOSEN?

Life does not stop happening in all its complexity and messiness simply because you have decided to tackle one area of difficulty. It is very likely that you will also have to cope with things that are not closely related to the IPT focal area you have chosen; for example, if your work situation becomes very pressured soon after a bereavement, or if a family member falls ill and needs your help and attention when you are embroiled in a dispute with your partner.

It is still helpful to continue to work on the area you identified as being most relevant to your depression even when other difficulties come up. Whatever the theme you have chosen, you will be working on developing your relationships, communicating more clearly and managing your symptoms of depression, so you can expect that the work you are doing in IPT will also help you to manage other challenges as they come up. Also, it is unlikely that the difficulties in the focal area will spontaneously get better when new difficulties appear, so sorting out persisting difficulties can free you up to attend to subsequent life events more effectively.

It is also worth considering whether work in the area you have decided to focus on might help with the new problem too. For example, if you chose to work on a dispute with your partner and then lost your job, you might find it easier to cope with the new problem if you could talk constructively with your partner about how to manage the practical and financial implications of the change. The new event happened in another area of your life but the original focus remains relevant in helping you to manage it.

An example: Susan

Susan had worked for the same boss for many years and when he retired she found it very difficult to adjust to a new, younger boss, who had a very different style and by whom Susan felt bullied. Susan had never considered early retirement and felt completely at a loss when she was retired on medical grounds. She planned to focus on this important role change to help her recover from depression. During her IPT Susan's sister died, following a short illness. Susan was saddened by her sister's death but could see that it had not been responsible for her depression, which had started months before her bereavement. She used the skills she was developing in IPT to help her to talk to friends about how she felt, but did not lose focus on the work she had to do to help herself to recover from depression and make a satisfying life for herself in her retirement.

Take some time to think about your own story and how each of the four interpersonal themes features in that story. Try to find as many examples as you can. Don't feel under pressure to choose one now – in fact, deliberately try to keep an open mind about what each one might offer to your recovery. The following chapters will guide you through building up the layers of your story to reveal the most useful direction for you to follow.

Summary

- IPT has four main interpersonal themes: change, conflict, loss and isolation.
- These themes relate to common difficulties in relationships, especially when you are depressed.
- Choosing a focus helps you to do what you can now, with what you have, where you are.
- It is exactly because our lives are complex that simplifying your focus is a good idea.
- A focus gives you a place to start. It does not try to tell the whole story.

Chapter 6

Understanding your depression

Nothing in life is to be feared, it is only to be understood.
Now is the time to understand more, so that we may fear less.

MARIE CURIE, NOBEL PRIZE WINNING PHYSICIST

What is depression?

In previous chapters we have frequently referred to becoming an expert in your own depression, and to creating a depression story for yourself and to share with the people in your life. These are useful ideas that we will come back to many more times. However, to make best use of these ideas we must first be clear what is meant by 'depression'. Is the depression referred to in these pages the same condition that you are living with? 'Depression' is a commonly used and misused word, and as we have seen, good storytelling uses language that the storyteller and listener understand. So let's take some time to establish if we are on common ground.

Low mood is something we all experience – an emotional response to the losses, disappointments or disagreements that crop up in all of our lives. The term 'depression' is often used interchangeably with low mood, sadness or unhappiness, when it refers to a depressed mood state. This depressed mood is typically unpleasant, temporary and changeable, and is often a reaction to immediate or recent circumstances; with time, or a change of circumstance, the emotional temperature changes and so does our mood. Also, such moods do not seriously interfere with how we manage our lives. We still go to work, keep up with our relationships and maintain our routines. Feeling low sometimes is just part of everyday life.

On some occasions, however, this common mood state becomes more serious and the recovery, which we would usually expect within hours or days, does not happen. This type of depressed mood is more persistent and often more intense than the passing low mood. It is more difficult to change this mood state and it lasts even when our circumstances change. Persistent low mood suggests a more serious problem, which might have a biological or psychological trigger, and is likely to have a greater impact on our lives. We might start to notice that other aspects of our lives are affected; for example, we feel less interested in other people, or our sleeping patterns become disrupted. The longer the depressed mood lasts, the more likely it is that other difficulties will start to develop.

When a broader set of common symptoms, such as trouble sleeping, memory problems and lack of interest or motivation cluster together, we are looking at the mood disorder that we call 'depression'. This is a psychological illness, which requires treatment. Typically, this kind of depression affects:

- our daily routines;
- our emotional balance;
- our ability to think clearly;
- our energy levels.

While a lot is known about this disorder, many details remain unclear. The rest of this chapter sets out some information about this kind of depression that may be useful to you. But don't worry – you are not expected to learn all of these details!

Becoming expert in your own depression is not going to be like studying for an exam. Read through as much as you can manage and think about how much of it matches your personal experience. The exercises later in the chapter will help you to think about your own experience of depression. You might find the rest of the chapter easier to go through one section at a time; and you can use this chapter as a reference, something to dip into when you want to think about one part of the picture more closely. You can move on to the following chapters even if you have not read all of the information provided in this one, and then return to it as necessary. Many of the details will also be repeated in future chapters, so there will be plenty of opportunity to become familiar with the characteristics of depression as they are described here.

Symptoms of depression

The symptoms used to diagnose depression are divided into core symptoms and other common symptoms.

- Core symptoms are:
  - ○ Sadness or low mood, most or all of the time.
  - ○ General loss of interest or pleasure in activities, even for activities that you normally enjoy.
- Other common symptoms are:
  - ○ Disturbed sleep compared with your usual pattern. This may be difficulty in getting off to sleep, waking repeatedly through the night, or waking early in the morning and not being able to get back to sleep. Sometimes the problem is sleeping too much.
  - ○ Change in appetite. This often involves poor appetite and losing weight, but a pattern of comfort eating and weight gain can also develop.
  - ○ Fatigue (tiredness) or loss of energy.

○   Agitation or, on the contrary, slowing down, slug-
     gishness.
○   Poor concentration, forgetfulness and indecisive-
     ness. For example, you may find it difficult to read,
     work, etc.
○   Feelings of worthlessness, or excessive or inappro-
     priate guilt.
○   Frequent thoughts of death. For many people
     thoughts such as 'Life's not worth living' or 'I don't
     care if I don't wake up' are common. For a smaller
     number of people, this may develop into thoughts
     and even plans of suicide.

Several additional symptoms are also commonly reported,
and these are included in exercise 6.1 below.

Symptoms alone do not confirm a diagnosis of depression.
We also look at how long the depressive symptoms have lasted
and the impact they are having on someone's life. Depression
will be diagnosed if:

• you have at least five out of the above nine symptoms,
  including at least one of the core symptoms; *and*
• your symptoms cause you distress or interfere with how
  you manage from day to day, such as affecting your
  work, family or social life; *and*
• your symptoms occur most of the time on most days and
  have lasted at least two weeks; *and*
• your symptoms are not a side effect of medication, or
  due to drug or alcohol misuse, or to a physical condition
  you have.

On the basis of how many symptoms you are experiencing
at any given time, and how severe their effects are, it is possible
to distinguish between mild, moderate and severe depression.
It is important to be aware of these distinctions when you are

thinking about options for treatment, which we shall come on to in a later section of this chapter. Essentially, the more symptoms you are experiencing, the more severe your depression:

- In severe depression, you would normally have most or all of the nine symptoms listed above, to the point that they interfere significantly with your normal routine and ability to keep up with day-to-day demands.
- In moderate depression, you would normally have more than five symptoms, usually including both core symptoms. The intensity of the symptoms and their impact can vary between mild and severe.
- In mild depression, you would normally have five of the symptoms listed, but rarely more than that, and you would be able to function normally most of the time.
- In what is called 'sub-threshold' depression, you would have fewer than the five symptoms needed to make a diagnosis of depression and so your mood disorder would not be classed as depression. However, the symptoms you do have would be troublesome and cause you distress. If this situation lasts for more than two years it is sometimes called dysthymia (see page 103 below).

Guidelines for diagnosis focus attention on common experiences, and clusters of symptoms that are useful to monitor. However, our individual experiences of depression vary and change over time. Looking at the list of common symptoms above, you can see that one person could be agitated, unable to eat and exhausted due to poor sleep, while another may struggle to get going, go back to bed several times a day and constantly snack to take their mind off their sadness. Both could be diagnosed as depressed. Because depression is a complex and variable disorder, and can affect individuals in so many different ways and to such different degrees, it's important that if you think you might be depressed, you see your doctor and get a proper diagnosis. The information in this section, and exercise 6.1, will be useful in seeking the support you need.

At the same time, while these descriptions provide a framework for thinking about depression, it is important to identify the specifics of *your personal experience*. It is not your fault that you are depressed, and the symptoms and effects described above make it clear that depression is a very difficult condition to live with. Exercise 6.1 will help you pinpoint how depression is affecting *your* life,

Exercise 6.1: Identifying your symptoms of depression

It is very helpful to use red, yellow and green highlighter pens when completing this exercise. You will find a copy of this chart in appendix 1. Make some copies, as you will be asked to rate your symptoms in this way every week while you are following this self-help programme.

Go through the list in the chart below and pick out the symptoms that you have noticed in yourself during the last two weeks. If you have noticed other symptoms, which are not on the list, write them in the blank boxes at the end of the chart.

Use a red highlighter pen to mark the symptoms that bother you most or all of the time, a yellow pen to mark those that bother you some of the time and a green pen to identify those that do not bother you. If you don't have coloured highlighter pens, draw a circle around the symptoms your experience most regularly, underline those that you experience sometimes and leave the symptoms that don't bother you unmarked.

Sadness	Little interest	No enjoyment	Poor motivation
Waking up during the night	Cannot get to sleep	Do not want to see other people	Cannot concentrate
Hopelessness	Forgetful	Taking part in fewer social activities	Cannot make decisions
Helplessness	Lost weight	Fewer hobbies or interests	Feeling life is not worth living
Low self-esteem	Feeling slowed down	Neglecting my responsibilities	Difficulty at work
Feeling guilty	Feeling agitated or on edge	Think other people do not like me	Easily confused
Feeling irritable	No interest in sex	Feel I have let others down	Sleep too much
Cannot get started	Unexplained aches and pains	Feel intolerant	No appetite
Blame myself for everything	Tearful	Bored	Overeating
No energy	Reduced sex drive	Always tired	Feeling bad about myself
Anxiety	Waking early	Want to die	Napping during the day

- Can you identify five or more symptoms that have troubled you most of the time for at least two weeks and which have an impact on how you manage at home or at work or socially?
- Which symptoms trouble you most?
- Are there any symptoms that trouble you now which did not when you first started to feel depressed?
- Have any other symptoms improved over time?

Mark the chart with the date, to help you to monitor what happens to your depression over time. Tell the people close to you, who might be on your IPT team, what you can about your experience of depression. Appendix 4 has a description of depression that you can share with friends and family. It might be helpful for the members of your team to read this information as a way of introducing the ideas before you discuss your own experience.

Rating your symptoms in this way will start to give you a measure of how your depression is at the moment and how it may have changed over time. We can often feel as if nothing changes when we are depressed, but on closer inspection we can see that the picture has changed more than we realized.

Our experience of depression is complex. Some symptoms are clear for anyone to see, such as appearing sad and tearful, not being able to sleep even when you are exhausted, or losing weight. Some symptoms, however, are more subtle and only become obvious because of their consequences. These might include becoming less productive at work because you cannot concentrate or missing appointments because your memory has become unreliable. Others symptoms might be invisible to anyone other than the person living with them, such as feeling worthless or thinking about death.

Remembering accurately how your symptoms have changed over time can be difficult. Ask someone close to you what changes they have noticed. Other people can help to fill out your picture of depression. Inevitably another person will have a different point of view from your own. This is not necessarily more accurate, but it can help to pick up on changes you may not have noticed: for example, they might have noticed changes in your behaviour, while you have been preoccupied by the change in the way you feel inside.

What do we know about depression?

Depression is the most common mental health disorder and can affect anyone, no matter what their age, background, nationality or gender. It tells us nothing about how intelligent or hard-working a person is and it is an illness that is no one's fault. Two-thirds of people worldwide will experience depression at some point in their lifetime, mostly in the mild to moderate range. Many of them will not know that this is depression; they might imagine, for example, that this is a normal way to feel, or believe they are being weak or lazy.

Depression often goes unnoticed, and studies in the UK have shown that only about half of all people with depression are diagnosed by their GPs. This is a strong argument for becoming your own expert, so that you can ask for the help you need. One of the main reasons for missing depression is confusing it with a possible physical illness, whether or not that illness is present, and missing the emotional impact. Again, this is a good argument for knowing all of the symptoms and being able to talk about them clearly.

Thoughts of death, and in some cases suicide, are a very frightening part of depression for many people. Most people with depression will think about death or dying, but only a very small proportion make plans based on these thoughts. The majority of people with depression do not plan to kill themselves or actually do so. However, two-thirds of those who do commit suicide have depression. The risk of suicide increases with the severity of the depression, additional anxiety symptoms and substance misuse, often because it may make the person more likely to act in an impulsive way. Men are more likely than women to commit suicide.

If you are troubled by thoughts of dying or life not being worth living, there is help available 24 hours a day. You should contact your GP or the Samaritans (call 08457 909090 or email jo@samaritans.org) or go to your local A&E department. People who are trained to talk about these difficult feelings can offer immediate support and help you to think about the longer-term options for managing depression.

Depression is typically an episodic disorder, that is, it comes and goes rather than continuing at the same pitch indefinitely. An untreated episode of depression lasts on average for four to six months, and many people suffering from mild depression will recover spontaneously, without any need for treatment. However, many people live with depression for much longer than six months. Research has shown that about half of people with depression are still depressed one year after being diagnosed, and for one in ten people depression will follow a chronic course, that is, it continues without recovery for many months and perhaps years. Responding early to signs of depression can help to limit the length of an episode, and this reinforces the importance of understanding the way in which depression works so that you and the people around you are forewarned to react quickly.

For many, depression is a recurring problem. About half of those who have been depressed in the past will face depression again in their lives, and the likelihood of further depression increases with each new episode. The risk of depression following a recurring pattern is greater if:

- you were under 20 years old when you had your first episode of depression;
- you have only partially recovered from a previous episode;
- your symptoms return when you stop taking anti-depressant medication; or
- you have experienced a severe episode of depression in the past.

It is important to understand that for many people, depression is something to manage rather than cure.

This can be very difficult reading if you are feeling depressed. However, it is very important to remember that depression is a *treatable illness* – and just by picking up this book you have already taken a very positive step in looking for ways to help yourself. Learning more about depression and how it works can equip you to manage the challenges of this illness much more effectively, to pick up on signs early and to take positive steps in managing its impact on your life. Responding quickly to the signs that depression is appearing or returning in your life can shorten the duration of the episode and help you to exercise some control over the depth of your depression. There are many things you and the people around you can do to influence its course, and the remaining chapters in this book will guide you through a very well-researched approach to managing depression and staying well.

Who gets depression?

We do not know exactly what causes depression and, as we have just seen, anyone can become depressed. While some people are more prone to depression than others, and while it can be the result of very difficult circumstances, it can also develop for no reason.

There is a higher risk of depression in people who have a physical illness that causes disability or pain, and between about a third and two-thirds of people with depression will also experience anxiety symptoms, such as worrying, social anxiety or occasional feelings of panic.

Depression is more common in women, one in four of whom will experience it at some time, than it is in men (one in ten), which probably reflects cultural norms and biological differences, as the most common time for women to become depressed is around pregnancy, childbirth and menopause. Men and women tend to describe depression differently. Men are less likely to describe feeling bad about themselves or feeling hopeless and are more likely to report fatigue, irritability, sleep problems and general loss of interest in their routine activities, the people around them and often themselves. They are also more likely than women to talk about anger, aggression, violence, reckless behaviour and substance abuse. Men, especially young men and older men who don't have a family, are at a higher suicide risk than women. Women are more likely to describe irrational feelings of guilt, sleeping excessively, overeating and weight gain.

There are a number of 'risk factors' for depression – that is, aspects of someone's personality or circumstances that might make them more likely to develop depression. The more risk factors that are present at the same time in your life, the more likely you are to experience depression. These factors include:

- loneliness;
- lack of social support;

- relationship problems;
- recent stressful life events;
- health problems and chronic pain;
- a past history of depression;
- a family history of depression;
- unemployment or underemployment (for example, only working part-time when you are able to work full-time);
- other mental health problems.

Many of these risk factors can be directly targeted through IPT, such as loneliness, lack of social support, relationship problems, stressful life events and health problems. By working on these difficulties through IPT you can reduce the risk of depression now and in the future and at the same time build up the social support that is known to protect against depression.

Why bother monitoring symptoms?

Let's think about why it is useful to look at your symptoms so closely. Symptoms are a reflection of your current situation. They are, in a way, a form of communication – telling you that something is not functioning as well as it should be. As such, symptoms can be useful if you learn how to read their message. They serve a function. The symptoms of depression are telling you that something is not right and it is time to take action. An early warning system, if you like.

So, to summarize, it's worth taking time to assess and monitor your symptoms, using the chart set out in exercise 6.1 above (and reproduced in appendix 1 at the end of the book):

- to make sure that what you are experiencing *is* depression;
- to learn to notice the circumstances that contribute to your symptoms changing;
- to confirm that the interpersonal problems you are

focusing on are directly relevant to your current depression;

- to signal when you should act or ask for help to challenge depression;
- to monitor your progress;
- so that you will know when you are no longer depressed.

Continue to monitor your symptoms regularly. Make a note of the day-to-day fluctuations, however slight they might be, and take time to look back over your notes each week to identify any changes in this pattern. Your expertise will develop with practice: you will become better able to identify the impact of depression and eventually to manage or banish its influence on your life.

Using copies of the chart in appendix 1, rate your experience of depressive symptoms, using your coloured pens or marking code of circling and underlining, every week while you follow this self-help programme. Complete a new form each week and use this to monitor any changes in your symptoms. As you start to feel better you will start to see a red page turn yellow and green, or fewer circles and lines being marked on the page.

What are the treatment options for depression?

Treatment recommendations reflect the severity of depression and are largely divided into treatments for mild depression and treatments for moderate and severe depression. Let's look at these different options.

TREATMENT OPTIONS FOR MILD DEPRESSION

There are several options for people with mild or persistent sub-threshold depression.

Self-help

This book is an example of self-help. Self-help resources have also been developed for other types of therapy, such as cognitive behavioural therapy (CBT). You can use self-help resources on your own, but it is often more helpful if you have someone to work with – for example, the IPT 'team' we have suggested in this book or possibly a mental-health professional, a partner, a friend or relative. Other people can encourage you when your motivation wavers and can help you to monitor the progress you are making. Some types of self-help, mainly based on CBT are also available online, where you are given a series of modules to work through over a period of (usually) eight to twelve weeks. Details of some useful and informative websites are provided in appendix 7.

Exercise

Research has shown that regular exercise often helps to ease the symptoms of depression. Aerobic exercise, which builds stamina, such as running and cycling, and anaerobic exercise, which builds strength, such as weight training and sprinting, have both been shown to have an effect. Regular moderate exercise, such as cycling on flat ground or swimming at a leisurely pace, is more effective than occasional light exercise, such as walking slowly. However, just getting started is a major achievement when you feel depressed, and finding something you enjoy and will continue to do over time is the first main goal. If you can involve someone else, so much the better: you can encourage each other. To help you distinguish 'light' from 'moderate' exercise, remember that during moderate exercise your heart rate will increase and you might start to sweat. This is what you are aiming for. You should still be able to talk but would not be able to sing. During light exercise, on the other hand, you would be unlikely to sweat and you could sing along if you took a soundtrack with you on your walk.

It is recommended that you do 150 minutes of moderate exercise each week to combat depression, which is around the same level that maintains good health overall. This total can be broken down in various ways, and would be the equivalent of 30 minutes' exercise five days a week. Some of this time might be spent on particular activities like running or cycling, while on other days the time could be built into your routine by, for example, getting off the bus a stop early and walking the last part of your journey briskly, or carrying a bag of shopping home rather than taking the car. Several examples and suggestions that will help you to plan your own routine are available via the recommended sources of information provided in appendix 7. To increase the chances of keeping an exercise routine going it is a good idea to include a mix of different activities, e.g. attending exercise classes, going running or cycling with a friend, and taking up a team sport. Make things easy for yourself by planning the types of exercise that are easier or more convenient for you to do and setting manageable goals.

Doing regular exercise can easily be combined with IPT and could create good opportunities to spend enjoyable time with other people.

Peer support

Spending time with other people who can understand your problems can be a helpful way to start talking about your feelings and difficulties. Self-help groups are usually run by a mental-health professional, who can provide useful information and help group members to monitor their progress. Again this could help you to create new opportunities to spend

supportive time with other people, which would work very
well alongside IPT. Ask your GP about local groups that run
in your area, or use the websites described in appendix 7 to
identify local resources and groups.

Anti-depressant medication

Anti-depressant medication is not usually recommended for
mild depression, but may be useful if other treatment approaches
have not helped, if you have had more serious depression in the
past or if you have found anti-depressant medication helpful in
the past.

TREATMENT OPTIONS FOR MODERATE OR SEVERE
DEPRESSION

More formal treatments are recommended when depression is
moderate or severe.

Anti-depressant medication

Anti-depressant medications are commonly used to treat moderate or severe depression. They can't address your relationship
difficulties directly, but can improve collaboration and teamwork with other people, and may ease many of the symptoms
which interfere with your daily routine, such as low mood,
poor sleep and irritability. Indeed, these changes have been
shown to occur even when people who are not depressed take
anti-depressant medication. When the burden of symptoms is
eased in this way, you may find you can function more normally, and this in turn may increase your ability to deal directly
with problems or difficult circumstances.

The effects of anti-depressants are not usually noticeable

immediately, and may take up to four weeks to become apparent. A common problem is stopping taking medication too soon, so that it does not have time to work. Research has shown that the medication is actually working from the moment you start taking it, but evidence of change takes longer to filter through because the chemical balance in our brains is gradually readjusting and our well-established patterns and routine take time to adapt. People sometimes feel concerned that anti-depressant medication creates a false high. In fact what is happening is that the false low of depression is being reversed. Chemical levels in your brain which have dipped while you are depressed are gradually adjusted upwards bringing you closer to your typical non-depressed level.

A standard course of an anti-depressant medication lasts for six to twelve months, and should be continued for *at least six months after your symptoms of depression have stopped*. This helps to make the effects of the medication more stable and long-lasting. You might think of it as similar to continuing to wear a cast on a broken bone for a period of time after the bone has healed, to protect against pressure on an injury that is still vulnerable and might be at risk of breaking more easily than normal. In just the same way, if you stop taking medication too soon, you run the risk of depression returning more quickly. When people have had more than one episode of depression, the length of time over which they take anti-depressant medication increases. After a second episode of depression the recommendation is to continue on medication for two years, and after a third episode or more the recommendation extends to five years. In all cases it is important to talk this over with your GP and monitor the effects of medication over time.

Although anti-depressants are not physically addictive, that is you don't need to keep taking higher doses to achieve the same results over time, they should still be gradually reduced over about four weeks as you come to the end of your treatment. This can prevent the withdrawal symptoms that some people develop if they stop their medication too abruptly. Our bodies become used to the medication and need time to adjust when it stops, just as they do when it is first introduced. This is why your doctor will tell you to reduce the dose gradually, and why it is very important to follow these instructions.

Finding the best anti-depressant medication for you can be a process of trial and error. There are several types of anti-depressants, each with advantages and disadvantages. If the first one you try does not suit you or help to ease your symptoms, your doctor may choose either to increase the dose or to give you another type to see if that works better for you. It is very important to monitor your response to a new medication carefully, and you should speak to your GP every two weeks when you start a new anti-depressant.

IPT can be used alone or with medication, depending on the current severity of your symptoms and your history of depression. Many research studies have reported on the benefits of combining IPT and anti-depressant medication, and this may be the most effective treatment for you if your depression is moderate to severe or you have been depressed in the past. Research also suggests that when IPT is used in the treatment of moderate to severe depression, it is most effective when used with the support and guidance of an IPT therapist.

Talking therapy

A number of psychological treatments have been found in research trials to be good treatments for depression. Many talking therapies can be safely combined with anti-depressant medication, and many people find that this is more beneficial than either treatment alone.

In addition to IPT, the talking therapies most often used in treating moderate or severe depression are:

- **cognitive behavioural therapy (CBT)**, which helps people to make changes in the way they think, feel and behave and to take a more realistic view of their situation and options;
- **behavioural activation**, which helps people to change patterns of inactivity and dwelling unhelpfully on certain thoughts or themes, both of which are common in depression;
- **couples therapy**, which helps partners work together on improving their relationship by improving their communication;
- **Dynamic Interpersonal Therapy (DIT)**, which focuses on identifying repeating patterns in relationships and helps to make the connection between past experiences and current interpersonal difficulties, using what happens in the relationship between you and your therapist to help you think about the problems in your life.

Conditions related to depression

There are several types of mood disorder. It is useful to be able to distinguish between them, and the close attention you will be paying to your specific symptoms and the context of your depression will help you determine whether one of these may apply to you.

POST-NATAL DEPRESSION

International studies have found that between 10 and 15 per cent of women develop depression after having a baby. Research suggests that marked changes in hormone levels may contribute to higher levels of depression around this time. Also, childbirth and all the associated changes are a prime example of the kind of major life event that can trigger an episode of depression in many people. The symptoms of post-natal depression are similar to those of depression listed above, may be mild, moderate or severe, and are treated in the same way.

SEASONAL AFFECTIVE DISORDER (SAD)

A small number of people – between 1 and 3 percent of the general population, mostly women – develop a yearly pattern of depression that starts in autumn or winter and stops in spring. Figures vary between countries, with higher rates in Europe and Canada than in Asia and the United States, reflecting different seasonal weather patterns. The symptoms are similar to those of depression at other times, but are more likely to involve oversleeping and overeating. Effective treatments include self-help, medication, talking therapies and light therapy.

COMPLICATED GRIEF

Between 10 and 20 per cent of bereaved people develop complicated grief after their loss. Complicated grief differs from the feelings experienced by most people who have lost loved ones because it does not gradually lessen with time unless treated, and the experience is often more intense or extreme. Complicated grief shares some features with depression, but also involves intense yearning for the person who has died, difficulty accepting the death, numbness and continuing preoccupation with the loss. It is thought to involve a mixture of symptoms of post-traumatic stress disorder (PTSD) and depression symptoms. Effective treatment involves anti-depressant medication and talking therapy.

DYSTHYMIA

We have already mentioned dysthymia or sub-threshold depression (see page 86 above). About 3 per cent of the general population and up to 36 per cent of people in mental-health settings in Western countries experience this persistent form of low mood and other symptoms of depression. Treatment involves a combination of medication and talking therapy.

BIPOLAR DISORDER

A very small number of people (about 1 per cent in the UK and 2 per cent in the United States) develop a psychological disorder in which they experience extreme mood swings from feelings of intense despair to equally intense feelings of elation. Men and women are affected equally. Treatment will usually involve medication (mood stabilizers) and talking therapy.

Depression in context

In IPT we have two simply stated goals:

- to reduce your depression; and
- to improve your current relationships.

If these goals are achieved one after the other, that's good. If they are achieved through each other, it is even better.

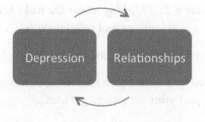

We often find that our relationships influence how we feel. You might struggle to get on with some people, or to get what you want from them, and this can lower your mood, leave you feeling guilty or keep you awake at night. With other people, you might feel relaxed and happy in their company and find that your mood is better when you spend time with them; you have more energy and feel interested in things again, even if only briefly. It will be equally important to work on the relationships you routinely associate with feeling worse and to deliberately seek out the people whose company makes you feel better. You can take advantage of these patterns in your recovery. Monitoring the overlap between your symptoms and your relationships can help you to gain some control over your depression, by managing and limiting the troublesome relationships and encouraging the more pleasurable ones.

As you start to monitor your symptoms and pay attention to the points in the day when your symptoms change, e.g. when your mood dips or you want to back out of a plan, try to identify what was going on at the time that contributed to the change in how you felt – for example, a conversation that upset you, an extra demand at work, missing someone who used to be in your life. This is the *context*. It will not always be obvious, but with time you will gradually be able to read how your symptoms and your interpersonal world interact.

Exercise 6.2: Thinking about the links between symptoms and relationships

Think of a time in the last week when:

- You spent time with someone, or thought about it, and your symptoms *got worse*.

- You spent time with someone, or thought about it, and your symptoms *improved*.

Write down the name of the person, the date and the situation.

Now think about the following questions and write down the answers in your notebook, listing them separately for each example:

- Which symptoms did you notice changing?
- How long did the change last?
- Did the other person know that your contact with them had that effect?

If you can, talk through your responses with someone in your IPT team.

If you find it hard to do this exercise because you have had little or no contact with other people in the last week, then ask yourself:

- Has your lack of contact with other people in the last week had an impact on your depression?
- What have you noticed when other people are not around or available?

It is quite common to avoid other people when you feel depressed, because you can't be bothered with company or do not expect to enjoy it. Sometimes it is the absence of relationships, rather than their presence, that depression responds to. So ask yourself:

- Have there been any times in the last week when you would have liked more company than you had, or when being on your own felt like part of the problem?

The correlation between symptoms of depression and relationship difficulties works both ways. What is going on in your symptoms can shape how you behave in your relationships for example, if you cancel plans because you feel tired and unmotivated. Similarly, what is happening in your relationships can have a direct impact on your symptoms, for example, if you find yourself lying awake in bed, unable to get to sleep, after an argument). Understanding and working on disentangling these links is one of our key objectives.

It can be useful to map out the links between your symptoms and your relationships in order to understand them more clearly. One simple way to do this is to make a simple chart which tracks symptoms and relationship triggers. A blank copy of a chart for doing this is provided in appendix 3: you can make copies of this or just draw up your own in your notebook. All you do is list the days of the week down the left-hand side of the page, and then put two headings at the top. Then, each day, under 'Depression' write down any changes in your symptoms of depression; and under 'Relationships' note any incidents or changes in your relationships. When you can see a link between two things in the different columns, draw a line between them.

Below are three examples of how this kind of chart might be filled in.

Chart 1. No connection between depression symptoms and relationships

	Depression	Relationships
Monday	Felt tearful	Didn't see anyone
Tuesday	No interest	Turned down invitation to go out
Wednesday	Slept better	Went to class at the gym

In this chart the depressive symptoms appear to come out of the blue: no links are made to what is going on in relationships. If this is how your chart looks, it is likely that some connections are being missed, and it may be useful to talk through changes in your symptoms with someone in your IPT team to generate ideas about any relationships issues that might be influencing how you feel.

When Suzanna (whom we shall get to know better in chapter 17) started to look at her symptoms she came up with chart 2 (below). She often felt tired and lost interest in plans but struggled to explain why. She found the unpredictable nature of her symptoms very distressing and felt as if she had no control over them.

Chart 2. Occasional connection between depression symptoms and relationships

	Depression	Relationships
Monday	Sad	Busy day at work, under pressure
Tuesday	Tired	Irritable with my partner
Wednesday	Felt guilty	Cancelled plans to go out

In this chart the picture is mixed, with symptoms and relationships sometimes seeming to change independently of each other and sometimes in relation to each other. It is possible that Suzanna's sadness contributed to her irritability and her guilt was a consequence of it, but she initially overlooked these connections. This is a good start, and what is happening in your relationships will not always explain any changes in your symptoms, but it would be unusual for this pattern to be completely absent or random. By tracking the two areas more closely, you will start to notice the main triggers for change in your symptoms.

As time went on, Suzanna became more aware of some of the links between her symptoms and her relationships. She was good at noticing the links when she had a big argument with her boyfriend and her mood plummeted or she lay awake all night, but still felt confused about what was happening around those times and when her relationships with other people had a more subtle influence. She found it very helpful to talk about those times with her IPT therapist, and often discovered links that she hadn't noticed through these discussions.

Chart 3. Repeated connection between depression symptoms and relationships

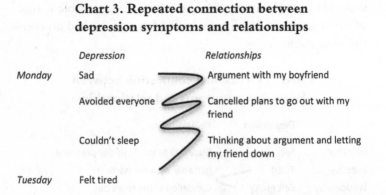

	Depression	Relationships
Monday	Sad	Argument with my boyfriend
	Avoided everyone	Cancelled plans to go out with my friend
	Couldn't sleep	Thinking about argument and letting my friend down
Tuesday	Felt tired	

In chart 3, the connections between symptoms and relationships are clear and evident on both days. This chart reveals very good insight into the ways in which our symptoms and relationships with other people respond to each other, giving Suzanna a good basis for working out which relationship issues or themes come up most often and could serve as a focus for recovery.

By the end of her therapy, Suzanna had become much more skilled at drawing out the links between her depressive symptoms and the fluctuations in a number of different relationships. She had learned to be vigilant when the types of exchanges that had previously overlapped with her symptoms were happening and used this awareness to plan how to avoid repeating these patterns. She noticed the subtle impact of small exchanges in her day and responded to them more quickly, rather than letting them build up and spill over later. She also deliberately targeted the positive links, and made spending time with the people whose company she enjoyed a priority in her week.

Exercise 6.3: Exploring the links between your symptoms and your relationships

On a blank page in your notebook, make a copy of the chart in appendix 3. Go back to the examples from the last week that you have just been thinking about in exercise 6.2. Write down the symptoms that you noticed in those examples on your blank chart. Then write down the relationship triggers or consequences in the second column. Draw a line between the items in the two columns each time you recognize a link.

- Can you follow the links back and forth in your own experience or are there some gaps you find it difficult to explain?
- Does talking to someone else about what happened help you to see links that you didn't notice initially? Ask one of your IPT team if they can help.

This is a really useful exercise to repeat, especially if you often feel that your symptoms come out of the blue. It takes practice to get to the point where you can routinely understand your symptoms in context and see the triggers and consequences that surround them. You will be reminded to repeat this exercise each week when you have identified a relationship theme to focus on.

You will already have noticed that these exercises require quite a bit of effort on your part – and of course it's not always easy to summon up the energy to make that effort when you are depressed. So the next chapter is devoted to looking at your own role in working towards your recovery, and how you can make it easier for yourself – including, crucially, by getting help from other people.

Summary

- Depression is a common and treatable illness.
- Depression is more than just feeling sad. It disrupts our daily routines, emotional balance, clarity of thinking and energy levels.
- Many people experience depression more than once, and it is often a condition to manage rather than cure.
- Difficulties in relationships, or the lack of relationships, can contribute to depression: these include loneliness and poor social support as well as problems in existing relationships.
- Self-help approaches can be helpful for mild depression.
- Moderate to severe depression often responds to talking therapies and anti-depressant medication.
- Monitoring your symptoms each week (using the form in appendix 1) will help to develop your expertise in managing your depression.
- Monitoring the relationship triggers associated with any changes in your symptoms (using the form in appendix 3) will help you to put your depression in context.

Chapter 7

Your role in your recovery

In the choice between changing one's mind and proving there's no need to do so, most people get busy on the proof.

JOHN KENNETH GALBRAITH, ECONOMIST

IPT takes a 'no blame' approach to diagnosis. It is not your fault that you are depressed, and blaming yourself or feeling blamed by others will not help you to recover – in fact, it will probably make you feel worse! However, a 'no blame' diagnosis is not the same as a 'no consequences' diagnosis. It is likely that you are experiencing difficulties in a number of areas of your life, including with family and friends and at work. When you are depressed, the inclination is to retreat into yourself, but that is difficult to do without a knock-on effect. You are part of a network of relationships, and when you change it has an impact on the rest of the network. You might find this difficult to imagine when you're feeling depressed. You might feel that you are not important, and that your contribution at home or at work is of little consequence. Lots of people feel that way when they are depressed. But when any part of a network changes the whole network is affected.

To see how your life, and the lives of the people in your network, might be affected by your depression, try answering the questions in exercise 7.1. Write your responses in your notebook.

Exercise 7.1: Thinking about the effects of depression on you and others

- What effect has depression had on your life?
- What effect has your depression had on the people around you?
- In what ways would your life and the lives of the people close to you improve if you were no longer depressed?

We have already looked at the need for a *story* when you are depressed – a story that can help you to explain why you are not yourself at the moment and guide you towards recovery. This story serves as a bridge between you and the people in your life when you are unwell. It makes clear the additional burden you are experiencing and invites the people around you to think about how they can support your recovery.

Negotiating around illness: using your story

Back in the 1950s, the sociologist Talcott Parsons looked at how people behave when they are unwell and also at the behaviour of the people around them. His focus was less on illness itself and more on the *negotiations* that happen between you and the people close to you when you're ill – for example, you might all agree that you won't be doing some things for a while. When you are unwell it is difficult to meet the normal expectations of others, and so you need to explain why this is. Your depression story is a useful tool in explaining this change to other people.

The main points that Parsons highlighted, and that are used in IPT, are captured in the diagram below.

ACKNOWLEDGING AND ACCEPTING DIAGNOSIS

When you are depressed you are hampered by an array of symptoms and often can't manage your daily routines as you ordinarily would. Living with depression can be like tackling life with one hand tied behind your back. So it is important to recognize that you are ill and to put some of your responsibilities on hold while you deal with the illness – e.g. you may take a few days off work or cut back on the jobs you normally do at home. This involves, first, understanding your symptoms as part of an illness and giving yourself permission to take a break; and second, agreeing this with the people who will be affected by this change. This is the negotiation. Making this temporary concession and agreeing to adjust your routines is a constructive way for you and the people close to you to respond to the reality of the symptoms of depression, acknowledging that they are not simply imagined or made up. This is an important step in your becoming an expert in depression. Depression is often misunderstood because it is difficult for other people to *see* it. With other illnesses there are test results on paper or an obvious injury, like broken bones. Depression is less visible, but is no less real and has no less of an impact.

Let's compare overcoming depression with adjusting to a chronic illness such as diabetes. If their diabetes is well managed, someone with this illness can still live a full and active life, even though they will need to make some adjustments in diet, exercise and medication. When a person understands the nature of his illness and how it works, he can use his knowledge to manage its impact and therefore to influence its course. At the same time, it is also very useful for the people close to him to understand the illness as well. For example, it will be particularly helpful for other people to know what to do if his blood sugar drops and symptoms flare up, because if this happens, he might become irritable and confused and may not be lucid. So the people close to him need to know what to do to see him through moments of crisis as well as help him in the more routine day-to-day adjustments.

There are obvious differences between a medical condition like diabetes and depression, but there also some important similarities. The person with depression and the person with diabetes both need to understand their illness and to monitor their symptoms or they will risk an acute flare-up. Both need to adjust routines around exercise, diet and, potentially, medication in order to stabilize their condition. Both need to have informed back-up to see them through times of crisis in order to avoid the risk of more serious illness and potentially serious harm. Depression is serious, and the implications can be just as problematic as for other illnesses.

Now think about your own situation and how you could apply these ideas by answering the questions in exercise 7.2.

Exercise 7.2: Thinking about the consequences of accepting your diagnosis

- Can you see that depression is an illness and not your fault?
- Which daily activity that really makes your heart sink could you set aside temporarily to give yourself a break?
- Which responsibilities could you pass to someone else, or share with someone, while you are recovering?

It can be difficult to think about what you can give up and whom you can ask for help. When depression undermines your sense of worth it is difficult to care for yourself properly, let alone ask other people to do the same. Sometimes this is easier to think about if you imagine first what you would stop doing, and what help you would ask for, if you were physically ill in another way, say if you had a bad dose of flu. Now try to keep this care-taking perspective in mind as you answer the questions in exercise 7.3.

Exercise 7.3: Giving yourself a break and asking for help

- Who could you ask for help?
- What could you ask them to do for you?
- What could you stop doing just until you felt better?
- Would any of this be helpful to you now?

ACCEPTING RESPONSIBILITY TO WORK TOWARDS YOUR RECOVERY

Being unwell is not only unpleasant for you, it is also undesirable for the people around you. You are part of a network, and each person in that network relies on everyone else to make his or her contribution for the whole system to work. If one person can't make their contribution, both that individual and the system as a whole feel the effects. Therefore it is in the interests of both the person who is unwell *and* their network to support a quick recovery.

This has two implications. The first is that, as the person who is unwell, you are expected to **make recovery a priority**, not set it aside for later, when you feel up to it or after more important things have been done. **You are important; your contribution matters**. It is important to get you well as quickly and efficiently as possible. The second is that it is just as much in other people's interests for you to be well as it is in your own. Therefore **it is entirely reasonable to look to others to help you** to make your recovery. This is a really important point to emphasize. It is not uncommon for people who have depression to recognize that support is available but to struggle to access it – 'I don't like to ask for help', 'They have their own troubles', etc. We will look at this in more detail below under the heading 'You and your IPT team'.

An important part of recovery is deliberately seeking out anti-depressant activities – that is, things to do that give you enjoyment and pleasure. One of the core symptoms of depression is having less interest in people and activities than usual and taking less pleasure from the things you do and the people you see. The activity and other person may be the same as they always were; what's different is how you respond to them. Depression therefore quickly limits both the things you do and the company you keep, and so the opportunities for enjoying yourself. It is not surprising that life becomes uninteresting if almost all the things that gave it flavour have been dropped from your routine.

The challenge, therefore, is to reintroduce being in company and doing activities *before* you feel like it in order *to* feel like it. It is tempting to try to tackle this the other way round, that is, to say: 'When I feel better I will do more, see more people, try new things.' Unfortunately, depression does not work like that – it is *through* doing more, seeing more people and trying new things that you will start to feel better. This might even mean that you have to persevere for a while before feeling the benefit. This is not the same as putting on a brave face and pretending something is better than it is. You might do things, see people and try new things and initially have to concede that it did little for you. You might even feel that it took more out of you than you got out of it. However, what you are doing is giving yourself the *chance* of a different experience, the chance of feeling a spark of pleasure or interest. And at first this might be little more than a spark – like a camera flash that briefly illuminates a space and lets you glimpse what is there before the darkness returns. Gradually you will start to find that, instead of just a single flash, you might have a cluster of flashes that keep the light on for a little longer. You might be able to string some of these together, or start to regain a sense of control over making the flash light up. Depression is good at robbing you of both your sense of control and your sense of hope, and a natural consequence is that you stop pursuing or creating opportunities to improve things. This part of the work we do in IPT is about creating opportunities, even if we have to wait for the results to catch up.

With all this in mind, start noting some ideas down for your-self by doing exercise 7.4.

Exercise 7.4: What can you do straight away to start making opportunities for improvement?

- Which daily routines do you need to improve, e.g. eating more healthily, taking regular exercise, etc.?
- Who can help you with this? What can they do *specifically* to help?
- Which hobbies or interests can you start to re-introduce so that the possibility of pleasure is built back into your day?
- Whose company do you enjoy? Make a plan to see that person.

YOU AND YOUR IPT TEAM

As you start to identify the responsibilities you might be able to set aside for a while and the pleasurable activities you can start to introduce, think about whom this might affect, e.g.:

- the people who expect you to do the things you are setting aside;
- the people you will ask to do something different or more often for a while;
- the people who, if they do not know about what you are doing, might inadvertently create an obstacle in the way of your achieving your goal;
- the people who would benefit from your recovery.

The people who come to mind when you answer these questions are the people it would be useful to talk to about your depression. In appendices 4 and 5 you will find information to share with the people in your life. Appendix 4 sets out information about depression and IPT, and explains the valuable role the people in your life can play in supporting your recovery. Appendix 5 provides a useful chart for you and your team to use in warding off future episodes of depression. Read over this information yourself and pass copies on to them.

IPT is not a private therapy, and you will benefit from it most if other people know what you are doing and are invited to help. This book contains lots of information and exercises to guide your efforts to feel better, but the bulk of the work in IPT happens when you put the book down and put the ideas into practice with the people in your life. This might feel daunting, but it is the biggest step you can take away from depression and towards feeling better.

Your IPT team are the people who will support and encourage you in the coming weeks. Your team might include any or all of a partner, friends, family and your IPT therapist. The size of your team is up to you. You might feel more comfortable sharing what you are doing with just one other person, or you might want to tap into the different kinds of support available from a range of people.

The members of your team should be people you trust, can spend time with regularly and feel able to talk with about your feelings and relationships. You will not be forced to tell anyone on your team anything you do not feel ready to discuss, but it is useful to bear in mind that having gentle and encouraging support when you are facing difficult issues and feelings can be very helpful – indeed, research has shown that it improves mental health generally, not just where people are depressed.

Your team might help you in a number of ways:

- **Companionship**: It's good to have someone to join you when you become more active, whether in taking exercise, socializing, picking up old interests or starting new hobbies and/or pursuing shared interests.

- **Building up the picture**: Each of the chapters in this book is broken up with a series of questions that help to develop your story. These could be used as the basis of conversations with the team members who support you at each stage. One of your team could ask you the individual questions and think about your answers and plans with you. This doesn't mean they have to take on the role of a therapist, but they can help you to stay on track and to keep going if your motivation dips.

- **Practical help**: Some team members might know relatively little about the detail of what you are doing but can still offer practical help that will allow you to spend time on the more personal or emotional aspects of this process. For example, someone might look after your children once a week to give you thinking time or perhaps time to talk to another team member.

- **Monitoring progress:** It can be very helpful to have someone who knows the goals you have set for yourself and who helps you to review your progress at regular intervals. This might highlight changes in your mood that you had not noticed, help you to refocus if you start to lose direction, and help you to think through the inevitable setbacks which will interrupt your progress at times.

Now that you have considered all these points, it's time to do exercise 7.5. Take your notebook and make a list.

Exercise 7.5: Choosing your IPT team

- Who will you invite to be on your team?

Now you are armed with information and support to begin work towards your recovery, it's time to start looking for the central theme of your own story that will provide a focus for you to work on. The next chapter shows you how to set about this by drawing up your own storyboard or timeline.

Summary

- IPT takes a 'no blame' approach towards the diagnosis of depression.
- Understanding and accepting depression is the first step in recovery.
- Working towards recovery is a priority.
- Recovery is a team effort.

Chapter 8

Understanding the story of your depression

I wanted a perfect ending. Now I have learned the hard way that some poems don't rhyme, and some stories don't have a clear beginning, middle and end. Life is about not knowing, having to change, taking the moment and making the best of it, without knowing what's going to happen next.

Delicious ambiguity.

GILDA RADNER, COMEDIENNE AND ACTRESS

How do timelines work?

It is very useful to have a timeline to help you to think about the overlap between events in your life, especially those involving other people, and your depression – the basic link that we focus on in IPT over and over.

A timeline, at its simplest, records the order of events as they happened over a specific period of time. For example, in the kind of timeline set out below, the events are set out clearly (above the line) against the months in which they happened (below the line), but the relationship between the events is not examined.

Jennie's timeline

Moved city	Found new Job	Started relationship	Left job	Relationship difficulties	
					TIME
Jan	April	July	Oct	Dec	

We can see that Jennie's timeline describes a year that involved a lot of change. The story starts with her moving to a new city and finding a new job, followed by starting a new relationship a couple of months later. Jennie then leaves her job after six months and the year ends with her relationship hitting a difficult patch. We know the basics of what happened and when. but we don't yet know if any of the events are connected, or how these events related to Jennie's experience of depression, if at all. This sequence could be the basis for a number of different stories. Jennie might have left her job because she didn't like it or because she had always been planning to start studying and just needed something to fill the months before her course began. The simple facts don't tell us whether it was a positive or negative event, planned or unexpected. The relationship could have come under strain because Jennie was feeling low about being unemployed, or because she was busy with new friends at college and had less time for her relationship. Or it might have been nothing to do with work: perhaps it just wasn't a good match. So, knowing what happened and when is useful, but not enough to make sense of the story.

A more informative timeline will help you to develop your story by highlighting how events are linked. Depression does not occur in a vacuum, so understanding what was going on at the time you became depressed is central to deciding what to do about it. If you can tackle the problems that led to your depression or keep it going, you have a much better chance of resolving the depression itself.

The next diagram, still based on Jennie's story, is a little more complicated but captures more of the story. As well as the timeline at the bottom, it includes a line up the side indicating how well or depressed Jennie was, with a dotted horizontal line marking the transition between feeling well and feeling depressed. It also includes a curving black line which shows the fluctuation in how depressed she feels. Now we can start to see whether events simply follow in sequence or might have an effect on what happens later. We can also trace the way depression developed and think about what contribution each event made to that process. For example, in this diagram the move to a new city appears to have been positive, as does finding a job and starting a new relationship. This is shown by the rising curve of the line that is tracking depression, heading in the direction marked 'not depressed'. Losing her job appears very closely tied to Jennie starting to feel depressed, with the black line dipping very sharply just after that happened. This suggests that Jennie may have found it difficult to cope with this important change. The difficulties in her relationship start a few months after the depression started, which suggests that these difficulties may not have triggered the depression but could be one of the consequences of depression continuing over several weeks. When the connections between the different pieces of information we hold begin to become clearer in this way, it becomes a little easier to start to understand what the story is about.

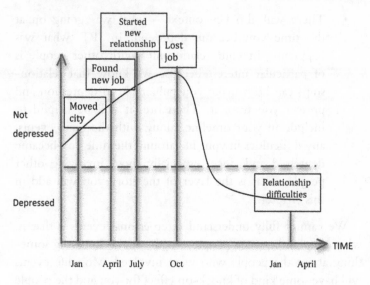

Preparing to make your own timeline

The timeline you will be developing is your own, and so you start this task as the clear expert. No one knows your story better than you do. Even when it feels confusing and overwhelming, you still know more about it than anyone else does. The IPT process will help you to make sense of your story and so of your depression.

Like any story, your story of depression will have several layers.

- There will be the story of your symptoms and how they developed over time. This is the story you started in chapter 6, when you identified the range of depressive symptoms you have been experiencing recently. This story might also come with some history, if you have experienced depression before.

- There will also be context – what was going on at the time you became depressed. In IPT, what was happening in your relationships with other people is of particular interest because we know that relationships can both make you vulnerable to depression and protect you from it. Therefore, it will be helpful to include in your timeline, along with the main events, any difficulties in your life around the time you became depressed and since, especially those involving other people. That is the layer of the story you will add in this chapter.

We cannot fully understand interpersonal events – that is, what happens between people – without also knowing something about the people who were involved. Most life events will have some kind of knock-on effect for you and the people around you. In Jennie's example above, she moved cities. This meant she had fewer opportunities to see her old friends, so she might have been trying to make some new friends through her job and by starting to date someone. Jennie's new friends and colleagues became less available when she left her job and her new relationship might have struggled to cope with the impact of depression at such an early stage. The way in which people rapidly appeared and disappeared in this story contributed to Jennie's vulnerability to depression. We will look at the characters in your story in detail in chapter 9. For now simply take note of the main people who were involved in the events and difficulties you identified above.

The three stages of your timeline

In building the picture of your depression that you will use in IPT, it is helpful if you start in the present and work backwards.

Initially, in exercise 6.1, you thought about all of the symptoms that you have been experiencing in the last couple of weeks. Next you will extend the picture to cover the weeks or months since you started to feel depressed recently. Finally, it will be useful to add some more detail about any previous experiences of depression you have had. The diagram below shows how these three stages build on one another to give you the whole picture.

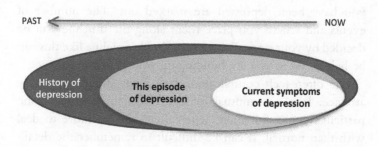

By doing this you can build up a rich and coherent story that can help you and the people close to you understand your current experiences and make plans for change. In IPT we are trying to understand the current interpersonal context for your depression – that is, the relationship issues in your depression story – in order to help you feel both less depressed and more effective in managing difficulties with other people. Our aim is to work in manageable chunks. Consequently we start with a simple timeline, *focusing on your recent experience of depression*, but in the full knowledge that it forms part of the bigger picture of your life.

Let's look first at the most simple timeline initially, in which the order of significant events of a period are written out.

	Event:	Event:	Event:	Event:
Start of				
recent				**Present**
period				
of				
depression	Date:	Date:	Date:	Date:

In this diagram the most important events during the time you have been depressed are marked out. The number of events and where you place them along the timeline will be decided by your story. Even a very simple timeline like this can be helpful when you are building up your personal story.

Life often feels complicated, with many things happening at once. It is not unusual for depression to develop during particularly stressful times, when there is even more to deal with than normal. It can be difficult to remember the details when you are depressed, and life might have started to feel like an overwhelming wave of pressure pushing you under. This simple timeline can help you to start to think about this turbulent period in a more constructive way. It is a first step towards planning how to get out of the depression by working on the most relevant relationship difficulties.

If you find it difficult to remember everything that has been happening in your life, look back over diaries and photographs from the time when you first began to feel depressed, or tap into other people's memories by asking them what they remember. This is where your IPT team could help, especially if they were around at the time you became depressed. They might be able to help you piece together the story.

Talk through what you are trying to do and ask if they can think of any other events or problems you might have overlooked. The idea is not to record every single thing that happened around the time you became depressed recently, but rather to focus on the main events, especially those involving other people, that were important to you and that had an influence on your symptoms.

- **Who can help you to construct your timeline?**
- **Who was around at the time that you started feeling depressed and is still around now? Ask them what they remember about that time.**

A very simple timeline outlines the events during the time when you have been depressed. However, depression rarely develops out of the blue, although it may sometimes feel like it. It is therefore a good idea to start your timeline a little *before* you became depressed. This will capture the things you were dealing with at the time, which may have influenced the way depression developed. The connections run two ways: what goes on with the people around us has an impact on how we feel and function, and how we feel goes a long way towards determining how we talk and behave with the people around us.

Drawing your own timeline

Let's think about pulling these ideas together to draw a more developed timeline. There are many ways to do this, using words, pictures or symbols. You can experiment to find out what suits you best. You can use your notebook, but often a large piece of paper and some sticky notes are best for this exercise.

STEP ONE

Copy the basic graph on to your piece of paper. The dotted line running horizontally across the middle marks the dividing line between feeling depressed and not feeling depressed. This allows you to mark out clearly the times when you felt well and the times when you felt depressed.

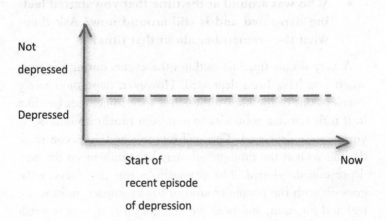

The solid horizontal line along the bottom records time. When did you first notice yourself becoming depressed recently? Try to remember the approximate date, e.g. 'last summer', 'February last year', and work forward from there. If you find it difficult to identify when the depression started, think about when you noticed it getting worse recently. Sometimes people describe not feeling fully well between episodes of depression but having periods when their mood and other symptoms dip more than usual. When did you notice the most recent major dip – perhaps when you became aware of changes in sleep or mood or enthusiasm for the things you normally enjoy? Mark this date under 'Start of recent episode of depression'.

Now mark out a regular series of intervals along the line between that 'start' date and 'now'. The units of time you use should reflect how long this episode of depression has lasted. If you have been depressed for six months, split the solid line into months. If it has been longer, it might be easier to divide the line into blocks of three or six months. The point is to use whatever scheme best helps you to record *your* experience. Two examples are included in the diagram below. Having regular intervals marked out will help to show how events unfolded over time. Leave a little space at the beginning of the solid line so that you can add details of what was happening just before you became depressed. In the diagram below you will see that 'start of the recent episode of depression' is noted a little way along the line.

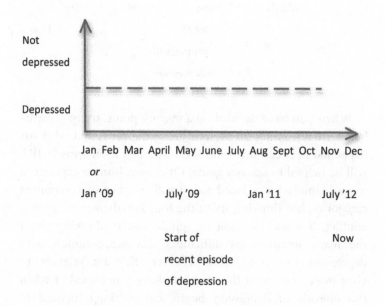

Paul's timeline, which we will see in context in chapter 15, is set out below as an example. Paul had been depressed for nine months, and so his timeline covered the last year and was broken down into three-month intervals.

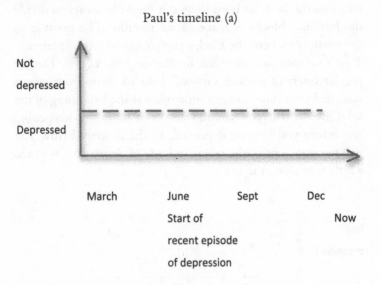

Paul's timeline (a)

Not depressed

Depressed

March   June   Sept   Dec

              Start of   Now
              recent episode
              of depression

When you have decided on a starting point, try to remember what was going on in your life at the time, and what has happened between that time and now. The focal areas in IPT will be helpful to use as a guide. Of course, human experience cannot simply be reduced to a small number of convenient categories, but thinking about the four key themes of change, conflict, loss and isolation can guide you in thinking about the many interpersonal difficulties that are common with depression and considering whether they are relevant to your story, starting at the time you have pinpointed as when this episode of depression began and working forward to the present.

Change or 'role transition'

When you first started to become depressed, was anything changing in your environment or routine that involved an adjustment in one of your roles – as parent, as partner, as employee, etc.? Having to adapt to change and to adjust how you operate from day to day is a common feature of life, but sometimes the nature of the change can unsettle you rather than propel you on to something new and exciting. So let's think about your routine – the structure of your day, the people who populate it, the expectations others have of you and how ready you feel to meet those expectations. Did any of that change around the time you're thinking about? Perhaps a relationship started or stopped. Did your work environment change – with promotion, redundancy or a period of leave? Did someone close to you experience a change in their routine that had an impact on you? For instance, did your partner lose their job, your parent or child fall ill, or an adult child move out of the family home? There might be all kinds of examples – take time to think over that period and consider all the changes you had to adapt to at the time.

Remember that not all changes are obviously either good or bad. Adapting to change is a very common life experience and some of the things on your list might be changes you feel you coped with. If so – well done! Sometimes the difficulty comes because there are so many changes all at once; sometimes because they happen so quickly and leave you feeling wrong-footed and poorly prepared. Sometimes a change takes so long to happen that you are worn down by the time it actually comes about, so that even something you expected or wanted to happen is hard to complete or welcome. You do not need to make any value judgements on the significance of the changes at this stage; simply acknowledge them. Write down on one of your sticky notes each of the changes you have faced since your recent episode of depression began.

Change in Paul's timeline

Paul had a number of changes on his timeline. First, the company he worked for was taken over and all of the staff had to reapply for their own jobs. This created a lot of tension at work and increased Paul's workload. Then, when he applied for his own job, he was very surprised to be unsuccessful and angry to have been replaced by a junior colleague. Although he was offered a job it was at a more junior level, so Paul left the company. This meant Paul was unemployed for the first time in his working life and he suddenly found himself spending all of his time at home. Before all of these changes had happened Paul had had a busy professional life and was a member of two sports clubs. When he became depressed he gave up his hobbies and spent more time at home with his family than he had done for a very long time.

Conflict

The second key theme is conflict. Again, this is a common element in almost all human relationships; it might be fleeting and trivial, or might be the main character of a relationship. When conflict is temporary and can be left behind because the central issue has been addressed, it can leave the people involved feeling closer to each other. Clearing the air and sorting things out can be a very useful thing to do – a bit like an emotional spring-clean. However, sometimes conflict will linger on, being only partly set aside with the issues not really resolved. Or it might have been tackled head-on but resulted in a stand-off without reaching an agreement. In either of the latter cases it is far more likely to have a negative impact on your mood and, over time, on other symptoms of depression.

Think about the relationships you were involved in at the time when you started to feel depressed. Were any of them going through a tough patch? Were you feeling less close to anyone or taking less pleasure in someone's company? Did you find yourself arguing with anyone more frequently than normal or carrying uncomfortable feelings like frustration, disappointment or resentment after spending time with certain people? Think about what happened to these disagreements. Were they ever sorted out? Did circumstances change? Are they still unresolved or only partly resolved? It is useful to take note of when relationships have not been working so well and think about how this experience influenced your mood and other symptoms. Make a note of any relationships that were in conflict at the time you became depressed, again using your sticky notes.

Facing a dispute in a close or significant relationship can feel daunting or frightening. When you are depressed it can be difficult to resist imagining the worst. You may fear that if you admit that there is a problem then the relationship will crumble under scrutiny. Try to be as honest with yourself as you can about any troubles you are experiencing in your relationships now, to give yourself the best chance of understanding what might be feeding into the symptoms of depression and keeping them going. Again, write down any recurrences of conflict, or new disagreements, on sticky notes, and take note of when the disagreements started:

- Some might have flared up around the time you got depressed.
- Some might have been around long before you felt

depressed, but affected you more once you were
depressed because you had less energy to bounce back.
• Others might have developed some time after you had
started to feel depressed, but because by then you were
feeling withdrawn and irritable you were less able to
manage them.

Conflict in Suzanna's timeline

Suzanna had an on–off relationship with her long-term
partner. They had been together for six years, apart from a
few months when they had split up a couple of years into
the relationship. Although the relationship had started
again, they often argued and would spend several days at a
time not speaking to each other. When Suzanna gave her
partner an ultimatum about the future of the relationship
one year earlier, he had refused to do as she wanted and
she became much more depressed. Suzanna had friends
at work but she rarely talked to them about her personal
life. However, she also felt angry with them for not offering her more support around her relationship with her
partner, and this regularly led to small disagreements and
fallings-out which made her depression worse at times.

Loss and grief

Many people experience something very similar to depression
when someone significant in their life dies, such as a partner or
child. That is not to say that everyone who is bereaved becomes
depressed, but rather that it is a common human reaction to
feel intensely sad at such times and for routines to be disrupted.
It is for this reason that depression is not diagnosed in the first
two months after a major bereavement; it is recognized that

the adjustment is almost always difficult and painful and is not an illness.

However, the majority of people report a slow change in their experience following bereavement, as they gradually learn to live with the loss. If this gradual progress does not happen it might indicate that the person has become stuck and depression has started to develop.

Had you experienced a bereavement around the time your depression started? Or was there an anniversary of a significant bereavement at that time? If so, write it down. Note when the bereavements happened and consider how they may have contributed to the change in your depressive symptoms recently.

There may well be bereavements earlier in your life that you still feel sad about. For the moment, only note those bereavements that happened around the time that you became depressed. We will come back to think about experiences further in your past later on.

Loss in Jean's timeline

Jean's husband had died three years ago. She had tried to build a life for herself by starting new jobs and spending time with her family but repeatedly found herself slipping back into depression. She became distant from her son because he criticized his father, and when she fell out with her daughter and thought that she might not be able to see her granddaughter she became distraught and could no longer find the will to get out of bed in the morning. She had expected to recover more quickly following her husband's death so initially overlooked its impact. Through her timeline she recognized that her current difficulties could be traced back over the three years since he had died.

Isolation

The fourth area in IPT is different in character from the other three we have just looked at. It concerns difficulties in starting or sustaining relationships and so may not involve a specific event, although these difficulties might overlap with times of change, conflict or loss when you feel more isolated than you usually do. Maybe making friends has always felt daunting; or maybe you find the boundary between an acquaintance and a friend baffling and so find yourself on the edges of relationships but not getting what you want out of them. We know from research that being socially isolated is strongly related to depression, and can make people more vulnerable to becoming depressed. Sometimes people live with isolation for a long time, and find it difficult to imagine anything else.

In IPT we do not try to force people to be in more relationships for the sake of it, but we do take seriously the vulnerability to depression resulting from insufficient support. What constitutes *sufficient* support will vary from person to person and might only be revealed when the need for other people to rely on becomes more obvious. Do you have enough support to see you through an unusually tough time, or would this stretch your resources too far? Often your degree of isolation becomes more apparent with change, for example, when someone you relied on is no longer available, or if you suddenly have to be around more people than normal and find this overwhelming, e.g. when starting a new job and having to get to know new colleagues. Finding relationships difficult is unlikely to feel new, but it may have become a bigger problem recently and fuelled your feelings of depression. If you have noticed not having relationships becoming more of a problem, jot this down on one of your sticky notes.

Or if you have noticed an increasing demand that you make contacts with other people when you do not feel confident or comfortable doing so, write down when that happened on a sticky note.

Isolation in Miranda's timeline

Miranda had always found it difficult to make friends and spent much of her time on her own. She had few friends whom she saw regularly, and she worked alone, often from home. Her social routine in recent months largely revolved around a work colleague who had befriended her. When her friend moved to Spain, Miranda found it very difficult to keep up the social routine they had shared and retreated back into spending much of her time alone in her bedroom. She felt lonely and frustrated but did not know how to change her situation.

STEP TWO

It might take a series of attempts to gather together all your relevant events. Don't worry if you can't quite remember the order in which things happened or all of the details. Just write down on sticky notes the events that make up your story as you remember them. Some events might overlap, as there are often several things happening in our lives at one time. Using the sticky notes can help you to build up the layered narrative of your story.

Now add your notes of the main events that happened during that period to your timeline. It may be easiest to simply note the sequence of events initially, that is, the order in which things happened, without trying to position them in relation to the vertical line indicating how depressed you were.

If you have difficulty remembering the order of events, move the notes around until you think it matches what happened. Think about whether the events overlapped with each other, clustered together or heightened the impact of other events at the same time. For example, losing your job and splitting up with your partner are both likely to feel bad, and each might feel worse if they happen at the same time. If events overlapped you can cluster the notes together to remind yourself that it was a demanding or busy time.

Once you're happy that you've got the events in sequence, now think about them in relation to how depressed you were at the time. If some events were clearly linked to being depressed, place those notes below the dotted line. If other events were not related to your depression, place them above the dotted line. The next diagram gives you an outline of how this might look, followed by Paul's timeline as a more concrete example.

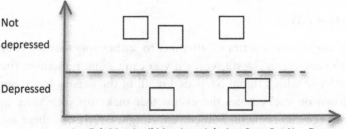

STEP THREE

Once you have placed the main events in sequence, and positioned them according to your level of depression when they happened, think about whether any of the problems have been resolved. For example, you might have had a big argument with your sister a few months ago but have worked it out since; or perhaps you lost your job, but have recently found a new one. Pay particular attention to the problems that are still around for you now and which contribute to your feeling depressed.

Paul's timeline (b)

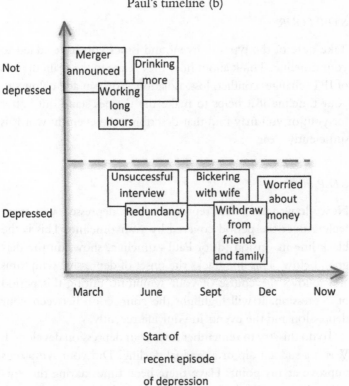

Not depressed	Merger announced — Working long hours	Drinking more		

Unsuccessful interview — Redundancy   Bickering with wife   Withdraw from friends and family   Worried about money

Depressed

March   June   Sept   Dec   Now

Start of
recent episode
of depression

In Paul's story, some of the problems that featured early in the story were no longer difficult for him: for example, he no longer had to worry about the company being taken over, he had stopped working long hours and he had also reduced the amount he was drinking. These past issues have been faded out on the next version of his timeline (c), and the remaining issues have been highlighted in bold type as ongoing difficulties. The boxes corresponding to the original sticky notes have been stretched to indicate that those issues have remained a problem over the months he has been depressed.

STEP FOUR

Take note of the types of event and issues you have added to your timeline. Think about how they relate to the main themes of IPT: change, conflict, loss, isolation. You can add colours to your timeline if it helps to make the themes stand out better for you; or you may find that describing the event in words is sufficiently clear.

STEP FIVE

Now draw a line that represents how depressed you were feeling over the period covered by your timeline. This is the black line in version (d) of Paul's timeline, shown in the diagram below. This line tracks the onset of depressive symptoms and follows the course of your symptoms during this period of depression. It will highlight the connection between your depression and the events in your life recently.

To do this, try to remember how your depression developed. Was it a sudden dip or a gradual decline? Did your symptoms improve at any point? Have there been times during this episode when you have felt worse than you do now?

Paul's timeline (c)

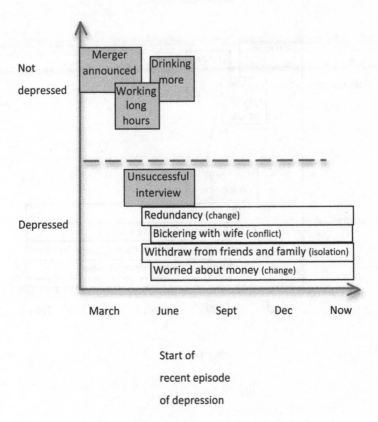

In Paul's story his symptoms of depression started quite suddenly after his unsuccessful interview. He has remained low
in the months that followed and has become very isolated.
Therefore his depression line dips sharply early in the diagram
and remains below the depression line until the present.

Paul's timeline (d)

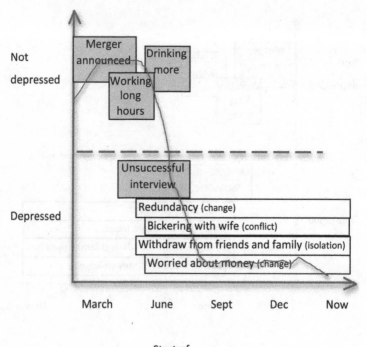

Start of

recent episode

of depression

STEP SIX

In this final stage of developing your timeline you add brief details of times when you have been depressed in the past. Note the date and the main issues during that period of depression, if you know what it related to.

Paul had been depressed once in the past, when his first business collapsed, almost twenty years earlier. He didn't receive any treatment at the time.

Paul's timeline (e)

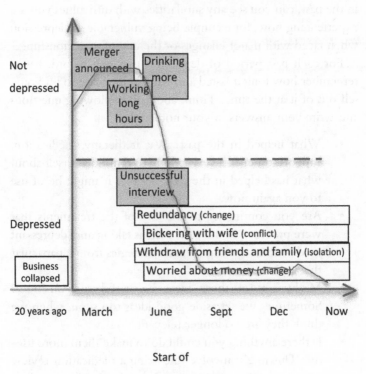

Start of

recent episode

of depression

Have you been depressed before? If so, what were the main difficulties you faced at that earlier time? Add the date and a word or two to describe the main events related to your past experiences of depression. In version (e) of his timeline, Paul has marked his previous episode of depression, some 20 years earlier. This also related to a period of change at work and may suggest that not being successful in his working life is an area of particular vulnerability for Paul.

When you think about times that you have been depressed in the past, can you see any similarities with difficulties you are experiencing now, for example being vulnerable to depression when faced with major changes or the end of a relationship?

For each past period of depression that you record, try to remember how long it lasted and what helped you to lift yourself out of it at the time. Think about the following questions and write your answers in your notebook.

- What helped in the past? Was it therapy, medication, support, time? It is very helpful to remind yourself about what has helped in the past, because it might be of use to you again now.
- Are you continuing to use any of the treatments that were provided in the past, such as taking anti-depressant medication, or using ideas or strategies from a particular therapy?
- Might any of these ideas be useful to you now? Sometimes we set aside good ideas too soon, when we think they are no longer relevant.
- Is there anything you could do to make them more useful? This might involve discussing a medication review with your GP or using strategies picked up in a previous therapy more regularly, for example, maintaining a regular routine around going to bed or relaxation exercises.
- Have less formal approaches been helpful to you in managing past episodes, such as talking to friends, taking exercise daily?
- Have you been able to use these less formal coping strategies during this episode of depression?
- If you're finding this kind of thing difficult to do for yourself at the moment, is there anyone who could help you to do it?
- What would you need to do to get this help and to start

using the strategies that you know have been helpful to you in the past?

When you have completed your timeline, think about what it tells you about your current experience of depression. Does it suggest what it might be useful to focus on to help you navigate your way out of this episode? You don't have to be sure about this at the moment. In fact, it is helpful to try to keep an open mind and consider as many possibilities as you can. This is another reason why it is a good idea to involve someone else in putting together your timeline. They might be able to see or imagine links that have not occurred to you yet, and that may open up other options for ways out of the depression you are experiencing.

I hope you will be starting to see by now some of the ways in which your relationships with the people around you may be intertwined with the story of your depression – and how some of those people can help you recover. In the next chapter we will look at your current relationships more closely when we set about making an 'inventory' or catalogue of them: what in IPT we call your own 'interpersonal inventory'.

Summary

- The timeline looks at the overlap between events in your life and your depression.
- The timeline helps you to distinguish between your current problems and problems you have already resolved.
- The timeline mainly focuses on your current depression, but is informed by past episodes of depression.
- The timeline looks at how the main IPT themes of change, conflict, loss and isolation feature in your story.
- Creating a timeline is an opportunity to involve other people in your story.

Chapter 9

Your interpersonal inventory

The profoundest impediments to our desire most often lie close to home, in our own bodies, personalities, friends, lovers and family.

JANET BURROWAY, WRITER

The characters in your story

One of the key tasks early in IPT is to make an inventory of your current relationships. This is an interesting task through which you will create a rich interpersonal context in which to understand your depression. In fact, it can be surprisingly informative about your depression and the most useful ways to find a path out of it. It is helpful to approach this task with an open and curious mind, as it will often reveal things about your own network of relationships that you had not previously realized.

Until now we have focused on developing the story of your depression – the symptoms, the context, and the events and relationships that have influenced its course. This is a very good start. However, IPT operates in the links between what is happening in your symptoms and what is happening in your relationships – in other words, which relationships make you feel better and which make you feel worse. Therefore it is very important to start to populate your story with the key relationships in your life.

Like any good story, this one is likely to be populated with people whom you are more or less drawn to and relationships you are more or less happy with. The inventory is not simply a list of people who can support you, although this information is crucial. It is a dynamic list of all the current relationships that have an impact on you and your depressive symptoms, whether positive or negative. By understanding more about your current relationships and the issues at play in them, we aim to understand more about your depression and, crucially, your way out of it.

It would be overly simplistic to divide your relationships into opposite categories like 'helpful' and 'unhelpful', but it can be useful to think of them in broad and flexible clusters. Some ideas are central to using IPT, so we want to make sure they inform the way you review your relationships. With this in mind, the most useful inventory will cover:

- the support available to you, the use you make of it and how this has changed since you have been depressed;
- the relationship difficulties you are trying to deal with and how significant these are for your depression;
- the four IPT themes of change, conflict, loss and isolation;
- how central each of these factors will be in your plan to overcome your depression.

One of the principles of IPT is seeking to achieve balance – balance in description, balance in perspective, and balance in your view of relationships. To that end, we will look at what is good and what is not so good about each of your important relationships. It is important to be able to tolerate having those aspects of your relationships that appeal to you and those that trouble you as part of the same picture. You might want to change the picture, but it is best to have seen the whole picture before you try to do so. It is the nature of human relationships that, individually, they satisfy some but not all of our needs – and in some cases they even frustrate our needs. This applies to very good relationships as much as those that are more like thorns in our side.

As with all of the tasks in this process, putting together this list is most usefully done with someone else. The very act of having to describe your relationships to someone else can give clarity to your thoughts. Ask one of your IPT team to help you complete this task. If you currently struggle to think of anyone who can help you, don't worry, you can work up to sharing the details of your list with someone else. Your inventory might even help you to find this person.

Getting an overview of your relationship world

A good way to start is by drawing a diagram of the network of people who surround you. This will give you a powerful visual reminder of the people in your network that you can update and change as you go on. The style of the diagram is not especially important: what's important is that it is clear to you. Blank versions of both of the types we're going to look at here are provided in appendix 2 which you can copy and try out for yourself.

You could use a pattern of concentric circles, which allows you to show how close you feel to each person. The diagram below shows Sharon's relationships mapped out in this way. It's her 'relationship world' that is being described, so she is placed at the heart of the picture. Working outwards from the centre, the first circle is where Sharon will put her closest relationships. These are typically the people we are most emotionally involved with and often those we spend most time with. Placing a relationship close to the centre of the diagram *doesn't* mean that the relationship is perfect – there might be things that are tricky about these relationships, too – but they generally hold a significant place in our life. Sharon has identified her partner, David, as her closest relationship and so placed him right on the inner edge of the first circle. The next person Sharon includes is her friend, Michael, who is slightly further away from her on the diagram but still in the first circle. This suggests Michael is important to Sharon and someone it will be useful to think about when completing the inventory. The next person on the diagram is from another area of Sharon's life: her work colleague, Claire. This is still quite a close relationship, but Sharon has distinguished between this friendship and her closest relationships by placing Claire in the second circle. Finally, Sharon has added her sister, Louise, to the diagram. She has placed Louise right at the edge of the outer circle, which suggest that they have quite a distant relationship.

When you draw up your own inventory, it's a good idea to begin by putting all of the people you want to think about on your diagram, and then go over the questions that are suggested later in the chapter for each person in turn. That's because it is helpful to have an overview of your relationship world before you start going into detail about each individual relationship – and the overview itself might already tell you something quite important. For example, it appears from this first diagram that Sharon has some close relationships but doesn't have very many people in her life. This might mean that there is quite a lot of pressure on those few close relationships to meet all of her needs; or it might mean that she is not very sociable and is satisfied with a small number of close friends. The questions that follow will help us to understand more about the basic picture that we get from this overview.

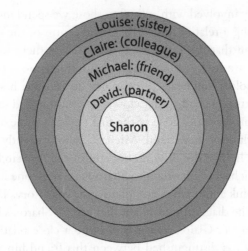

Another way of creating your inventory is to draw a spider diagram, like the one below. Each additional relationship is added in a new bubble. There is a lot of flexibility with this type of diagram, e.g. the people you feel close to can be added nearer the centre of the diagram and other people further out; family members or colleagues might cluster together, especially if you tend to see them together.

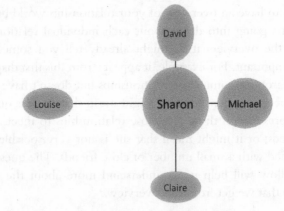

Whichever style of diagram you choose, aim to collect all of the information on a single page, to help you to get an overview of what your current relationships – your interpersonal world – look like.

Exercise 9.1: Creating your inventory

Use a blank page in your notebook to draw up your own relationship inventory. You can use a copy of either of the diagrams provided in appendix 2. Add the names of the main people who are in your life, as described for Sharon above. Focus on your current relationships, and especially those who influence your experience of depression, rather than trying to make a complete list of everyone you have ever known. Focusing on current relationships will make the task more manageable and more useful in understanding your depression now. Make sure you include the people who help to lift your depression *and* the people you associate with feeling worse. The relationships included are likely to range from intimate to more distant, and from happiest to troublesome.

When you have populated your diagram, look over the people you have included, and think about the following questions:

- How many people did you include?
- Does it surprise you how many or how few people you included?
- What does your diagram tell you about how involved you are with other people at the moment?

- How has depression changed the way your network would normally look?

You might like to write down the answers in your notebook, or discuss them with someone in your IPT team.

When you have completed exercise 9.1, try to think of a story that captures the essence of each relationship you have included on your diagram. It might be a simple anecdote or an important moment in the history of that relationship. Remember, stories can capture more than simple facts; they contain a sense of how the relationship feels. If someone is helping you to complete this task, tell him or her the stories.

Now take another look at your diagram and think about these questions:

- Which areas of your interpersonal life are represented in your list e.g. family, friends, work colleagues, etc.?
- Are any groups missing – e.g. people you share an interest with, such as sports, politics, book club, etc.; or people who you do not see regularly, perhaps because of distance or changing routines, but whom you still regard as friends?
- Does this list include the people you come into contact with as part of your daily routine, e.g. people you live with, who you spend time with during the day or in the evenings or at weekends?
- Have you spent time with anyone in the last month who is not on the list?

If any of these questions prompt you to think about people who are not already on the list, consider adding them. The aim is not to complete a 'final' or 'correct' version, but simply one that reflects your current relationships. There will be many more opportunities to revise or add to your inventory, either because the picture expands or because you develop a clearer sense of how you want it to look and start to take steps towards achieving that.

Taking a closer look

When you are satisfied that this list is reasonably representative of the people who are in your life and who influence your experience of depression, start thinking about each person in turn. This can take some time, depending on the length of your list, but try not to rush through it. You might find yourself feeling quite emotional when you look at some relationships, and working through the sequence at your own pace will help you to examine each relationship more fully; so it can be helpful to complete this task over a few sittings. While you're doing this, you can add anyone else who comes to mind. It is not unusual to think of other people you want to add some time into the process of putting together your inventory, once you have started to examine your interpersonal world more deliberately in this way.

Exercise 9.2: Beginning to explore your relationships

Taking each person in turn, think about the kind of relationship you have with them. A series of questions and prompts are set out below to guide you through this process. Sketching out a brief overview of each relationship in your notebook that addresses the key points highlighted in these questions will give you a good foundation on which to build a more detailed picture. Share what you feel comfortable about with the person who is helping you with this task.

- Is this a relationship you chose and still choose to be in? When and how did it start?
- What is the story of this relationship?
- Is this a relationship that has adapted in response to your changing needs and circumstances?
- Is this a relationship that has kept going through good and difficult times? What difficulties have you faced in this relationship and how have you come through them?
- How has this relationship featured in the story of your depression recently?
- How might this relationship contribute to your recovery?

Consider what strengths your notes reveal within your network – for example, adaptable relationships that you have chosen to be in and that have lasted over time; and also the vulnerabilities they highlight – for example, an inflexible network, or one that has been forced on you, or one whose membership changes rapidly and unpredictably. Write these down in your notebook and use your discussions to consider patterns you had not recognised before now.

The questions set out below in exercises 9.3 and 9.4 will guide you in filling out the sketch you have just made for each of your relationships. Think about the questions for each relationship in turn, and try to use them as guides to prompt you, rather than just as a checklist. Add stories about the relationships to bring the inventory to life. This will help you to home in on specific details rather than noting only general patterns or broad conclusions, which can often miss out some of the more interesting and valuable information.

The questions ask you to consider several different aspects of each relationship, more than you can easily hold in your mind at once. So it's a good idea to take simple notes about each relationship as you consider each set of questions. A summary table is provided below, after the questions, to help you to gather this information together. This will help you to summarize your thinking and may help you to pick out patterns that repeat across your relationships. This will also be useful to you later when you are monitoring your progress. It is likely that you will have much more to say about many of your relationships than you have space to record in the summary table. Write your full notes in your notebook and use the table to summarize your responses, as in Charles's example on pages 165–7. The summary chart also includes space for you to summarize your thoughts on how each of the four key themes of IPT – change, conflict, loss and isolation – may be connected with your relationships. We'll look at these connections, through another set of question prompts, in the next section of the chapter.

For now, let's start with the practicalities.

Exercise 9.3: Reviewing your inventory (1): contact and routines

Ask yourself, for each person in your inventory:

- How often are you in contact with each other? How happy are you with this amount of contact? What change would you make to this, if any, to make it better? How do you think the other person feels about the amount of time you spend together?
- Is your contact face to face, by telephone or email, through text messaging or a mixture?

Are you happy with this type of contact? What change would you make to this, if any, to make it better? How do you think the other person feels about the type of contact you have?

- How would you describe the time you spend together and what you do together?
- Does one of you take main responsibility for staying in contact, e.g. getting in touch, suggesting things to do, or is this shared between you? Are you happy with the balance of responsibility for keeping the relationship going? What change would you make to this, if any, to make it better? How do you think the other person feels about the way your time together is organized?
- Has the routine between you changed since you have been depressed? If so, in what ways has the relationship changed? What change, if any, would you like to see in this relationship? How do think the other person feels about the changes, if there have been any?

Exercise 9.4: Reviewing your inventory (2): help and support

Now think a little more about the emotional and supportive characteristics of each relationship.

- Does this person know that you have been feeling depressed? If yes, how did they find out and how have they responded to this information? If not, what has stopped you sharing this with them? Do you think they might suspect even if you have not told them? Are you happy with how much this person knows about your depression? What change would you make to this, if any, to make it better? How do you think the person feels about you being depressed?

- Is this someone you would normally be able to speak to about your feelings or when something is troubling you? If yes, when was the last time you did that, and did you find it helpful? Has this changed since you have been feeling depressed? If so, how has it changed? How do you think the other person feels about being asked for this support?

- Is this someone you can go to for practical help or advice that might not relate to how you are feeling, e.g. to give you a lift somewhere or pick up some shopping for you? If yes, when was the last time you did this, and was it helpful? Has this changed since you have been feeling depressed? If so, how has it changed? How do you think the other person feels about being asked for this support?

- Would you describe this as a flexible relationship – one that can adjust to a change in circumstances for either of you – or does it tend to stick to a set routine that is difficult to change? Has this changed since you have been feeling depressed? If so, how has it changed? What change would you make to this, if any, to make it better? How do you think the other person feels about your routine together?

- Do you think this is a two-way relationship with give and take on both sides? If not, how would you describe the balance in this relationship? In healthy relationships it is common for each person to be interested and involved in the other's life. This does not need to be a perfect balance, but most relationships work best if you both make a contribution and accept the balance that exists. To evaluate this in your relationships, look back over the previous questions and ask them in the opposite direction, i.e. does the person talk to you about their worries or come to you for practical help, etc.? Has this balance changed since you have been feeling depressed? If so, how has it changed? What change would you make to this, if any, to make it better? How do you think the other person feels about the balance in your relationship?

Here's the chart for your summary notes. Add more columns if you need to.

Name of the person				
Relationship with the person				
How much contact do you have?				
Does the person know about your depression?				

Can you speak to the person about your feelings?					
Do you see each other socially?					
Can you ask the person for practical help and advice?					
Is this a flexible relationship?					
How would you describe the give and take in this relationship?					
Are you satisfied with this relationship?					
Has this relationship changed since you've been depressed?					

Has this relationship been affected by a change?					
Has there been conflict in this relationship?					
Has this relationship been affected by a bereavement?					
Do you feel the connection is poor in this relationship?					
Will this person be in your IPT team?					
How will this relationship feature in your plan?					

This inventory is particularly useful in clarifying the relevance of each of the IPT interpersonal themes – conflict, change, loss and isolation – to your relationships. Again, use the questions in exercise 9.5 as prompts to help you.

Exercise 9.5: Reviewing your inventory (3):
interpersonal themes

Consider how each theme features in your inventory:

- Are any of your relationships going through or influenced by a change? What kind of change? Is this welcome or unwelcome? Are you managing to adapt or finding this a struggle? Highlight any relationships that are going through a change that contributes to your depression.

- Are any of your relationships in conflict? What is the conflict about? Are you working together to sort out the conflict or stuck in the middle of a dispute with little idea of how to resolve it? Highlight any relationships that are currently in conflict that contributes to your depression.

- Are any relationships missing because of bereavement? Have any of your current relationships changed significantly following bereavement? Has the bereavement overlapped with the period in which you have been depressed? Highlight any lost relationships that contribute to your depression.

- Have you found it difficult to think of people to include in your inventory? Is this because there are few people in your life just now or because the relationships you have do not feel very important? How would you like this to be different? Would you like more people, closer relationships with some people or other changes? Highlight in your notebook any current relationships that you would like to develop.

When you have filled in the summary table, take note of any gaps this may reveal in your inventory, e.g. limited or no social support, or an absence of give and take in most relationships. This can sometimes be easier to see when the summary is completed – for example, when a blank row stands out. Alternatively, you might discover some imbalance, for example a lot of detail in one column and gaps under other relationships, suggesting that a lot is expected of one particular relationship and less is asked of other people. This might put that relationship under strain and could make you vulnerable if the relationship changed in any way or became unavailable for a period of time. This could highlight a need to develop other relationships to create more balance or to make you less vulnerable if anything changed the routine in your most significant relationship.

Charles's interpersonal inventory

Charles was in his mid-fifties and had suffered from depression on and off for over fifteen years. Between periods of depression he felt very well and had an active social life with his long-standing friends. He had regular contact with these friends and they were often in each other's homes and spent weekends and holidays together. They shared many hobbies in common, such as hill walking and cooking, and often spent time doing these things together. Charles was confident that he could call on his friends at any time for practical help and would readily offer the same in return. Charles had never married, but was close to his friends' partners and looked on their children as if they were his own nieces and nephews. He saw them as his substitute family and mostly felt satisfied with this situation. The major gap revealed in Charles's inventory was that none of his friends knew anything about his depression. He felt ashamed of his illness and did everything he could to conceal it from them. He had managed to make excuses when he first became depressed and spent less time with his friends, but he found this increasingly difficult to do as the episodes of depression recurred. This caused tension in one friendship in particular. Stephanie confided in Charles when she had difficulties and encouraged him to talk to her in turn, but he found this very difficult to do and was afraid he would seem to be a burden. He knew that she had been hurt by his silence and unexplained withdrawal in the past, but he struggled to change this pattern. Charles had been brought up in a strict and unemotional family, where feelings were never discussed. Despite this, he had felt quite adrift after his parents died soon after each other ten years earlier. He had a very distant relationship with his only brother and felt that his main contribution was to give him money occasionally.

Charles's summary table appears below.

Name of the person	Frank	Peter	Stephanie	Joanne	Mark
Relationship with the person	Friend	Friend	Friend	Neighbour	Brother
How much contact do you have?	2-3 /week	Most days	1-2 /week	Daily	1/every few months

Does the person know about your depression?	No	No	No	No	No
Can you speak to the person about your feelings?	No	No	No	Occasionally	No
Do you see each other socially?	Yes	Yes	Yes	Yes	Occasionally
Can you ask the person for practical help and advice?	Yes	Yes	Yes	Yes	Yes
Is this a flexible relationship?	Yes	Yes	Yes	Yes	No
How would you describe the give and take in this relationship?	Balanced	Balanced	Take more than give	Balanced	Give more than take
Are you satisfied with this relationship?	Yes	Yes	No	Yes	Mostly
Has this relationship changed since you've been depressed?	See less often when depressed	See less often when depressed	See less often when depressed	See more often when depressed	No

What are your goals in the future for this relationship?	Maintain as it is	Maintain as it is	To be more open	To be more open	No change
Has there been a change in this relationship?	No	No	Some tension about status of relationship	No	No
Has there been conflict in this relationship?	No	No	Occasional small arguments when I am low	No	Ongoing squabbling, no change
Has bereavement affected this relationship?	No	No	No	No	Less close since parents died 10 years ago
Do you feel the connection is poor in this relationship?	Personal life isn't known but good friend	Personal life isn't known but good friend	Sometimes feel lonely because we aren't as close as I'd like	No	Have never really been close
Will this person be in your IPT team?	Yes	Yes	Yes	Yes	No
How will this relationship feature in your plan?	Steady support and companion	Steady support and companion	A relationship to work on making closer	A good friend to make more use of	Won't feature significantly

Exercise 9.6: reviewing your inventory (4): overview

- What has completing this task told you about your current relationship network?
- Have you been surprised by any of your responses? In what way?
- What have you discovered about your network?
- What ideas has this exercise given you about the changes you could make to ease your depression?

Over the past few chapters you have taken a close look in turn at your symptoms of depression, at the events in your story (through your timeline), and at the relationships in your life (through your interpersonal inventory). Together, your timeline and inventory create the interpersonal context of your depression. Equipped with this information, you are now in a good position to select a focus to work on. This is what we shall be looking at in the next chapter.

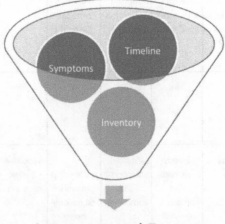

Interpersonal Focus

Summary

- Your interpersonal inventory reveals the characters in your story.
- A useful interpersonal inventory covers supportive relationships, troublesome relationships, persistent themes and plans for change.
- Your relationship inventory is a current snapshot and will develop and change in the weeks ahead.
- Creating your relationship inventory is an opportunity to discover more about your relationships as well as describing what you already know.
- Creating your relationship inventory will reveal the many ways other people can contribute to your recovery.

Chapter 10

Finding your story and selecting a focus

Courage is grace under pressure.

ERNEST HEMINGWAY, WRITER

The exercises you have been doing as you have worked through the last few chapters will help you to identify a specific inter-personal difficulty that will be your main focus as you try to resolve this episode of depression – in other words, the central theme of your story. Your story is, of course, more complex than a single theme. However, trying to address *all* the current issues in your life at once is likely to be overwhelming. By making too many demands on you, this would probably result in little progress, keeping you depressed for longer. By focusing on a single central theme you aim to achieve **maximum change by manageable means**.

The focus you choose will relate to one of the four themes you have already been looking at, each of which links into a helpful way of approaching the problem, as summarized in the chart below.

It is likely that you will have become aware of several of these themes cropping up in your story, probably more than once. Sometimes they may have been connected with passing events, such as successfully changing your job (change); at other times they might relate to a stage of life, such as leaving home for the first time (isolation/change). Feelings of loss might have come up in many contexts. It can feel tricky to choose between the themes, to decide what should take centre stage and what will remain in the background, at least for now.

Conflict Examining a repeating conflict in an important relationship and supporting better communication to reach an agreed solution.	**Change** Mourning the unwanted loss of a valued or significant role and adjusting to the needs and demands of the new role that is created in its place.
Loss Mourning the loss of an important relationship and developing current and new relationship to meet your needs now and in the future.	**Isolation** Understanding repeating patterns that interfere with making or maintaining meaningful relationships and laying a foundation for more successful relationships.

The focus you are going to select doesn't try to explain your whole history of depression, or even all the things that have happened since you became depressed this time. To do that might stretch back over several years, more than one period of depression and many overlapping events. That would be too unwieldy a task and could be quite confusing, as you try to link back and forth in time and across competing stories. Also, you might have put issues that were important in the past behind you and feel no need to stir them up again. The focus you select now forms part of your bigger story, but will only try to target the key issues during your most recent period of depression. The focus you select is the main theme now, and, as in any good story, it is most useful when it is set in the context of how this story developed and how it can be brought to a good conclusion.

Deciding on which focus will be most useful for you typically involves making a choice between options. It is not about finding the 'right answer', because many different strands will feature in your story. It is about deciding what will be useful to focus on *right now* in order to move things on. This will be determined by:

- its relevance to your depression;
- its match with the timing of your depression;
- the potential for change in that area;
- the support available to you in making this kind of change.

Ideally, the theme you focus on will be highly relevant to your depression, will have been troublesome throughout the period when you have been depressed, will have scope to change and will be something you can engage other people to help you to manage.

By now you will have created several diagrams and noted down lots of ideas or thoughts on the questions you have been asked so far. This should have built up a good picture of your symptoms, the episode of depression, the main events that have influenced you during the time you have been depressed and the relationships that have featured in that story. You might feel confident that you know what your depression is about – or you might feel a bit nervous about trying to choose between several different themes. Having a number of competing difficulties does not mean you cannot use IPT. It is exactly *because* there are so many different issues pulling you in different directions that narrowing your focus and reducing your goals at this stage will be helpful. Don't be alarmed if it seems that there are a lot of issues and you are unsure which direction would be best for you. You will have an opportunity to think through each of the options, and you will be supported in putting it all together in a useful and optimistic way. It will be very useful to involve your IPT team in talking over the different options, but *you* will remain in control of the focus you take.

Exercise 10.1: Organizing your story

Use the bubble diagram below to organize your story. Make a copy on a large piece of paper or in your notebook.

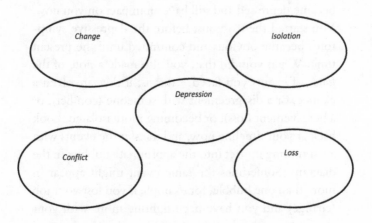

In chapter 6 you identified all of your current symptoms of depression. Write your symptoms in the centre circle.

For example, Paul would add these symptoms:

Depression
Cannot sleep at night and lie in bed all morning; cannot get going; no interest in anything; sad and bored all the time; irritable with everyone; cannot concentrate; wish I was dead.

In your timeline you identified all the events and relationships that had an impact around the time you became depressed and still have an impact on you now. You started the story just before the depressive symptoms became obvious and continued until the present time. When you did that, you also made a note of the *kinds* of events you faced – that is, if they involved a change, or a disagreement with someone (conflict), or a bereavement (loss), or becoming more isolated. Look back at your timeline now, and transfer the events with a continuing impact into the appropriate bubbles in the diagram. Sometimes the same event might appear in more than one bubble, for example if you lost your job (change) and you have been fighting more with your partner since that happened (conflict). In that case, add it to both bubbles, highlighting the relevant feature in each case.

- Do you notice one type of difficulty standing out or are there several possibilities to consider?

For example, the details Paul wrote down made it clear he was likely to choose between change and conflict as his focus:

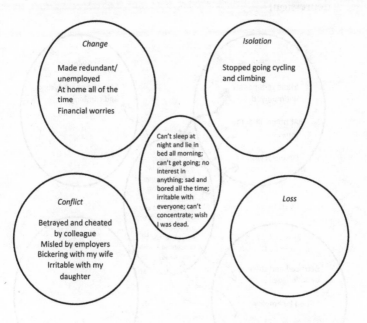

Now look at the issues in the outer bubbles, and for each one that you think contributes to your depression, draw a line between the issue and the depression bubble in the centre. You can use thicker lines for the issues that you think make the biggest contribution to your depression and finer lines for less problematic issues.

- Take note of where most of the lines linking to depression originate.

For example, Paul would add his lines like this, highlighting the two-way relationship between the various changes and conflicts he faced and his ongoing depression:

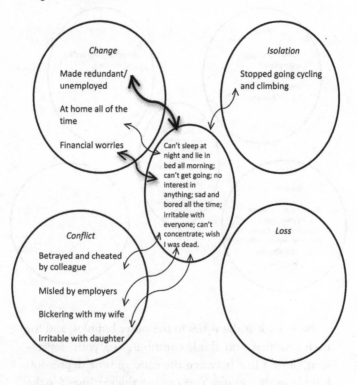

In your interpersonal inventory, you reviewed all of your current relationships. Many of the people in your inventory will have been involved in or affected by the events from your timeline. Write the names of the people who are most closely involved with each event in the appropriate bubble.

For example, Paul would add:

Change

Made redundant/
unemployed
(boss, family)
At home all of the
time
(Anne, Louise)
Financial worries
(*family*)

Loss
Stopped going cycling
and climbing (*club
members, Gerry, Peter
etc.*)

Can't sleep at
night and lie in
bed all morning;
can't get going; no
interest in
anything; sad and
bored all the time;
irritable with
everyone; can't
concentrate; wish
I was dead.

Loss

Conflict
Betrayed and cheated
by colleague (*Tom*)
Misled by employers
(*Frank*)
Bickering with my wife
(*Anne*)
Irritable with daughter
(*Louise*)

It's likely that your drawing is getting quite full of information now. So stop here and take a good look at it.

- Which circles have the most outstanding (unresolved) problems?
- Who is involved in these problems?

- Who can support you to manage each of these problems?
- Does this fit with your idea of what your current depression is primarily about?

Let's go back to the reasons why you might choose a main theme to focus on:

- its relevance to your depression;
- its match with the timing of your depression;
- the potential for change in that area;
- the support available to you in making this kind of change.

By doing exercise 10.2, ask yourself how each event/relationship that you've identified as currently troublesome matches these requirements.

Exercise 10.2: Distinguishing between focus and context

1. **Did this event/person contribute to my depression starting, either directly or as an immediate consequence of another triggering event?**

   (**Yes**: consider as possible focus
   No: consider as context)

   Example: Paul's depression started immediately after he was made redundant and so this role change should be considered as a possible focus.

   He didn't start bickering with his wife until he was home all of the time, so this is a consequence (context) not a trigger.

Similarly, he didn't completely withdraw from all of his hobbies and social routines until after he became depressed, although he had been doing less when he was working very hard. This is likely to have made him more vulnerable to becoming depressed and is likely to contribute to depression continuing.

Bickering at home and withdrawing from friends makes depression more difficult for Paul to manage, but neither contributed to his becoming depressed at the start of the story. Being made redundant is the key issue.

2. **Does the event/relationship continue to contribute to my depression now?**

    (**Yes**: consider as possible focus
    No: consider as context)

    Example: Losing his job, bickering with his wife and being isolated all contribute to Paul's depression now. Being made redundant makes the biggest contribution to how he feels.

3. **Has this event/relationship always been difficult, and is it something I managed more effectively before I was depressed?**

    (**No**: consider as possible focus
    Yes: consider as context)

    Example: Paul had not faced redundancy or unemployment before. This is a new issue linked to his current depression.

    He bickered with his wife and missed family and sports club events in the past, especially when he was working longer hours, but he had not become depressed when this happened previously. It is not surprising that difficult situations feel worse when he is depressed.

4. **Is there reason to think that this event/relationship could improve?**

   (**Yes**: consider as possible focus
   No: consider as context)

   Example: Paul cannot change his redundancy but he can change how he responds to it. He can change his relationship with his wife and his social routine. His wife is actively supporting his recovery and his social routine is available to pick up again.

5. **Do I have the support I need to make a change in this kind of event/relationships?**

   (**Yes**: consider as possible focus
   No: consider as context)

   Example: Paul is supported by his wife and could have more support from his friends if he asked for it. He may need to develop more support, as he dedicated so much time to work that he did not concentrate on developing many supportive relationships outside of work.

Both the exercises you have done so far in this chapter should help you to distinguish between the background detail, the overlapping events or minor issues, and the main theme of your story. For example, Paul was vulnerable to depression because he was in a stressful situation, stopped using his positive stress management techniques, including exercise and spending time with friends, and increased activities likely to have a negative and destabilizing effect on his mood, such as drinking. It was against this background (in this context) that he became depressed when he faced the major change of losing his job. The *context* made him vulnerable, but would have been unlikely to lead to depression without the significant *role change* that came about with unemployment.

- What are the background details in your story, e.g. history of depression, history of similar types of difficulties, temporary or circumstantial changes that interfered with your ability to cope?
- What are the overlapping issues in your story, e.g. background conflict, difficulty accessing support, difficult or stressful events that you were managing successfully?
- What is the main focus of your story?

Exercise 10.3: Telling your story

You can tell your story in whatever way you feel comfortable. Try using the template below to sketch out the main points. This won't give you your final story and doesn't include the personal details that will make it your own, but it will help you to get started. Remember, this is only the story *so far*. It isn't finished, and it doesn't have to be tidy and perfect. It is simply a way to get started, and you will add to this story step by step.

- **I know I am depressed because**: (describe your depressive symptoms)
- **I first started to feel depressed**: (date when depression started)

- **At the time that I started to feel depressed, the main interpersonal difficulties I faced were**: (describe circumstances)

- **Since then my depression has**: (describe how symptoms have changed or developed)

- **The main interpersonal problem I faced when I started to feel depressed has**:

  stayed the same / improved / worsened

- **The other interpersonal difficulties that I faced around the time or since becoming depressed are**: (describe additional difficulties)

- **The other interpersonal difficulties have**:

  stayed the same / improved / worsened
  (describe what has happened)

- **These additional problems have made it easier/more difficult to cope with depression / have made no difference**

  (describe their impact)

- **I have poor / adequate / good social support available**

- **I use my social support**:

  never / occasionally / frequently

- **The main theme of my recent depression has been**: (choose one)

  Change   Conflict   Loss   Isolation

- **When I tell my story to my IPT team, they think the main theme is**:

  Change   Conflict   Loss   Isolation

If opinions differ among your support team on the most useful focus, talk over your different points of view. Ultimately *you* decide which focus you would like to take, but it can be useful to look at your situation from a different angle from time to time. This can prompt ideas that may never have crossed your mind otherwise. If you still feel unsure, take some time to read through the individual chapters on each focus (chapters 14, 16, 18 and 20) and the case examples that go with them (chapters 15, 17, 19 and 21) to give you a better idea of what each one involves before you make your decision.

Let's draw the threads of this chapter together by looking at Paul's story.

Paul's story

I know I'm depressed because: I feel depressed and tired most of the time. I am angry with everyone and feel like lashing out. I fight with my wife and shout at my daughter when they've done nothing wrong. They try to be understanding, but I am difficult to live with. I drink more than I used to, which doesn't help and brings me down, and I feel like a failure. I cannot sleep and lie in bed wishing I wouldn't wake up the next day and that it was all over.

I first started to feel depressed: Nine months ago.

At the time that I started to feel depressed, the main interpersonal difficulties I faced were: I was made redundant from a job I had worked in for fifteen years. I had been working extra hours for months to try to secure a promotion. It came as a complete surprise and turned all of my plans upside down. I felt betrayed by my colleagues (one in particular) and misled by my employers. Home life quickly became tense, even though I know my wife supports me. I had neglected my family life because of work but then found myself spending all of my time at home because I couldn't face seeing anyone. It was the first time I had been home so much of the time in years. I generally hid away in my office on my own.

Since then my depression has: Gradually worsened. I feel like I sink further into depression every day. I no longer go out or see any of my friends. I have given up all my hobbies and worry about how we are going to manage financially. The more I stay home, the more difficult it seems to face the outside world, but the longer I go without making any progress, the more I feel like a failure.

The main interpersonal problem I faced when I started to feel depressed has:

<u>stayed the same</u>

i.e. I am still the same

The other interpersonal difficulties that I faced around the time or since becoming depressed are: Arguments with my wife; becoming very isolated, worried about money and how the family will manage if I don't find a job.

The other interpersonal difficulties have:

<u>worsened</u>

e.g. I bicker more often with my wife, I never go out with my wife or to the cycling and climbing clubs any more, and the longer I am unemployed, the more I worry about money.

The additional problems have made it <u>more difficult</u> to cope with depression: I find it very difficult to use the support that I am offered and I don't do anything that would take my mind off my problems or to give myself any pleasure.

I have <u>adequate</u> social support available – mainly from my wife, but it feels like too much to expect from one person. There are opportunities of companionship in my sports clubs.

I use my social support <u>never</u> – I don't talk to my wife about how I feel even though I know she would listen, and I don't see any of my friends any more or go to my sports club.

The main theme of my recent depression has been:

<u>Change</u>

When I tell my story to my IPT team, they think the main theme is:

<u>Change</u>

Now that you have chosen a theme as your most useful focus, at least initially, we can move on in the next chapter to consider your goals – and, most importantly, to see how you can set goals that are *achievable*.

Summary

- Finding your story and choosing a focus involves a deliberate choice between different options.
- The focus of your story doesn't try to cover the whole

story but rather aims to highlight the area most useful for you to concentrate on.

- Your story will guide you towards one of the main interpersonal themes – conflict, change, loss and isolation – as your most useful focus at this time.
- Your focus will explicitly link your current depression and current interpersonal difficulties.
- Your story will highlight how other people can contribute to your recovery.

Chapter 11

Setting achievable goals

Do what you can, with what you have, where you are.

THEODORE ROOSEVELT,
26TH PRESIDENT OF THE UNITED STATES

Once you know the area you are going to focus on it is very useful to set some goals to work towards. It's really important that these goals should be clear, relevant and achievable. Working towards any goals when you are depressed is an uphill struggle, and if you are not sure what you are trying to do, or feel you have no chance of getting there, it can leave you feeling like Sisyphus in the Greek myth, endlessly pushing the same rock up the same hill only to watch it roll back down to the bottom again.

It is therefore very helpful to think of goals as part of the process of recovery, not simply the end point. **The very act of setting a goal is an anti-depressant activity in itself**, and you will potentially see the effect of your efforts towards it long before the ultimate goal is actually achieved. This idea is captured very well in the popular book *Zen and the Art of Motorcycle Maintenance* in which the author, Robert M. Pirsig, describes learning to distinguish between the process and the result. The main character in the book sets out to climb a mountain with a group of Zen monks. During the climb he focused on his goal, which was to reach the summit. The scale of the climb overwhelmed him and the continual reminders of how far he had to go sapped his energy and will to continue. By defining his goal in terms of completing the climb he set it out of reach, and the goal worked against him. In contrast, the monks were able to continue their climb because they used the summit in a different way. The peak guided them and helped them stay on track, but they were not so distracted by it that they failed to take advantage of what each step on the way had to offer. Being on the journey was an end in itself.

Setting goals does not guarantee that they will be achieved, but the simple act of identifying a realistic goal does increase the likelihood of success and creates opportunities for small victories as you move towards your objective. Sometimes just telling someone else what you want to achieve is a way of committing yourself to the plan. Planning and imagining the way ahead are more difficult when you are depressed, and so people with depression tend to set fewer clear goals; this means fewer recognizable achievements, which then confirms an inner sense of being 'stuck'. By imagining and talking about the ways in which your situation could be improved, and what you need to do to make this happen, you can begin the process of change. This is more than wishful thinking; it is making the apparently insurmountable achievable by breaking the journey down into practical steps and using the support available to you.

General goals and personal goals

A small number of general goals can be identified for each of the focal areas in IPT. These offer a useful starting place, but you'll need to break them down and personalize them if they are to be helpful in motivating you to make changes. The general goals are:

Change:

- Mourn and accept the loss of your old role.
- Start to see what is or could be positive in your new role.
- Improve your self-esteem by developing the skills you will need in your new role.

Conflict:

- Make initial changes to encourage basic communication, for example cool down heated arguments or warm up a cold war.
- Identify and, where necessary, adjust expectations about the relationship and improve communication to bring about a satisfactory resolution.

Loss:

- Mourn your lost relationship.
- Re-establish interests and current relationships.

Isolation:

- Reduce isolation.
- Develop new relationships.

Each of these goals describes an ultimate aim – a bit like getting to the top of the mountain. They will be helpful to you if you can describe what they would mean for you personally and identify the practical steps that will be involved for you in getting there.

It is therefore useful to break your goals down into stages:

- short-term goals – for the next week or two;
- medium-term goals – for the next month or so, perhaps by the time you get to the end of this book;
- long-term goals – thinking to the future and keeping progress going.

Goals in these various categories will look very different from one another, even though they're all geared to movement in the same direction. For example, let's imagine Annette is trying to recover from a relationship break-up – that is, a major *change of role*. She might initially feel very hurt about the way the relationship ended, and unable to move on. Annette is initially immobilized by depression and her feelings about losing the relationship, and this prevents her from imagining what she will do next. Imagining herself in a new relationship or being happy to be single is out of reach at the moment. In order to mourn the old role and free herself from some of the painful feelings that hampered her, she has to think deliberately about what was good and bad in the old relationship, to create a more balanced picture. Her avoidance of such thoughts might have made it very difficult to look at her new single role, and so she has not identified what options are available to her. If she started to do that, she would be able to develop a clearer idea of what skills, supports and routines she would need to make the most of the opportunities now available to her, and she could focus on developing new skills and relationships.

An initial short-term goal might involve Annette spending

some time each day thinking about the things that she enjoyed and the things that had been difficult in the relationship, or talking to a close friend who could help her by adding a different perspective on her time in the relationship. It can be useful to set a time limit on this type of plan, e.g. thinking about the relationship for thirty minutes each day. This can help to focus your thinking, contain thoughts that might run across your day, remind you to balance your thinking, and create time for other things and other people.

A medium-term goal might be for Annette to have reviewed as many of the good and bad things about the relationship as she can remember, and to discuss her experience with three people who knew her while she was in the old role (girlfriend to her ex-partner), e.g. mutual friends, people who knew her before and during the relationship, etc. By doing this she would create a more balanced view of the relationship than was originally available to her.

A longer-term goal might involve Annette identifying all of the relationship skills she had developed and used in her old role, which she could still use now, and actively transferring those skills into opportunities in her new role (as a single woman). She could also take note of any difficulties that she experienced in her old role and think about how she could prevent the same problems occurring again.

Each of these steps will help Annette to achieve her general goals of mourning and accepting the loss of her old role in a manageable way, and identifying and creating a positive new role that she feels she can manage. If the goals are not broken down into manageable steps like this and don't follow a specific theme, it is quite likely that she will continue to feel overwhelmed and remain depressed for longer.

It is really helpful to involve other people in this process. They can help you to come up with ideas on how to break down goals that feel too big to tackle into manageable chunks, and to monitor and support your progress. In this way your IPT team become your 'goal buddies', helping you to keep on track and continue moving forward at a pace that you can manage.

They can also help you to celebrate your successes. It is very useful to set milestones to mark your progress and to plan how you will celebrate your achievements. In the example we have just looked at, this might include doing something enjoyable with your team when you have completed your list of all the good and bad things about your old role. This can help to motivate you, and makes each step really feel like part of the process – much better than waiting until you get right to the top of the mountain! Set your milestones in advance and keep track of your progress between each set of goals e.g. between your short-term and medium-term goals. Write your goals, and your milestones, in your notebook and keep track of your progress with your IPT team.

You might feel unsure about how long it will take you to work towards some of your goals, and at first the distinction between short-, medium- and long-term goals might be unclear. Working this out is itself a very helpful part of the process. Some of your medium-term or longer-term goals might rely on other short-term goals being completed first, and so it is helpful to think about the most useful sequence. One way to do this is simply to write the initial goals that come to mind on a series of sticky notes and move them around to find the most useful and realistic order in which to tackle them.

In the example outlined above, the person would first have to identify which friend she wanted to speak to, and then explain about depression, and what she was trying to do, before completing her first goal. Her friend might then help her to think about who else it would be useful for her to speak to, which she would need to do before completing her medium-term goal of talking to a number of people who could provide helpful and informed perspectives on her time in her old role.

Hitting the target

The type of goals you set can greatly increase the likelihood of making progress and accomplishing your ultimate goal. Descriptive goals are more helpful than vague wishes. Think about the difference between 'I wish I liked my job' and 'I am going to be in a better job within three months and I am going to sign up to a recruitment agency today to help me to find it'. Focusing on what *you*, rather than other people, are going to do will also increase the usefulness of your goals. Much of this comes down to planning in advance, and again this is something other people can help with. Let's look at what makes a good goal.

A popular way of approaching goal setting is by setting SMART goals. SMART goals are:

- **specific** – clearly defined, including what, who, when, how;
- **measurable** – success can be clearly demonstrated and quantified;
- **achievable** – realistic, taking into account the resources available;
- **relevant** – clearly linked to the problem to be solved;
- **timely** – there is a clear and realistic timescale for achieving the goal.

This may be easier to understand with an example.

An example of a vague or general goal for Annette might be: 'I want to be less upset about my relationship break-up.' This could mean a variety of things and gives no ideas about how to achieve this goal.

A SMART alternative goal would be: 'I want to be able to think in a balanced way about what was good and what was difficult in my last relationship.'

Specific: My specific goal is to be able to remember what was good and bad about my last relationship without being emotionally overwhelmed.

Measurable: I will assess my progress by monitoring the balance of good and bad memories when I think about the relationship and noting how upset I feel when I think about them.

Achievable: To achieve this goal I will set 30 minutes aside each day to think through individual examples or periods of time in my last relationship. I will discuss these examples with someone else at least once a week to help me make sure I am building a balanced picture and thinking about my time in the relationship from different perspectives.

Relevant: By focusing on specific examples from my last relationship I will remain focused on the change that has been difficult for me.

Timely: I will have recalled and talked about a series of memories of the relationship with at least three people in the next month.

Specific goals will help you to focus on what *you* are going to do. Breaking the goal down into individual tasks and short periods of time can help you to plan your progress towards it and to monitor whether you are on track. This can also help you to assess how achievable your goals are. Research has shown that the most effective goals are neither too easy nor too difficult. If goals do not pose some degree of challenge they risk being dismissed as insignificant, and so they aren't pursued. If they stretch you too far, they might put you off starting in the first place.

It is important that your goals focus on what *you* are going to do and not the changes you would like to see in someone else. This makes sure that the goals you set are achievable for you and progress is under your control. For example, if your goal is 'I want my husband to listen to me', your success depends on what your husband does or doesn't do. If your goal is 'I want to communicate clearly and in a way that my husband can hear', you can develop skills to bring this about and you are in control of the progress you make.

It can be very helpful to talk this through with someone else to make sure you achieve this balance. Depression might diminish your confidence so much that you believe you cannot do anything, or it might make you intolerant of your own temporary limitations and lead you to set challenges that are too ambitious and inevitably lead to failure. By weaving your goals into your depression narrative you can check that they relate to the central theme and gradually expand your plan as time goes on.

Balance short-term goals over the next weeks, which will maintain momentum, with medium-term goals that help you to measure progress, and longer-term goals that will take a broader perspective and fit the recent episode into your bigger depression and life stories.

Exercise 11.1: Setting your goals

- Identify the general goals that relate to your chosen focus.
- Personalize the goals to reflect your own story.

- Identify your goal buddies.
- Set a short-term goal, a medium-term goal and a long-term goal for each of your personalized general goals above, with your buddies' help.
- Discuss with your buddies what they can do to help you to achieve your goals.
- Identify the milestones when you will reward yourself for making progress and decide what that reward will be. Ask your buddies to help you to monitor your progress.
- Start working towards your first goal.

Whatever goals you have chosen, and whichever of the four key themes you have chosen as your focus, it's pretty certain that in pursuing them you're going to need to communicate effectively with other people. This can be very difficult when you are depressed, so the next chapter is devoted to helping you see how you might be able to develop this all-important skill.

Summary

- Goals are part of the process as well as the end point.
- It is helpful to break down your goals into short-term goals, medium-term goals and long-terms goals, all leading in the same direction.
- Using SMART goals clarifies what you are going to achieve, how you are going to do it, when you are going to do it and how you will monitor your progress.
- Involve other people in planning your goals, monitoring and supporting your progress, and celebrating your successes.

Chapter 12

The process of communication

The real art of conversation is not only to say the right thing at the right time but to leave unsaid the wrong thing at the tempting moment.

DOROTHY NEVILL, WRITER AND SOCIETY HOSTESS

Communication is a two-way process, not a solitary activity. It involves *exchanging* information between two or more people. Sometimes you are *giving* information and sometimes you are *receiving* it. You swap back and forth between these roles when you are communicating. You could say something clearly, but if the other person is not listening the communication will not work. Similarly, you might be listening closely, but if the message is not clear the communication will fail. Effective communication relies on information being clearly delivered and clearly received. Improving communication therefore is about clarifying not just what we say but also what we hear. Good communication is saying it in such a way that it can be heard.

The good storyteller

Who do you know who is a good storyteller? Someone you enjoy listening to and who can hold your attention and make you want to hear more? This might be someone who tells stories for a living, such as a favourite writer or film-maker, or someone in your personal life, work life or past, such as a particularly inspiring teacher. Whoever it is, think about what it is they do that captures your attention. Is it the words they choose, the details they include, the way they speak, the ways the story is built up or something else? Try to identify at least three things that make them a pleasure to listen to. If you can, ask them how they do it and what they enjoy about their own stories. Take note of these details, because it is often best to learn from what works.

Depression and communication

Our ability to communicate comes under threat in a number of ways when we have depression.

The first is that there is simply less communication. If your instinct is to withdraw into yourself and hide away from other people, there will be fewer opportunities for you to speak and fewer opportunities for others to listen to you, and vice versa.

The second threat follows on from this. If you talk less, more communication will be based on interpreting behaviour rather than direct discussion. Does cancelling an arrangement mean you are angry, struggling or uninterested? Communication becomes more fragmented and vulnerable during depression, and leads to much poorer understanding.

A third threat relates to the perceived worth of what you have to say. When motivation and interest are low it can be difficult to think of things to say. If you are doing less than usual and turning the same problems over in your mind there will be fewer events to talk about, and if you do say what you have been doing you might worry that it will be too boring or insignificant to be worth mentioning.

Finally, it is common for depressed people to anticipate a hostile or uninterested audience to anything they want to say, and so silence can be used as a way of protecting against this threat.

Such breakdowns in communication can be powerful in keeping the depression going.

The reasoning brain and the emotional brain

Most good stories are built up in layers. These include events, problems, feelings, different points of view and a thread that holds them all together. A good storyteller is also aware of the person who is listening and can adjust the way the story is told to pique their curiosity and hold their interest. This whole process involves many areas of brain activity, including those areas responsible for memory, speech, listening, reasoning and emotions. Some of this activity is deliberate and planned, such as working out the structure and point of the story (reasoning brain), while other parts are more instinctive and automatic, such as feelings and reactions to events described (emotional brain). Both parts are necessary and add to the quality of the communication. Emotions bring the facts to life and the structure of the story gives the feelings a meaningful context.

Juggling all these different elements of telling a story can be tricky at the best of times. When you are depressed it is an even bigger challenge. Our memories and ability to plan may not be very good when we are depressed, and our ability to communicate effectively can be easily pulled off track. Our emotions are often closer to the surface and can spill over in unexpected ways. This is a particular risk if you are trying to talk about things that are emotionally significant to you. It is easy for automatic reactions to override a poorly worked out plan when you are depressed, so that the message you're trying to get across, or your response to what someone is saying to you, gets drowned in a flood of feelings.

This leads to another key element of successful communication: timing. This is very important. Talking about emotionally significant events or issues is generally most effective when emotions are calm, rather than when the emotional centre of activity in your brain is at its most active. If you want to tell someone about feeling angry, it is best to do this when you are not feeling angry. When you are feeling relatively calm, the reasoning and planning part of your brain will be activated and the emotional system will be less likely to undermine the process. If you try to talk about being angry when you *are* angry, the emotional brain centre will interfere with the reasoning brain centre, and your message will be lost in the intensity of the emotion you convey and the emotion provoked in the other person.

In this way we can see communication leading by example. Calm and planned communication invites a calm and considered response. Emotional and unpredictable communication is likely to provoke the same turmoil. If you want your communication to succeed, it is to your advantage to send an invitation from the thinking part of your brain to the other person's thinking brain and leave emotions at a distance on both sides.

This is, of course, easier said than done when you are feeling depressed, and when the people around you might be agitated or critical and struggling to understand the changes in you recently. It is very helpful under these circumstances to think of communication as *a process rather than an event*. By thinking of it as a process you start to imagine it as something that continues to happen. The process carries on: everything does not need to be said at once, as it might do if communication were a one-off event. Depressed people often become frustrated when they forget to mention something in a discussion or get distracted by the force of someone else's argument, feeling that they have missed their opportunity, as if the opportunity stopped when the conversation did. In IPT, curiosity rolls on and asks: 'What happened next?' When was the next time that you or the other person could send out an invitation from the reasoning brain so that the communication could carry on, step by step, working towards an understanding?

How do we communicate?

We communicate in all kinds of ways. Studies have shown that when we talk about emotions, as you might do when tackling relationship problems, only a small proportion of the communication consists of what is actually said out loud: most of the message is conveyed through paraverbal and non-verbal signals. What does this mean? Well, we communicate basically in three ways:

- **verbal communication** – what we say;
- **paraverbal communication** – how we say it; and
- **non-verbal communication** – what we do while we are saying it.

When these three elements of a message match and reinforce each other they result in good communication. For example, I say I am delighted to see you in a bright and cheerful voice, smile broadly and open my arms to hug you. However, if different elements contradict each other, the communication process begins to break down and it is unclear what message is being sent and what should be understood. For instance, suppose I say I am delighted to see you, but sound cool and avoid eye contact. What are you to understand? Offering a consistent message therefore increases understanding, clarity, trust and rapport, while an inconsistent message confuses or misleads the listener and leads to tension, mistrust and confusion. With so many different elements in play at once, it is not difficult to see why communication can get into difficulty.

Let's look at each of the elements in turn.

VERBAL COMMUNICATION

This refers to the spoken or written words that we use when we communicate. They might be well chosen, specific and beautifully put together, or exaggerated, sloppy and vague. The usefulness of the words relies on a shared understanding of what they mean to the person speaking and the person listening. Think back to the different uses of the word 'depressed' we considered in chapter 6.

Your ability to use words effectively will partly depend on how well developed your vocabulary is *on the subject under discussion*. For example, knowing the name of every part of the emotional centre in the brain will be of little use in talking about the feelings it produces. Verbal communication is therefore not a matter of intelligence or academic learning but of having the words to say what you need to in a way that can be understood. This can be difficult when we are talking about depression, because some experiences feel beyond words or beyond the understanding of the people who are listening. This is one of the reasons why a vocabulary to talk about depression is deliberately developed early in IPT.

PARAVERBAL COMMUNICATION

This term covers the ways our voice gives clues to the feelings and attitudes that lie behind the words we choose. These include our tone of voice and the pitch, speed, clarity, abruptness and flow of our speech, and strongly influence how what we actually say is understood. Imagine you're sitting in a restaurant and something catches your ear from three or four tables away. Even if you cannot hear the words, you can often guess the gist of what is going on from the sound. You can almost certainly distinguish between excited delight and an erupting argument.

We might use paraverbal communication deliberately for emphasis, e.g. shouting when we're angry or squealing with pleasure, but we also use it unintentionally, and perhaps unknowingly – and in these instances it can reveal more than we realize. For example, your voice might shake when you are nervous or become clipped when you are irritated. The paraverbal element is missing in most examples of written communication, which makes it more vulnerable to misinterpretation, especially if it is in a very brief form like text messaging. Have you ever found yourself in an unexpected disagreement after a text message was misunderstood? Capital letters, underlining, exclamation marks, etc. are sometimes used to try to recreate something of this element of communication, but text messaging is rarely a good method to communicate something important.

Exercise 12.1: How meaning changes with emphasis

Look at the following sequence of sentences. The written words remain the same, but the stress changes – and as it does, it changes the meaning of the sentence. Read each sentence aloud, each time stressing the word in bold italics.

I did not say you were to blame.

I *did not* say you were to blame.

I did not *say* you were to blame.

I did not say *you* were to blame.

I did not say you *were* to blame.

I did not say you were to *blame*.

Try to identify the different meanings in each sentence. Ask someone else to do the same and see if you both understand each example in the same way.

NON-VERBAL COMMUNICATION

This covers the wealth of activity that surrounds the words you use and how you use them, and includes eye contact, facial expression, movement and position, posture, gestures and touch. All these can also, intentionally or unintentionally, reveal feelings, attitudes or intentions. It is important to be aware that non-verbal communication is likely to increase when we feel emotional: in these circumstances the planned and deliberate can easily be ambushed by the unintentional and reactive. Consider the conflicting elements in the message when someone says they are fine while they have tears rolling down their cheeks. As with each of the other messages in your communication toolbox, non-verbal communication is most effective when used in combination with the other elements, and most vulnerable to being misunderstood when used alone. Non-verbal communication might be used to:

- **repeat** the verbal message, e.g. nodding when saying you agree;
- **complement** the verbal message, e.g. a pat on the back when saying well done;
- **underline** the verbal message, e.g. pounding the table when making an important point.

But it can also:

- **contradict** the verbal message, e.g. rolling your eyes while saying you agree;
- **replace** the verbal message, e.g. slamming a door without saying a thing.

In the last two examples the message is less clear because in the first the verbal and non-verbal communications suggest different messages and create confusion, while in the second there is no verbal element, which creates ambiguity. This sort of mismatch is often evident in depression, when the reasoning brain is vulnerable to being ambushed by the emotional brain and the amount of direct communication often decreases. Patterns of ambiguous and contradictory communication fuel depression.

Exercise 12.2: Identifying strengths and weaknesses in communication

Use the information given above about the three types of communication to think about how you communicate, and identify your own communication strengths and weaknesses. This picture will help you to identify ways to communicate more effectively. Discuss this with your IPT team.

Non-verbal communication can be easily misused and misunderstood, so it is useful to spend a little time looking at some examples in more detail.

Eye contact

We often rely heavily on eye contact to gauge what is happening with another person. In Western culture good eye contact is interpreted very positively and suggests interest, attention and credibility. (However, this interpretation is not universal: in many Eastern cultures, for example, direct eye contact would be perceived as rude.) Eye contact is often used to check if the listener is following what is being said and to regulate the flow back and forth in a conversation. This convention is so powerful that breaking contact for just a few seconds too long can create tension or lead to the conversation breaking down. In a similar way, too much eye contact can quickly start to feel intrusive or threatening.

Exercise 12.3: Using eye contact

Think about how eye contact works in your own communications. It can be more difficult to hold eye contact when you are depressed, as it suggests a confidence and interest that you might not feel. However, avoiding eye contact can make even simple exchanges feel unnecessarily awkward. Practise looking at people when you are speaking and take note of the effect.

If you find this difficult to start with, try to follow a five-second cycle – focus on one eye for five seconds, then the other eye for five seconds and then the person's mouth for five seconds. If you feel uncomfortable, look to the side (which is what we often do when we are thinking about something that has been said) and then go back to the five-second cycle again. Counting to five might be a little distracting at first, but gradually you will get used to looking at someone when you communicate and will notice how powerful this can be in engaging other people.

Facial expression

This is a feature of communication that the person listening has much more access to, and perhaps awareness of, than the person speaking. We all look at people's faces for hints about what they are feeling. The use of facial expressions to convey and understand emotion is such an important part of human interaction that the pioneering nineteenth-century biologist Charles Darwin argued there was a biological basis to a basic set of facial expressions – that is, we are hard-wired to show basic emotions like anxiety and despair in a universally recognizable way. Much of the research that has been done in the century and more since Darwin put his idea forward has supported this. The use of facial expression to convey what is going on inside someone was also appreciated by another great figure of the nineteenth century – the novelist Charles Dickens. In order to capture facial expressions accurately, Dickens would watch himself in a mirror while repeating his characters' dialogue in order to discover how they would look; this enabled him to describe the characters in a way that would suggest their inner lives to his readers. He observed the outside to learn more about what was going on inside the person he was writing about.

Exercise 12.4: Interpreting facial expression

When you are listening to people talking, use opportunities to note what their facial expression adds to what they say, and what the impact is when words and expression do not match. If you find this difficult to do in real conversations, watch a TV programme or film with the sound turned down: identify as many emotions as you can over ten minutes and then watch the same clip again with the sound on and rate your accuracy. It can be interesting to do this with someone else and to compare notes on what you each pay attention to and how you interpret what you see.

Movement and position

Where you stand and how you move can also influence how
you feel during a conversation. This can be as simple as whether
you move towards or away from the other person, and how
fast or slowly you do this. Rapid or unexpected movements
can be unsettling, and can lead to the person who is trying
to understand the movement feeling ambushed by a sudden
approach or abandoned by a sudden turning away.

'Personal space' refers to the free space around you that you
see as your own. The distance you maintain between you and
another person signals something about the type of relationship
you have. Intruding on this space can create a strong emotional
reaction and is likely to work against any attempt to communicate. The need to re-establish a comfortable distance interrupts
communication, and an awkward dance backwards and forwards can develop if this is not sufficiently understood. While
preferences vary between people and cultures there are general
norms for what is appropriate in different types of relationships
and situations. These are summarized in the diagram below.

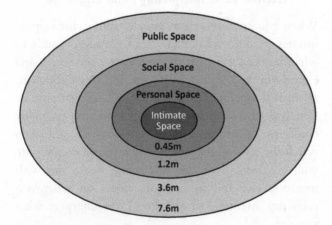

You will notice that the concentric circles in the diagram above look similar to those you may have used to draw your interpersonal inventory. Personal space means literally the physical distance between you and another person, while your interpersonal inventory illustrates emotional closeness and involvement. Neither scheme is set in stone: the position of any person in your interpersonal world can move closer or further away on either diagram. And so the way personal space is measured might also give us clues about the status of a relationship: for example, when it is going well a person may, literally and emotionally, be allowed into the personal or intimate space, but when there are difficulties it may be more comfortable to keep the same person further away from us. However, if this is not explained or mutually understood it can easily derail communication. When we are depressed it might be tempting to keep people at a distance to protect ourselves against the emotional reaction that is triggered when this space is violated. Alternatively we might feel an urgent need for physical and emotional closeness, to support us when we are struggling. For the people around you this can create an unexpected distance, leaving them feeling shut out and confused, or a new demand to stay close and help you to carry the burden of depression. In either case clear communication is crucial to understanding this change and ensuring that your needs are met.

Exercise 12.5: Thinking about personal space

Take note of how it makes you feel when someone breaks the unspoken rules about personal and social space by standing too close to you or too far away. For example, it can be unsettling, and make you question whether you have fully grasped the situation you are in, if someone steps into your personal space or retreats back into public

space immediately after being introduced, or if someone
you know repeats this pattern each time you meet. Is
this an issue with anyone you struggle to communicate
with now? Has your level of comfort for physical closeness changed since you have been depressed? Have you
told other people about that change?

Posture

When people want to communicate they signal it by facing
towards each other and mirroring each other's posture and
movements. This helps to create a good rapport, putting the
other person at ease and conveying understanding. You might
match posture by standing or sitting so you are both at the same
level, or if you're walking keeping a similar pace, neither rushing
ahead nor lagging behind. You might add to this by mirroring
the other person's expression, such as smiling at someone who
is smiling. This should be distinguished from mimicking, or
copying exactly, which can have quite the opposite effect and
can come across as mocking. As with eye contact, attention
is signalled by turning your face and body to face the other
person and keeping your posture open; closed postures, such
as sitting with arms and legs crossed, or turning in the opposite
direction, discourage communication. Sunflowers are one of
Nature's best illustrations of an open, attentive posture as they
face the sun and follow its trajectory across the sky throughout
the day. Their attention is fixed and constant.

Exercise 12.6: Practising use of posture and movement in communication

When you're talking to someone, see what happens if
you match an aspect of your posture or movement to

the person you are speaking with. This will inevitably involve you paying closer attention to the person in order to mirror their behaviour. Take note of how this makes you feel and whether it helps to keep the other person's attention.

Gesture and touch

Gestures and touches can be a very powerful way of underlining a message or signalling that the message has been heard. There are many deliberate body movements that are used to communicate a message directly. Think about the impact of nodding to encourage someone to continue talking or to indicate understanding, interest or agreement, and the contrary impact of frowning, yawning or rolling your eyes. Touch can be used to reinforce a point – for example, a handshake or hug signals the warmth or intimacy of a greeting, while touching someone's arm can emphasize attention or sympathy. Just as touch can signal encouragement, withholding touch might indicate a difficulty.

The use of touch obviously overlaps with the issue of personal space, and will be strongly influenced by personal preference. Some people will be tactile with most others around them, while others feel uncomfortable touching or being touched outside their most intimate relationships. A mismatch in approaches can create communication problems: for example, a tactile person can unintentionally provoke a defensive or even hostile reaction in someone who does not like to be touched. This is a form of communication that should be used with caution if preferences on each side are not well understood.

Our feelings about touch may change when we are depressed, either because we have a greater need for closeness to diminish feelings of loneliness, or because we feel a greater reluctance to be close or tactile with other people.

Exercise 12.7: Thinking about touch

How do you use and respond to touch as part of your communication style? Has this changed since you have been depressed? Have you talked about this with the people close to you, or has it created an unexpected change?

THE WHOLE MESSAGE: CLARITY AND CONSISTENCY

Effective communication relies on a coherent and consistent message being delivered and received through these different routes. When communication is clear the verbal, paraverbal and non-verbal messages will confirm, repeat and reinforce each other. Poor communication involves muddled messages, with conflicting elements pulling the speaker and listener in different directions and creating confusion about what to pay attention to and which part of the message best conveys what the speaker means. It's best to consider non-verbal elements of communication together, as reading too much into a single signal can be misleading. Also bear in mind the context of the conversation, as this will help you to make sense of the signals you read. The context in which a conversation takes place can influence people's behaviour enormously. You're unlikely to behave exactly in the same manner at work, at home and on a night out with friends. It's a good idea to read the signals in the light of the context, taking into account the opportunities and limitations this will create. Consider the overall consistency or inconsistency of a message and be prepared to ask the other person if something is unclear.

Listening deliberately

The give and take of communication means that the way we listen is just as important as what we say, how we say it and what we do while we're talking. Just as we can deliberately choose our words and use our body language to back up our message, we can be deliberate in the way we listen. Listening in a deliberate way focuses our attention firmly on the person who is speaking. The aim is to understand as clearly as we can what the other person is trying to say. To do this we have to shift attention away from ourselves and onto the other person temporarily. This is the difference between waiting to speak and listening to what is being said. In the first case, your attention is likely to be on yourself and what you think and want to say. When we are focusing on ourselves and not listening to the other person, our responses often change the direction of the discussion and risk losing the original point. In the second case, our attention is on the speaker and what he or she is trying to say. The point is not to decide whether we agree with what is being said or to react to it, but to hear the message that is being conveyed. When we listen deliberately to what the other person is actually saying, our responses are likely to stay focused on the original point and to reinforce that we are listening to the speaker. Of course, we may want to think about whether we agree or consider how to respond at some point, but we will be in a much stronger position to do both of those things if we have clearly heard everything that is being said in the first place.

Listening deliberately involves using your whole body, not just your ears. We use our ears to pay attention to the words used and how they are said; we use our understanding of paraverbal communication to start to speculate about the meaning of the words. Our eyes will add another layer to our listening by adding information on body language and the wider context.

Many of the non-verbal communication techniques described above can be used to signal to the other person that you are listening to them, such as nodding or facing the person in an open posture. Sensitive use of touch will add another layer, interpreting or offering encouragement through direct contact.

In order to listen in this way it is important to be as free from distractions as possible. Your ability to listen deliberately will be diminished if you are likely to be interrupted by people not involved in the discussion, watching TV out of the corner of your eye or thinking about work deadlines for the following day. It is no coincidence that therapy sessions are booked in advance and take place in a private room. Meaningful communication often requires planning and preparation.

There are also a number of verbal communication skills you can use to show you are listening and help communication lead to a better and shared understanding. When communication is in trouble it is often because only part of an intended message is expressed or heard. The process gets interrupted, taken off track and misunderstood. Under these circumstances it is easy for communication to break down completely or to escalate into an argument, both of which lead to less communication rather than more. There is a range of simple but useful skills that will help you to keep communication focused, improve the chances of understanding more clearly, and leave both people involved feeling that it was worth taking the time to talk things through. We'll take a look at the main techniques now.

REFLECTING WHAT IS SAID

This is saying back, *in your own words*, what you have heard and understood: 'So let me check, I think you are saying . . . Have I got that right?' Using your own words, rather than repeating the other person's words parrot fashion, is a very direct way of showing that you have been listening and thinking about what has been said. It is important then to check if what you have understood *is* what the person was trying to say and to listen to their response when you ask: 'Have I understood what you are saying? Have I missed anything?' If you have understood correctly, the communication has been successful and can carry on if there is more to say. If you have not understood, you can invite the person to explain again and prompt them to clarify what was confusing or unclear the first time. This allows the two of you to share the responsibility for keeping the communication on track and reduces the chances of misunderstandings leading to the discussion breaking down or escalating into an argument. It is useful to use this pause and check approach during the discussion to keep it on track, rather than waiting until everything has been said, when it will be too difficult to remember all of the detail. The frequency of your reflections should be guided by how much you can remember, especially if this has been affected by depression; it's often helpful to work with small chunks of information. It would be disruptive if this kind of feedback were offered at the end of every sentence, but it's often a good idea when one or two main points have been made or if the conversation is about to move in a different direction.

REFLECTING FEELINGS

This is a similar process to reflecting what has been said, but focuses instead on the speaker's feelings, and so involves very important information in significant communication about relationships. You might base what you say on the person's own description of how they are feeling, or on your own observation of how they appear to feel from their body language. It is very important to remember that you cannot be directly aware of what another person is feeling and can at best interpret the signals that are offered e.g. going red in the face, crying, sighing. So your impressions should always be carefully checked with the person to see whether it is accurate – e.g.: 'You seem sad, are you?' This may prompt the person to offer more detail than was available at first. 'I do feel sad, but I am also frustrated.' It is often difficult to read the full range of emotions that a person is feeling, but if you pay careful attention to those that are easier to see this can open up discussion on other feelings that have been concealed or are subtler.

CLARIFYING

This involves a request for specific information or explanation on a particular subject or point that has not been clearly understood, e.g.: 'Will you tell me more about . . . ? What did you mean by . . . ?' This acknowledges that you need more information in order to understand and prompts the speaker to explain in a way that improves your understanding. Clarifying questions specify the particular subject you want the person to expand on, e.g. 'How did you feel about that?', 'Would you give me an example of when that happened?', but the focus stays on the person speaking.

OPEN QUESTIONS

The examples of clarifying questions above are all open questions in that they invite the person to say more. The invitation can also be offered in a more general way, e.g. 'Can you tell me more?' 'How have you been this week?' Here the subject is largely left up to the person who is speaking. These questions are helpful in discovering what someone thinks, feels, expects, etc., but can also be used to keep the discussion on track, e.g.:

'How does that relate to what you were saying a moment ago?'
A combination of general and increasingly specific questions,
each of which picks up one point from the previous answer,
can help to prompt a more detailed account, e.g. 'How have
you been this week?' . . . 'What happened to upset you on
Tuesday?' . . . 'How did you feel about that?' . . . 'Did you say
how it made you feel?'

CLOSED QUESTIONS

In contrast, closed questions invite little response and can typically be answered with a yes or no. These questions tend to
focus more on the view of the person posing the question than
the person answering, and to close down further discussion,
e.g.: 'Do you think that's fair?' 'Are you really going to do
that?' Closed questions can be useful if specific facts or plans
are needed, but should be used sparingly to avoid the discussion
simply becoming a way of confirming what you already thought.

SUMMARIZING

Pulling together the main ideas and feelings expressed in the
conversation to show you have listened and understood allows
you to confirm that the impression you will be taking away
from the conversation is the one that was intended. A summary
should be succinct and clear, highlighting the two or three main
points that you have heard. It can be useful both in the middle of
a long or complicated discussion, to make sure important points
are not lost, or at the end of a briefer discussion. Summarizing
allows you to focus on the overall message. You'll have noticed
that a summary is provided at the end of each chapter in this
book, highlighting the main points from the much longer
description of the ideas that forms the body of the chapter.

You may already use several of these skills, but they can be more difficult to persevere with when you feel depressed or are trying to talk about emotional subjects. It's a good idea to remind yourself of the skills you have and to make time to practise them. You don't need to use them all every time – indeed, it might seem a bit awkward to attempt to use them all in simple day-to-day conversations. You can still practise using them, though: for example, whether or not you need to reflect or clarify important points in a conversation, you can practise listening as if you were going to. This builds up a habit of listening deliberately so that it will be easier for you to do so, and to use the techniques described above, when you are faced with more difficult discussions.

Exercise 12.8: Practising deliberate listening

Practise listening deliberately in your day-to-day conversations. Imagine what you would say if you were going to reflect the main point you have understood from each conversation. Try to find one opportunity each day to prompt someone to say more by reflecting and checking you have understood the main points they have been making.

Communication style

As you have been doing the exercises in this chapter you might have started to notice some patterns in the way you and the people around you communicate. Some people like to talk at length and in lots of detail while others like to get to the point quickly. Some people tend to dominate conversations while others like to stay in the background and make fewer contributions. Each individual's communication style is likely to be relatively consistent across relationships and situations.

- What have you noticed about your own communication style?

Depression can have a very direct impact on the way you communicate. It can make a normally lively person seem quite muted and reserved. It might make you feel less tolerant of the people around you, or more likely to be uncharacteristically snappy or inflexible.

- What have you noticed about the way you communicate since you have been depressed?

UNHELPFUL STYLES OF COMMUNICATION

Certain styles of communication, described below, tend to act as barriers to good communication. These are very often seen when relationships are in conflict and are much less common when relationships are working well. They also appear more often when someone is depressed and so can put relationships at risk.

- **Attacking or aggressive**: This style of communication is harsh and critical. It focuses on blaming and criticizing other people and is constantly looking for fault. Questions feel like an interrogation, rather than genuine interest, and there is a tendency to shame or embarrass other people.
- **Preaching**: This style of communication focuses on telling other people what to do. It is full of judgements and tends to label other people's problems and faults. It is quick to give advice and full of statements about 'You' and very few about 'I'.

- **Bullying**: This style of communication is domineering, takes control and overrides others. This is a juggernaut style of communication, clearing everything in its path. It makes a show of being powerful by threatening others and giving orders.
- **Passive:** This communication style is almost invisible. It involves almost no direct contribution to communication and tends to bend to anything that is suggested. It always agrees with what has been said, in order to avoid conflict, whether or not this agreement is actually felt. It is difficult to know what the passive communicator thinks or feels because both thoughts and feelings are concealed.
- **Passive aggressive**: This is an indirectly aggressive, ambiguous and manipulative style of communication. Cooperation is passively resisted and undermined. It relies heavily on non-verbal communication, like silent treatment, rather than clear messages, and attempts to control others without appearing to, for example by sabotaging an unwanted arrangement by being late or forgetting to bring something that was required, while blaming the error on someone else.

Exercise 12.9: Observing styles of communication

- Do you recognize any of the unhelpful styles of communication in yourself or in the people around you?
- In what way can you see this style in your verbal communication, your non-verbal communication and your paraverbal communication?
- In what way can you see this style in the verbal, non-verbal and paraverbal communication of the people around you?

- How does this style of communication, in your-self and/or in other people, contribute to your current experience of depression?
- Have these styles of communication in you and the people around you become more obvious or rigid since you have been depressed?

A HELPFUL AND EFFECTIVE STYLE OF COMMUNICATION

The constructive alternative to these unhelpful styles of communication is *assertive communication*.

- **Assertive:** This communication style involves openly and clearly expressing your feelings, objectives and requests in a way the other person can hear. Verbal and non-verbal communication styles are well matched. This form of communication acknowledges your right to your feelings and goals, and invites other people to consider them in their response. This does not mean forcing your position on to someone else but it does guard against automatically conceding your position in favour of another person's and it lays the ground for a well-informed next step in the conversation or relationship.

In her book *Brilliant Communication* Gill Hasson identified two conditions for assertive communication – confidence and empathy:

- **confidence** that you can communicate well; that you can put your points across directly and clearly, without apology or manipulation; and that you can ask for more information and clarification if the message you receive is not clear;

- **empathy** enabling you to imagine the listener's position, feelings and attitudes and to hold these in mind to help you to communicate your message in a way they can hear; and, by paying close attention to the information provided, to imagine the experience and feelings described from the speaker's point of view, whether or not you agree with or wholly understand their perspective.

This might feel quite a challenge when you are depressed – at a time when your confidence has been knocked, and it is difficult to lift yourself out of your own point of view to imagine someone else's. Fortunately, these are skills you can practise and build up over time.

Reviewing communication styles and skills

Look back over the picture you have built up during this chapter. Is it possible that some of the problems you have experienced have arisen because of a mismatch in communication styles – e.g. one of you likes to get to the point quickly and the other likes to go over all the details carefully – rather than a lack of communication skills? If so, understanding the mismatch more clearly might help you to plan how to use your skills more effectively.

If you have noticed gaps in your communication or listening skills you can use the exercises in this chapter to help you to fill in the gaps. Key points to remember are:

- Pay attention to non-verbal messages.
- Make sure verbal and non-verbal messages match.
- Listen carefully so that your response will be better informed and will show you have been listening.
- Identify the main skill gap you want to fill and practise using that new skill at least once every day.

Exercise 12.10: Practising helpful communication habits

Practise communicating directly and positively in day-to-day situations. For example, say 'Good morning' and smile at someone on the way to work; ask a simple question like, 'Have you had a busy day?', when you buy a coffee or some shopping; make a point of asking someone if they have anything nice planned for that evening before you leave work. Practise eye contact and non-verbal encouragement in small moments and you will gradually find they become a useful habit.

It is always helpful to learn from what works well, so when you feel satisfied with a conversation you have with someone, make a note of what happened. Likewise, reflecting constructively on conversations that don't go so well can give you some useful insights into how things might be improved.

Exercise 12.11: Successful and unsuccessful conversations – what works?

First, think of a recent conversation you had that went well.

- What did you do that helped the communication to work?
- What did the other person do that helped you?
- Ask the other person what they think works well when you talk to each other.
- Consider how closely your communication styles match and how this contributes to the success of your time together.

Now consider the conversations that are less successful.

- Are you still doing the things that are successful in other conversations?
- If not, what stops you from doing these helpful things?
- How could you bring those skills into these difficult communications to make them more successful?
- Does the other person do the things you find helpful?
- If not, which things do they miss out?
- Do either of you do things that do not happen in your more successful communications?
- Who does what?
- How well do you think your communication style matches the other person's communication style?

An example: Stella

Stella loved to talk and to recount things that had happened. She was animated and vivid, and felt as if she were back in the moment as she described an experience. This often meant that she got carried along by the emotion of the story she was telling and could become quite worked up or agitated if it was about something that had upset her. When she was worked up she was less aware of the person she was telling the story to and so it was difficult to interrupt or contribute until the story was over. Many of her stories were quite elaborate and lengthy, and she found it very satisfying and helpful to retrace the sequence of events in detail to examine how things had turned out.

Stella's husband, Frank, did not especially like stories. He liked information to be presented in a clear and factual way and for detail to be kept to a minimum. When he was talking, he was succinct and got to the point as quickly as possible. He was good at identifying the important points in a discussion and had little patience for details he saw as irrelevant.

When Stella and Frank tried to talk about emotionally charged incidents they found it very difficult and often ended up arguing. Stella did not feel that Frank was listening to her, and felt rushed and under pressure to make clear what she was herself struggling to understand. She felt hurt and let down when Frank would give up near the beginning of her story and walk away. Frank felt overwhelmed by the detail and emotion that Stella's stories involved, and felt concerned that she upset herself by reliving the detail so closely. He wanted to protect her and help her to set the upset aside, but found that his efforts to do this appeared to upset her more, and their attempts to communicate with each other routinely fell apart.

Over time Stella learned what she needed from her communications and where she could find it. She came to understand the difference between her style and Frank's, and no longer took his responses as a personal attack. She learned to edit her stories and to speak in a more factual way with Frank, which helped to reduce the number of arguments between them, and meant she could take advantage of the helpful and practical suggestions that Frank often made. However, Stella continued to find it helpful to talk in more detail about her experiences, and so she did this with her girlfriend Julie. Julie's style was much closer to Stella's and she could readily listen for a long time. The two of them would set the scene and pick their way together through the events and feelings of the story, comparing what had been intended and what actually happened. By recognizing the differences and similarities in communication styles between her and the other people in her life, Stella was able to deliberately focus on the strengths in each style and take advantage of what they had to offer, while reducing the frequency of unsatisfactory communication by entering into fewer mismatched exchanges.

Principles of good communication

It can be tempting to imagine that other people have no difficulty in finding the right words. Most of the time, however, this is not true. Clear communication has usually been thought through and planned. Following a few simple principles can significantly improve the quality and clarity of your communication.

Principle one: Start with your purpose – what you want the other person to know

Signal when something is important and needs careful attention. It is helpful to state clearly one or two main points you want people to take away at the start of a discussion – this makes it clear what you want to talk about, thus preparing the other person for what you might be going to say, and helping them to listen more effectively. If you drop an important message into the middle of a bigger conversation it is likely to be missed or lost.

Principle two: Think about how you say it

You now understand the importance of the way in which you make your point. Your point is less likely to be heard if it is made in a way that makes the listener feel defensive or distant, for example if you start with a criticism or accusation. When making an important point, it is helpful to keep your tone of voice calm and neutral, and take your time when speaking. This will give both you and the person you are talking to time to think. In addition to thinking about how you deliver your message, it is important to think about the other person's communication style. Do they like you to get to the point or would they prefer that you take time explaining? Match what you say to what they can listen to most readily. For example, you might simply present some key points to someone who has a very succinct communication style, while you could use a more fully fleshed-out story with someone who is interested in details.

Principle three: Understanding the other person's perspective will help you to communicate more effectively

Having a different point of view from someone else does not have to be a problem. Good communication is not about persuading other people round to your way of thinking; it is about *being heard*. You will both be in a better position to work out a solution if you understand each other's position clearly. It is helpful to present your thoughts and feelings clearly and directly because this will inform any decision you and the other person make together.

Set the scene for the person you are going to talk to. Consider what they already know and what they need to know in order to follow what you are going to say. If they need

more information to be able to understand, provide that first.
Consider how they feel about the subject you are going to
raise. If this is a subject that will provoke strong feelings in
them, you may have to proceed slowly and gradually rather
than moving quickly through everything at once. We think
more slowly when we are emotional, so it will be important
to pause regularly to allow feelings to settle. Be prepared to
have more than one conversation; if either of you finds your
feelings start to take over, it's a good idea to call it a day and
start again another time. Also consider the wider setting, such
as where and when the conversation happens. This should be
convenient to both of you and not just determined by one of
you suddenly deciding it is time to talk. You might have been
awake for hours thinking something over, but it is unlikely that
waking your partner at 3 a.m. will lead to a useful discussion!

Principle four: Make sure there is time for questions

Sometimes this is as simple as slowing down when you speak
and remembering to pause after you have said something
you want the other person to pay attention to. This might be
enough to allow them to ask any questions they need to. If they
do not ask questions, you can ask if there is anything else they
need to know to be able to understand what you are saying,
and if they have been able to follow what you have been saying
so far. Do not let this sidetrack the discussion. If another subject is introduced, acknowledge that it might be something to
discuss at another time but you would like to finish the original
discussion first. Make sure that your main points have been
covered before moving on to anything new.

Practise using these principles in your conversations with your
IPT team. Think about whether they make it easier for you

to make the point you want, and ask your team members if it helps them to understand what you are trying to say. When you have mastered these principles in the safe environment of these relationships, you will feel more confident about using them in more challenging or unpredictable settings.

We've talked quite a lot in this chapter about how your feelings can affect communication. In the next chapter we'll look more closely at feelings, and investigate some ways to manage your own emotions in the context of your relationships with other people in your life.

Summary

- Communication is a two-way process.
- Depression often undermines good communication.
- When and how you communicate are just as important as what you say.
- You communicate with your whole body.
- Listening is just as important as speaking, in good communication.
- Matching communication styles can help you to tell a story in a way that can be heard.
- Know what you want to say and why you want to say it.
- Think about how you say what you say and what the other person can hear.
- Always leave time for questions.

Chapter 13

Understanding emotions

It is easier to act yourself into a new way of feeling than to feel yourself into a new way of acting.

HARRY STACK SULLIVAN, PSYCHIATRIST

Feelings and communication: keeping the airwaves open

Our feelings create a consistent background hum to our day. We tune into them more or less closely at different times, yet they set the quality and character of most of our experiences. When we feel cheerful we barely notice small frustrations, but if we are feeling irritable the same frustrations are likely to catch our attention and gain importance. In general, feelings fluctuate around a middle ground, with occasional bursts of intensity that pass relatively quickly. When we are depressed, feelings like sadness or hopelessness can dominate virtually every waking moment of our day, while other feelings like enthusiasm and pleasure seem impossibly out of reach. Not only does the strength of our feeling change when we are depressed, but our sense of control also diminishes, creating a potentially frightening and unfamiliar experience that we do not know how to stop.

The ability to read one's own and other people's emotions is hugely important in determining how well we manage day to day and the satisfaction we feel in our relationships. Much of the time this is a relatively silent process, which relies less on our ability to understand what is said and more on reading the cues and signals that pass between us and the people around us.

When our ability to regulate and predict our own emotions is disrupted it has a powerful effect on our relationships. The white noise created by a constantly intense emotional world can make it much more difficult both to send out and to receive clear emotional signals. Our feelings might be unfamiliar or confusing, making it difficult to share our experience with friends and family. If the signals that other people send out have to fight through the depressive fog that surrounds us, we might find ourselves working with only part of the picture, with even the messages that do get through becoming distorted or confused by the interference. It might be hard to distinguish which signals are our own and which are coming from other people. It is not difficult to see why confusion and misunderstanding creep in, often reinforcing the self-doubt and blame that depression created in the first place. An encouraging finding in research is that the difficulties in recognizing and talking about feelings that we often experience when we are depressed often ease when the depression lifts.

How emotional skills can help you

Understanding and talking clearly about how you feel is a central part of recovering from depression and managing your relationships. By creating a coherent story of your depression you become more attuned to your own feelings and how you respond to people and events. In sharing your narrative you achieve greater clarity in telling this story to the people you are close to, so that they too have a chance to understand, and any mismatches in communication can be smoothed out.

Research has repeatedly shown that understanding and managing your emotions well leads to better mental health, more successful relationships and greater satisfaction in life. Developing your emotional awareness and communication skills is therefore likely to be really useful to you in recovering from depression and relationship problems. The cluster of skills that are involved can be useful in a number of ways. Let's look at a few of the main ones.

- Recognizing and naming your feelings is a useful internal guide, helping you to be clear about your own reactions to events and people. This *self-awareness* in turn can help you to regulate your responses. You will have more control over what you feel, how strongly you feel it and for how long. You will gradually be able to tolerate painful feelings both when you are alone and when you are with other people. Resisting the urge to automatically withdraw when you are upset or angry reduces your isolation and helps you to tackle the problems that trigger these feelings more directly.

- Self-awareness plays an important role in our relationships, too, and improved self-awareness can become a foundation for better communication with other people – what we could call better *interpersonal awareness*. By sharing your feelings and inviting other people to do the same, you can pinpoint the most important issues to be addressed in your relationships. Reading the emotional temperature and its effect on how well you communicate helps you make better decisions on when and how to say what you need, which in turn increases the chances of a good outcome.

- Finally, *gaps in our emotional experience* can also provide useful clues. Pleasure and happiness are among the first feelings to be stifled in depression. These feelings can seem out of reach when we are depressed, and if our day-to-day routine changes we might find that there are fewer opportunities for pleasure and satisfaction. This 'treasure hunt' for long-relinquished feelings is a central part of the process of recovery.

Given that there are so many potential advantages to using your emotions, it is useful to understand the ways in which you currently make use of your feelings and which opportunities are being missed. Let's consider each of the examples described above – self-awareness, communication and filling gaps in your experience – to help you to think about the role emotions currently play in your life. You might find that you are already tapping into some of these opportunities, while others offer new options or will require new skills to take full advantage of what your emotional world can offer.

Self-awareness

Being aware of what you are feeling is the first step towards a healthier emotional experience. This involves recognizing an internal change and accurately identifying which emotion or emotions are involved. At a basic level this means that you know when what you are experiencing is an emotion, and can distinguish it from a physical sensation (e.g. heart racing) or a thought (e.g. I am a bad person). Our feelings, sensations and thoughts often get confused, and when this happens it can reduce the accuracy of what you tell yourself and other people about what you feel.

SENSATIONS, THOUGHTS AND FEELINGS

Let's look more closely at the two examples I've just mentioned to understand the difference. When your heart races – that is, your heart rate increases – you feel a physical sensation in your chest. This might happen for a number of reasons, e.g. you are about to speak in public, you have just had an argument or you have been running. In each case the *physical sensation* will be the same, reflecting the physical reality that your heart is beating more quickly. However, the *emotion* that goes with that sensation will probably be quite different in each example. You might feel anxious about public speaking or angry about the argument and you might have thoroughly enjoyed your run. Anxiety, anger and pleasure are the range of *feelings* potentially associated with the same physical sensation.

'I am a bad person' describes a *thought*, not a feeling. The thought expresses a belief you have or a conclusion you have drawn. As yet, the thought does not describe any related feelings. The person expressing this thought might feel sad, guilty or indifferent about this belief or conclusion. You can often tell the difference between a thought and a feeling by trying to describe it in a single word: this is usually easy for a feeling, e.g. 'sad' or 'anxious', whereas a thought is typically described in a sentence, e.g. 'I am a bad person'. This can become confusing because the 'thought' sentence is often one that is *phrased* in terms of feeling: 'I feel that I am a bad person', which is misleading. Both thoughts and feelings are useful pieces of information, and if you can distinguish between the two you can produce a richer description of your experience.

Suzanna's thoughts and feelings

When Suzanna tried to describe how she felt when she had down days she would say, 'I couldn't be bothered'. Implicitly she seemed to be describing lack of interest and perhaps low energy, but it was ambiguous because her feelings were indirectly communicated in her conclusion that she 'couldn't be bothered'. This was her only guide for herself and the only explanation she could offer to her friends when she cancelled plans. Given this was all she had to go on, she routinely retreated under her duvet for the rest of the day and her friends felt confused and upset by her lack of interest. When she learned to distinguish between her thoughts and feelings she realized that when she *thought* she couldn't be bothered she sometimes *felt* sad that her boyfriend didn't want the same things from their relationship that she did, sometimes disappointed that her friend had not asked what was troubling her, and sometimes anxious about how long it had been since she had spoken to her boyfriend following an argument. By distinguishing how she felt from what she thought and naming individual feelings (sad, disappointed, anxious, etc.), she began to understand what triggered her feelings more clearly and could explain her feelings and responses to the people who were involved and those who could help her.

Many of the feelings that are part of depression are unpleasant, and you might have found yourself trying to tune out or distract yourself from them. Trying to hold painful feelings at arm's length can be an exhausting part of depression and might have blunted your awareness: if you tune out in order not to feel bad all the time, you gradually lose track of subtle emotional changes. Breaking this down will involve relearning how to pay attention to the subtle emotional shifts that happen from moment to moment.

Julie's fear of overwhelming sadness

Julie described trying to distract herself from feeling sad by keeping busy all the time. She felt exhausted by the effort, but was afraid that if she let the feelings in she would not be able to cope. Like many depressed people, she worried that if she started to cry she would never stop. When she started to pay attention to changes in her feelings, she did feel sad some of the time, but she also noticed times when she felt a little better, even if only briefly, and times when she felt angry or bored or relaxed. When she stopped resisting her feelings and acknowledged the highs and lows, she started to feel more in control. She noticed that her feelings changed over time and she learned ways that she could influence her mood. She said that allowing herself time each day to think deliberately about how she had been feeling acted like a sponge that soaked up the feelings she had been afraid would drown her. Noticing and naming her difficult feelings drew them together and freed her up to do and feel other things at other times, rather than being constantly on guard and reminding herself of the threat.

EMOTIONAL VOCABULARY

Having become more aware of these emotional changes, it is helpful to *name* what you are feeling. This is especially useful if you can do it at the time you are having the feeling, so that this 'real-time feedback' can guide your response. However, sometimes feelings tumble over each other or change quickly, making it more difficult to be sure what you are feeling in the moment. On those occasions it will be helpful to take time later to look back on how you were feeling and trace the ways this changed from moment to moment.

In order to name your feelings you must have an *emotional vocabulary* – a selection of words that you can use to describe your feelings. The vocabulary might cover just a few basic feelings or might be more fully developed, allowing you to make subtle distinctions in the quality or strength of the feelings described. When we are depressed we often find it easier to think of words for negative feelings than positive feelings. Consequently, our positive feeling vocabulary might be neglected and underused. This bias rarely provides a balanced picture, and repeatedly paying attention to our negative feelings at the expense of our positive ones can prolong the feeling and lower our sense of control.

It is useful if our emotional vocabulary describes both:

- the *type* of feeling, e.g. happy or sad, and
- the *strength* of feeling, e.g. content/delighted or down/ miserable.

Margaret's emotional vocabulary broadens her perspective

Every week Margaret's friend asked about her depression. Every week Margaret said there had been no change and she felt as depressed and hopeless as she had the week before. However, over the weeks Margaret looked brighter, she cried less often, she took more care of her appearance and recently she'd had her hair done. Margaret's friend commented on this and said that she was feeling confused because what Margaret said and how she appeared no longer matched. Margaret realized that she had become so used to feeling depressed over the months of her illness that this had simply become her norm and she had stopped really looking at how she felt. In the week that followed Margaret paid close attention to how she felt each day and noticed that she was less depressed on several days: some days she actually enjoyed and occasionally she felt happy. When she was next asked about how she was feeling, she described the many different feelings that had featured in her week, both positive and negative. Broadening her perspective in this way helped her to focus on her successes and gave her ideas about what kinds of things it would be helpful to do again. It also helped her to use the support her friend offered to understand the setbacks that continued to bring her mood down.

Exercise 13.1: How well developed is your emotional vocabulary?

Let's start with some basic feelings. Can you think of a time during the last week when you experienced any of the feelings described in the table below? Tick the box for each feeling you recognize in the *last week*.

Happy	Sad	Hurt	Anxious	Confused
Caring	Angry	Lonely	Guilty	Inadequate

Was it easier to think of examples of some feelings than others?

Each of the headings in the table represents only one of the words you could use to describe these types of feeling. You might have chosen a different word to capture your feelings. For example, you might have said 'miserable' or 'empty' instead of 'sad', or you might have chosen 'interested' or 'loving' instead of 'caring', etc. Changing the word can subtly change what you are communicating and gives you an opportunity to describe your feelings more carefully. If you would have chosen a different word to describe any of these feelings, copy the table below into your notebook and add your alternative words in the empty boxes.

Happy	Sad	Hurt	Anxious	Confused
Caring	Angry	Lonely	Guilty	Inadequate

- What do you notice about the words you have added?
- Do they describe stronger or milder feelings than the words we started with?
- Copy the table below into your notebook and add three words under each heading to describe different intensities of the feelings e.g. 'happy'

could change to 'content' (mild), 'cheerful'
(moderate) or 'delighted' (strong).

- Which of these words best describe your experience in the last week?
- Ask someone else for ideas if you find it difficult
  to think of examples for each feeling.

	Happy	Sad	Hurt	Anxious	Confused
Mild					
Moderate					
Strong					
	Caring	Angry	Lonely	Guilty	Inadequate
Mild					
Moderate					
Strong					

- Which additional 'feeling words' would you
  add to capture the full range of your current
  feelings? These feelings might not have been
  captured at all by the previous lists. Some examples have been suggested in the table below.

Expand the table in your notebook and try to add as many more feeling words as you can. To prompt yourself, try to think about all the feelings you can remember having over the last two weeks.

Interested			Embarrassed	
				Pleased
		Bored		
	Comforted			

By completing this exercise you will already have started to develop quite a full emotional vocabulary. Take some time to think about each of the feelings you have identified and think about how each feeling has featured in your experience of depression. Think about each of the feelings you recognize in turn, and write your answers to the questions below in your notebook.

- Have you experienced this feeling recently more or less often than you typically would ?
- Would you like to feel this way more or less often?
- Have you felt more or less in control of this feeling recently than you typically would?
- Have you told anyone else that you feel that way?
- Who would it be useful to tell?

STANDING BACK FROM YOUR FEELINGS

Using your self-awareness involves looking at your emotions in a neutral way rather than reacting to them or being taken over by them. In order to think about all of the feelings that are stirred up from day to day you have to stand back to find some perspective rather than acting from within the experience. This starts to make the complex and changeable nature of our feelings very clear and starts to give you distance from the feelings surrounding depression.

This change will not happen immediately. It will take regular practice over the coming weeks and months to notice your feelings and to be able to identify them accurately. Use the lists you have created to help you to think about your emotional experience from day to day.

- Take five minutes each day to identify the different feelings you have had that day. Add any new feelings you notice to your list of feeling words.

As you become more aware of your feelings you will start to recognize how often they change and what you can do to make that happen. Depression tips the balance towards negative rather than positive feelings, but this bias can gradually be reversed as you begin to manage rather than be managed by your feelings. This kind of emotional resilience (see p. 24) uses self-awareness as the basis for action, because change won't happen unless we do something to bring it about. Knowing we feel sad isn't enough to change it, but it is useful if it encourages us to do something that will change how we are feeling. Similarly, knowing we are happy isn't enough to make it last, but deliberately doing the things that have made us feel that way in the past will make it more likely. Awareness is crucial, but we must act on it if it is to be of use in our recovery.

Maria's awareness of her anger

Maria regularly felt angry with her son. When she was angry she would shout and criticize him and feel out of control. Within minutes of doing this she would feel terribly guilty and ashamed and would ask her son to forgive her. Every time this pattern repeated itself, Maria felt more and more hopeless and her son found it more difficult to accept her apology. As Maria started to monitor her feelings she realized that her angry feelings did not come completely out of the blue, as she had originally thought. She noticed that she was much more likely to become intensely angry when she felt under pressure or tired. When she took notice of these early warning signs she was able to let her son know how she was feeling and they worked together to avoid arguments. Maria also took these early signals as a prompt to do the things that helped her to relax, such as going for a walk. By taking this action and sharing how she felt with her son she was able reduce how often she became uncontrollably angry. This success in turn reduced the general sense of pressure and apprehension that she felt and meant that there were fewer angry exchanges.

Although in IPT we mainly focus on the here and now, you will also be asked to think about experiences you have had in the past. This might be the quite distant past, when you think over the relationship you had with someone who died, or your experience in a role that you have had to give up, or it might be the much more recent past, as you think about an argument you had a few days ago. Each of these is an opportunity to think and talk about how you felt *at the time* and your feelings about it *now*. Tracking the changes in how we felt then and how we feel now is an important part of our self-awareness and will reveal whether our feelings have remained the same, e.g. 'I was furious with him then and I'm still furious with him now', or have changed over time, perhaps softening, e.g. 'I was furious with him then, but I can see he was trying his best and did not mean to hurt me and I feel sad that we did not manage to work it out', perhaps hardening, e.g. 'I was furious with him then and I am convinced he did not care about my feelings at all and blame him for all of the problems we had'. Noticing your response at different points on your emotional journey can help you to think about the progress you are making and if you are moving in the direction you need to in order to move on from your depression.

Interpersonal awareness

As you learn to tune into your feelings more closely you'll also start to notice the situations that trigger those feelings. Feelings rarely appear out of the blue, even if they might seem to sometimes. Usually our emotions change because of something that happens to us or because of emotionally charged thoughts we have. As you have been developing your personal story about depression, you have been looking at the ways in which your depression symptoms are linked to your current relationships. You might feel sad or guilty about one or more of those relationships. You might feel confused and hopeless about what to do to solve serious problems. You might struggle to motivate yourself to tackle difficult conversations or adjust to unwanted changes. Tracing your feelings back to the relationships and related issues that have triggered them will be an invaluable guide to targeting your attention in IPT.

As you gain perspective and learn to step back from your feelings, you will become more practised at considering your response rather than simply reacting. This will be valuable in helping you to stay with the people and conversations you need to in order to sort out your current difficulties. The vocabulary you have developed to clarify your own feelings can be integrated into your discussions with other people. Adding information about your feelings, and being genuinely curious about how other people feel about the situation you're facing, will improve the quality and effectiveness of your discussions. This will help you to understand each other better and to make better plans to do what is needed to solve any problems you are facing.

It is helpful to think about feelings happening in sequence rather than as a single event. Young children often display very quick changes in their emotional state. Imagine the small boy who is heartbroken when his mother insists on holding the frame of his bicycle when they cross the road but is instantly gleeful when she lets go and he can cycle off into the park. This kind of emotional 'switching' is less common in adults, although you may have experienced more of it while you've been depressed. As adults we learn to tolerate small frustrations without being unduly affected and to enjoy pleasures while still being able to contain our excitement. Relatively few occasions in life merit or require a very intense emotional reaction.

As feelings build up, there are opportunities to change course and limit the emotional fallout. For example, if you are bickering with your partner, you can probably feel yourself becoming tense and your voice becoming clipped and your heart rate increasing. You are being given warnings that the situation could escalate. If you and your partner continue on this course it is likely that there will be an argument, during which you might feel angry, hurt or frustrated. However, if either of you pays attention to these signals and suggests that you put off further discussion until you both feel calmer, it is likely that the tension will drop, you will begin to relax and might even feel pleased with yourself for having effectively managed the situation and avoided more conflict. This example is important because it highlights the possibility of using early warning signs to prevent painful feelings further down the line. Your awareness of how you are feeling gives you the opportunity to plan ahead and avoid predictable problem situations, as shown in the diagram below.

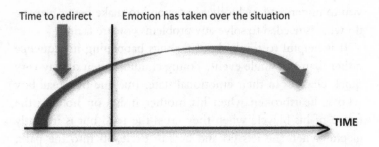

Time to redirect   **Emotion has taken over the situation**

TIME

This is not to suggest that you should always use awareness of your feelings to avoid difficult situations. There may be conversations that are important to have, indeed necessary in order to sort out difficulties. Knowing when to have these conversations will play a big part in their success. The aim is to:

- resolve conflicts positively by staying focused on the present;
- choose your arguments carefully;
- forgive faults rather than blame;
- end conflicts that cannot be resolved.

Continuing an argument when you are angry and want to have the last word is very tempting, but rarely leads to a positive outcome. Similarly, having an important discussion when you are too poorly motivated to make any of the points that are important to you or to express yourself clearly, because you are feeling depressed and hopeless, is likely to lead to a conclusion that will be unsatisfactory in the long run. It is useful to be atuned to your feelings so that you can use your awareness to notice and describe how you feel, but this relies on you thinking clearly when you talk about your feelings. It is useful to think in terms of an optimal window of opportunity when communication is clearly helped by your being emotionally aware, but not overwhelmed by it.

Too little emotion	Window of opportunity	Too much emotion

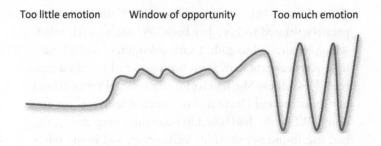

Reading emotional cues in your friends and family will also help you to decide when to approach important conversations and when to wait until a better time can be found. When you have important discussions you want a constructive outcome. Being able to read when someone is receptive to what you have to say is an important part of your planning. So, starting a difficult conversation when the other person is so angry they cannot think straight or so tired they cannot concentrate is not a good idea, as you are unlikely to achieve what you are hoping to.

New or unacknowledged feelings

A final advantage of this emotional awareness is that it will help you to examine and express feelings that do not normally receive sufficient attention. These might include painful feelings that are buried below layers of other feelings and have not felt safe or acceptable to talk about. We often worry that our feelings are not acceptable and try to censor ourselves by remaining silent. Often, when we finally express them, we will find that such feelings are in fact quite common.

Diane's uncomfortable feelings

When Diane's baby daughter died she felt empty and desperately wanted to have her back. Yet she also felt relief, which in turn led to guilt. Diane's daughter had had multiple physical problems from birth and had required care round the clock. She had had many medical crises during her short life and Diane had not been able to relax at any point. While she had loved her daughter very dearly, she had also found her short life exhausting, and in the midst of her own sadness she was relieved to be released from the constant worry and panic just below the surface.

Uncomfortable feelings are often resisted or rejected as unacceptable. We may label them as 'bad' feelings. However, keeping these feelings inside us often requires a huge amount of energy and can in fact prolong their influence. The effort this demands directly contributes to the fatigue and guilt that are so common in depression. While it's quite understandable that you don't want to feel bad all of the time, it is not possible to block your emotions indefinitely, and attempting to hold them at bay often creates additional problems as well as masking what the feeling might usefully tell us. Remember, feelings are communications.

Learning to think of feelings as emotional responses at a given moment, rather than being either 'good' or 'bad', can be a significant turning point. Feelings are not facts, and they do not make you a better or worse person. They simply mark a response at any given time and will inevitably change as time passes. This is just as true of uncomfortable feelings as it is of positive feelings, such as happiness and compassion, which can seem all too fleeting in depression. To change with time is the nature of emotional experience. Observing and accepting our feelings, rather than reacting and judging them, can help to bypass the guilt and self-blame that make depression worse.

Actively seeking out positive feelings is another way to expand your emotional experience. Admittedly, this is difficult when you do not want to do things or see people. But cutting out opportunities to feel good prolongs depression. Pursuing 'anti-depressant' activities and company will promote pleasure and feelings of satisfaction, and will begin to loosen the grip depression has on your life. It can take time for positive feelings to come back, but this process can be helped by making a deliberate effort, that is, looking for positive experiences rather than waiting for them to find you. As Harry Stack Sullivan suggests in the quotation at the head of this chapter, it is a way of acting yourself into a different feeling. This is likely to start in small ways. You might try using your interpersonal inventory to identify the people who lift your mood, and deliberately spend time in their company. Or you could find activities that give you brief flashes of pleasure and build those into your routine until they provide a constant beam of light.

In the remaining chapters we will continue to look at ways in which you can not only manage what feels uncomfortable but pursue what feels positive to regain emotional balance in your day-to-day experience, as we examine four case studies, each focusing on one of IPT's four core themes.

Summary

- Your feelings are the background noise of your day.
- Your ability to predict and regulate how you feel is disrupted by depression.
- It is helpful to recognize and acknowledge your feelings.
- Awareness will help you to communicate clearly about your own and other people's feelings.
- Use the emotional temperature to identify the best windows of opportunity for talking.
- Pursue opportunities for positive feelings.

Chapter 14

Theme one: changing roles

We must be willing to let go of the life we have planned, so as to have the life that is waiting for us.

E. M. FORSTER, WRITER

An unwanted 'role transition', that is, moving from one role to another, often feels like stepping off an anticipated path. The road you were following might have come to an unexpected end or curved off in a direction you didn't anticipate, with the effect that you feel, at least temporarily, disorientated and unsure what to do next.

Let's take each word in turn, because they each reveal something important in understanding this kind of difficulty.

Role

Roles operate on many different levels. On an individual level you have roles that relate directly to yourself, like being your own caretaker. This involves, for example, eating properly, taking the rest you need, and being kind to yourself when life is difficult. This kind of role is often abandoned when we are depressed, undermining our ability to recover, and re-establishing this caretaker role is one of the first objectives in IPT (see chapter 7).

But 'role' is more often an interpersonal idea, that is, something that works between people. For example, as I act in the
role of writer I do it with a version of you, the reader, in
mind. Imagining what you need as a reader helps to clarify the
objectives of my role as writer. Usually, roles operate in relation to other real people in your life. For example, you might
be a caretaker to your children or parents, partners and friends.
You might hold responsibilities in your role as an employee or
employer – responsibilities that will shape the daily routine of
your life, dictating how and with whom you spend your time.
Juggling these various roles can feel immeasurably harder when
you are depressed. Expectations you once coped with can feel
overwhelming and threatening.

Our roles are also the scaffolding for the communities and
society we live in. We rely on each other to perform our roles
in the way we and others expect in order that we can all get on
with life. You expect the bus driver to arrive on time and to
take the planned route, in order for you to meet your responsibilities, such as getting to work on time.

So we hold many different roles – son, daughter, partner,
parent, friend, employee, customer, leader, audience member,
etc. – and they vary in how important they are in our lives. Each
role has routines associated with it, which reflect what we do
in the role, and with whom we do it. Roles also involve basic
rules, which reflect the expectations, rights and responsibilities
that define and set limits on the role. Parents spend time with
their own child, set rules around bedtime and provide food and
shelter, but the same expectations and responsibilities would
not apply with a child they didn't know. How flexible the routine and rules are depends on the specific role and the people
involved. Your routine might be quite flexible in your role
as friend with a number of different people, but less so when
you act in the role of employee and go to work in the same

office, at the same time and with the same people every day. When people hold similar expectations about the roles they hold for each other, the relationships usually run smoothly. They each know what to expect and that is what they get. When our expectations differ, however, trouble is rarely far away.

Transition

Life is dynamic and we frequently face change. Jobs are offered and lost, relationships start and stop, children grow up and move away, parents grow older and need more support. No matter what we do, life continues to move on and we try to keep up. Most transitions, or changes, are managed success-fully: needing only a brief period to adjust, we transfer our skills from one situation to the next, our relationships adapt to new routines and we move on. However, the frequency with which we typically change roles can both help and confuse us when we are trying to understand a difficult role transition. You might be asking yourself, 'If I manage change most of the time, why not this time?' In this chapter we will explore the way depression interferes with our ability to manage some changes.

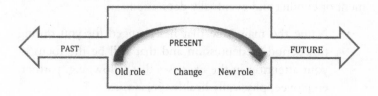

Transition describes a process of change – in this case, a change of role, as summarized in the diagram above. There are three points of particular interest in this process:

- the old role;
- the change in role;
- the new role.

Mismatches in expectations, which interfere with the smooth running of our roles, are more common after a change, and might arise at each of these points:

- you might not want to give up the old role (e.g. when breaking up with someone you did not want to break up with);
- you or the people around you might not know what to expect in a new role (think of your confusion on the first day in a new job);
- you might not want to conform to the demands of the new role (e.g. being forced to retire when you don't know what you will do with so much free time).

Depression can directly undermine your ability to adapt to change – to feel confident that you can meet new demands, or to tolerate the pain of losing something or someone you did not want to give up. You or the people around you might become inflexible in your routines, which leads to disappointment or conflict and eventually depression.

- Name the main role that has changed for you during this period of depression and that will be the focus of your attention in the exercises that follow, e.g. partner, employee, physically healthy person, etc.
- Draw a simple timeline (refer back to chapter 8 for a reminder) to mark out the significant events around this

particular change. These will be expanded on in later exercises.

For example, Paul's role changed from being employed to being unemployed, and his basic timeline would look like this:

| Merger announced | Longer hours; drinking more | Unsuccessful interview; leave job | Spending time at home alone | Money worries; bickering |

| Feb | Feb – April | April | April to present | June to present |

The wider context

Depression is not an inevitable consequence of change. On most occasions we can manage change successfully and with relatively little fuss or disruption. However, from time to time we may struggle with change, particularly when we are depressed, and so it is helpful to consider some of the features that might influence why this can happen.

THE SIGNIFICANCE OF THE ROLE YOU LOST

Significant roles such as partner, employee, etc., tend to involve a deep emotional and practical investment and have a strong impact on many areas of our life. Change in these significant roles usually causes much more disruption than would be the case with change in casual or occasional roles, such as being a member of a gym class. The ripple effect of losing a significant role will reach out much further and may create a number of difficulties, such as consequent changes in social routine, financial security, living situation etc.

THE DESTABILIZING EFFECT OF THE CHANGE ON OTHER RELATIONSHIPS AND SUPPORTS

Just as our roles do not exist in a vacuum, so changes in our roles don't happen without wider consequences in our relationships. The people around us often change when an important role changes, and this can sometimes make it more difficult to cope because several routines are disrupted at once. For example, after a divorce, socializing might feel more difficult if you are the only single person in a group of married couples. At other times people are literally not available in the way they used to be following a change. If you move city, despite still having relationships in your home town you will be, at least temporarily, more isolated.

A mismatch between our current needs and resources will increase our vulnerability to depression. This might be revealed in a number of ways:

- Some people have a network of supportive relationships but will be unable to use them for practical reasons, such as physical distance or time demands. In this situation, deliberately seeking out those supports or developing new local supports will be important in managing the risk of depression.
- Others have support available in their network, but resist asking for help. Directly challenging this impulse, and making more active use of the support available to you, is important in this case.
- Others, with few supportive relationships, will be more vulnerable after a significant change because they have little

back-up to support them in facing the additional demands of their new role. In this situation it is important to be proactive in developing new supportive relationships.

Exercise 14.1: What support is available to you in facing change?

- Can you relate to any of the scenarios described above?
- What can you do to build up the support you have available during this period of change?
- Identify one person you could ask for support or one opportunity to meet new people who could support you, and be proactive in making contact with them.

CHANGE BROUGHT ABOUT BY SOMEONE ELSE

Coping with change that is the result of someone else's action can be complicated: it may make you feel less in control, and may involve feelings of betrayal or abuse. Think of the difference between being bullied out of your job and leaving your job voluntarily, or being left by your partner rather than deciding together to end the relationship. Research has repeatedly shown that painful or frightening events instigated by other people are often found to be more distressing and more difficult to recover from than painful events in which another person was not actively involved.

GENERAL STABILITY AND COMPETING DEMANDS

The general stability of the bigger picture is also important in determining how well you cope with change. If several areas of your life change at the same time, and several routines are disrupted, it might be more difficult to use your normal coping strategies. People vary greatly in the number of demands they are comfortable dealing with. Some people thrive on juggling lots of things at once, while others prefer to be more methodical and work through one thing at a time. This will influence their respective vulnerability to depression if they are faced with several competing demands at once, with the first person likely to cope well but the second person quickly feeling overwhelmed.

These various features of change, and their likely impact, are summarized in the table below.

Feature of change	Impact of change
Significance of the role	Impact increases with significance of role
Support available and support used	Impact decreases when support is available and used
Others' involvement in creating change	Impact increases with others' deliberate involvement
Stability in the wider environment	Impact decreases with wider stability

By considering each of these features in turn you can begin to understand why a particular change is more difficult at a particular time. Let's use Margaret's story to illustrate this.

Margaret's story of change

Margaret faced many changes around the time that she became depressed. Her relationship with her partner had become more and more difficult over the past year, and this came to a head when he announced unexpectedly that he did not want to continue their seven-year relationship. Margaret had been aware of problems but did not want the relationship to end. She had found it very difficult to focus on the problems with her partner because she had faced many competing demands in the months leading up to the separation. Her elderly father had fallen and broken his hip. He was making a slow recovery and required regular assistance. Margaret made a 45-minute train journey to his home on four evenings a week to spend time with him and prepare his meals. She was close to her father and enjoyed time with him, but found his increased dependency frustrating and the extra travel very tiring. Around the same time Margaret was given a promotion at work. She enjoyed her job and was very pleased about the promotion, but as it involved managing other staff for the first time she experienced some anxiety in trying to cope with the new role and tended to work extra hours on the nights she did not visit her father in order to keep up. Given all of these demands, Margaret had less time to socialize with her close friends, whom she would normally have tried to meet once a week. She missed their company but felt that all of the other demands had to come before her social life. This left Margaret feeling very isolated in managing a period of considerable change and she became increasingly depressed.

Significance of the role that changed	Role as partner was very significant	More impact and greater vulnerability to depression
Support available to manage change	Good support available but not being used	More impact and greater vulnerability to depression
Another person's act/decision	Separation was her partner's decision	More impact and greater vulnerability to depression
Stability in wider environment	Little stability in wider environment	More impact and greater vulnerability to depression

Exercise 14.2: The wider context of change

Copy the table below into your notebook and describe your own experience of role transition in the blank boxes.

Which role changed?

Significance of the role that changed		
Support available to manage change		
Another person's act/decision		
Stability in wider environment		

Are there ways that you can change this picture now? For example:

- Spend time with friends and let them know what is happening.
- Set aside some demands temporarily to allow you to focus on the major change.
- Take control of those parts of the change that you can. Ask for help to do this.
- Negotiate how the change happens, even if you cannot stop it from happening.

These details add important layers to your depression story and begin to explain why this particular change is so difficult for you now. Add this information to your personal story so that these background details can be used to explain the impact of this change for you.

Monitoring your progress

It is important to continue to monitor your symptoms of depression and to track the ways in which they interact with your attempts to manage this particular role change. Fill in the symptom table each week (see appendix 1) and use exercise 6.3 in chapter 6 (see page 109) and appendix 3 to help you to clarify the links between your symptoms and your relationships. It will be useful to look more closely at occasions when you can see increases in your symptoms coinciding with issues related to the change.

Where are you stuck?

The significance of each part of the change – the old role, the manner of the change and the new role – will vary from one individual to another. The story may be one of unwilling loss, one of being surprised or let down, or one of being unsure or reluctant.

Letting go of what has been lost

Accepting the way the change happened

Adapting to new circumstances and demands

- Are you finding any specific part of the change more difficult to cope with than others?

How do you feel about the old role? You may feel anything from a preoccupied sense of longing for things to be how they were to relief and a sense of 'good riddance'. Consider the difference between John Lennon and Paul McCartney's song 'Yesterday', in which they captured struggling to let go, idealizing the memory and shying away from the future, and Gloria Gaynor's outlook when she sings 'I Will Survive', in which she looks back on a relationship in which she was hurt and treated badly and from which she wants to move on. Both describe losing a relationship, but from very different perspectives.

- Write in your notebook how you feel about the role you have given up.

In some cases, it may not be letting go of the past that is the hard part. The need to move on might seem clear, but the way the change happened might be difficult to get past. Imagine a relationship that has run its course and is drifting towards a natural conclusion. This might be on course for an amicable separation until one partner simply drops out of contact without a word of explanation, leaving the other feeling betrayed and hurt. It may not be the end of the relationship itself that is the stumbling block, but the way it happened. Recognizing the impact of the way a change comes about can reveal important clues in trying to understand your reaction and the link to how you feel now. Has the way your role changed been a stumbling block to moving on?

- Write in your notebook how you feel about the way your role change came about.

Even if the change itself is not seen as a bad thing, and the manner of the change is not distressing, the outcome can still be unsettling and may contribute to you feeling depressed and hopeless. Many women and men actively plan to have children but find the reality overwhelming (indeed, post-natal depression is very common). In these circumstances, and others where a new role brings a whole rush of demands, depression can flourish. This situation can be especially challenging when the demands of the new role remain unclear, for example in adjusting to a long-term physical condition or waiting months for medical retirement to be confirmed. The move from the familiar to the uncertain is rich ground for depression to take root. How does the prospect of taking up your new role make you feel? Does it contribute to you feeling depressed?

- Write down in your notebook any concerns you have about your new role.

Notice what preoccupies or troubles you each day, perhaps lowering your mood or keeping you awake at night. Note whether this relates to a particular stage of the change, e.g. you find yourself thinking about the good times that you miss; dwelling on the painful way the change happened; or feeling confused or unclear as you try to manage your new situation. You might find yourself reacting to each of the stages of the change at different times. That is not unusual. The point is simply to try to pinpoint your own personal obstacles to moving on.

Building a balanced story of the past

When we give up an important role we are more comfortable if what we feel now corresponds with the way we remember things in the past, e.g. feeling sad about losing something good or angry about being treated badly. However, you might get stuck around a role transition because the issues are more complex or involve contradictory feelings. There might have been both good and bad things about your old role. We sometimes find it difficult to think about all the different elements that made up a lost role. Some aspects might remain very clear while others get lost along the way. For example, if you feel a strong sense of loss about giving up a role you might focus a lot of attention on the things you miss about that role and pay less attention to the difficulties you had in it. This could create a memory that fails to capture important features of the role you have given up. To guard against this kind of partial or biased memory it is helpful to go over the role you have given up in detail, allowing yourself to think about the enjoyable and diffi- cult things about the role and hold both sides of the picture in mind at the same time. Considering the overall balance of the picture is undoubtedly more of a challenge, especially when you are feeling depressed and your memory and concentration are not as reliable as they would usually be, but it safeguards against getting unnecessarily stuck by only remembering part of the picture.

IPT is a therapy about change. It is also primarily about the here and now, and so it could be tempting to think that you will be served by putting all your energy into making the new role work. While this is the long-term goal, it is useful to spend some time initially remembering the old role. This way you can make sure that you acknowledge and understand your loss, leaving you free to move on. The aim is not to persuade you that the change did not matter, but to help you to understand why it mattered so much.

Reviewing the old role can also clarify which losses associated with this role change are *necessary* and which *unnecessary*. Some things are necessarily given up when a role is given up or taken away – e.g. status attached to being the boss, intimacy with a specific partner – while other aspects of your experience might survive even when the role disappears, such as friendships with the people you used to work with or interests you once shared with someone else. When you are depressed it can be difficult to make subtle distinctions, and there is a tendency to imagine everything is lost. Leaving a job does not necessarily mean giving up all the relationships you had with former colleagues, but it might mean reorganizing some of them to be friendships. By looking at the old role first you can check whether there is anything from the past that would be useful to take with you as you face the future.

It can be difficult to fill out the story on your own, especially if you find it easier to remember one side of it. It is therefore a good idea to involve your IPT team in building up the story, including people who knew you at the time you were in this role. It can be very interesting to hear a familiar story from someone else's perspective.

Exercise 14.3: Getting help to fill out the story of the old role

- Who will you invite to help you?
- Were they directly involved with you when you were in your old role, e.g. someone you worked with in a job you have lost, or who socialized with you when you were still in a couple or before you had children?
- What do they remember about you in the old role? Ask them about both the good and the bad things.
- Did you go to this person for support about any aspect of the old role? What do they remember about that?
- What have they noticed since that role has been lost?

Our roles change and develop over time, perhaps moving from uncertainty to familiarity, from excitement to routine, from pleasure to disappointment. There may be a series of significant events that pushed the story forward, or it might have gently plodded along until a final more or less dramatic conclusion. Take time to think over the whole story of your old role and to think about how you responded to the ways it changed over time. Don't be tempted to rush over these questions. You may find that you have to come back to them more than once to gradually build up a representative picture.

Exercise 14.4: Thinking over the old role

- What were the high points of the old role, the experiences or opportunities that gave you pleasure and that you miss?

- What has been hardest to give up?
- What were the difficulties in that role?
- How serious were these problems?
- Did anyone help you to manage those problems? If so, who?

Some of these questions might be difficult to answer, especially if you remember the role being particularly good or bad. It might feel tempting to dismiss examples of the other side as not mattering now, but this is an opportunity to consider all that has been lost in this role change, and thereby to give yourself the best chance of moving on.

Sheila's reflections on her old role

Sheila found it particularly difficult to think about her old role. She had been married for twenty years and in the last few of those her husband had been sullen, aggressive and at times violent. Sheila could not understand why she felt depressed after finally ending the relationship, when she thought she would only feel happy to be free of it. She felt ashamed and confused by her sadness. Taking time to remember all aspects of her old role, though, she gradually started to remember a different story. In the early days of the relationship, she remembered, her husband could be quite charming. This is what had first appealed to her. They had been good friends and shared similar ideas of having a family. Sheila had never imagined a life for herself that did not involve marriage and children, so when the opportunity to leave her overbearing parents presented itself she had not hesitated. Later, her husband withdrew from her when he lost his job and he began drinking more. The occasional violence started a few years into the marriage, by which time they had three small children and Sheila believed she had to put up with her lot to protect her children's home. She imagined for some time that things would get better again but she gradually lost hope. She slowly realized by going back over her story that she felt sad to leave behind the early days of the marriage and the hope that things would go back to the way they had once been. She was also sad to leave behind what she thought it meant to be in a family, and had not yet discovered her new role in her reorganized family group.

Exercise 14.5: Creating a timeline for your old role

- Create a timeline of the old role, highlighting the most successful and happiest times, and also times that were more difficult. Include as many examples as you can remember.
- Was there anything about this role that contributed to you being depressed now?

In these exercises we are trying to build a balanced picture that includes both the good and the not so good aspects of what is now past. It is important to include the good times. These will be the times that you need to mourn, and remembering them will help to make sense of why you feel so sad about letting this role go. However, it is also important to remember what was not so good, so that you have a balanced memory of what you are leaving behind. Those who are close to us may talk down the old relationship or the old job in a misguided attempt to make us feel better now that has been lost, but that is just as unlikely to be a fair reflection as an idealized view in which nothing was wrong. It takes courage to look at the good and bad side by side, and the people you involve in this exercise will be of more help if they are tuned into what you are trying to do.

Building bridges between past and present

As you start to think about the old role more broadly, and perhaps a little more dispassionately, try to pick out the threads that could run through from the old role into the here and now. These might be:

- **relationships** you imagined were lost when you gave up the old role but that can be adapted to your new role, e.g. former colleagues who can become friends;
- **skills** that you used in the old role that can be usefully transferred into your new role;
- **activities** that you did in the past and that you could share with different people now;
- **support** you found in a lost role that is available from someone else in your life now, e.g. someone new to confide in or socialize with.

Each of these examples suggests ways in which aspects of the old role can be adapted to be of use to you now. Some of the details might have changed, but neither relationships nor activities have to be lost entirely, and keeping these threads going can provide an important sense of familiarity and continuity in an otherwise unfamiliar situation.

Exercise 14.6: Looking for continuity

- Who would you like to continue to see after the change? What adjustments will be necessary in the relationship for this to happen?

- What skills did you use in the past that you could still use now? Will any adjustments be necessary for this to happen, and who can help you make them?
- What things did you use to do that you would like to continue after the change? Will any adjustments be necessary for this to happen, and who can help you?
- Make a plan of how to reintroduce each of the unnecessary losses you have identified into your life now. Talk to the people close to you if you struggle to imagine ways to do this. Borrowing from other people's imagination is part of the team effort towards your recovery. Put your plan into action and monitor your progress with the people who are supporting you.

Agnes: keeping what doesn't have to be lost

When Agnes was retired compulsorily on medical grounds she felt time stretching out before her like a black hole. She felt at a loss to know what to do with her time and felt alone in facing this challenge. She had been used to running a busy office, with colleagues constantly around and a diary full of appointments and things to do. She assumed that she had lost all of those relationships and that there was no place for the skills and knowledge she had built up over thirty years once she had retired. When she started to distinguish between the necessary and unnecessary losses of her retirement she gradually realized that she was giving up more than was called for. She began to appreciate that she had friends as well as colleagues in her old workplace and that those friends remained interested in her. She had assumed that as she was not doing anything with her time she would have nothing to offer in conversation and did not want to bother them. When she did arrange a lunch with her ex-colleagues she found she was warmly welcomed. Her former workmates reminded her that the buzz of activity was not always as enjoyable as she had remembered and was often simply exhausting and frustrating, and to her surprise they envied her the luxury of the time she now had. This prompted Agnes to explore the middle ground between chasing never-ending deadlines and dreading endless empty days. She started to keep a diary again and made sure she had something planned for each day. The familiarity of the routine boosted her confidence. She also volunteered her services to a local charity. Her organizational skills were immediately recognized and put to very good use. Agnes felt useful and as though she had something to contribute. She developed new relationships with other people who volunteered for the charity, some of whom were also retired, and this reduced her sense of isolation and gave her more opportunities to meet new people and gain new experiences.

How did the change happen?

Change can come about in many ways. It is important to be aware of how prepared you felt for the change that happened in the role you have been focusing on. The predictability and speed of a change can strongly influence how we try to adapt: for example, when things suddenly take an unexpected turn this can be very disorientating. Many people describe feeling that the change that led to their depression came out of the blue, and this can make it much harder to accept. It might simply seem unreal. We often strive to cope with change by trying to make sense of it. A good story will do this. Even if it has twists and turns, it guides you through the unexpected so that you can see how you got from beginning to end. If chapters of the story are edited out, or the motivation for certain characters to act as they do is concealed, the story is frustrating and feels incomplete. Many people get stuck in depression because they are struggling to make sense of an unexpected change.

Change can come about suddenly, leaving us feeling ill-prepared. Or it might be a long, slow process that leaves us feeling worn down by the time it is finally complete. Either sequence can leave us feeling wrong-footed. Think about how the details of the change – e.g. its timing, whether it was predictable, how much support you had – influenced your ability to adapt and contributed to your depression. The time around the change is just one sequence in the bigger story, which includes the old and new roles, but it is one that is worth zooming in on to understand the impact in detail.

Exercise 14.7: Focusing on the change itself

- Describe the period around the change scene by scene. There might have been a single moment when everything changed, or your role might have been transformed over a more gradual process that took days or weeks. Try to focus on the time when you finally knew the change was happening, but expand this description as much as you need to give that moment a meaningful context.
- Use the storytelling sequence from chapter 4 to build up the layers of this story, including the

physical setting, your feelings at the time and other people's perspectives.

- Share this story with your IPT team and fit it into the bigger story, which continues on after the change happens.

This change of role marked a time of stress and loss for you, and the support you had around you at the time will have been an important factor in how well you coped. Having close friends in whom you can confide, and using them to talk about your feelings, is known from research to be a highly effective defence against depression. Depression is more likely to develop when we don't have any support, or if we don't use it at stressful times.

Exercise 14.8: Examining your support at a time of change

- What support did you have to help you immediately after the change?
- What support have you had since then?
- How did you use the support that was available at the time and since?
- What impact has this had on your success in adapting?
- Add these details to your narrative and discuss them with your IPT team.

The extent to which you agreed to the change happening and felt in control of the process will also influence your response. Leaving your job voluntarily and being sacked will both result in you being out of work, but are likely to provoke quite different reactions.

Exercise 14.9: Examining the nature of the change and your use of support

Copy the table below into your notebook and use it to consider how the predictability of the change, whether you agreed to it, and the amount of control you had over it contributed to the difficulties you have faced. In the second column, describe the aspect of the change highlighted in the first column, and in the third column note how this influenced your response, e.g. whether it made it easier or more difficult to adjust.

Agnes' story is given first as an example, followed by a blank table for you to fill in.

	Aspect of the change	Impact
How *predictable* was the change?	Very unexpected. Had never considered retiring early. Medical retirement was a complete shock.	Made it much more difficult to adjust.
Did you *agree* to the change?	Did not agree to retirement until the very end.	Made it more difficult. Felt I had failed.
Did you have *control* over the change?	I had no control over the bullying at work that forced my retirement.	Made it more difficult. I felt angry and ashamed.
Did the change result from another *person's* act/decision?	My new boss's decision after he bullied me.	Made it more difficult. I blamed him for ruining a job I loved and forcing me into this situation.
How *quickly* did the change happen?	It dragged on over two years before I was finally retired.	I was worn down and had lost all confidence by the time I was retired.

What *support* was available to help you manage the change?	No support for my boss. Support from other staff and my husband.	Other people's support helped a lot and helped me to realize it was not all my fault.
What support did you *use* to manage the change?	I was very reluctant to talk to anyone other than my husband at first. Later I talked more to former colleagues and friends.	I felt isolated and worthless at first. Talking to people boosted my mood and gave me confidence to try new things in my retirement.

	Aspect of the change	Impact
How *predictable* was the change?		
Did you *agree* to the change?		
Did you have *control* over the change?		
Did the change result from *another person's* act/decision?		
How *quickly* did the change happen?		

What *support* was available to help you manage the change?		
What support did you *use* to manage the change?		

Again, this exercise will be even more useful if you involve someone else. Sometimes we miss signs of difficulty or change in our own lives, especially when they are not what we want to see. Other people, one step removed, might be better placed to read these signs. Invite someone from your IPT team to help you to specifically consider the time around the change. Not only can this help you to understand the change that has happened, it might also suggest ways to avoid similar difficulties in the future, e.g. by reading signals more clearly or asking for help sooner.

How you felt then and how you feel now

Change can feel frightening, exciting, upsetting, intriguing or irritating, among many other feelings. Our emotions can change rapidly as we are faced with change, go through it and then look back on it. It is useful to pay particular attention to the feelings triggered by this change and to note whether and, if so, how they may have changed over time. This can be very helpful in pinpointing where you have become stuck in the transition.

Take time to think carefully about the feelings you had *when the change happened* – on the day, in the moment, in the days that followed. Look back over diaries you might have kept or photographs of the time if you have them. This can help to prompt memories that you've pushed to the back of your mind. Did you tell anyone how you were feeling at the time? Did you feel understood? Did you feel supported?

Exercise 14.10: Feelings at the moment of change

Copy the table below into your notebook. In the first column, write down each of the feelings you were aware of at the time – for example, you might recall anger and sadness but also relief. Note all the feelings you remember – or perhaps there was just one single overriding feeling in that moment. If you remember more feelings later, you can add them to your list.

Next, think about how you feel about the change *now* and write those feelings in the second column. Do these feelings relate to the same things that prompted the first list, or has your focus changed? For example, Agnes used to focus on how angry she felt at her ex-boss but now she focuses on how lonely her retirement feels.

Feelings at the time of the change	Feelings about the change now	Changes in my feelings over time
1.	1.	
2.	2.	
3.	3.	
4.	4.	
5.	5.	

- Does anyone else know how you feel now?
- Do you feel understood?
- Do you feel supported?
- Who could you talk to about any ways in which your feelings have changed over time?

In the third column, note any ways in which your feelings have changed over time. Discuss this with your IPT team to help you to track what has happened to your feelings. The list below suggests a number of ways in which feelings change over time. Which of your feelings have remained, and which have changed or been replaced by different feelings as time has passed? Monitoring change over time can be helpful in developing perspective. Our feelings generally do change as time passes, sometimes becoming more intense, often becoming less so. You might continue to have strong feelings but perhaps less often. Using the two lists as a prompt, think how your feelings at the time and now compare in terms of:

- type of feelings, e.g. anger or loneliness;
- focus of your feelings, e.g. on my ex-boss or on missing the company in the office;
- strength of feelings, e.g. overwhelming or something you can cope with;
- frequency of feelings, e.g. every day or every week;
- ability to talk about these feelings to someone close or someone who would understand.

In chapter 13 you were encouraged to take a few minutes each day to deliberately think about how you are feeling. Take note of any changes that become evident in your feelings as you repeat this exercise over the weeks you are using IPT. Feelings may not change overnight, but try to identify any subtle changes that start to happen from week to week and month to month.

Patricia: understanding change

Patricia was shocked when her five-year relationship with her partner ended. She felt it came out of the blue and she struggled to make sense of the change. As part of thinking about her old role she read through a diary that she had kept during the early part of the relationship. She was surprised to find how often she mentioned feeling uncertain about the relationship. She had never spoken to anyone about her insecurity and suspicion, and instead had locked these feelings in her diary. When even this became too unsettling, she stopped writing the diary and tried to ignore her own feelings. She was surprised to discover how many of the feelings she had described in her diary still resonated at the end of the relationship. She began to understand that her reluctance to address the problems had led her to try to ignore them. Before reading the diary Patricia had felt agitated and anxious when she thought about the relationship ending. She felt she had missed something and repeatedly went over the same scenarios to try to make them fit with what had happened. She said she was afraid to consider another relationship because she did not want to be taken by surprise again. Reading the entries in the diary reminded her of details that she had pushed to the back of her mind and she became more confident that she would be able to pick up signs of problems next time around. She realized that hiding her concerns from the people who cared about her had made her more vulnerable. She started to talk to friends about how she was feeling and for the first time was able to talk openly about what had been good and bad in her relationship. This helped her to remember the relationship in a more balanced way, and she no longer felt agitated when she thought of its ending. Her focus turned more to the friends who were in her life now, and she thought about the lost relationship less and less as the weeks passed.

And so to the present . . .

> Inside every toilet roll a ship's funnel is waiting to get out. (Ian Hamilton Finlay, Scottish writer and artist)

Where have you come to in this story of change? Some changes create their own new role, for example those from being married to divorced, childless to parent, employed to unemployed. With others, the destination will be less clear, and what was familiar is simply replaced by uncertainty. How does the new role look to you as you start to focus on it more closely? If it was something you felt forced into, you might feel reluctant or angry. If you chose to make a change and it has not worked out, you might feel disappointed and ashamed. Take time to think about how you feel about taking up your new role and what you need to do to make it work.

Given that this change has proved challenging and has been closely tied to your depression, it is likely you will have some negative feelings about it. It is also possible that you are underestimating and overlooking your skills and your ability to cope with this new challenge. Depression has a way of doing this, fuelling negative feelings, doubts and reservations that get in the way of positive attempts to explore what the new role has to offer and how you can make it work for you.

Exercise 14.11. How do you feel about your new role?

Start by naming the feelings you have as you face the new role. Write the list in your notebook, and include all feelings of which you are aware. Discuss this with you IPT team if it helps you to think about your role now.

Do you have any positive or neutral feelings about taking up this new role, such as curiosity or excitement? Change isn't only about what we give up but can also create new possibilities that can lift the burdens of the past away from you. Add to your list any positive or neutral feelings you have about your new role.

Now let's try to put those feelings into context and think about the expectations you have created of the new role.

Most roles – parent, retiree, new boss, patient – involve some form of day-to-day routine and being around other people. Your day might be divided into work time, family time, social time etc. Each role will account for part of your day and will influence:

- where you are, e.g. office, home, cinema;
- what you are doing, e.g. paperwork, making dinner, relaxing;
- who you are doing it with, e.g. work colleagues, family, friends.

The *new* role might interrupt any or all of these routines and require us to think of new ones. Consider just two possibilities:

- A new mum who used to go to work now doesn't see colleagues and friends each day and instead stays at home with a young baby. A nine-to-five routine is replaced with being on call twenty-four hours a day. If she wants to see other people she has to plan and make time to see them, as they may not feature as a routine part of her new life.
- When a relationship breaks up we might spend more time alone. Home life and social routine no longer automatically provide company, so we have to actively seek out people to do things with. If other relationships are not used to fill some of these gaps we might feel isolated and lonely.

Exercise 14.12: Looking at new routines

- What is the day-to-day routine in your new role?
- How does this differ from your old role?
- Who does your new role bring you into contact with?
- How does this differ from the old role?
- Who could be added to this routine?

The new role is by definition new, so you might still be unclear about what is expected of you. You might need to develop some new skills or relationships to manage in the new role, e.g. in childcare, in starting new relationships at a new job or in organizing your time without work. Do not overlook the resources you already have in your existing network. Routines may have to change, but adjusting to change is part of good relationships, especially the relationships that continue with us through life.

Exercise 14.13: Looking at new skills

- What do you know about the new role and what is expected of you?
- Are there things about this role you do not understand or know how to do?
- Who could help you to understand more clearly what is expected?
- Which of your existing skills will be useful to you in this role?
- What new skills will you need?
- Which of your existing relationships can help you in this new role?
- Do you need to develop new relationships? What opportunities can you see to do that?

Most changes produce a ripple effect, and changing one role can trigger changes in others. Losing your job might mean more time with family; ending a relationship might mean more time with a wider group of friends. This knock-on effect can be used to create opportunities that would not have existed when you were in the old routine, such as retraining after losing a job. Most roles involve limiting ourselves in some way, e.g. not doing certain things because your partner does not enjoy them or giving up hobbies because they do not fit with your working hours. While you may accept these limitations more or less willingly, they can be cast off when the role they related to is left behind. Giving up any role, even a valued one, almost always has some benefits, and your review of the old role may have highlighted some of these for you.

Try to be open to possibilities you had not previously considered. When you first embark on a transition it is very difficult to have anything other than a limited perspective. The old role obscures your view, and the possibilities that the new role has to offer might be quite well hidden. Initially you might see the new role in terms defined by the old one, e.g. divorced is no longer married, unemployed is no longer employed, retired is no longer working. As the depression lifts, which it will do, you can start to consider what possibilities there are for defining the role less negatively; e.g. 'divorced' might mean free to pursue the training you always put off, 'no longer employed' might mean free to consider the balance of responsibilities in your home life and how these are negotiated with your partner, 'retired' might mean having scope to discover new activities and people who would never have featured in your working life.

Exercise 14.14: Looking at the benefits of role change

- What limitations in your life have been removed since you left the old role?
- What opportunities are available now which were not in the past?
- What are the advantages of not being in the old role?

Depression is very effective in undermining this kind of problem-solving approach, and as a consequence genuine possibilities tend to be swamped by the overwhelming impact of change.

James: acknowledging opportunities after change

When James lost his job he was angry, embarrassed and worried about the future. He focused on having been good at his job and how much he would be missed. He defined himself as a teacher and repeated this over and over – 'I am a teacher, that's what I am.' After listening to this many times, his wife interrupted him and reminded him that he was also her husband and their son's father. She explained that they had missed him when he had worked every evening and weekend and they were looking forward to spending more time with him and being able to put family life first. She agreed that there were problems to sort out and wanted to find a way for them to do that as a team rather than James holding all of the responsibility as he had done at work.

Change as a process not an event

As you have been adding layers to your story of change, one by one, you have been tracing a journey from your past through your present and into your future. This journey does not stop. You set some personal goals when you first decided to look at this change, and these can be helpful signposts to keep you moving in the right direction. You have been challenged by an event which created an opportunity for depression to take hold. Your ability to make decisions and to motivate yourself was affected and you became stuck. Understanding what you have lost and what is expected of you now will have given you a clearer measure of the challenge and helped you to get moving again. Acting on that understanding and being open to the opportunities that will be revealed or created is the process through which you will turn depression into health and continue your journey.

Remember to rate your symptoms of depression every week (using the table in appendix 1). Think about how working through this change influences your symptoms, and each week identify two or three points where symptoms and difficulties related to the change overlap to think about in more detail (using the table in appendix 3). Talk to your IPT team about these difficulties, and use the suggestions in this chapter to help you to manage them more effectively.

The next chapter illustrates the ideas we have explored in this chapter and earlier chapters by looking at Paul's story of role change.

Summary

- Role change involves giving up an old role, tolerating a period of change and adjusting to a new role.
- Poorly matched expectations can make a role change more difficult to manage.
- Having and using good social support is a key strategy in successfully managing a role change.
- It is important to distinguish between necessary and unnecessary losses following a role change.
- Many relationships and skills can be usefully transferred from the old to the new role.
- Monitoring how feelings change can clarify the ways a role change has stalled and how to move it on.
- Alongside the loss come new opportunities, which become clearer and more accessible as depression lifts.

Chapter 15

Paul's story

Paul was a 45-year-old man who had been made redundant from his role as team leader in a finance company nine months earlier. He had worked for the company for fifteen years and his redundancy came as a complete shock. Paul had never been depressed before and was unsure what psychological therapy could offer him, but had been encouraged by his wife to look for help.

In the months leading up to his redundancy, the company Paul worked for had been involved in a merger, which meant that staff had to compete for a smaller number of jobs. This had been a high-pressure time, but Paul believed his position in the company was secure and went into his interview feeling confident. Following the interviews, Paul's colleague was offered the job Paul had expected to get and Paul was invited to apply for a much more junior role. He felt it would be impossible to accept this kind of demotion and that he had no choice other than to take the redundancy he was offered. He found this experience humiliating and soon became depressed.

Paul made his attitude to asking for help clear early in the therapy process. He repeatedly explained how important he had been in his job and how he had risen through the ranks to a senior management level. He prided himself on having been a good manager and having supported a number of staff when they had faced emotional and practical difficulties. However, he made it very clear that he saw asking for help as something for his junior staff, not for him. This said a lot about how he thought his relationships should operate and explained something of his current isolation, which was a factor in sustaining his depression.

Paul's vulnerability to depression had been exacerbated by the importance to him of his working role, the removal of that role as a result of someone else's decision, and his tendency to isolate himself, which cut him off from potential sources of support. The knock-on effects of the role change, which created problems at home and money worries, all served to compound the impact of the original change.

Paul drew up a timeline summarizing the story of this period of depression – see opposite. (Take a look back at chapter 8 if you need a reminder of how this was constructed.)

Paul's symptoms interfered significantly with his daily life. One of his main problems was how poorly he slept. He typically stayed awake until 2 a.m., then slept fitfully until around 6 a.m., when he would be wide awake but stay in bed. By about 8 a.m. he would be tired again, and so he had fallen into the habit of sleeping until late morning, when he would wake up feeling sluggish and guilty for having wasted half the day. He drank coffee throughout the day to try to get himself going, but was caught in a pattern of brief peaks and prolonged troughs in energy. He often felt disconnected from his own body because the build-up of caffeine in his system meant that he felt sluggish when he wanted to be more energetic and agitated when he wanted to relax. Paul felt down most of the time and had no interest or motivation. He couldn't concentrate for long and so found it difficult to occupy his time, which left him feeling bored, irritable and very critical of himself.

Paul's timeline (e)

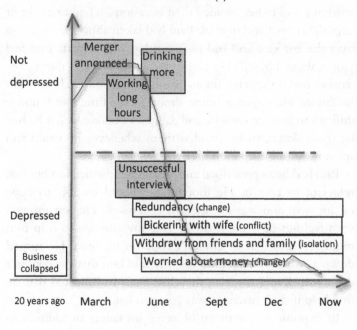

Start of
recent episode
of depression

Paul thought about death and imagined not waking up in the morning, but didn't plan to hurt himself. His wife told him directly that she did not want him to die and that she was afraid that he would think about it and tell himself she would be better off without him. Paul thought his wife was clever to have anticipated how he might try to justify this to himself and 'cut him off at the pass'.

Paul had not been in touch with colleagues from work since leaving his job and had also been avoiding his friends for several

months. He hadn't told his parents or his sister that he wasn't
working, and either avoided their occasional telephone calls or
kept them brief and neutral. Paul had taken almost no exercise
over the last year and had put on 5 kg, which made him feel
worse about himself. He comfort-ate and snacked during the
day but had no appetite for an evening meal and rarely ate with
his family. He stayed at home almost all the time, but found it
difficult to be with his wife and daughter because he felt he had
let them down, so he avoided them whenever he could and
spent most of his time on his own.

Paul had been prescribed anti-depressant medication but was
reluctant to take it. He thought he should be able to cope
on his own and was ashamed to be unwell. He was gripped
with feelings of being a failure and any attempt to help him
reminded him that he couldn't cope on his own. He turned
down all offers of help until his wife told him that she couldn't
cope with living the way they had been and insisted that he
find help if their marriage was going to last.

In response to the threat of losing his family in addition to
everything else, Paul started sessions with an IPT therapist.
Talking about the diagnosis of depression in therapy was
painful for Paul, but he reluctantly agreed he was troubled by
many of the common symptoms. Despite this, he struggled to
adjust to the implications of being ill. He found it very difficult
to imagine what adjustments he could make to increase his
chances of recovery, as he had already dropped almost all of
his daily routines. To help him to think about this, his active
role in his recovery was emphasized. It was explained why he
would need to know more about the nature of depression and
how he could use this information to make decisions about
which routines it would be useful to keep going and which
would need to be adapted. The basic objective was to try to
increase Paul's anti-depressant activity and to minimize the

routines that reinforced depression. Paul was keen to overcome his depression but struggled to imagine how IPT could help when he didn't want to see anyone.

Paul was encouraged to draw up an interpersonal inventory as a basis for starting to think about how his symptoms and relationships were linked to each other, and whether his relationships could be used more effectively to help his recovery. Paul's interpersonal inventory proved to be very revealing. Since leaving work he had actively resisted all contact with ex-colleagues (Tom, Bob, Frank, Christine, Neil). This dramatically reduced his social routine, as his job had often involved social engagements with company clients and colleagues. His extended family lived in another part of the country so he rarely saw them and didn't speak to them for weeks at a time. In practice he had reduced his social world to his wife and daughter.

It was obvious that this picture revealed very little about Paul's interpersonal world before he had become depressed. In order to get a better measure of how much this had changed, Paul expanded the inventory to show how it would have looked six months before he became depressed. At this point there was an explosion of relationships on the page. His life was full of people, both professional and personal contacts. When he had been working, Paul would have business dinners two or three times each week. He travelled regularly as part of his job and was often taken out by the companies he worked with. He worked as part of a team of six who would regularly attend corporate events together, and Paul considered the other five friends as well as colleagues. He also described hobbies that he had enjoyed in the past but had almost entirely given up. He had been an enthusiastic rock-climber and cyclist, and had belonged to clubs for both. He had enjoyed the mental and physical challenges and the teamwork in organizing trips and climbs.

His social life with his family had been less active, but his wife and daughter would sometimes join him at family events and social evenings in his sports clubs. Paul had been married for twelve years and had an eight-year-old daughter. Paul and his wife had spoken about having another child but had given up after his wife had had two miscarriages. Over time Paul's focus of attention increasingly turned to work and he admitted that he had neglected his family and thrown himself into his job. He had worked very long hours, and had routinely prioritized the job over family life in recent years. He described his wife as a strong and supportive woman, but he felt he had left her to act as a single parent for much of their daughter's life. He described his daughter as a timid, shy child and said with some pain that he believed she felt awkward and uncertain around him. He felt very guilty about this and blamed himself for having let both her and her mother down. Paul couldn't see how he could improve his family relationships feeling as he did, despite his wife's active support, and repeatedly came back to not being in his job and so not earning money to support the family, which was the only contribution to family life he could see that he made.

Repeating the inventory exercise helped Paul to set some short- and medium-term goals. He realized how isolated he had become, and while he did not want to see his former work colleagues he agreed to make contact with one or two people from his sports clubs. He said that over the coming weeks he would like to return to some form of exercise and thought cycling would be the easiest to do. Initially he planned to do this on his own but also agreed to discuss going out on some short rides with individual members of his cycling club. Paul could not imagine returning to the full timetable that he had once had and hoped to balance activities at home with his family with a cycle ride every other week.

Paul's interpersonal inventory

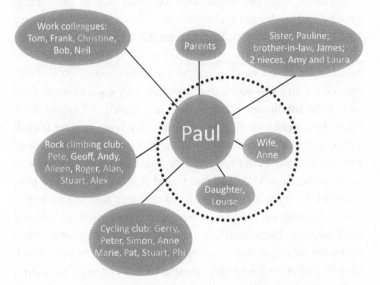

Paul agreed that he needed to look back at the experience of losing his job and said he would like to feel less angry about what had happened and to be able to imagine what his future life would look like. As a medium-term goal he agreed to make contact with former clients to identify what opportunities existed for him when he felt ready to return to work.

One of the main things the inventory revealed was that before Paul became depressed he had had a more balanced social routine and a network of friends both at work and outside the company. Since leaving work he had withdrawn from almost all of his relationships because he felt ashamed and didn't want to tell people he wasn't working. When we looked at the extended picture more carefully we began to see more opportunity for Paul to re-engage with other people gradually without running significant risk of having to talk about work.

Paul was able to identify a small group of friends who had no connection with his work. One of them was in his cycling group, and – despite feeling unsure about it – when Gerry invited him for a coffee Paul accepted.

When the two men met, Paul noticed that after a brief mention of Paul's work situation the conversation quite easily moved on and was much like the chats they used to have. Paul found this much easier than he had anticipated and enjoyed the hour they spent together. He repeated this with another friend, Peter, and was surprised to find that Peter was optimistic about the opportunity Paul's redundancy could offer. Peter had been made redundant twice and had found that being forced to plan consciously what he was going to do next had led to better things turning up for him. These conversations were unusual for Paul, who had effectively avoided all contact and discussion about his work life since leaving his job, and he was very struck by how different his friends' perspectives were from his own.

Despite being depressed, Paul's communication style was that of someone who was used to being in control. There was very little sense of a relationship during initial therapy sessions, other than that between a performer and his audience. It was clear that he was making a great effort to hold himself together, but this also had the effect of holding other people at a distance. He would talk at length, often leaving little or no space for a response and not appearing to need one. In fact, it appeared that he actively wanted to *avoid* a response that might in any way question or interrupt his litany of achievements and bring him more in touch with his current, more vulnerable state. Paul was clearly preoccupied by his old role and it seemed very difficult for him to think about it in any other way than the one he was used to.

Despite avoiding contact with anyone from his former workplace, Paul often found himself thinking about his time there, especially the period leading up to his leaving the company. When Paul was asked to apply for the job he had expected to get, he was competing with a junior colleague whom he had recruited to the company. He felt sure he would be successful and that his colleague would be offered his assistant's post. In practice the opposite happened, and Paul felt humiliated, angry and betrayed by the colleague who was successful. The whole process happened very quickly, with the interview, outcome and offer of redundancy all happening within a day. Paul clearly remembered watching his colleague being invited into their manager's office first and realizing that he hadn't got the job he had expected. This happened in front of his team: he couldn't bring himself to acknowledge what was happening, and no one in the team spoke to him as the situation became clear. When he spoke to his manager, Paul became very angry and felt there was little he could do to repair the situation. He immediately left the office and was signed off work. He left the company without seeing any of his colleagues again. In looking back over this sequence of events, it was clear that Paul had not felt at all prepared for the change he faced, had had almost no opportunity to adjust when the situation had moved on so quickly, and had had no support from the people around him at the time. Paul remembered his wife being very supportive and caring when she discovered what had happened, but he felt so wounded he found it difficult to accept her support and withdrew into himself.

Paul's preoccupation with what had happened provided a good opening for reconstructing the change in more detail, and adding the background to this period. Paul initially spoke with anger and a sense of betrayal about that time, initially running over and over the same sequence of events. In order to help him break into this repetition, Paul was asked to gradually add more layers of detail to the story he found himself repeating. These included visually reconstructing the physical environment, asking him to tell the same story from other people's perspectives, including that of the colleague he felt betrayed by, and tracing his feelings about the events at the time and into the present. We also looked closely at whom he had spoken to around the time of the work change, and the quality and nature of these discussions.

Paul began to remember how much pressure everyone had been under at the time, with a number of his colleagues also facing competitive interviews for their own jobs. He also conceded how difficult it would have been for anyone to approach him in the very short time between the outcome of the interview being revealed and his leaving. He remembered that he had received phone calls and text messages in the weeks after he left, but he had not returned any of them and they gradually stopped. Paul began to appreciate how rigid his version of events had become over time and how many gaps he had filled in about other people's views and feelings. After discussing this several times he began to feel curious about some of his ex-colleagues, and eventually he called the person he had been friendliest with on his team, Bob. His former colleague was pleased to hear from him and said he was glad to have an opportunity to tell him how sorry he was about the way he had been treated. He told Paul that the team had been concerned about him but didn't know what to do when he had not returned their calls. He gave Paul a brief update on how much pressure they had all been under since the merger, and they ended the call on good terms. Paul described feeling some relief that he wasn't still in the endless routine of deadlines, travelling and crisis management.

This conversation, and his more open review of the period when he had left his job, helped Paul to think more broadly about his years with the company. He remembered with both pleasure and sadness the challenges and excitement of a busy and important role. He had enjoyed working with his team and relished the intellectual challenge he had faced when he had had to find solutions for the companies he worked with. He also acknowledged that he had felt under considerable stress much of the time and on occasion had found it difficult keeping pace with the work. When this had happened, he withdrew into himself and tried to manage by working harder and over longer hours, but had found this difficult to sustain. He drank significantly more during the last three to four years in the job, and he recalled with some embarrassment that this had had a detrimental impact on some of his early meetings with his new prospective employers – for example, he had sometimes arrived late and poorly prepared, and had struggled with feeling unwell and tired.

Paul was able to recall previous periods when he had felt similarly overwhelmed by the stress of his job. He was confident that he typically performed well but had a tendency to drink more when under stress, as was common in that corporate culture. He realized that the period when his drinking increased overlapped with a decrease in the time he spent cycling and climbing, and that this lack of balance in his life had contributed to the difficulty he experienced. He initially said these incidents were infrequent and preferred to emphasize the many examples of his successes and details of the industry awards he had won. He described feeling stimulated and powerful in his job and enjoying the status of his role. Gradually, though, he began to acknowledge that he had also begun to feel more tired by the routine of long and unsociable hours than he had used to, and had begun to think about cutting back and finding a way to change his role. Towards the end of these discussions he revealed he had had a two-year plan to work towards leaving his job and had hoped that the merger would have been his means of giving up the pressure he had found increasingly difficult to manage.

Throughout therapy Paul was encouraged to deliberately discuss his time at work with his wife. He asked her about what it had been like from her perspective when he had reacted to work pressure by just working harder and drinking more. He hadn't talked to his wife about this before, and felt much closer to her when he realized how much support she had offered him over so many years. This also gave them an opportunity to talk about what they expected from each other now and to plan ways to make their family life more of a priority.

During this time Paul's mood had been gradually improving and his energy and motivation increased. Taking up cycling again helped him to sleep better and also prompted him to improve his diet and start to take care of himself physically.

When Paul started to talk about the plans he had had for leaving his job he started to remember what he had wanted from that change, which included more time to spend with his wife and more time for his hobbies – and he noted that he had now had both of those things. He was encouraged to talk about this in detail with his wife. They were able to review their financial situation methodically, and this gave Paul a much clearer time-scale to think about finding a new job, reducing the pressure he felt to find an immediate solution. He began to contact former clients and was offered a few short-term contracts for specific pieces of work. This further eased his anxiety about the family's financial situation and allowed Paul to return to a working environment gradually rather than jumping straight back into the old pattern of stress and overwork. Paul involved his wife in all his decisions about the jobs he accepted, and they made a clear plan for how he would like to balance his work and family time in the future. Through picking up his work contacts Paul started to become clearer about the opportunities that were available and others that he could start to create for himself. When his sixteen weekly sessions of therapy ended he had not found a new full-time job, but felt optimistic and was slowly developing projects in areas that interested him.

Paul deliberately made time for the sports that he had enjoyed in the past. He recognized that this had an immediate positive effect on his mood, both because he was more active and because he enjoyed his friends' company. He was surprised by how many of his clubmates had faced similar problems with low mood or unemployment in their own lives, and was encouraged by their support and hearing their stories of how they had struggled and coped. In the past Paul had used sport as an escape, throwing himself into the physical activity but making little of the relationships that were available to him. He saw this now as a missed opportunity and began to look forward to the company as much as the physical challenge. He also deliberately involved his family in all the social events in the cycling and climbing clubs in order to link up the different parts of his life more fully.

At the end of his treatment, Paul was no longer depressed. His mood was generally good and he had a number of interests. His sleep had greatly improved and he had much more physical and mental energy. He was still concerned about the future, which remained uncertain, but felt more confident in his ability to cope and knew that there were people willing and able to help him. He continued to take his anti-depressant medication, which he had been so reluctant to use at the start of treatment. He understood that, having been depressed, he could face similar problems in the future. He wanted to do all he could to reduce this risk and agreed to use medication, support from the people around him and exercise in trying his best to avoid a recurrence in the future. He felt apprehensive about finishing therapy and was surprised by how much talking had helped. He recognized that talking to one person had helped him to start talking to several more, and that many of these relationships would still be available to him in the future.

Chapter 16

Theme two: interpersonal role conflict

Loneliness is never more cruel than when it is felt in close propinquity with someone who has ceased to communicate.

GERMAINE GREER, ACADEMIC AND WRITER

Disagreements in relationships are virtually inevitable. Simply having a disagreement does not in itself necessarily tell us anything about a relationship, certainly not that it is in trouble. Being able to constructively express and hear different points of view is a strength. Avoiding disagreements and silently enduring differences of opinion might create a more harmonious picture on the surface, but could also conceal a deeper vulnerability.

The relationships we have with other people are complex and fluid. They develop over time, and consequently we have periods that are better and worse, and more and less satisfying. The balance of give and take generally moves back and forth over time, rather than remaining steady. Changes in our relationships might reflect something happening within the relationship itself, or the circumstances and external demands influencing the relationship at any given time. Often it will be both. When a relationship hits a more difficult period, this can be stressful and unsettling, perhaps even distressing. However, these difficulties are also a very basic part of life. If we accept that difficulties will happen, the issue becomes less about whether or not we have a disagreement in a relationship, and more about what to do when this becomes a pattern.

The distinction between a one-off event and something that happens again and again is important. In this context, it is the difference between a disagreement that feels temporary and fixable and one that feels stuck and unsolvable. In the first scenario it is more likely that we will see the disagreement as being *about* something – that is, focused on an issue or event, such as forgetting an arrangement. However, when disagreements play out over and over again, they can become confused with our attitudes towards the other person or people involved, so that the focus is on the people who are disagreeing rather than the issues they are facing. This is the difference between being angry *that* (something has happened) and being angry *at* (someone). For example, in this repetitive pattern I might take missing an arrangement as evidence that you don't care about me and are selfish. When a dispute is personalized in this way, it can feel much less open to change, and can create the feelings of hopelessness that are characteristic of depression.

Disagreements happen in healthy relationships but they rarely run on over time; instead, problems are named and tackled and a solution is worked out. Then we move on and leave the disagreement behind. The disagreement is not allowed to take over the relationship, and once it has been addressed, day-to-day life returns to normal. Effectively, both parties to this kind of relationship are on the same side. There doesn't need to be complete agreement on everything, but shared goals are clear and remain steady, even when the relationship has taken a brief deviation around an obstacle. The disagreement might be seen as an interruption to normal proceedings, but does not fundamentally change the course of the relationship.

Relationships that fall into a repeating pattern of disagreement are less likely to navigate around diversions. Once the pattern has been established, it is much more difficult to see the way ahead, and responses tend to become rigid and less helpful. Individual disagreements are only partially addressed, or perhaps frankly ignored, and so there is little sense of things being sorted out as examples accumulate over time. The relationship does not manage to throw off the original disagreement and so it hangs around and recurs, sometimes in an obvious way, but often lurking in the background waiting for any opportunity to resurface. This can be fertile ground for arguments that lose focus, as issues are cast up from the past, highlighting how poorly these have been addressed previously.

IPT and interpersonal conflict

Relationship conflict is in many ways the most obvious of the four focal areas in IPT. When our relationships sink into patterns of conflict and disagreement, and it becomes a struggle to maintain a good quality relationship with another person, it is easy to see the impact on our mood and other symptoms of depression. The conflict might be obvious, with arguments and fallings out, or subtler, with an unspoken sense of disharmony despite relatively few overt signs of disagreement. Being in dispute with someone often makes us feel sad, frustrated and anxious for the future, or hopeless about an unsatisfactory present.

It is not unusual for our relationships to change when we feel depressed. You might enjoy other people's company less and notice tension in a number of your relationships. Feeling intolerant and irritable with other people is very common in depression. We feel less motivated to tackle difficulties and our confidence in what we have to offer a relationship is often low.

These changes are understandable in the midst of depression, but won't necessarily be the main focus in IPT. As your mood, energy and motivation improve, so typically does your enthusiasm for other people, and the general tension eases. Some relationships, though, face more serious difficulty, and these will be more central to the changes you need to make. The relationships that are likely to benefit most from close attention are usually caught in a repeating pattern of conflict. This might be regular arguments or long-lasting quiet resentment, neither of which will seem easy to sort out.

In deciding whether or not to focus on disputes in your IPT, you can use your timeline and interpersonal inventory to try to identify the way this kind of conflict has contributed to your story. If this is a useful focus for you, disputes in your close relationships are likely to have featured as you built up your story. While you have been feeling depressed you may have noticed an important relationship becoming more problematic: perhaps you have had arguments more frequently, or have been feeling less satisfied with it.

Selecting a relationship to focus on

The strategies in this problem area are generally more useful if you can identify a particular relationship to focus on. There is a good practical reason for this. You will be asked to think about what happens in the relationship in detail, and this is difficult to manage if you are trying to think about several relationships at the same time. The understanding and skills you will acquire can of course be applied to many different relationships, but it is easier to develop them by focusing on just one relationship at first.

It might be quite obvious to you which relationship you need to make changes to – you might see that one of your relationships is not going well and may have struggled to work out how to move things on – but even when it is obvious it can be difficult to see where to go from here. You might feel hopeless and unable to imagine how things can change, and as a result reluctant to target this as the basis for your recovery from depression. The relationship might be a particularly significant one for you – a partner, your children's parent, your boss, a best friend – and sometimes simply acknowledging that there is a problem can highlight the relationship's vulnerability, which may be quite frightening. If you feel too apprehensive about the consequences to take action at the moment, take time to read through the remainder of this chapter to help you to think more about the options that are available before dismissing a challenge that frightens you.

Taking time to observe

When you have identified the main relationship in difficulty, take time to look carefully at the way you and the other person relate to each other. Learning about how the relationship works will guide your efforts to improve it. This sounds simple, but can be tricky to do when emotions are running high and it is tempting to react rather than just observe. The ultimate goal is for you to be able to make informed and well-reasoned decisions about your relationship, rather than continuing to get caught up in emotional and impulsive reactions and unhelpful repeating patterns. To do this you must first gather as much detail as you can on how the relationship is currently working.

By now, you will be familiar with the role of constructive curiosity and gathering more information in IPT. By building up additional layers of the story, we can see what is happening from different angles. Imagine yourself as a director on a documentary about your relationship, gathering basic information before a decision is made on where it would be most interesting to point the camera. Your task is to observe and record, but not – just yet – to try to influence the course of the events you see. Of course, your role is more complex because you are both a participant in the relationship and the observer. It is tempting to try to rush and change things, but that will risk misdirecting your energy in unproductive ways. The first step is to research your subject.

Exercise 16.1: Observing the relationship

- Pick out two or three typical examples of times you have spent together in the last week. These might be arguments, attempts to make a decision or plan together, or periods of silence if there was little communication between you. The most useful examples will have been linked to a change in your symptoms of depression, e.g. a drop in your mood or a sleepless night subsequently.

- To help you to stand outside the scene, try describing each example from more than one point of view to someone in your IPT team. For example, you might start with your own point of view, the one you know most about. Next, tell the story from the point of view of the other person involved, i.e. the person you had the argument with. This is how the other person *would* tell it, if asked – not how you think they *should* tell it. You do not have to agree with this version, simply see the scene from another angle. Then tell the same story from the point of view of a neutral observer – perhaps someone who was there, or if no one else was present, a fly on the wall.

- Discuss what this reveals that was not so obvious from your original point of view.
- This exercise works best if you can discuss each version with someone you trust. If this is difficult to do, you can still go through the exercise on your own by writing the descriptions in your notebook and working towards sharing your ideas with someone else.

As you recreate each occasion in your mind, try to remember as many of your words (unless, of course, you have chosen to focus on episodes of silence), thoughts and feelings as you can. You will probably find there are quite a few gaps at first. This will improve with practice and as you learn to pay closer attention to how you communicate. Remember, communication is about listening as well as talking. What can you remember of what you heard the other person say? Were you listening deliberately (see page 213) or were you distracted by your own thoughts and feelings? Again, this is something that will improve with practice. Add as many words, thoughts and feelings as you can to each version you describe. Pay close attention to the gaps that you may have filled in automatically to make sense of the information that was available to you. These will be points to check in future conversations.

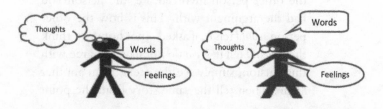

Responding rather than reacting

It is crucial to understand the difference between *responding* and *reacting* when you are trying to change a pattern of conflict. The key differences lie in the preparation and thought involved before acting.

Reaction is usually emotional and influenced by past experiences, instincts and habits rather than thought – such as routinely flying off the handle after even minor irritations. Reactions form the basis of many rigid and repeating patterns across relationships. A reaction is likely to be impulsive, with limited attention to context and longer-term consequences.

Response takes time and involves making a choice. Responding is a deliberate process that involves several elements:

- **Seeing the big as well as the little picture.** The little picture might focus on an individual argument, but that is part of a bigger picture of the whole relationship, which can help to put individual incidents in a meaningful context.
- **Remembering your objectives.** These will include your objectives in this conversation, and your bigger objectives for the relationship. Think about whether they complement or contradict each other. For example, you might be tempted to criticize a fault, but this could interfere with the bigger plan of encouraging better teamwork. Think about whether your immediate goal contributes to your overall goal. Are you risking the long-term goal for short-term gain?
- **Making a choice.** You will have choices about how to respond to any given situation. Take time to consider all the options and make a deliberate choice that takes the context into account and is most likely to contribute to your long-term goal.

These elements are summarized in the diagram below.

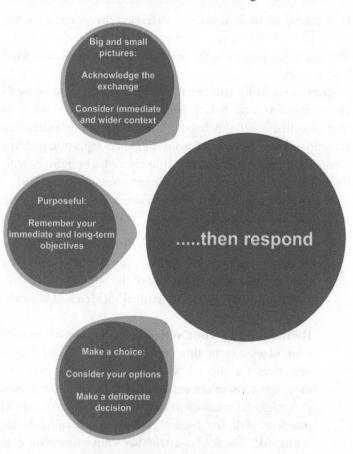

Big and small
pictures:

Acknowledge the
exchange

Consider immediate
and wider context

Purposeful:

Remember your
immediate and long-term
objectives

.....then respond

Make a choice:

Consider your options

Make a deliberate
decision

If you *react* to an argument you are more likely to repeat unhelpful habits, whereas if you *respond*, you open up the possibility of changing those patterns of behaviour. Responding involves a degree of choice that is missing in a reaction. The following sections will look at how you can prepare your responses and limit your reactions.

What stage is the dispute at?

Now you are going to use the examples of your time together recently to describe the general character of your relationship at the moment. We call this homing in on the *stage* of the dispute: that is, putting together a broad description of what your communications and interactions with the other person are *usually like* at this time. By doing this you identify both how it looks at the moment and how that fits into the bigger story of this relationship, particularly while you have been depressed. Thinking about a dispute in terms of the stage it is at reminds us that there has been a period before the current stage and there will be something to come after it, as illustrated in the diagram below. This challenges our sense of being stuck and invites us to step back and look at the current nature of the relationship in a bigger context. The ideas in this chapter will help you to understand how the difficulties developed and what you can do to change them.

Less depressed; improved relationships

Using support in your network

Improving communication

Stage of the dispute

Developing conflict

Context

Start of period of depression

THE STAGES

Incomplete negotiation

In some relationships both people are aware that there is a problem but have become like adversaries in a battle. In these relationships there may be some attempt to problem-solve or to talk about the difficulty, but with little success. If the dispute has become stuck, and the same difficulties keep coming up, it is likely that the strategies being used to tackle the dispute are not working, or are falling short of what is needed in some way. The challenge is to make the strategies that are being used more effective. If you are arguing over and over again, particularly if you are covering the same ground without moving on, it will be useful to stop this pattern repeating by identifying when the pattern starts and interrupting it early. This tips the balance in favour of healthy communication, and limits repetitive and unhelpful exchanges. This is a stage of *incomplete negotiation*, that is, a negotiation that falls short of a solution, as illustrated in the example below.

Lin: incomplete negotiation

Lin chose to be with her partner against her parents' wishes. She thought they were being conservative and old-fashioned in their objections, and she made a stand against their control by entering into the relationship. This created a split in the family, with her parents refusing to speak to her while she was still with her partner. When Lin and her partner started to have arguments and the relationship became very unstable, Lin started to think that she had made a mistake in choosing her partner over her family. She blamed him for her unhappiness and felt guilty that she did not feel as loyal to him as he was to her.

Her resentment and anxiety that she had made the wrong choice fuelled their disagreements, but her feelings were not directly talked about and instead they had many arguments over trivial things. Lin found it difficult to understand the pattern of petty niggling and criticism, which was her indirect way of saying she was unhappy and unsure about her decision. Chipping away at the relationship by trying to correct unimportant differences did not help them to make progress and blocked the way to genuine discussion of the more important differences between them.

Impasse

When relationships go back and forth over the same old ground many times it can become exhausting. This is especially true when you are depressed and your energy and motivation are already low. Under these circumstances you may find that you retreat from each other. This isn't a formal decision to end the relationship, and that might not be what either of you wants, but the experience can be like living on the outside of a relationship while still being part of it. You might feel on your own and disconnected rather than part of a team. Under these circumstances it will be important to find ways to become more involved in the relationship again. In the scenario with Lin, things needed to be cooled and contained; here they need to be thawed and mobilized. This is a stage of *impasse*.

Mary: impasse

Mary wanted her husband to share the housework with her following his retirement. She was very reluctant to ask for what she wanted directly, because her husband had a short temper and she feared she would upset him.

Her attempts to raise the subject in the past had often deteriorated into bickering and bad feeling, and so she had stopped mentioning it. Rather than asking for what she wanted, she would talk around the subject and drop hints that she hoped he would pick up on. When he did not respond she felt disappointed, resentful and helpless to change her situation. They argued less, but Mary's depression did not improve because she felt just as dissatisfied with the current arrangement as she had when her husband had first retired a year earlier.

Ending the relationship

A third stage arises when the differences between you are serious enough for you to agree to end the relationship. However, before you reach that stage it is a good idea to take time to look at the relationship carefully and consider the ideas outlined below on how to improve your communication and to clarify what you both expect from the relationship. Sometimes the problem is not that change is impossible but that neither of you knows how to make changes. If the relationship does end, the suggestions below on how to communicate more effectively can be helpful in negotiating a mutually acceptable separation rather than going through an acrimonious split. In these circumstances it will be useful to look at chapter 14 on role transition.

Active renegotiation

These descriptions of the various stages at which a relationship might be are not rigid or mutually exclusive. Many disputes fall somewhere between incomplete negotiation and impasse, edging closer towards and further away from each at different times. The goal from either starting point is to move towards *active renegotiation*: that is, constructively talking about your differences and identifying ways to change that both of you find acceptable. It is important that any solution is acceptable to everyone involved if it is to have a chance of working. Consequently keeping the other person in your dispute informed about what you are trying to do is crucial.

Involving the other person

You will know by having read this far in the book that IPT is not a private therapy. It works most effectively when other people know what you are trying to do and get involved to help. This is particularly true when you are trying to address a dispute with someone you are close to. IPT can help you both to understand the problems and to negotiate a better balance in your relationship. Many of the exercises described in this chapter are most effective if you both do them, but you can still do them on your own if you don't feel able to do them together initially. However, do try to involve the other person as soon as possible.

• Have you told the person you are in dispute with that you are depressed and that you would like to work on making changes in your relationship to help your recovery?

This is an important conversation to have. Let's think about the purpose of it.

Depression and relationship difficulties interact and sustain each other. It is not your fault that you are depressed, but you and the people you have relationships with will feel the impact of this illness, and knowing about depression is going to be one of your weapons in fighting it. As you become expert in monitoring the way depression affects you, you will be better able to target your efforts to make effective changes in the relationship in dispute. The same is true of the people you have relationships with, especially the person you are going to focus on. If they understand the nature of depression, they can see more clearly where the battle lies – with the illness, not with you – and they can become one of the team working towards your recovery rather than one of the obstacles in your way. Easing your depression and improving your relationships will be of benefit to both you and the people you have relationships with.

However relationship difficulties start, they are maintained by contributions from both sides. It is almost impossible to keep an argument going on your own! You might be able to start an argument, and you might try very hard to finish it, but it needs both sides to contribute in some way – one to provoke and the other to react. If either person does not play their part, the argument tends to grind to a halt. When we are in a dispute with someone, we often feel unhappy about how the other person behaves towards us. It can be tempting to accuse or blame them for how bad we feel. When we are feeling depressed, we are also much more likely to feel guilty, and perhaps assume responsibility and blame too often. Whichever ways this tendency runs, it is rarely helpful to think in terms of blame. Rather than blaming the other person, or accepting blame too automatically, it is better to *understand* what is keeping the dispute going. By understanding how both people contribute to the repeating pattern, you will have a much better idea of how to bring about change.

There are two points that are particularly useful to cover when you talk to the person you are having difficulty with. One is that you are depressed; and the other is that you are trying to sort out the problems that contribute to your depression, including the problems in your relationship. In chapter 6 we looked at the nature of depression and the information you need to start to become an expert in this illness. A summary of this information is included in appendix 4 for the people around you to read. You might like to take a copy of this to give to the person in the relationship you are working on. Just as understanding depression and what you can do about it will help motivate you to make the changes necessary for you to feel better, so the same information can help other people to understand how they are being indirectly affected by your illness and what they can do to help and improve the situation.

Exercise 16.2: Beginning to involve the other person

- Ask _____ (the person you are focusing on) to read the information in appendix 4 and then make time to discuss it together.

Monitoring your progress

It is important to track the links between your depression and the conflict you are focusing on (using the form in appendix 3). This will help you to monitor your progress and to home in on the most important and relevant experiences in your week. Also, rate your depressive symptoms every week (using the form in appendix 1) and try to identify the main incidents related to the conflict that have contributed to how you felt. Experiences in the week related to the conflict and a change in your depression symptoms will be useful to look at in more detail.

Exercise 16.3: Starting to observe your relationship

Think back over the last two weeks, to the occasions when you and the person you are having difficulty with were together.

- How would you describe your time together – tense, enjoyable, distant, close, confusing?

- Did you argue? If so, how often?
- If there was an argument(s) did you work it out or was it left unfinished?
- What was your contact like between arguments? Did it feel as though an argument was just under the surface even if it didn't blow up?
- Did you actively avoid spending time with each other?
- Were there enjoyable times together, free from tension and disagreement?

These questions will help you to think about whether your relationship is best described as at a stage of *incomplete negotiation* or *impasse*. The first would involve more arguments, unfinished business and heightened tension. The second would have fewer flare-ups but there would be a persistent sense that there is something to be sorted out in the background. It is quite likely that you will recognize features of both patterns.

- What has the main pattern been recently?
- Ask the other person to read the paragraphs above about incomplete negotiation and impasse and to say which pattern they think describes your relationship at the moment.
- Discuss whether it would be useful to start to set limits on the arguments you have, or to try to talk a little more to break into the silences.

Are you still able to enjoy each other's company, even for short periods of time? It is encouraging if this enjoyment hasn't disappeared entirely. If you don't have any enjoyable time together, finding ways to build it back in will be an early target. These plans don't need to be elaborate. They might include going for a walk together, watching a movie or eating a meal together – anything that you used to enjoy that has been allowed to disappear from your routine. These plans don't have to start with talking openly about your relationship difficulties; just get used to being in each other's company again, as a first step.

Michael

Michael and his housemate had become embroiled in a series of arguments over their respective share of the household bills in recent months, and despite a number of very heated discussions they had not managed to find a solution they both found entirely acceptable. A once-good relationship had become tense and irritable, and they gradually retreated from spending time with each other, which created a very uncomfortable atmosphere in the home they shared. They had fallen into the habit of sitting in different rooms and could spend several hours without seeing each other despite being the only people in the house. To increase the time they spent together, Michael started reading in the living room, where his housemate usually sat, rather than in his bedroom. He checked out that she didn't mind first and mentioned that it was nice to have some company. They did not speak for much of the time, but they occasionally had a cup of tea together, when they would chat about what they were reading. This simple change resulted in more pleasant time together than had been the case for many months and provided a calmer atmosphere in which they could approach the more difficult discussion they still had to tackle.

The big and the small picture

When you have identified the current stage of the dispute, whether it is incomplete negotiation or impasse, it is useful to remember that this phase is part of a bigger picture. The relationship you are in has its own history and its own time-line, which started before the disagreements and will hopefully continue after the conflict has been resolved. You might have come through similar difficulties in the past, or perhaps this is the first time the relationship has faced this kind of challenge.

Exercise 16.4: Your relationship timeline

Sketch out a timeline of the relationship, as you did with your depression, and consider how the relation-ship has developed over time. Ideally, do this with the other person in the relationship, to help you to think about the bigger picture together. If this is difficult, start to think about this with one of your IPT team and share your thoughts with the person involved in the conflict when you feel ready.

Go back to how the relationship started and try to remember what has been good about it in the past and how you have managed difficult times previously. Use the diagram and questions below to guide you.

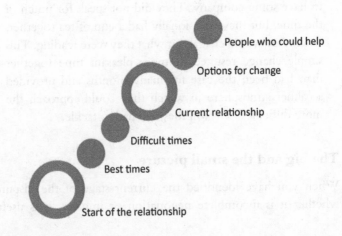

People who could help

Options for change

Current relationship

Difficult times

Best times

Start of the relationship

- When has the relationship worked well?
- What contributed to the good times? Consider factors both inside and outside the relationship.
- When have been the most difficult times in this relationship?
- What or who has helped you to get through difficult times before now?
- Have you tried to use things recently that have helped in the past?

The timeline will help to remind you of the big picture, and it might also suggest some clues to what will be helpful in sorting out the problems. The best solutions are not always new ideas. Sometimes it is a matter of reminding yourself of your own good ideas and skills – things that you may have quickly forgotten when you became depressed. If you have come through similar difficulties in the past, think carefully about how you did it and whether any of the things you did then could be useful to you now.

The role of communication

In chapter 12 we looked at the importance of communication in keeping relationships going and making them better. Movie scripts are good examples of how to communicate several types of information at once. A movie script includes lots of detailed information which helps to make the description on the page become a meaningful picture in your mind. To do that it must communicate more than just what is said. Of course, that is important; but the setting, the way things are said, intentions and feelings are also described. Consequently this form of storytelling is a good guide to follow when you are thinking back over moments of conflict in the last week.

SETTING THE SCENE

A good movie script creates scenes that you can see in your mind. It sets out the physical setting, the context, the time of day, etc. As you think back over important moments of conflict in the last week you will start to gradually build up the descriptive layers, just as you did when practising storytelling in chapter 4, and setting the scene will be the foundation layer.

Exercise 16.5: Setting the scene

Go through the questions below for each occasion you thought of in exercise 16.1 – examples of recent exchanges in the dispute that were linked to a change in your depressive symptoms. You might find it easier to write your own thoughts in your notebook initially, but then discuss them with the other person involved or one of your IPT team.

- Where were you physically?
- What time of day was it?
- Who else was there, or were you and the other person alone? Do different examples have different audiences?
- Did you both anticipate having a discussion (or argument), or did it start spontaneously, without planning?
- Was the argument face to face or indirect – e.g. on the telephone, or by text message or email?
- Did the argument carry on from one setting to another, such as starting at home but continuing at work or when you went out?
- Were you both in the same space, such as sitting or standing in a room together, or moving

        between spaces, for example, walking out of the
        room, shouting through walls?

- Had either of you been drinking/taken drugs or
  missed a night's sleep before the argument?
- Do you think that the setting of the discussion
  contributed to its becoming an argument?

Quite often when you start to look at examples in detail
like this you discover that so far you have not been telling the
whole story. This is not deliberate. We often start our stories
in the middle – at a point of crisis or dramatic change. This is
especially true when we are depressed or anxious, because then
our perspective tends to narrow. We are less likely to focus on
the events leading up to or following a problem, and instead
become fixed on the actual crisis or argument. Remember the
diagram of the story arc (see page 44)? This can be used to
describe individual episodes as well as summarizing a whole
story, as illustrated in the diagram below.

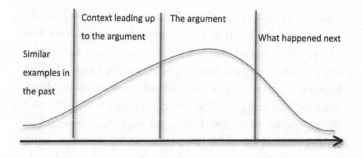

Exercise 16.6: Filling out the scene

Add the following details to your description of each
recent incident:

- What had happened in the lead-up to the argument, e.g. an argument earlier in the day, a bad day at work, feeling exhausted after a poor night's sleep? Add any details you think are important.
- Does this help to explain why a discussion became an argument?
- How could you change this to reduce the like-lihood of an argument in the future – e.g. not raising important issues when you are tired or hungry or via text messages, or reacting when someone else does the same?
- Could anyone else help with this? What would they have to do?
- Discuss your ideas with the person involved or with your IPT team.

Emma

Emma was concerned about how much her friend drank. She dropped hints that she would like her to drink less but Emma's friend did not appear to notice and noth-ing changed. During one night out with friends Emma became agitated when her friend continued to drink after she had stopped. They had been out for a meal and then gone on to a club. Everyone, including Emma, had shared wine at the meal but Emma did not want to drink any more when they moved on. When her friend con-tinued to drink Emma became concerned she would get very drunk and they would not know how to get home from an unfamiliar part of town. Emma confronted her friend in front of their other friends and told her she was worried about her drinking and wanted her to stop. Her friend was embarrassed to be challenged in this public and unexpected way and reacted angrily. The conversation quickly descended into an argument, with several of their friends offering opinions and suggestions, which aggravated the way both Emma and her friend felt. As the argument escalated, Emma became more upset and went home alone, feeling even more depressed.

A week later Emma asked her friend if they could talk about what had happened on the night out. They arranged to meet when they had time on their own to talk it through. They had both been upset by the argument and took the opportunity to discuss how they felt. Emma explained her concerns and realized that her friend had had no idea how she felt or how difficult it was for Emma to go out when she wasn't sure if she would have to be responsible for getting her friend home safely at the end of the night. Emma also realized how embarrassed her friend had felt on being challenged in front of their other friends, and how difficult it was for her to understand Emma's point when she was not prepared for a serious discussion and so many other things had been distracting her.

WHAT WAS SAID?

The next stage of breaking down the conflict is to reconstruct in detail what was said during important discussions and arguments. Most of us find this difficult to do at first, especially when we are depressed, so don't worry if it takes some practice. We tend to remember our conclusions more easily than the way we reached them. This is a problem if our line of reasoning hasn't been reliable, because we might misinterpret what was said. Your ability to remember more of what was said will improve with practice, and you might be surprised to find how many useful clues come back to you.

We don't typically remember all the details of our conversations. We generally edit our memories quite heavily and focus on the gist of what was said. This is often useful. After all, if we reran every conversation in real time in our heads, we would never manage to move on to anything new. However, it also means we are usually only working with part of the picture. The way in which we select out information to remember is fairly predictable. It is generally easier to remember our own contributions to a conversation than someone else's, especially when feelings are running high. Our memory is also influenced by how important we think the conversation is: we tend to remember more from conversations we thought were important at the time than those that seemed less significant. The net result is that important messages are easily missed or forgotten, especially if feelings were running high, there are lots of competing messages and the significance of what is being said wasn't understood at the time.

Mary: how conversations can go astray

Because she was reluctant to ask for what she wanted directly, Mary often led up to a request with a long and meandering introduction, which included lots of detail that had little to do with the main request. Mary's husband often got frustrated by these long stories with no obvious point to them, and either interrupted her or simply walked away. This often meant that the conversation was over before Mary had made her point, or that she lost the thread because her story led her around such a circuitous route. On the few occasions when she did actually make her point, her husband rarely responded, as he did not distinguish her main point from the wealth of other details that had come up.

To get into the habit of remembering conversations in more detail, it can be useful to think of these episodes as scenes in a fictional drama, with you as the director, not one of the main actors. Instead of being preoccupied with your own lines and movements, you are focusing on how the scene works, what moves it from one moment to the next. At this point the rights and wrongs are less important than the *how*. Practise tracking the way situations unfold by watching TV or movie scenes in which the characters have important discussions or arguments.

Exercise 16.7: Watching an argument unfold

- Watch a scene from a movie or TV show in which two people have an argument.
- Immediately after watching, try to remember as much as you can about what each character said, and the order in which they said it (reconstruct the dialogue).
- Rate how clearly you think each character made their point.
- Restate each character's main points in your own words.
- Rate how well you think each character heard or understood the point the other person was making.
- If the argument escalated, identify three contributing factors, e.g. tone of voice, choice of words, physical setting, etc.
- If the argument was resolved, make a note of three factors that contributed to the positive

> outcome, e.g. listening carefully, finding what they agree on, staying calm, etc.

- Ask one of your IPT team to watch the scenes with you and compare your descriptions. Do either of you pick up on things the other missed?

Most people find this exercise quite tricky to do at first. You will probably remember some details and completely forget others. You might find it easier to remember details about the character you feel sympathetic towards and more difficult with characters you do not like or do not agree with. Remembering complex information in detail like this is a skill and one you will be able to develop. This is not a memory test, however: the aim is not to recall absolutely everything but to pick up on a number of different strands well enough to follow the ebb and flow of a conversation and to identify when and how it goes off track and when and how to bring it back.

Exercise 16.8: How your own conversations unfold

Now think back over recent arguments or important conversations in the relationship you are working on and repeat the process in exercise 16.7 with them. Then ask yourself the following questions about each instance:

- How did the discussion unfold – in a straight line to the main point or around the houses and never quite getting to where you intended?
- Do the same topics come up (directly or indirectly) in several recent episodes, or does the subject vary in a random way?
- Were you both talking about the same topics

or was there a battle about the direction of the conversation, with each of you trying to set the agenda?

- Were you talking about what you wanted or intended to talk about?
- If not, why not? Did you try to make your point but get distracted, or hint at your main point and hope that would be enough for you to be understood?
- Was your experience influenced by depression, perhaps because you had been feeling depressed and so felt less able to express yourself, or were you left feeling more depressed after the argument?
- Discuss your thoughts with one of your IPT team.

You will inevitably know more about your contribution than the other person's. In time you will invite the other person to look through the director's lens with you, and you will try to work out together where your communication tends to go off track. For now, though, you are simply learning how to stand back and observe for yourself.

Communication routinely relies on our filling in gaps and working with our best guesses when we don't know all the details, for example about another person's feelings, intentions or understanding. This usually works well enough and allows communication to flow, but it can be less reliable when you are arguing or have strong feelings about something. Later on in this chapter, you will check if the way you are both filling in the gaps is giving you a sufficiently accurate impression of the other person in this dispute, but for now we're focusing on you.

IT IS NOT ONLY WHAT IS SAID, BUT HOW IT IS SAID . . .

A single conversation can be interpreted in many different ways, depending on which words are stressed, whether they are shouted or whispered, whether they are blunt or subtle, and how we move when we say them. These are features of non-verbal communication, which we looked at in detail in chapter 12, and along with information about the scene they give a measure of the emotional temperature of an exchange. For example, a conversation taking place between two people who are sitting alongside each other talking in hushed tones will look and feel quite different from one in which they are standing up, facing each other and speaking in raised voices. Both will look and feel different from a conversation that moves from room to room, with one person leaving and the other following to carry on the conversation. What is actually said could be exactly the same in each of these scenarios, but they are likely to be interpreted quite differently.

Exercise 16.9: Gathering information about non-verbal communication

As you build up the descriptions of your recent exchanges, add a layer that describes the non-verbal information:

- Where you were in relation to each other (close, far apart, in different rooms etc.)?
- What was your posture (sitting, standing, walking, etc.) and that of the other person?
- How did you and the other person move (were you still, agitated, gesturing, etc.)?
- What *kind* of language did you use (measured, vague, exaggerating, swearing, threatening, insulting, etc.)?

- What was the volume of the exchange (under the breath, shouting, escalating, fading away, etc.)?
- Describe these details to one of your IPT team.

Arguments often speed up, get louder and use more extreme language, with each of these aspects feeding off the others. This *escalation*, which doesn't usually make things any clearer, can happen for a number of reasons:

- One person *does not feel they are being heard or understood*, so they speak more loudly, urgently and forcefully to try to get their point across.
- One person *does not want to hear* what the other is saying, so attempts to drown them out.
- Emotions are aroused and both people find it more difficult to control the way they express themselves.

Ironically, in most cases escalation leads both participants to listen and hear less effectively and either to shut down or to redouble their own attack. At this stage communication has broken down, and is often more like two monologues than one dialogue between two people.

Exercise 16.10: Assessing non-verbal communication

- What impact did the way in which the conversation happened have on its effectiveness in your examples?
- What impact did it have on you and your symptoms of depression?
- What impact would you say it had on the other person?
- Discuss these details with one of your IPT team.

GETTING TO THE POINT

This is about the *take-home message* – the point of your communication. In arguments we can often find ourselves talking
about a variety of different subjects, not all of which are central
to what we want or need to talk about. Take note of what is
being talked about in the examples you are looking at, and
think about whether you are getting close to the points that are
important for you.

It is just as important to notice what has *not* been said as
what *has*. When you think back over recent exchanges, do
you find that there are important things that you wanted to
say that have not been said directly? Try to be honest with
yourself here and be clear about what you *actually said* – not
what you meant to say, not what you implied, and not what
you think any reasonable person would understand (all of
these can be fertile ground for misunderstandings in disputes).
Let's make sure the script is useful to you and to the person
listening. Remember, the better the importance of the topic
is understood, the better the content of the conversation will
be remembered. If your most important messages are getting
buried or sidestepped entirely, it is easy for them to be missed
and forgotten.

The key questions to ask yourself are:

- Have you said explicitly what you want the other person
  to know and understand? And, on the flip side:
- Have you heard clearly what the other person is saying?

Exercise 16.11: The take-home message

Think about the main things you *wanted to say* in each
of the arguments you have identified. Be warned: this
might be quite different from what you actually said!

Summarize in one or two sentences what you wanted the other person to know and understand.

- In each of the examples you have described so far, *what was your intended take-home message?*
- Ask the member of your IPT team who has been helping you with these exercises if they understood this message from all they have heard so far.

If you can be clear with yourself about the main point of your communication, you have a greater chance of hitting this target when you talk to someone else. The goal is to match your intention to the discussion that happens.

- From now on, try to identify your one or two main points before starting important discussions in this relationship, and monitor how often these points are made (you might like to look back at the 'Principles of good communication' on page 226).

As the two key questions above indicate, this process works both ways. When you look back at your recent arguments, can you identify the other person's take-home message? This is something to check out with them.

- From now on, when you have a discussion in this relationship, offer the other person a brief summary of what you have understood they have said and ask them if they agree.

If you did understand correctly, you are reinforcing the message that you were listening and are trying to understand. If you have not understood, or the points were not made clearly, this creates an opportunity for the other person to clarify.

- Likewise, whenever you have a discussion, ask them to do the same for you – to summarize what they understood from what you said.

Again, you will have created a chance to clarify if there have been misunderstandings, and to correct them when necessary. You can start to use these techniques right away to help you to stay focused and ensure you understand each other.

Mary: getting the point across better

Initially, Mary found it difficult even to acknowledge to herself what she wanted. She had become so used to putting other people first and setting her own feelings aside that she struggled to identify what would make her happy. As she gradually became more aware of how she felt and what she wanted, she realized how little of this had ever been said directly, and how little opportunity there had been for her husband to understand how she felt and what she needed. She slowly began to talk about her feelings with her husband and to ask directly for the things that would improve her mood. This proved challenging because her husband was not used to her making any kind of requests, and so had to adjust to no longer having everything entirely his own way. At times he could be slow to respond, and Mary had to hold her nerve in making her requests. Often this was enough, and the routine at home gradually started to change towards a more balanced picture. Mary then had to learn to express her pleasure at this change, to show her husband that his efforts were appreciated so that this new way of communicating would continue.

Issues and key difficulties

As you have been reflecting on recent periods of conflict in your chosen relationship, you will have started to develop a clearer understanding of what you think are the main issues in your disputes. These are the issues that repeatedly come up and that you have not found a way to sort out. You might already have a good idea about what drives your dissatisfaction, and hopefully you are now getting a more detailed picture of whether these issues are given due attention in the conversations you have, or whether they become lost somewhere in the distraction and noise that arguments can create.

Exercise 16.12: Pinpointing the main issues of disagreement

- Identify the main issues you disagree about in the relationship you are focusing on. Try to state the issues simply and factually, rather than focusing on who is to blame, what you want or how it makes you feel. For example, 'we don't agree on whose responsibility it is to do the housework' rather than 'she never does anything' or 'I want him to do more around the house'.
- Do you think that the person you are in conflict with would identify the same issues?
- If not, what do you think their main issues would be?

While it is useful to think about what the dispute is about yourself, and to talk this over with your IPT team, an important next step is to make time to talk about what the key issues are with the other person involved. Hopefully by now you have already started doing more enjoyable things together and been thinking about how you have fallen into unhelpful patterns. Now you have an opportunity to apply what you have learned to the important issues facing you.

Let's summarize the main points about how best to conduct these discussions:

- **Context or background:** Planning when and where to talk is important and can affect the outcome of any significant conversation. Both of you should know and agree that you are going to talk about things that are important to each of you. Do not spring an important discussion on the other person without warning. A mutually convenient time should be agreed when you will both have time and privacy to talk – and that doesn't mean a few minutes grabbed when your children are not around or when you are out with friends.

- **Content:** If you are going to discuss potentially difficult issues about your relationship that are important for either or both of you, you should both have time to think about this before and after the discussion. This will give each of you an opportunity to plan what you want to say (your *take-home message*) and afterwards to consider how to *respond* to what you heard, rather than simply *reacting* in the heat of the moment (see page 307 above).

- **Manner:** It is possible that one or both of you might feel upset or worked up about what you are discussing. Agree in advance that if the emotional temperature starts to rise sharply, or if you start to feel more depressed, making it difficult for you to express yourself clearly, you will agree to postpone the rest of the discussion until you are both calm and can express yourselves clearly and listen attentively. Be sure this means *postpone* and not *cancel*. Agree when you are going to come back to the discussion and stick to the plan. If there is a reason why one of you cannot stick to the agreed plan, be clear that another time should be arranged as soon as is convenient to you both.

- **Ongoing process:** Expect to follow up on the discussion after you have both had time to think. Remember that *good communication is a process, not a one-off event.*

Give and take: negotiating expectations

When relationships are working well it is a sign that our needs and expectations are being met. That is, what each person wants and needs from the relationship is roughly what they get. The match doesn't need to be exact for a relationship to work, but it needs to be close enough for the balance to feel satisfying.

Many people struggle to make their expectations known. This might be because we are not sure what we want, or because we have difficulty clearly expressing what we want. In many relationships, the idea of expectations has never been spoken about at all. Most relationships don't have a period of open discussion early on when the parameters of the relationship are spelt out. Instead, we typically start a relationship with someone we like or want to spend time with and the relationship evolves naturally over time, with differences or important issues negotiated as they arise.

Let's think about what it means to have expectations. It is not the same as telling the other person what they have to do or how they have to be. Expectations are much more useful if they are framed in terms of ideas about what you need and want from the relationship and what you will contribute to the relationship. If your expected relationship and actual relationship are similar, you will feel satisfied; if they are dissimilar, you are likely to feel dissatisfied. Understanding how your relationship differs from your expectations of it will give you a focus for discussions to bring these two pictures more closely in line.

When our expectations are not met in a relationship, or when the two people in a relationship do not have the same expectations, the differences can lead to conflict, dissatisfaction and depression. Imagine a partnership in which one person expects fidelity and the other does not, or parents who expect to set ground rules for a teenager who expects total freedom. The difference in itself is not necessarily a problem, as differences are generally to be expected in human relationships; but the failure to find acceptable common ground can be problematic. In IPT we call this *non-reciprocal role expectations* – a fundamental mismatch between what you want and what you get in a relationship. The process of examining past exchanges in detail that you have been working through in this chapter so far is designed to help you to identify areas of mismatched expectations and to consider the options open to you to resolve these differences.

In some cases, simply clarifying the difference is enough to start negotiation on acceptable common ground: for example, an employee and manager might negotiate around the freedom the employee has in planning their daily routine. In others, when a particular expectation is not considered crucial, one member of the relationship may accept that their expectation will not be met, e.g. a husband might accept that his wife doesn't share his interest in camping and they won't do this on every holiday. Expectations of this kind that aren't met in one relationship may well be satisfied in another relationship without detriment to the first, and where expectations are clarified and revised or redirected in this way, conflict can be reduced because the solution has been agreed. The issue becomes more pressing when the expectation is regarded as crucial by one person in the relationship but is not met by the other. More active and supported negotiation will be required to address these differences.

Tanya: revising expectations

Tanya was very intelligent and enjoyed heated debates about challenging subjects. She enjoyed being intellectually stimulated and respected people who had inquisitive and questioning minds. When Tanya started her relationship with her boyfriend she imagined he would enjoy the same things and expected to be able to debate and discuss a wide range of subjects with him. Tanya's boyfriend had little interest in the subjects Tanya liked to talk about. He was quieter and more reflective, and felt uncomfortable in the heated debates that Tanya would initiate. He had much better emotional insight and awareness than Tanya and was often good at calming her down if she became worked up in a debate that then turned into an argument. Tanya often did not notice this because his contribution was quiet and understated. Many of their initial arguments were fuelled by Tanya's disappointment that her expectations were not being met. As they worked on their difficulties they began to appreciate which expectations of involvement in each other's interests they shared, and also the ways in which their expectations differed. When Tanya began to rely more on her university friends for intellectual stimulation and to her partner for emotional support and companionship she found a way to use the best of what each relationship offered and focused less on the inevitable gaps.

IDENTIFYING NON-RECIPROCAL EXPECTATIONS

As you have been thinking about your recent exchanges, you will have identified the key areas of disagreement. These are the issues that repeatedly come up in arguments or predictably trigger symptoms of depression. Having identified what the key issues are for each of you – e.g. how you share responsibilities for childcare or finance, how much time you spend with other people, how much freedom you have to run your team the way you want at work, etc. – it is now useful to look at the ways in which your expectations differ.

The first step is for each of you to describe your personal expectations about each issue as clearly as possible. Once you have clarified how close or far apart your expectations lie, you can start to think about whether there is any common ground and how you might try to bridge the gap.

If your goal is to keep the relationship going, both of you will need to be flexible in order to find a solution. Rigidly holding out for what you want, exactly as you want it, or being faced by the same from the other person, will simply flip you back into the dispute. It is important to be willing to give what ground you can in negotiation and invite the other person to do the same.

OPTIONS

Simply understanding more clearly how your expectations differ can in itself be very useful. Many disputes are fuelled by poorly understood ideas about what the other person actually wants. Talking more openly about what you want and trying to understand what the other person wants can make quite simple solutions more obvious than they had been when you were arguing or avoiding speaking to each other.

In some relationships, though, recognizing more substantial differences might be useful but not sufficient to sort out the problems. Here you will need more active discussion on the common ground that may exist between you on the key issues and how this can be used to come to an agreement that you could both accept as 'good enough'. This might involve accepting that one or the other or perhaps even both of you have expectations that might not be entirely fulfilled in the relationship. Continuing the relationship is given priority over meeting a specific expectation, which may need to be modified in the light of your better understanding.

A variation on this route is for one person in the relationship to give up something that they had previously expected to have. Discussing your respective needs and expectations may reveal little or no scope for a particular expectation to be met. This may feel more challenging, depending on the expectation in question. It may be possible to meet some expectations elsewhere in your network of friends and family, so that you can meet this need without asking it of this relationship – as Tanya did with her desire for lively debate. In some cases, the need or expectation in question might have been specific to this relationship, for example, when partners decide whether or not to have children, and in such cases one of you may need to set the expectation aside for the relationship to continue without further dispute. In making such a decision it will be important to consider how important the particular need or expectation is to you. Not all expectations are equally important, and many of us get used to setting some of ours aside when it becomes clear they are not going to be met. Again, this may be a matter of weighing up the relative importance of the need or expectation in question against the general quality of the relationship. For example, Tanya decided to give up her expectation that she would enjoy heated debates with her boyfriend because she was able to satisfy that need with her university friends and she recognized that her other equally important needs, such as emotional support and companionship, *were* being met by her boyfriend. So it is important to be honest with yourself and with the other person about which needs and expectations are the most important to you in your relationship.

However, it is important that it isn't always the same person in the relationship who gives up their needs and expectations. It is particularly important to monitor this if you are feeling depressed and as a result may be more vulnerable to feeling guilty and less worthy. If a particular compromise or the pattern of compromise creates additional feelings of dissatisfaction or resentment, it is not a good plan for the future. If you find that you are routinely giving in to the other person because you feel low, guilty or unworthy, you won't have tackled the mismatch in your expectations and your relationship is at risk of slipping back into the pattern of disagreements that you were trying to resolve.

Using your network as a resource

In the exercises above, we have asked you to focus on one particular relationship. However, when you do this it is easy to lose track of all the other people you have relationships with. Your wider group of friends, colleagues, neighbours and family can be useful in your recovery in many ways. Individual relationships do not exist in a vacuum; they respond to all of the pressures and opportunities that surround them. Imagine your relationship network as like a jigsaw, made up of many interlocking pieces. No single piece can make up the whole picture, just as no individual relationship can meet all of your needs.

REPEATING PATTERNS ACROSS RELATIONSHIPS

You have been working hard to understand what contributes to an unresolved dispute in an important relationship. To help you to work out whether the problems you have identified are specific to that relationship or part of a more general pattern, it is also useful to ask yourself whether you have faced similar issues in any of your other relationships. Often we experience similar difficulties with a number of different people, but we might manage those difficulties in different ways, depending on who the other person is and what situation we are in. How you manage disagreements with your partner might be quite different from how you manage disagreements at work or with your parents.

- Do you face similar difficulties to those you have identified in any other relationships?
- If you do, have you found effective ways to manage those difficulties with other people?

If you have successfully managed similar difficulties in other relationships, it is important to remind yourself that you have useful and relevant skills to manage this kind of difficulty and have already been using those skills effectively. For example, you might be very good at resolving disagreements between colleagues at work, using a different approach from that you use at home. It is easy to overlook how competently you manage certain things when you feel depressed, and tempting to dismiss such achievements as irrelevant or mere coincidence. However, this can stop you from using ideas and skills already familiar from one area of your life in another area that is proving more difficult. Try instead to take careful note of the skills you already use to manage these problems in any part of your life. The challenge is then to work out how to transfer the skills you already have to the current situation.

You might feel anxious about the idea of trying something new in a relationship that is tense or where you expect a strong reaction. It might therefore be helpful to try some of the communication skills you have been developing with other members of your network, just as you have been doing with your IPT team. You could do the same with the skills you have used effectively in other areas of your life. As you learn to talk more openly about your emotions and to be clearer about what you want or need, you can start to introduce these communication skills into discussions in other relationships, maybe including some where there is minor conflict. This doesn't have to be in response to a disagreement; it can become a way of communicating more clearly in general. As you have been doing with your IPT team, you could ask for feedback from each person you talk with. Did they find it easy to understand what you were telling them? Was the additional detail useful and of interest? By practising in this way, you can gain confidence in bringing the new skills you have developed into play when you come to tackle difficult conversations.

You may feel that you have difficulties in other relationships similar to those in the relationship you have been focusing on. If so, it may be useful to try tackling these difficulties first, using the skills you have learned. It may be that the other relationships feel less threatening to focus on because they are less important, or because you have a clearer sense of the other person's willingness to try to find a solution with you. For example, it might feel easier to talk to your best friend about a comment that upset you than to tackle this kind of discussion for the first time with your critical boss. Again, success with one relationship can give you the confidence to try to use your new skills in a more important relationship or one that is more difficult.

Remember to rate your symptoms of depression every week (using the table in appendix 1). Think about how living with interpersonal conflict influences your symptoms, and each week identify two or three points where symptoms and difficulties related to this conflict overlap to think about in more detail (using the table in appendix 3). Talk to your IPT team about these difficulties, and use the suggestions in this chapter to help you to manage them more effectively.

The next chapter illustrates the ideas we have explored in this chapter and earlier chapters by looking at Suzanna's story of role conflict.

Summary

- Make your point; don't bury it.
- Disagreements are pretty much inevitable in relationships and can be healthy, as long as they do not become established as a pattern.
- *Reacting* is impulsive, paying little attention to context and the longer-term consequences.
- *Responding* involves holding on to both the big and the small picture, remembering your objectives and making choices.
- Relationships can become stuck in *incomplete negotiation*, with the same argument repeating again and again, or *impasse*, where you have stopped talking.
- Both kinds of 'stuck' conflict are assisted by *active negotiation*, which involves making expectations clear and working together to find acceptable common ground.
- IPT is not a private therapy and it works most effectively if you let other people know what you are trying to do and ask them to help.
- When you have learned to stand back and observe your

disagreements from a distance, you can invite someone else to look through the director's lens with you and work out your differences together.

- Paying attention to context will help you to tell the beginning, middle and end of your story.

Chapter 17

Suzanna's story

Suzanna was first diagnosed with depression after breaking up with her partner, three years before starting IPT. She had had periods of very low mood since she was a teenager, and in hindsight thought that these might also have been depression, but she had never before asked for help or received treatment. This time, following a friend's recommendation, she spoke to her GP. She found counselling and medication helpful, and restarted the relationship that had broken down. However, she continued to feel very sad and unmotivated, especially when she stopped her anti-depressant medication, and she had experienced increasing difficulties in her relationship during the last year. She started IPT to help her to manage recurrent symptoms of depression and relationship difficulties more effectively.

Suzanna described several symptoms of depression and anxiety to her therapist. She was easily upset and tearful, especially following arguments with her boyfriend, and described feeling very unhappy most of the time. This left her feeling out of control, and she was generally irritable with the people around her. She said that much of her current sadness related to the state of her relationship with her partner, but she also felt guilty about 'almost everything'. She did not think about dying but described feeling worn out by her situation. Her sleep was relatively undisturbed but her concentration was poor and she said she easily became exhausted, mentally and physically. This created some difficulties at work, where she was a project manager, responsible for coordinating efforts on several jobs simultaneously. Suzanna was still going into work but felt she had used up all of her energy by the end of the day. She had not been able to tell anyone at work about the strain she was under, and this was creating its own pressure, as she worried that she would be found out in not coping as she normally would.

She described routinely putting things off, feeling little motivation or interest and regularly cancelling plans. She was in touch with her friends, mainly because they worked together, but she made fewer suggestions about doing things together and had spent much less time with them outside work over the last year. She had previously been at the heart of the group, but was now happy to stay at home or occasionally go to the gym. She described always feeling anxious and physically tense, and finding it very difficult to relax.

Suzanna agreed that she had been consistently depressed for the last year, after a fluctuating pattern of symptoms for the two years before that. She was encouraged by the idea that this was an illness that could be treated, rather than something she just had to put up with, and said she felt closer to her 'real self' when she had been taking her medication. She had tried stopping her anti-depressants twice, but on each occasion her symptoms became worse. Each time the medication was restarted Suzanna felt her symptoms improve, but this had not been enough to manage the greater difficulties of the last year. The information her therapist gave her about the nature of depression, emphasizing that it is a common, episodic and recurring condition, helped her to think about what she would have to do to manage its impact on her life and highlighted to her that it was a condition she would have to address more actively and over a longer period of time than she initially anticipated.

Suzanna recognized that retreating from most of her relationships and activities was a feature of the depression and was contributing to keeping it going. She was still going to the gym occasionally and agreed to make this a twice-weekly routine because she recognized that exercise lifted her mood and energy levels. She still had to battle with low motivation, however, and so attended classes rather than exercising on her own because this encouraged her to go and gave her some light-hearted company.

Suzanna also planned to ask her partner to help her with the household jobs that were building up. She had found her daily routines more difficult to keep up with and was frustrated by the mess that had built up in her flat. She had tried to conceal the mess when her partner visited, but this was no longer possible and she found that they bickered when he made comments about the place being untidy.

When Suzanna completed her timeline with her therapist, it revealed a two-year period during which she had dipped in and out of depression and a clearer and prolonged episode of depression over the last year. The main incidents were the split – a role transition, and then the ongoing conflict after the relationship resumed. (For a reminder of how the timeline is constructed, take a look back at chapter 8.) Her symptoms had been consistently worse following an argument with her partner in which she had said that they should move in together and he had refused. She became hopeless about the future of the relationship and worried that they would split up again. Most of the other areas in Suzanna's life had been stable during this three-year period and so the conflict with her partner stood out as the main factor contributing to her depression.

Suzanna's timeline

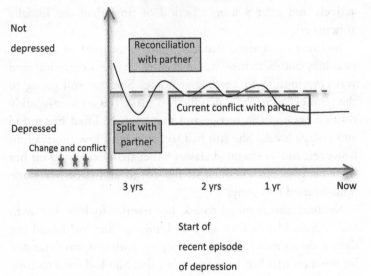

Suzanna began to recognize that she had had periods of depression dating back to her teenage years (marked with stars on the diagram above), although a diagnosis had never been made and she had not received treatment. Her therapist suggested that this pattern of untreated depression might have increased her vulnerability to becoming depressed again. Suzanna first recalled feeling depressed as a teenager following a major falling-out in her family that had resulted in her sister leaving home. This had left Suzanna alone with her parents, both of whom drank heavily. Suzanna's mother did not speak to her absent daughter again and for a while Suzanna only had erratic contact with her sister. Suzanna felt depressed and abandoned to a difficult home life, and as soon as she was able to she also left home. She did not make contact with either of her parents again before they died.

After leaving home, Suzanna initially worked in an office with kind but much older women and then studied at college, this time with much younger peers. Feeling out of place in both environments, Suzanna suffered from recurrent periods of depression over some time. She sought comfort in a long-term relationship with a man she did not love but who she hoped would provide security. This relationship proved unsustainable and she eventually left, once more experiencing some depressive symptoms. It was soon after this relationship had ended that Suzanna met her current partner. She moved city and job to be with him, and her next episode of depression followed the break-up of that relationship two years later, when Suzanna felt they did not share the same level of commitment to the future of the relationship.

With the help of her therapist, Suzanna created her interpersonal inventory, and together they discussed the range of people in her life. This showed that all her current friends were work colleagues, or people she had worked with until recently, but she did also have a social routine with her colleagues. The stability in her home and working life over the last three years had allowed Suzanna to establish a wider network of friends than she had had previously, and within this she had people she could talk to, people she could ask for practical help and people she could spend time with socially. However, Suzanna realized she was not getting as much from many of these relationships as she would have liked. She felt that few of her friends really understood her current difficulties, but conceded that she also found it very difficult to talk about problems and tended to back away from other people when things were not going well. Her relationship with her partner was confirmed as the one that was causing her the greatest dissatisfaction.

With both of her parents having died, and having lost

contact with her sister and extended family, Suzanna said she felt she had let go of family relationships a long time ago. Her only concern related to them was that she would become more like her mother, who she believed had also been depressed. Suzanna had not maintained other friendships over her life, and routinely broke off contact with people when she moved job or hit any kind of disagreement. She also realized that a series of long-term relationships with partners had stopped her from making more friendships with other women. It became apparent that, while she had developed sufficient skills to make relationships with the people around her, Suzanna found it hard to address any difficulties in those relationships, or to keep them going when the people were not immediately at hand. Consequently, she had repeatedly found herself making a group of friends only to leave them behind when she changed job or moved, and so was constantly faced with having to start all over again.

Suzanna's interpersonal inventory

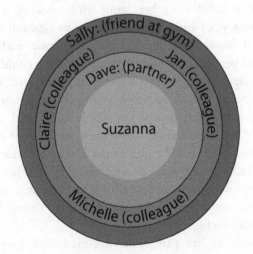

Suzanna and her therapist agreed that the focus of her IPT would be the dispute between Suzanna and her partner, with a second goal being to think about the way in which she generally sorted out disputes with her friends. The need for this wider focus was soon clear when Suzanna had a disagreement with one of her girlfriends, which she dealt with by ignoring her friend's attempts to contact her. This withdrawal was her typical reaction when she felt hurt or disappointed, and it had led to many previous friendships breaking down. This example demonstrated how vulnerable her relationships were and how difficult she found it to talk through disagreements.

Each week when Suzanna reviewed her depressive symptoms with her therapist, the link between her depression and her relationship with her boyfriend was clear. Several difficulties which appeared to have started early in her life, such as unclear communication, struggling to feel she belonged and side-stepping discussions around difficulties in relationships, were clearly played out in her current relationship. Although these were long-standing patterns of behaviour it was quite clear that the patterns would all be addressed even when the focus of her therapy was consistently on her current relationships.

Suzanna set a number of goals, which related to both her partner and her wider group of friends. Her first short-term goal was to invite her partner to set aside one evening a week when they would do something enjoyable together. Another short-term goal was to invite a colleague to join her at a class at the gym once a week. Her first medium-term goal was to learn ways to talk to and listen to her partner that did not either conceal her feelings or escalate into heated arguments. She also wanted to use her improved communication skills to talk more openly about her feelings with a small number of friends and to ask for help when she felt low. Her third medium-term goal was to make an agreement with her partner that they would

not continue with the current pattern in their relationship,
whereby they fell into days of silence following an argument,
and that they would make contact within twenty-four hours of
an argument. Her long-term goal was to discuss plans for their
future with her partner and to make her own plans depending
on the agreement they came to.

To improve her understanding of the conflict with her partner, Suzanna began by describing their daily routine. They did
not live together but spent five nights of the week at Suzanna's
flat. Over the last year they had largely stopped going out
together, now only doing so about once a month, usually to
the gym. While Suzanna had been depressed, her partner had
kept many of his own routines going, such as playing football
or meeting his friends for a drink, and this meant he would
be out during the early part of at least half the evenings he
stayed at Suzanna's. In the past Suzanna would either have
joined him or arranged to see her own friends on those evenings, but now she would wait at home alone. The mismatch
of their routines meant there was little or no conversation on
many evenings, and it was little better when they were at home
together, as they would generally watch TV in silence until
going to bed.

Suzanna described feeling bored and unhappy with this routine but had little energy to try and change it. She was reluctant
to bring it up in conversation with her partner because she felt
it was her fault that they no longer did things together – it was
her routine that had changed, not his – but she also felt hurt
that he seemed to carry on without her without any difficulty.
Suzanna said this reinforced her sense that she was not important to him, and when she tried to speak to him about it the
conversation quickly deteriorated into an argument and she
became anxious that her worst fear of another split would be
realized. Suzanna's therapist pointed out how many depressive

symptoms were evident in this response – low mood, little energy or motivation, guilt and self-blame, feeling worthless – and they discussed the way depression contributed to Suzanna's difficulty in identifying the range of options open to her.

Following another argument with her boyfriend after they had been to a party together, Suzanna used her therapy session to try to understand how the argument had come about and what she had been feeling. She realized that she had felt under pressure from her partner to go out and had been irritated when he left her to talk to some other friends soon after they arrived. Suzanna remembered thinking that she didn't know why she had bothered going out, especially as she hadn't wanted to. By the time her partner came back to her, some time later, she was feeling very irritated and was quick to accuse him of not caring about her evening and taking her for granted. This quickly deteriorated into a public argument when her partner reacted angrily, and Suzanna left soon afterwards to go home alone. She did not speak to her partner for several days afterwards, and during that time was unsure if the relationship had ended. When her partner subsequently contacted her she described feeling so relieved that she did not mention the argument again and tried to carry on as if nothing had happened. Suzanna recognized that this was a familiar sequence of events and said it left her feeling hopeless and unmotivated.

This provided a good opportunity for Suzanna and her therapist to look at the link between this relationship and Suzanna's depressive symptoms, and also at the support she might seek from friends. Following the argument, Suzanna had felt low and tired for several days. She backed out of all her plans, took two days off work and lost interest in everything around her. She had some contact with friends, however, when two of her colleagues called to find out how she was, which gave her the opportunity to challenge the guilty feelings she had experienced, as she discussed what had happened with them and they were able to suggest to her that she was not entirely to blame. Once back at work, she described how having friendly company around her had helped and her depressive symptoms had become less intense.

When Suzanna and her therapist examined her exchanges with her partner in detail, it became clear that the relationship was at the stage of impasse; in other words, neither of them was making an active attempt to sort out their difficulties, even though they both felt dissatisfied with the relationship. She and her therapist were able to start to speculate about some of the issues that needed to be addressed, such as Suzanna not feeling valued in the relationship, neither she nor her partner making time for the other, and uncertainty about their respective expectations of the relationship. The habit of allowing frustrations to build up and then launching into discussions driven by accusations and anger was agreed to be unhelpful.

Having identified the stage the relationship was at, and the communication problems involved, Suzanna and her therapist decided that she would focus on learning to talk about difficult and emotional issues more promptly and more calmly. Suzanna's history suggested that she hadn't developed effective communication skills for this kind of emotionally charged situation, and usually relied on walking away from relationships when difficulties arose. Suzanna did not want to walk away from her partner, so she needed to learn new ways of communicating with him. She recognized that they both contributed to the current pattern in their relationship, both by putting off important discussions without making time to return to them later. This had happened following the first break-up, and Suzanna conceded that they had tried to pick up the relationship without directly addressing the difficulties that had led to the split in the first place.

Suzanna clarified what she wanted from the relationship was to live together and have a future, but she was much less clear about her partner's hopes and expectations. She recognized that her wish for a more definite commitment was often an unspoken theme of their arguments but they had rarely discussed it directly. Her partner had been in an unhappy long-term relationship before meeting Suzanna and this had been something they had had in common when their relationship began. However, they had rarely discussed their respective responses to their past experiences, and while Suzanna had hoped he had seen their relationship as an opportunity for a fresh start, as she had, she had since come to fear that he had been put off making another serious commitment altogether. It became clear they had previously addressed any differences in expectations by means of ultimatums rather than constructive discussion. Suzanna realized that they now had a good opportunity to start to examine their expectations of the relationship and to assess what common ground there might be and where any differences might lie.

As a first step towards improving her communication, Suzanna's therapist helped her to examine and to learn to tolerate the emotional obstacles, such as fear of disappointment, which prevented her from taking steps towards her goals. It became clear that Suzanna had limited awareness of her own emotional state, and mostly said she 'couldn't be bothered'. Her therapist encouraged Suzanna to find other ways to describe her feelings. With help, Suzanna started to build up her emotional vocabulary, which in turn helped her to understand the range of her emotional responses and the expectations and hopes that they related to. She decided to try talking about her own feelings, rather than guessing her partner's, when she started discussions with him and rather than trying to force immediate decision about their future, to develop a clearer understanding of each other's expectations and feelings.

Developing her self-awareness and communication skills helped Suzanna to spend her time with her partner more constructively. She used her skills to achieve her first goal, which was to spend time doing something enjoyable with her partner each week. This change in routine reduced some of the background tension which had preoccupied and exhausted Suzanna, and allowed for her to focus some attention on her wider network.

She described how she had felt let down and unsupported by her friends, who had made few enquiries about her relationship with her partner. She had reacted to this in the past by withdrawing from them and cancelling plans, which made her sense of isolation worse and left her feeling even less supported. Parallels between Suzanna's relationships with her partner and her friends, in terms of unclear communication and uncertain expectations, were clear. Suzanna and her therapist discussed several examples, and each time it was possible to see a link back to her depressive symptoms when she felt tired and unmotivated following a confusing or disappointing exchange with the people in her life. By addressing these patterns in relationships with her friends and colleagues Suzanna was able to experiment with making changes in how she communicated in a safer context, where the issues did not seem so overwhelming nor the risk of change so alarming as with her partner.

Suzanna also gradually turned more to her friends to talk about how she felt and to fill the companionship gap that had emerged over time. She made more effort to see friends, rather than withdrawing from them as she had done in the past. As a result she felt more interested in and enthusiastic about making plans. She noticed that she was thinking and planning more clearly, and described feeling enthused by making these changes. Suzanna practised talking more openly with two of her friends in particular, Sally and Michelle, and took advantage of the routine they had established of going to the gym together on a regular basis. This routine consolidated the already reasonably close relationship Suzanna had with Michelle, who became a good friend rather than just a friendly colleague, and created a marked improvement in Suzanna's relationship with Sally, who had previously been on the edge of her social network. Suzanna found that her friends responded well when she could describe how she felt and what was worrying her more vividly, and they readily offered her support and encouragement. Suzanna began to look forward to their time together and found it very helpful to have their feedback when she sometimes struggled to organize her thoughts clearly. She would occasionally practise with them before speaking to her boyfriend about issues that were important to her, as she found that by discussing things in advance with people who were supportive, she felt more confident in expressing herself to her partner.

Over time Suzanna and her partner discussed many of the issues that they hadn't spoken about in the early stages of their relationship. On some occasions these discussions started to drift back towards arguments, but they had learned to notice the signs and when this happened to delay any further discussion until they both felt calmer. Importantly, they learned to agree a time to come back to these discussions and stuck to their plan, which allowed them to make much more headway than they ever had in the past. They were able to think about their mutual responsibility for the difficulties they had been experiencing and to talk openly about what they both wanted for the future. For the first time in their relationship, Suzanna's partner expressed a willingness to talk about moving in together, and they both agreed to take time to plan this together. Suzanna said she felt happy with the prospect, and was reassured that there were no longer topics that were off limits and that they were both willing to compromise on issues where necessary.

Suzanna felt some apprehension as she came to the end of her IPT, as she had come to rely on the therapy sessions as opportunities to sort out her thoughts and plan ahead, and was particularly concerned about the risk of falling back into depression in the future. However, she knew that she could now turn to her friends, as she had already done, to help her to examine her feelings, and discussed with her therapist the ways this could help to protect her against depression. She and her therapist took time to go back over what she had learned and consider how she would use her new skills and knowledge in the future. She identified the potential triggers for symptoms returning or deterioration in her relationships, and made a plan with her partner and friends about how to manage any dips in her mood in the future. By the end of her sixteen weeks of IPT, Suzanna no longer felt depressed and her relationships were more stable and rewarding.

Chapter 18

Theme three: grief and loss

There is no pain so great as the memory of joy in present grief.

AESCHYLUS, GREEK WRITER

Grief and loss are everywhere in depression. Indeed, it is difficult to imagine a depression story without them. So it might seem odd to apply the idea of grief and loss solely to depression that follows bereavement. In IPT we separate out depression after bereavement from other losses to acknowledge the special investment we make in relationships, and the distinct impact of a death. This particular kind of grief will be the focus of this chapter. Our social nature as humans means that our well-being relies on our close bonds with other people. We often make sense of ourselves through our relationships, and to permanently lose a significant relationship can provoke great uncertainty and self-doubt, especially if the loss is shrouded in depression. Unresolved grief is a person's struggle to maintain a relationship while at the same time facing the reality of the loss.

It is useful to take a moment to clarify the language that we use when we talk about grief. *Bereavement* is the experience of having lost someone through death: the practical reality of the event. We typically use *grief* and *mourning* to describe ways of responding to the event, with *grief* mainly focusing on the feelings, e.g. loss, sadness, emptiness or anger, and *mourning* capturing more of the behaviour surrounding these feelings, e.g. attending a funeral service, sharing memories with other people. Therapy cannot change the fact of the bereavement, but it can help you to re-engage with the mourning process and in so doing gradually reduce the pain of your grief.

Understanding responses to bereavement

Several studies have shown that losing a very close relationship with the death of, for example, a partner or a child, is the most stressful and painful experience a person can face. They have also shown that immediately after this kind of loss most people feel sad, lose interest in life, can't sleep or eat properly, and think about dying themselves: a pattern normally seen in depression. A diagnosis of depression is not typically made immediately after bereavement, however. This initial response to bereavement for many people is not illness, but the typical pain of loss expressed through our bodies, thoughts and feelings.

Over the weeks and months following a bereavement, most people gradually pick up the routines of life again: they begin to eat regularly, sleep and feel rested, and take some pleasure in doing things and in the people around them, even if this is accompanied by sadness that the person they have lost is not there to share it. They may feel waves of sadness and distress, at times as intensely as in the days immediately after the loss, but these gradually become less and less frequent. Similar feelings are often triggered by specific reminders or significant dates e.g. anniversaries or birthdays, but are less likely to appear randomly over time. The change will be gradual for most people and painful for many, but the slow process of adjusting to a new life slowly moves on. In the simplest terms, life changes and we live with the loss as part of our ongoing experience, without continuing to be defined by it.

This process of recovery can sometimes feel confusing, because grief and mourning are not exclusively about pain: they can also involve relief, happiness or a sense of peace. Sometimes we can embrace these feelings as part of our complex emotional response, but at other times they can provoke feelings of guilt and shame because we misunderstand them to mean that we didn't care or are disloyal. Our responses to our relationships are as complex and contradictory in death as they are in life. Positive feelings about a bereavement can be a natural response to the departure of a valued individual, but can also be our response to the end of an exhausting and painful time, such as a long illness. Research has shown that positive feelings such as relief, happiness and a sense of peace after bereavement can be a sign of greater resilience and a better outcome in the long term.

This process of accommodating and learning to live with a loss is a healthy response to bereavement. It will usually involve feelings of sadness combined with understanding and acceptance that this is the nature of life. It will very often also involve letting go of the relationship that has been lost.

Bereavement, depression and IPT

This gradual recovery will be delayed, and might even stall completely, if depression also develops. When, after bereavement, we also become depressed, we get stuck, and our experience of grief persists and becomes more far-reaching. Grief remains our predominant experience; rather than becoming a significant and remembered, but not dominating, episode in our life story, it comes to define us.

Around 15 per cent of people who are bereaved continue to experience symptoms of depression one or two years after the death. For these people, depression tends to involve a range of symptoms that are not typically experienced by someone who is simply grieving. These include:

- strong feelings of guilt, which are not related to the bereavement;
- thoughts of suicide or a preoccupation with dying, which are not solely about wanting to be with the person who died;
- feelings of worthlessness;
- slowed physical movements and markedly reduced activity;
- inability to work, socialize or enjoy any leisure activity;
- hallucinations of the deceased, or hallucinations which are not related to the bereavement.

When these symptoms last over time they mark out depression over and above usual grief, and signal a need for an active response to help with recovery. It is important to be clear that in these circumstances therapy is targeting *depression*. No form of treatment can take away the reality of your loss or make this less significant in your life. However, if the depression is treated, it becomes possible to resume the process of mourning and adjustment, as the majority of people manage to do.

When they first wrote about depression associated with bereavement, the psychiatrist Gerald Klerman and his colleagues who developed IPT described the bereaved person as having a 'crippling attachment'. This captures the idea of being stuck, mentioned several times already, which so often leads to depression. When a relationship with someone who has died continues to be the most important relationship in someone's life, this inevitably restricts their chances of living fully with the people who are still in their life. To enter into those relationships with enthusiasm now might either feel disloyal or simply

have lost all appeal. The reduced circle of life starts to look
very much like the reduced circle of depression, and for some
people these two patterns become one and the same. If we are
bereaved and become depressed, this interrupts the painful process of mourning, and we are likely to distance ourselves from
our current relationships, perhaps becoming preoccupied with
the lost relationship. The IPT approach to recovering from
grief looks at this preoccupation and avoidance, and supports
mourning and reconnecting with the people around you. In
many cultures mourning is a social process, not simply because
sharing the experience of loss with other people offers more
support, but because the very act of turning to other people
is part of the process of recovering, as it connects you to the
present rather than the past.

Using your timeline

If you are using IPT to help you to recover from depression
linked to bereavement, it will be most useful to you if bereavement features in your depression timeline and you can see the
connection between that loss, the start of your depression and
how you feel now. For some people bereavement will coincide
very closely with the start of the depression and it will be clear
that this is what triggered it. However, the connection is not
always so clear, and sometimes the impact of the bereavement
or its links to your current depression can fall out of sight.

Jean

Jean felt depressed after her husband died but managed
to lift herself out of it for brief periods by keeping active,
taking on new jobs or devoting her time to her grandchildren. As time passed, however, she found each new

project more tiring and less effective at holding back the depression that never felt very far away. Whenever she could not keep herself occupied she felt the full weight of depression once again. While from the outside it seemed quite clear that her current distress was linked to her husband's death a few years earlier, she had lost sight of the connection. She saw other people move on after going through similar losses and thought that because she had felt better at times there must be some other reason why she was struggling so much with depression. It was not until she was able to tell her story and follow the bereavement theme through it that she understood how little she had been able to mourn. In trying to explain her story to her therapist, she understood more clearly what was driving her depression.

If you have experienced several bereavements one after another, it can be difficult to trace the relationship between the grief and your depression. The repeated assault of multiple losses can increase the likelihood of depression, leaving you feeling exhausted. Or it could be that your ability to adjust to a major loss has been undermined by the subsequent losses, which distract and divert your energy and attention. It can be difficult to know where to focus your attention in order to move on. As well as the direct loss through bereavement, you may also be suffering wider consequences, for example if you become financially vulnerable or lose your home and neighbours when your partner dies.

John

John's young son died in an accident and he had no time to grieve before discovering his wife was pregnant. The couple lost their second child through miscarriage and in the two years that followed both of John's parents died. By the time he tried to talk about it to his IPT therapist, he was emotionally exhausted and had already withdrawn from most of his relationships. When he looked over the sequence of events, he could distinguish between the impact of losing a child whom he had known and loved and one whom he had yet to meet. He also distinguished between losing his young son so cruelly early and his parents, whom he saw as having lived good and full lives. He felt the weight of each loss, but could also see how his son's death was most closely linked to his depression and how all of his subsequent losses had used up his energy in a way that had prevented him from mourning.

Signs of grief are not always immediately obvious, and this can prevent us from receiving the help and support that we need. Someone might appear quite unaffected for weeks or months after bereavement and only react much later, perhaps after an anniversary or another loss. It can be difficult to understand the mismatch when something relatively minor appears to trigger a bigger reaction in us. This confusion can complicate our ability to mourn and may increase the possibility of depression because there are missing parts to the story. Look at your own timeline. Did your distress follow on immediately after your bereavement or after a delay?

Peter

When Peter's wife was diagnosed with cancer he stopped working in order to care for her in her last year. When she died, he did not appear to mourn and went straight back to work the next week. Five months later a neighbour, whom Peter knew a little, died. In the weeks that followed his neighbour's death Peter's mood dropped; he became very tired and unmotivated, and had to stop work. He felt confused and guilty to have responded this way after his neighbour's death when he had apparently responded so little to losing his wife, and went through numerous medical tests to try to find an explanation for his poor health. When he started to talk about how he felt some time later, he began to understand that his symptoms were a delayed reaction to his wife's death.

Your grief story

Your grief story will capture a number of features which may help to explain why you have developed depression. IPT guides you in looking more closely at how each part of the story influences your mourning. The likelihood of depression developing after bereavement is influenced by:

- the nature of the relationship you have lost;
- the events around the death;
- the support you used at the time and afterwards;
- the quality of your relationships now.

As with all areas of work in IPT, it is best to make the journey to recovery with companions. Consider who in your IPT team you could usefully talk to about what you are doing. Ideally, involve people who can share memories of the person who has died and can help you to build a balanced picture of the relationship you have lost. Also think about who may be able to help you to move forward and be part of the network of relationships that can meet your needs now.

As you start this process, are you in the weeks or months immediately after your loss, or approaching a significant date that reminds you of your loss, such as an anniversary or birthday? It is not uncommon for grief to be experienced in waves, which can be disconcerting and confusing. Initially it may feel that these waves are continually crashing over you, while later there are moments of reprieve in the emotional assault. It can feel alarming when intense grief returns after a period of relative calm. This is entirely natural, but the experience may be prolonged and exacerbated by depression, which will reduce your ability to tolerate the ebb and flow of the unfolding experience. It is also very common to feel your grief more intensely when you are confronted with certain reminders, such as significant dates or events. This does not mean that you are going back to the start of the whole process, although it may feel like it in the moment. With time, you will be able to recognize the predictable increase and decrease in your response. As your depression begins to ease, you will also be able to manage and plan around predictably difficult times more carefully, allowing you to mark those times you wish to without being taken over by them.

Many people who are bereaved start therapy as they approach one of these more difficult times, e.g. an anniversary. It can be very helpful to have extra support around those times. If a particular aspect of your loss looms very large for you, you may well find it best to home in on the exercises in this chapter that deal with the features of the relationship that are preoccupying you at the moment, rather than trying to force yourself to work through them systematically as they are presented. For example, if you find yourself mostly thinking about the final days with the person you have lost, start with the exercises that focus on the period around the time the person died (exercises 18.8 and 18.9). Alternatively, if you are most comfortable thinking about good memories, you could work through the exercises in the order in which they are set out and gradually expand the range of memories as described. Exercise 18.1 will help you identify the particular focus of your grief.

It is important to continue to monitor the links between your depression and your grief. Continue to rate your depression symptoms weekly (using the form in appendix 1), and when you notice a change in symptoms, think about whether or not the loss you have experienced is contributing to how you feel. You can use the form in appendix 3 to help you here. When your symptoms and grief overlap, it will be useful to look at what was happening at that particular time in more detail.

Remembering your relationship

Remembering the relationship that you have lost is an important part of mourning and recovery. It is likely you are already thinking about the person who has died, and you might notice that some memories come to mind easily, while others are more difficult to recall. The process of mourning is helped if you can remember the relationship in a balanced way. This includes remembering the happy and fond memories that can be a comfort, and also the more difficult times that crop up in every relationship. A balanced memory of someone does not idealize or criticize the relationship but remembers the whole.

Building up a balanced picture takes time and will draw on your memories from across the whole relationship. This can be an emotional process, and so it is important to take it gradually. Trying to piece the picture together too quickly may leave you feeling overwhelmed, unable to keep up with the feelings that come with the memories, and may risk triggering more symptoms of depression. Taking it slowly can help you to acknowledge the following important points:

- It is safe to remember.
- You can be confident that you can remember and still get on with day-to-day life.
- You can bridge the gap between the past and the present without feeling trapped in either.
- You can cope with remembering all of the relationship.

If you find it difficult to think about some parts of the relationship, use the support you have already identified in your IPT team. It might be useful to ask the person you have chosen to talk with if they would ask you some simple questions or prompt you with their own memories, so that together you can build up a picture that covers the highs and lows of the relationship.

If you find it difficult to tolerate talking about your memories at first, remember there are other ways that the people around you can help. For example, arrange a specific time and place to speak to or meet with someone after you have spent time thinking about the person who died. You might want to repeat this arrangement throughout the time you are using these exercises. This will help you to practise stepping in and out of the past, and will build up support in your current relationships. Other people can accompany you if you visit places with specific memories or significance, e.g. the graveside or a favourite place you visited when the person was alive.

Diane: grieving through dreams

When Diane's daughter died she often found that she would dream about her at night. She had mixed feelings about these dreams. She welcomed getting lost in her memories, but it often took her a few minutes to come out of the dream when she woke in the morning, and each time she realized that it was only a dream the painful reality of her loss hit her again. This left her shaken and irritable in the mornings and caused arguments with her husband, who struggled to understand what was behind her mood. At first Diane did not tell her husband about her dreams because she was afraid he would tell her she had to move on. When she did eventually tell him she was surprised to hear that he felt jealous that she had dreams that he had not been able to have. He gently encouraged her to tell him about what she remembered and what she saw in her dreams. This helped them to start talking about many different memories, some captured in Diane's dreams, some triggered by the feelings the initial scenes provoked in them both.

Following your memories and tracking the link to depression

Memory often doesn't work in strict chronological order. It is unlikely that you routinely think back to the first time you met the person who died and recall the relationship step by step as it happened. You probably think a lot about some of the times you had together and not very much about other times. You might be drawn to certain types of memory, e.g. the happy ones rather than the sad ones, or particular times in the relationship, e.g. the final days rather than early memories. Depression can make it more difficult to move between memories, as you would normally do, and it is not uncommon to dwell on some memories at the expense of others. Notice which memories of the lost relationship come up most often for you. Take particular note of the memories that trigger a change in your symptoms of depression, e.g. the memories that keep you awake at night or prevent you from doing something.

Don't feel you have to rush through these memories; they are part of the story. Take time to remember, but also notice if you begin to revisit the same memories several times.

Exercise 18.1: Thinking about your memories

Notice which part of the relationship you focus on most often. Do you:

- Think back to the good times and find it more difficult to think about difficulties in the relationship or around the time the person died?
- Think about the time around the death and have more difficulty remembering all the stories that went before?
- Go over unfinished arguments or unspoken thoughts and find it more difficult to remember the bigger picture?
- Find it easy to move between happy and sad memories, and between recent and more distant times? Or do you find yourself running over the same examples again and again?

How do these memories affect your symptoms of depression?

Focusing exclusively on one aspect of a relationship is common in depression, but it can conceal the variety of experiences that make up most relationships and may fuel depressive symptoms such as guilt or hopelessness. Sometimes memories offer us comfort, but focusing persistently on one part of the relationship might also mean you avoid thinking about things you find more difficult. You may feel you have little control over the memories that fill your mind, and some may be so painful or dominant that it is as if they have wiped out everything else. Focusing on a limited range of memories or a particular period in the relationship makes it more difficult to remember the relationship in the balanced way that is most helpful to mourning. Again, if you find that you have become focused on one part of the relationship, it can be helpful to involve someone else who can gently encourage you to add other memories by asking simple questions or sharing memories of their own.

Notice how you feel about the memories that come to mind most easily. Do they comfort you or make you feel sad? Do any of the memories that come up from day to day trigger your depression symptoms, e.g. feeling sad, lying awake or feeling guilty? Sometimes depression keeps you stuck in a repeating loop, and finding a way to break out of the loop can make the symptoms less intense. When you notice a link between your memories and your depression, take time to think and talk with your IPT team about how the memory and your symptoms are connected. It can be difficult to think of ways out of these loops, and another point of view can very helpful.

Jennifer: breaking out of the loop

Jennifer had always enjoyed gardening with her husband, who had kept a large vegetable garden that she used when preparing meals for the family. After her husband died she lost interest in gardening and avoided making the meals her husband had enjoyed. Mealtimes became a chore and she felt irritable when she looked out at the rotting patch at the back of her garden. She avoided going into the garden because she found it painful to be reminded of the many happy days they had spent there together. She planned to pave over the vegetable patch to block out the memories, but was discouraged by her daughter, who

pleaded on behalf of Jennifer's grandson: the little boy had
always been promised that he could help to pull up the
vegetables when he was old enough, which he now was.
With her grandson in tow, Jennifer was able to revisit the
garden and share her memories with her new gardening
assistant. Her pleasure in her new memories helped her
to manage the pain of what she had lost and to remember
the many good times she had been afraid to think about.

Exercise 18.2: Sketching out the story of your relationship

Now, in your notebook, or with your IPT team,
choose a starting place for your story of the lost relationship. This should reflect the memories you return
to most often. Notice whether these memories trigger
your depression or temporarily ease the symptoms you
experience. Allow yourself to simply have these memories and, if possible, share them with your IPT team.
When you are satisfied that these memories have been
revisited in detail, try to gradually introduce additional
memories. This is your opportunity to expand your
story backwards and forwards to cover the whole history of the relationship.

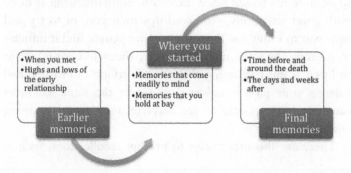

- When you met
- Highs and lows of the early relationship

Earlier memories

Where you started
- Memories that come readily to mind
- Memories that you hold at bay

- Time before and around the death
- The days and weeks after

Final memories

Relationships develop over time. Try to capture the journey through the course of your relationship in the selection of memories you think and talk about. You will have discovered more about each other over time, and found your way through highs and lows. If it is your partner whom you have lost, you may have moved from the first days of a romance to becoming established and building a routine together. You may have moved from living separately to adjusting around each other's daily routines. Perhaps you had children together and went through the anxieties of being new parents, managing teenagers, perhaps seeing your children grow up and leave home and having to adjust to being just the two of you again. Or perhaps you lost a parent, and your memories stretch back to childhood and through growing up; or you lost your own child, and are acutely aware of the gaps in your story and the times you did not have together as well as the shorter journey through life that you were able to share.

Talking to other people who knew the person who died can be a great help in opening up your memories. Each person will have their own store of memories, some of which will overlap with yours and some of which will be new to you. This is similar to what happens when people gathered together at a funeral share their stories. It may be that the people around you have stopped telling these stories, especially if some time has passed since the death. Sometimes this is done with good intentions – to avoid upsetting you, or to try and help you to move on. Sometimes other people find it difficult to go over the same memories many times and are reluctant to listen again. Explaining that you are trying to broaden and balance your picture rather than repeat the same examples can help other people to see ways to assist your mourning and recovery.

There are also other ways to prompt recollections, such as

looking through photographs or saved letters, visiting places you went to together. The way places look, smell and sound can be powerful triggers for our memories. Again, it will be good to share these experiences with someone else, ideally at the time or at least just afterwards, to help you to sort through what you feel.

- Which places would you like to visit to recall fond memories?
- Are there places it is more painful to visit, e.g. the scene of an accident or a family home you haven't yet been back to?
- Who could support you to spend time with your memories and then to step back into the present?

Frank: revisiting the family home

Frank had not been able to visit his mother's home since her death. He had used to visit her two or three times a week on his way home from work, but had been out of the country when she suddenly fell ill and died, and had not had an opportunity to say goodbye. Frank had felt afraid that if he saw the house and his mother was not there he would not be able to cope with the reality of her death. He had avoided talking about this for several months after his mother's death and made excuses to avoid joining his sister and brother when they started to clear out the house. Frank's sister was concerned that he would regret not seeing his mother's home for a final time before it was sold and suggested that they go there together. Frank took up her invitation and was surprised by the many different memories this triggered, many of them happy, as he had spent so much enjoyable time

there. He was very grateful to have his sister with him
and they laughed and cried and talked and acknowledged
how important this had been in allowing Frank to continue his recovery from depression.

What have you lost?

Exercise 18.3: Working out what you have lost

In your interpersonal inventory (see chapter 9) you
listed the kinds of support you get from your current
relationships, e.g. someone to talk to, someone to hang
out with, someone to help you out when you need an
extra pair of hands. Now ask the same questions that
you used while putting together your inventory about
the relationship you have lost.

- What kind of support did you get from that
  relationship?
- What support did you offer?
- How did you spend your time together?
- What do you miss most about this person?
- Was there anything about this relationship you
  would have liked to change?

Part of adjusting to a loss involves transferring some of
your expectations of the relationship you have lost on to the
people around you now. The person you have lost cannot be
replaced, but some of the ways you behaved around each other
and supported each other might be re-established in other relationships. This is not an easy process and may continue to feel
unsatisfactory for a while. This struggle is captured in a four-
year-old child's touching response to her daddy's reassurances

after her mother's death that many people loved her: 'But when mummy was not dead I didn't need so many people – I just needed her.' This longing for a single person can seem irresistible when you are bereaved, but your inventory will remind you that for nearly all of us life is made up of more than one relationship, and that these relationships overlap and duplicate in what we give to them and what they provide for us. By allowing yourself to consider how they overlap, you are starting to distinguish between the necessary and unnecessary losses following your bereavement. There will be some things that are lost for ever when you lose someone important to you, and these can't be replaced, even in other relationships. These are the losses it is necessary to mourn. However, there will be other things that you will, in time, be able to get from your existing and new relationships, which will help you in the future. Depression can sometime blind us to these possibilities. These are the unnecessary losses that many depressed and bereaved people suffer.

Can you think of aspects of your lost relationship that also feature in your current relationships – or could do, given the chance: e.g. someone to talk to, to spend time with, to share interests with? Thinking about the lost relationship in this way starts to break it down into the different functions that make up all relationships. You might find that all of the routines you developed with one person cannot simply be transferred on to a single other person, but many of them might find a place in a number of your relationships. Look over your interpersonal inventory again with your IPT team and try to identify the opportunities for support and company that are still available with the people around you and which may help to limit the unnecessary losses you endure as you learn to live with your loss.

Exercise 18.4: Beginning to develop other relationships

- Who can you share some of your routines and activities with now?
- Who would welcome the support you used to offer in the lost relationship?
- What changes will be necessary to develop the potential in these other relationships?

Pete: filling the gaps

Pete became depressed after his best friend died. They had been involved in almost every area of each other's lives – they shared a flat, worked together and socialized together. Pete felt like his whole life had been taken away, because this relationship had featured in his life in some way every day. Pete quickly recognized that he would not be able to find one person to support and accompany him in all the different ways his friend had done. However, when he looked at each area of his life he found people who could meet some of his needs e.g. other work colleagues whom he got on well with, other friends who had been part of his normal social routine, and his girlfriend, who now spent more time at home with him. Several of these relationships, which had not been fully developed in the past, offered potential to start to fill some of the gaps that had been created when he lost a central relationship in his life.

Managing memories and emotions

Exercise 18.5: Remembering the bad times as well as the good

- Think about the timeline of the whole relationship, which will include the good memories as well as the more difficult times.
- Draw this timeline in your notebook, to help you to hold the different features of the relationship in mind at once. Think about how the relationship flowed in and out of good and difficult times.
- Share this balanced picture with your IPT team and notice what happens to your depression symptoms when you look back on the ebb and flow of the big picture of your relationship.

You might feel reluctant to think about the difficult times in the relationship you have lost. You may even wonder what the point would be of doing so. It is a very human instinct to take comfort from what was good and to focus on that. However, often when people become stuck in the process of mourning it is because they find it hard to remember the whole of the person and the whole relationship. As a result, they may idealize what they have lost or feel overwhelmed by regret at unresolved difficulties.

People often have a sense of unfinished business when trying to come to terms with a death. You might not have had an opportunity to say goodbye as you would have liked, or to sort out disagreements. When you are depressed, you are more likely to blame yourself for past differences, perhaps questioning why things that seem of little consequence now were allowed to mean so much when the person was alive. Alternatively, there might have been quite significant differences between you that still seem important. You might realize that the efforts you each made to overcome these differences fell short in some way.

The range and intensity of the emotions involved in mourning can be very difficult to navigate. These feelings may mirror important features of the lost relationship, such as irritation or disappointment when a difficult relationship ends. When some feelings are much more prominent than others they can create a skewed impression of the relationship as a whole and may provoke feelings of guilt and shame. It's traditional to frown on 'speaking ill of the dead', but this prohibition fails to acknowledge the many and varied experiences in our living relationships. The difficult feelings you may have had about the relationship do not simply disappear after death, and if you try to banish them this can itself cause problems. Many people who experience depression following bereavement use a lot of their already limited energy in trying to ignore or deny difficult feelings that say something important about the relationship they have lost.

Anger is a common but often unexpected feeling after bereavement. Feeling angry does not necessarily indicate that there were problems in the relationship – you might feel angry at having been abandoned, or at having been left to sort out problems that have emerged since the death. This might have been exactly how you would have felt had the person still been alive but left you to face these difficulties for some other reason. Such feelings may change with time, but they are less likely to do so if you feel you are unable to name and acknowledge them. Under these circumstances, they are more likely to feed into the depression you are already feeling.

Other feelings may reflect genuinely unresolved difficulties that were part of the relationship. Many relationships fall short of what we hope for or expect, and disappointing or painful relationships can be much more difficult to mourn than happy and satisfying ones. It can be very frustrating when our attempts to sort out problems or to have our hurts acknowledged come to nothing, and the resulting resentment and disappointment can intensify in mourning. This underlines the importance of building a balanced story, in which you acknowledge the difficulties as well as the pleasures, to reflect the relationship you have lost. The aim is not to repeatedly rake over painful memories for the sake of it, like scratching at a wound, but rather to clear away the debris, examine the wound carefully and attend to the injury to let it heal. It may be helpful to reread the chapter on emotions (chapter 13) to help you to think more closely about this painful emotional part of your experience.

Try not to rush over memories of more difficult times or frustrations in the relationship. Focusing *only* on what was good or what was difficult stops a balanced memory from developing and reinforces the link back to depression. You may have spoken to people in your life about difficult times in the relationship when they were happening; if so, you may find it useful to speak to them again now. They can help you to remember the challenges that came with the relationship and also how you found ways through those challenges to keep the relationship going.

Exercise 18.6: Remembering difficulties in the relationship

- Were there difficulties in the relationship?
- Were those difficulties something you could talk about and try to sort out, or were they ignored?
- Was there anything that you couldn't sort out that feeds into your depressed feelings now?

Niall: remembering difficulties in a marriage

Niall was reluctant to speak ill of his wife, as he saw it. They had been married for thirty years and had three daughters. After she died, he initially spoke only about how good a woman his wife had been and how she had always thought of other people. It took some time for Niall to be able to mention how anxious his wife had been and how reluctant she had been for him to spend time in any other company. Niall had been a sociable character and was interested in other people and their stories, but strangers made his wife uncomfortable and she would complain and criticize if he talked to someone she did not know. Over the years Niall did less and less outside of their home, until in the final years of their life together they saw hardly anyone other than each other and their daughters. Niall felt guilty both when he recalled how much he had resented the way he felt limited by his wife and when he experienced relief at now having the freedom to act in a way that he wanted.

Sometimes looking at the lost relationship in detail can reveal opportunities that are available now in a way that they weren't in the past. It is not uncommon to have to make compromises in relationships, as Niall did above. Sometimes we give up things quite willingly, recognizing such give and take as a routine part of being in a relationship; in other cases it might be a difficult sacrifice. Recognizing that these constraints no longer apply can open up opportunities to spend our time in new ways, e.g. taking up a hobby we didn't have time for in the past, or spending more time with friends or family we didn't see very often.

Exercise 18.7: *Thinking about new opportunities*

- What opportunities are available to you now that were not available during the relationship?
- Discuss this question with your IPT team and write the possibilities you identify in your notebook.
- Would taking up any of these opportunities help in your recovery?

Diane: recognizing new possibilities

Diane's daughter was severely disabled from birth. She required constant care, and Diane hadn't felt able to trust anyone else to look after her. As a consequence, Diane had almost entirely given up her social life. She had joined in on family events, but had not been out with her friends or with her husband since her daughter's birth. Immediately after her daughter died, many of Diane's friends offered their support and company to help to see her through. She spent more time with a number of these friends than she had done in all the years of her daughter's life. As the acute pain of her loss started to ease, Diane began to take pleasure in their company and was able to enjoy not having to rush home or constantly having to listen for her daughter and so only giving a fraction of her attention to the person she was with. Diane felt these relationships develop and found a balance that had been beyond her reach when her daughter was her chosen priority.

Remembering the time around the death

One feature of all bereavement stories is the passage covering the time around the death. The details will be different in each person's story, including who was affected by the death, how sudden or predictable the death seemed, and what opportunity there was to say goodbye. The way in which someone dies can have a significant impact on how we grieve and how we recover and on the difficulties we face afterwards, and can increase the likelihood of developing depression.

An anticipated death, perhaps after an illness, might provoke a mix of sadness and relief that the person's suffering has ended, or it could be overshadowed by distressing memories of the person's deteriorating health. An unexpected death may leave a deep sense of shock and confusion because there was so little warning or time to prepare. Shock and confusion can also arise even when the death was anticipated, for example, when family members take time to rest and the person dies in the short time they are away. Reluctance to accept the possibility of death can prevent us from preparing for it, and so we may experience the event as if there had been no warning. Death following an accident may trigger anxious feelings about the fragility of life and anger that the accident was not avoided.

Death in violent circumstances is shocking and is likely to provoke fear and anger against those who carried out the violence. When the pain of loss we feel is the result of someone else's actions we tend to experience more and stronger symptoms, which create a further challenge for mourning. An example of this is suicide, which is painful and complicated for those left behind, especially if you were involved in discovering the suicide. The conflicting feelings of sadness, anger, self-blame, shame and abandonment, the search for unattainable answers, stigma and the risk of negative reactions from other people all increase the risk of depression under these circumstances. Having supportive friends and family has been repeatedly shown to assist mourning following a suicide.

For some people the absence of a clear story, because details are missing or memories are avoided, keeps them trapped in an unproductive loop of mourning, unable to fill the gaps and thereby to make sense of their loss.

Ellen: stuck in uncertainty

Ellen's friend died when she took too much pain-relief medication. Ellen believed that her friend had deliberately ended her life following a period of ill-health. Others insisted that it had been an accident and would not accept Ellen's suggestion. No one had witnessed her friend's death and so Ellen had no means of resolving the question of exactly how it came about. She felt increasingly isolated in her grief as she felt she was mourning something that other people were not. She found it very difficult to move past her constant questions about the death and to deal with the distress that the uncertainty caused her, and she gradually became depressed herself.

Exercise 18.8: Thinking about the time of death

Think back to the time leading up to and surrounding the death in as much detail as you can. This might be a short period of time, if the death was sudden, or it might stretch over weeks or months, if there was a long illness. Describe the time around the funeral and the days that followed when formal ceremonies were replaced by daily life. This may have been a particularly distressing time for you, and so it is important to use the support you have from your IPT team as you piece together the memories in detail.

•   How did the person die?

- Were you present? If not, how did you hear of the death?
- How did you react to news of the death?
- What happened in the days following the death?
- Was there a funeral service and did you attend?
- Is there somewhere you can go to remember the person, e.g. a grave or memorial? Have you gone there?
- Does the way the person died make it more difficult for you to mourn?

Gradually build up the detail of this part of your story by considering the events from different angles. The set of questions above prompted you to think about the events as they happened. Now think back over the same events, but this time focus on how you were feeling.

- How did you feel when you first heard of the death?
- How did you feel at the funeral?
- How did you feel in the days and weeks that followed?
- Have any feelings surprised or upset you, e.g. anger, blame or others?
- When were you first aware of feeling depressed?

The story around the death may involve a number of people, including you, the person who died, the other people who are mourning and the network of people who might help. As you work through the steps of your own story, pay attention to who else features in the story and what contribution they made.

- Was the person who died prepared for their death?
- How did other people respond to the death?
- Did you have support around the time of the death?
- Did you support other people?
- What has happened to the support you give and receive as time has passed?
- Did disagreements develop among mourners after the death?
- Were you involved in any disagreements?
- How do you feel about the people around you now?

This stage in the story raises questions about 'what happens next' for many people. Some will believe that death is final, while others will believe in some form of afterlife. Many more will feel that they simply don't know. Facing a significant bereavement can focus your faith or cause a loss of faith, or might mean you are caught between different belief systems at the same time, such as when parents offer an explanation of heaven and eternal life to their children that they do not believe themselves. The rituals that surround death may have brought you into contact with religious organizations or belief systems that were unfamiliar to you or, conversely, are central to your understanding of what this event means.

Exercise 18.9: Beliefs about death

Think about how your own beliefs about death, and those of the person who died, have shaped your experience. Discuss this with your IPT team.

- How have your beliefs about what happens after death influenced your experience of bereavement?
- Have your beliefs changed or been challenged by this bereavement?
- Do the people close to you share your beliefs or have they been a point of disagreement?
- Do you hold similar beliefs to the person who died?
- Was the funeral a religious ceremony?
- Have you sought support from a faith group?
- Whom can you talk to about what you believe happens next?

Use your IPT team to gradually develop a more detailed story covering the time around the death. Ask them about their own memories of that time. Developing this story will help you to grieve by integrating a very painful time into your bigger story. Try to continue to trace the story beyond the time of the death into the weeks and months that followed, bringing you up to the present. Pay particular attention to how other people have been involved and any opportunities to involve people who are in your life now.

Developing existing and new relationships

One consequence of focusing on the person who has died is that it can be more difficult to give your attention to the people who are still in your life. The commitment required to remember the person you have lost can limit the emotional energy you have left for others. Your friends and family might have been understanding at first and accepted seeing less of you as part of the grieving process. However, as other people start to pick up their routines again, you might have started to feel more alone and out of sync with the people around you.

People vary in how their response to bereavement changes over time, and this can be particularly difficult when you are depressed. Other people might have appeared to adjust more quickly than you, and it may be difficult to imagine that they would still understand or be sympathetic to your distress. Or you may feel reluctant to lean on other people who are also mourning, and your guilty feelings may get in the way of your receiving the support you need. The withdrawal that is very common after bereavement can become the norm, especially when depression dampens any motivation for or interest in once-enjoyable activities or company. Many depressed people describe feeling irritable with the people around them, who serve as a reminder of the one who is not there, and may resent them for carrying on with life when their loved one cannot. It is not difficult to see how the process of mourning can stall if you become isolated in this way, and how your current relationships can start to appear increasingly out of reach.

Research has shown that supportive contact with other people increases well-being just as less supportive contact increases depression. Your recovery from depression, therefore, will involve more supportive or pleasurable contact with other people. You have already been working on this with your IPT team: by sharing your memories and involving them in your efforts to adjust, you have built up support in the here and now. Next, try gradually extending that contact to include other people.

You have already spent some time thinking about the people who remain in your life while working on your interpersonal inventory (chapter 9) and exercise 18.4. Recovering from depression involves making the most of the opportunities these relationships provide for you. Your pleasure in friends and family might only come in brief flashes at the moment, but it is important to notice those flashes: however fleeting they seem, those brief periods of enjoyment and pleasure are the building blocks of your recovery.

Often, re-establishing our routines with other people involves doing the things we used to do *before* we feel like doing them. The company and activities you used to enjoy aren't necessarily less enjoyable now; it's just that it is harder for you to feel the enjoyment when you are depressed. Picking up simple and familiar routines with other people creates small opportunities to start enjoying those activities and people again. It is often easier to start with familiar routines, such as hobbies you used to enjoy or a weekend catch-up with family or friends, and to build up gradually from there. This is more difficult when you are depressed, so don't force yourself to do things at length, but instead build in small opportunities increasingly regularly.

Exercise 18.10: Doing things and seeing people again

- What hobbies could you pick up again?
- Who could do this with you?
- Plan to do one thing each week that you used to enjoy. Gradually add one extra thing each week, however small, to build up to a pleasurable activity each day.
- Ask your IPT team to help you to think of things you might enjoy doing again and invite them to do them with you.

Recovery from depression is not about feeling happy all of the time. That is not the way we live life, and it would be exhausting to try. Happiness and pleasure are passing feelings, just as sadness usually is. A healthy life involves a whole range of feelings and being able to move between one feeling and another without getting stuck. In depression, your emotional experience is limited and it is more difficult to change how you feel. Seeking out pleasurable activities and company will help you to rediscover lost experiences and put you back in control of how you feel.

As your routine builds up, it can offer clues about new relationships you may need to develop. Some of the things you want or need might be available in your existing relationships, and so it makes sense to start by looking to them. However, bereavement might create gaps in your life that will need new relationships to fill them, for example with companions who can share your interests or someone to provide practical assistance with things you did not learn to do yourself in the past. Bereavement may be the first in a series of changes, with a ripple effect across other areas of your life. For example, you may have lost your financial security and had to move home and make new relationships with new neighbours or at your children's new school. It can feel very unsettling when a series of unwanted changes follow one after the other. Using the support that is available in your existing relationships can help you to bridge the gap between old and new routines and to explore the possibilities in the life you now face. If your bereavement has triggered a number of subsequent changes you might find it useful to read the chapter on role transition (chapter 14), which overlaps closely with this process.

Some of your existing relationships might also change as people are thrown together in new ways as a result of the death. You may need to reassess certain relationships and consider unexpected opportunities. Some opportunities may be welcome, such as having time for people you may have seen less often in the past; others might cause a dilemma, such as the challenge facing siblings who don't get on and, having relied on their mum to keep them up to date with each other's lives before she died, now have to decide whether to do that themselves. These changes in relationships may generate unexpected disagreements and arguments. Chapter 16 will help you to work through any unexpected conflicts in a constructive way.

Each of these possibilities highlights the importance of thinking about the people around you. Just as you have paid very close attention to the lost relationship, now pay close attention to your remaining relationships. It might be necessary to sort through the problems that bubble up when everyone is upset in order to gradually build up the relationships that will serve and support you during and beyond your loss.

Finally, remember to rate your symptoms of depression each week (see appendix 1). Think about how learning to live with your loss influences your symptoms and identify two or three examples when symptoms and difficulties related to the loss overlap to think about in more detail each week (see appendix 3). Talk to your IPT team about these difficulties and use the suggestions in this chapter to help you to manage the difficulties more effectively.

Summary

- Mourning is a process, not an event. The process can be restarted if it has been delayed or stalled.
- Remembering the relationship you have lost is an important part of mourning and recovery.
- A balanced memory of someone does not idealize or criticize the relationship but remembers it as a whole.
- Our responses to our relationships are as complex and contradictory in death as they are in life.
- Start with the memories you are drawn to and work out from there.

- Recalling the difficulties and uncertainties in relationships is as important as remembering the good and certain things.
- Tapping into other people's stores of memories will open up your own and build a bridge between past and present.
- The person you have lost cannot be replaced, but you may be able to recreate some of the ways you related to each other and supported each other in other relationships.

Chapter 19

Jean's story

Jean described feeling depressed after her husband Bill died, but managed to lift herself out of her depression for brief periods by keeping active, taking on new jobs or devoting her time to her grandchildren. As time passed she found each new project more tiring and less effective at holding back the depression that never felt very far away. When she could not keep herself occupied, she felt the full weight of depression descend once again. While from the outside it seemed quite clear that her current distress went back to her husband's death, she had lost sight of the connection. She saw other people move on after similar losses and thought that because she had felt better at some times during the three years since her bereavement, something else must be behind her persistent distress.

Jean's struggle was eventually revealed when she had an argument with her daughter. Jean had come to rely on her time with her grandchildren as the only enjoyable experience in her week. She had not explained to her daughter how important this was to her, and in fact hoped that her pleasure on these occasions would conceal how bad she felt the rest of the time. When her daughter unexpectedly announced that the family was going away on holiday, Jean felt panicked and devastated. She could not imagine coping for two weeks without the children and reacted angrily to the news. Jean's daughter was surprised by her mother's response and an angry argument developed, after which Jean returned home and went to bed. She did not get up again until three days later, when her daughter visited and found her in her dressing-gown in the middle of the day. At this point Jean told her daughter how much she was struggling and agreed she needed more help.

When Jean started to tell her story, she set the scene by saying it had all started when Bill died, but did not appear to pick up on her own clue and described feeling confused and embarrassed by how she felt and how she had behaved. She was very self-critical and did not understand the role depression played in her story. She thought she should simply pull herself together, but said she had tried this many times without success and now did not know what else to do.

Jean was carefully guided through all of the symptoms of depression by her IPT therapist, and she recognized many of them. She felt down most of the time, the only exception being when she saw her grandchildren. She said they were her only interest, but although they gave her pleasure she also found them very tiring, so could only manage an hour or two in their company at a time. At other times she stayed at home, often not getting out of bed or dressed unless she was expecting a visitor. Although she stayed in bed a lot of the time she did not sleep well, lying awake for hours at night and then napping on and off during the day. She had given up cooking for herself because she did not see the point of cooking for one, and she generally felt sluggish and found it difficult to get going. Jean said she did little to occupy her time; she no longer watched television or read magazines because she could not focus on anything and quickly lost the thread of the story she was watching or reading, which she found frustrating. Jean often thought about dying but had no plans to hurt herself and could not imagine doing so. She had few friends outside the family, having spent most of her adult life in the company of her husband's family, whom she had seen only very occasionally since Bill's death.

When depression was described as an illness, Jean said she was relieved to have a way of explaining all that was troubling her because she felt like she was falling apart. She had difficulty thinking of ways in which she could give herself a break, but did agree that it would be useful to talk to her daughter about being depressed.

When Jean started to draw her timeline with her therapist's help, she began with her husband's death three years earlier. She had been depressed twice before, following the birth of each of her children, but had not received treatment and her symptoms had gradually improved over time. Jean said this was one of the reasons she found her current situation so confusing, because despite her efforts she had not been able to pick her life up again as she had done in the past.

Her husband had died of cancer one month after he had been diagnosed and Jean described it as a terrible shock. She said that although she had known about the diagnosis, Bill had not wanted to talk about it, and she felt as if she had leapt from diagnosis to death in a single step. She described feeling like a child and not understanding what was going on. She attended the funeral in a daze and could not believe he was really gone. She said she felt as if she were just waiting for him to walk back through the door. She said she found this very difficult to understand, because while she knew he was dead it did not feel as though that were true.

In the months that followed her husband's death Jean had taken a job in a local shop. She had retired from her job in a local factory just before Bill died, as both had just reached retirement age, but she did not see the point of retirement now he was no longer there to share it with her. She said the job lifted her mood for a while and she enjoyed the company, but she found the hours too long and had to give it up after a few months. When she no longer had a routine, her mood sank further, she found it difficult to motivate herself and her sleep remained very poor. Given her difficulty sleeping, she took a part-time job in which she was always on the night shift, hoping that this might make not sleeping seem less of a problem. Although she managed the shifts, she quickly became very isolated outside of work because her day had been turned on its head. When her daughter had her second baby, Jean decided to give up the job because she already missed seeing her first grandchild and did not want to miss out on the new baby.

Jean enjoyed her time with her family but felt she had nothing else in her life and went back to alternating between afternoons with her grandchildren and mornings and evenings on her own, when she would do very little and just wait for time to pass.

Jean's timeline

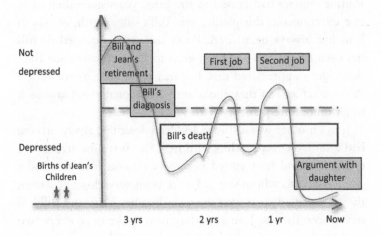

Jean's interpersonal inventory revealed a small number of close family relationships but few relationships beyond this circle. Jean was very close to her daughter, son-in-law and two grandchildren, who lived near to her. She saw them three or four times each week and often looked after her grandchildren. She also had a son, but he and his wife lived at the other end of the country and although they spoke on the telephone from time to time they didn't see each other very often. Jean had not spoken to her children about how she felt, and she said she was ashamed that she did not know how they felt about their father's death.

During her marriage Jean had spent most of her time with Bill's family and had seen little of her own. Bill preferred it this way as he did not get on with Jean's family. Jean said that she had never particularly liked her husband's family, although she had never said this while he was alive, and she had not been keen to keep in touch with them following his death, so most routine contact had ceased in the three years since then. The one exception in this picture was Bill's sister Ruth, of whom Jean had always been fond. Ruth had never married or had her own family and had been keen to support Jean since Bill's death. Jean appreciated this, but had done little to encourage the contact and so they spoke only occasionally and saw each other quite infrequently.

Jean's mother was still alive and Jean described always having had a difficult relationship with her. She was now living in a care home and Jean visited her every month. Jean also had a sister, Mary, to whom she had once been very close; however, they had drifted apart over the years because Mary and Bill had never been friends. Jean and Mary now spoke once every two or three weeks and visited their mother together.

Jean's interpersonal inventory

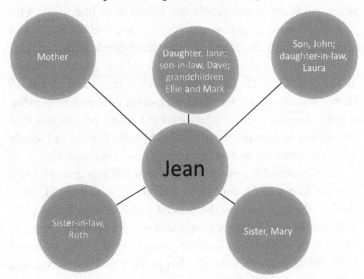

After she had gathered her story together, Jean agreed that the main focus was Bill's death, and her difficulty in accepting that he was gone and finding a way to build a life for herself now. Jean had given up a number of relationships to focus on her family and had made a number of compromises to fit in with Bill's expectations. She had had very little opportunity to prepare for such a significant loss, and her social and emotional withdrawal meant that she had had almost no support in coming to terms with the change in her life, with the result that she was stuck in a state of incomplete mourning and depression.

Jean set herself some realistic goals. The short-term goals were to get up and dressed by 9 a.m. each day, whether or not she was going out or expecting a visitor, and to reduce how often she went back to bed for a nap during the day. She also planned to continue to see her grandchildren regularly, and to speak to or see someone else each week. She identified her sister and Ruth as the people she would most like to see. Her first medium-term goal was to visit her son and his family and to talk to Ruth about going on a short break with her. Her second medium-term goal was to be able to ask her children about how they felt about their father's death, and to talk to them about how she felt. Her long-term goal was to develop a more flexible routine that involved more people and that helped her to manage those times when she felt sad and lonely without retreating to bed and hiding from everyone else.

Jean described a sense of disbelief that Bill was gone and said she felt like a child, unable to take in the information, even though she had been to the funeral and had visited his grave. She said she could not see how she could get on with a new life because she still felt as if he were going to walk in the door, and if he did and saw that she was happy he would be very angry with her. Jean said that saying this out loud made her realize that it wasn't going to happen, but she still didn't know how to get past the feeling. Jean was encouraged to talk about her relationship with Bill to clarify which parts of the relationship were so difficult to let go.

Jean's initial thoughts tended to focus on the things she was going to miss without Bill. She could not imagine what she would do without his company. They had been married for thirty years and had brought up a family together. Jean said they had never had much money and it had often been difficult to make ends meet. They had looked forward for years to their retirement, which Jean thought would be an opportunity for them to relax and spend more time together, with fewer money worries, and so it felt even more of a blow that Bill had died just as they were reaching that time in their lives.

Jean said that Bill had had relatively little to do with the children's care when they were growing up. She explained that they came from a generation in which the man and the woman had their own jobs to do and neither interfered with the other. She described this as an unspoken agreement and just how things were done. As she described this, Jean recalled an example from early in their married life when she had miscalculated some of the household bills and they were unable to pay their rent at the end of the month. Jean described fretting about this for days and not being able to tell Bill because it was her job to manage the bills and she was afraid he would be angry with her for making a mistake. After days of worry she eventually had to tell him, and although he was not angry with her he told her she would have to ask her parents for a loan to cover the rent. Jean was embarrassed to do this, but felt she had no choice and the matter was never discussed again. She said this was quite typical of how they managed problems.

As she recounted this story, she and her therapist noted that this was very similar to what had happened when Bill died. Jean recalled that he had been very frightened by his diagnosis and did not want to speak about it. He did not mention it again until he had to be taken into hospital a month later, and two days later he died. Jean said she felt she had been left on her own to cope with his death, just as she had been with so many other things in their life, and this contributed to how she felt now. Jean said she felt embarrassed when she looked back to the days in the hospital when she could now see that the nurses were trying to tell her how ill her husband was and that she should take the opportunity to say goodbye to him. However, as Bill still did not want to talk about it, Jean did not pick up on their prompts, and his death came as a terrible shock. Jean had gone home after the end of visiting time that night, and had received the call at home to tell her Bill had died. Jean's son returned to the hospital and took charge of the initial arrangements, and Jean did not see Bill again until he was in the funeral home. Jean and her therapist talked about how difficult it had been for Jean and her husband to work together when difficulties came up, and how often Jean had been forced to manage on her own, just as she had tried to do after Bill's death. Not being with him when he died made it all the more difficult for Jean to accept such a sudden loss.

Jean had enjoyed cooking, and she and Bill would eat together every evening. They had a familiar routine in which Jean would prepare the meal and Bill would wash up, and it was the time of day when they would chat the most. After Bill died Jean lost interest in cooking and relied on snacks throughout the day to keep her going. She said it felt pointless to make all the effort to prepare a meal for one, and eating alone just reminded her that her husband was gone. Her poor diet left her feeling tired and sluggish, and this made it even more difficult for her to motivate herself. When Jean talked to her daughter about what was happening, she invited Jean to have dinner with her once a week. Jean enjoyed the company and having a proper meal, and made a return invitation as a way to get back into a habit she had lost. She also invited someone else to have dinner with her on one other night every couple of weeks – often Ruth or Mary – and gradually her interest and motivation improved, and mealtimes became something to enjoy again rather than a reminder of what she had lost. Jean said she initially resented being encouraged to be around other people when she did not want to be, but gradually started to appreciate and look forward to the company.

Jean said that after Bill died she had found it very difficult to talk about him or hear his name mentioned without becoming upset. Her son and daughter were very aware of their mother's distress and so gradually stopped talking about their father in front of her to avoid upsetting her. However, Jean found that she also missed hearing Bill being mentioned and feared he was going to be forgotten. She started to resent other people for appearing to move on so easily when she could not. Looking back, she realized that neither she nor her children could win in this situation, and that the only way to move forward was to explain to them what she was trying to do and think about how to use the support she knew they would offer.

Jean continued to hesitate about talking directly to her children about Bill. She felt guilty that she didn't know how they felt about their own loss, and believed that she had let them down. She was also concerned about what they might say. Jean thought that her daughter would be understanding, but was worried about her son, who had had a more difficult relationship with his father. When they had spoken about Bill in the months after his death her son had been critical of his father, and Jean had said she could not bear to listen to what he had to say. They had not spoken for weeks after that, and when they picked up contact again they both avoided the subject.

As it became clear how much of Jean's story involved avoiding talking about difficulties and problems, she was encouraged to talk about aspects of her relationship with her husband that she had found hard to think back on. Jean became very tearful when she described her husband's previously undisclosed binge drinking, which she had found very difficult to cope with. She said this had happened for much of their married life and had added to the burden of running a household on very little money. Towards the end of his life, Jean discovered that her husband had been holding back money to allow him to go drinking with his friends. She had been so hurt by this that she had considered leaving him, and had gone as far as looking into renting another place to live. When she told her husband of her plans he became very apologetic and asked her to stay. Jean said that their relationship improved in the months that followed and he drank far less often, but then he was diagnosed with cancer and his death followed very swiftly. Jean said it had all happened so quickly that she did not feel she had been able to keep up with all the feelings this provoked. She said it was as if, just after getting him back, she had lost him all over again, and now there was nothing she could do.

Jean felt very guilty that she sometimes felt angry with her husband for not fighting harder to stay with her, as she believed she would have done for him. Jean was aware that the thought was illogical, because Bill had died of a very aggressive form of cancer and had had no choice about how long he survived, but she still felt angry. Denying this feeling used up a lot of Jean's energy and stopped her from being able to mourn her loss. This feeling of anger also provided clues about some of her feelings towards her husband during their life together. Some of her most difficult times had revolved around Jean's feeling that he was putting his friends before his family and leaving her to struggle with managing their children and household on very little income. His sudden death seemed like another example of his leaving her to manage on her own, and in time she recognized that what she was feeling now related to many unspoken feelings she had carried throughout their marriage. Jean felt that the timing of Bill's death made all this even more difficult to manage. In the months before his death she had finally managed to tell him how unhappy she felt about his behaviour and had been aware that he had made a conscious change. The future she had hoped for seemed at last to be within reach – only to be snatched away again. To ignore the uncomfortable mix of feelings surrounding Bill's death would have been to drop a central thread that held Jean's story together and made sense of her continuing battle to come to terms with her loss.

Jean did not want to talk with her daughter about the difficulties she had had with Bill when he was drinking. As a mother, she wanted to protect her daughter and her view of her father; and she also wanted to retain some privacy around personal details that had not been discussed with her children while her husband was alive. She was, however, aware that she needed to talk to someone about some of the difficult memories she had uncovered because otherwise they could pull her mood down and leave her still feeling guilty and frustrated. Jean decided to speak to her sister, who had previously confided in her about difficulties in her own marriage.

Jean had been very close to her sister when they were growing up but had seen much less of her after she married as Mary and Bill did not get on very well. By the time Bill died, Jean and Mary were only seeing each other when they visited their mother together. Mary offered her sister practical support and comfort in the early stages of her grief, but as time passed and Jean became more depressed and less motivated to do anything outside the home, they drifted apart again. Now Jean remembered how close they had once been and how they had enjoyed many of the same interests, e.g. craftwork and hillwalking. She realized she had let both activities slide as she had become preoccupied with her close family life and because they did not interest her husband. Mary was delighted when Jean suggested they try going on some of their old walks together, and both women found that it was much easier to talk to each other when they were occupied in doing something they enjoyed, so that emotional conversations could blend into the other routines they were building up together.

Jean felt less concerned about the risk of undermining her husband's memory in her sister's eyes and so felt able to talk more freely about her experience of the difficulties in the marriage. Talking to her sister and hearing about Mary's similar experiences helped Jean to recognize that many of the problems she had experienced were very common in married life. She was also able to balance the memories of very difficult times with memories of working out their difficulties and moving on to more settled periods when she had felt happier in the relationship again. She felt less angry with her husband and remembered the efforts he made to change as well as the times he fell into old habits, and this reminded Jean of why she had stayed with him rather than giving up on the marriage.

Jean had found it more difficult to talk to her son after Bill's death because he had spoken so directly about his father's drinking. She realized that she had been avoiding her son because she could not face him criticizing Bill. As she got used to talking with Mary about both the good and the difficult times in the marriage, Jean felt more confident about being able to speak with her son. She still worried that she would get upset, but felt more able to manage this if it happened. Several weeks after starting therapy, Jean decided to call her son and explain the work she had been doing. She explained how upsetting she had found it when he became angry at his father, but said she no longer wanted that to get in the way of their having a close relationship. Jean's son invited her to come and visit him and his wife, which Jean agreed to do for the first time in four years.

Jean was both nervous and excited about the trip. To help her to prepare for it, she talked with her daughter about how she was feeling. This allowed them to discuss her daughter's reaction to her father's death for the first time. Jean was relieved to hear how well her daughter had been supported by her husband, and was reassured that even when she felt upset she could continue talking to her daughter and the upset feelings would pass. This conversation helped to relieve the guilt Jean felt about having been unavailable to her daughter in her grief.

Jean stayed with her son for a week, and they managed to speak about Bill without arguing. The conversation then moved on and focused on her life now, and her son encouraged her to make plans for her future. In response to this encouragement, Jean went on a day trip on her own at the end of the week. She felt immensely pleased with herself for doing this, and saw that some of the plans she and Bill had made for things to do together, which she thought had been completely lost, could be put into action after all if she thought about them in a different way.

Jean had hoped to travel around the country more with her husband when they retired, and had assumed she would have to give up this plan after he died because she had never gone on holiday with anyone else and hadn't wanted to travel alone. Jean told Ruth about the plans she and Bill had had and how disappointed she was to see them come to nothing. Ruth suggested that they try going on holiday together to see if some of the plans could be saved. A short weekend trip proved very enjoyable and Jean realized that her sister-in-law actually shared more of her interests than her husband had done. She was still very sad not to share the trips with Bill, but happy to have found another way to carry out her own plans.

By the end of her time in therapy Jean was no longer depressed. She continued to feel sad at times, but could tolerate those feelings and they did not disrupt her daily routines. Her sleep had improved considerably and she had joined a craft group at her local community centre, which extended her regular routine beyond the family circle. In fact, she said she was glad the therapy was coming to an end because the appointments clashed with another group she wanted to join, and that was how she would prefer to use the time. She spoke openly to her daughter, Mary and Ruth about the therapy ending, and they discussed how they would maintain the routines they had built up. Jean had slowly become more expert at monitoring her depression and had learned how to tune into her day-to-day feelings rather than seeing every day as the same. She shared information about depression with her daughter and Mary, and they made clear plans about what to do, including going back to Jean's GP if the same pattern of symptoms and withdrawal returned in the future.

Chapter 20

Theme four: isolation

Solitude is fine but you need someone to tell that solitude is fine.

HONORÉ DE BALZAC, WRITER

When solitude becomes loneliness

Being alone is neither good nor bad. It might be necessary at times, to do the things that are important, and quiet time is often welcome when the demands and noises of the day are ringing in your ears. Choice is crucial to the quality of this experience. When we make a positive choice to be alone for a while it can feel like an opportunity, a break, something to be savoured. When we haven't chosen it, especially if it goes on for longer than we want, being alone can become being lonely.

Most people feel lonely at some time in their life. It is a common consequence of change or loss, when there is a delay between changes in your situation and you and the people around you adjusting to catch up – for example, when you change job and it takes time to get to know your new colleagues. On other occasions everything else may remain steady, yet you lose your connection with the people you are close to, for reasons that may be unclear, such as drifting away from a once-close group of friends. As with other feelings, loneliness generally passes with time and as other people come into your life and routines. In some situations, though, the experience may go on for longer, suggesting that there may be a gap between what your relationships offer you and what you need. When this happens, you may become isolated – which is where the fourth focal area of IPT comes in.

Recurrent relationship difficulties

Repeated problems in starting relationships or keeping them going lie at the heart of isolation. These relationship difficulties tend not to be fleeting or related to specific situations, as might have been the case when we looked at changing roles, managing conflict or adjusting after bereavement. On the contrary, difficulties related to loneliness and isolation may have been a fairly constant theme across most of your life. These problems are likely to have been evident when you completed your interpersonal inventory (chapter 9) – indeed, you may have found that a difficult task to complete.

Some people may have developed only a few relationships. This might be because they find meeting people difficult, feel wary of getting close to other people or are unsure how to move from acquaintance to friendship. Perhaps they feel shy around other people or anxious about social situations; perhaps they are reluctant to trust other people owing to difficult past experiences; or it may be that long-term depression has repeatedly undermined their enthusiasm for relationships.

In contrast, some people are able to start relationships, but regularly find them unsatisfactory in some way. This might be because they do not last, creating a rapid turnover of relationships, or because they do not develop beyond initial acquaintance, so that a deeply felt connection is never established.

Alternatively, you might have established relationships but still feel isolated within them, owing to problems managing disagreements or achieving intimacy, or feeling that you are being taken advantage of. These characteristic patterns might undermine a number of relationships and create a vulnerability to depression because they are so difficult to break out of.

This brief overview illustrates how varied the difficulties can be when isolation and loneliness are significant issues in your depression. This can be difficult to grasp because, unlike the other themes we have discussed, which relate to specific events – changing role (chapter 14), managing conflict (chapter 16), and coping with loss and grief (chapter 18), this area often involves examining the *absence* of events. The main challenges are to try to identify the kinds of difficulty that have repeatedly prevented you from making or continuing satisfying relationships, and to understand how these difficulties relate to your depression.

Isolation is widely recognized as a challenging theme to address. A basic assumption behind IPT's interpersonal approach to managing depression is that recovery will be the result of a team effort. When you are isolated, however, establishing a small supportive team might be more appropriately seen as a goal rather than a starting place. This can make a self-help approach to this area particularly problematic, because not having a team to support you may emphasize your isolation in a way that feels unhelpful.

However, if this applies to you, don't be disheartened! There are a number of ways in which you can use this chapter constructively, including:

- working with an IPT therapist, who can provide regular support;
- using the ideas in this chapter in combination with the

ideas in another chapter to focus on a specific relationship difficulty that is currently troubling you – changing role (chapter 14), managing conflict (chapter 16), or coping with loss and grief (chapter 18);

- improving the quality of a small number of existing relationships;
- using these ideas to prepare you to join an organized source of support, such as a course of therapy or a relationship skills group.

Janine

Janine was twenty-four years old and had been depressed for over five years. She found it very difficult to go out and spent most of her time alone in her bedroom in her parents' house. She had never had a job and the only people she had direct contact with were her immediate family. Janine often felt very bored and lonely and tended to comfort eat to distract herself. As a result she had gained a significant amount of weight and she found that this trapped her in her bedroom even more. She felt ashamed at the prospect of meeting people who knew her and would see the physical change in her appearance and discover she had been doing nothing for so long.

One of the few people Janine saw other than her parents was her cousin, who would drop in and chat to Janine every couple of weeks. When her cousin announced that she had been offered a new job that involved her moving away, Janine's mood dropped and she felt panicked that she would have even less contact with the world beyond her bedroom walls. Although Janine felt unable to say this directly to her cousin, her distress was evident, and with her cousin's and mother's support and encouragement she agreed to speak to her GP about her mood and difficulty going out. Janine's GP recommended that she talk to someone, and referred her to an IPT therapist. Janine felt very wary of talking to someone she didn't know, but also saw that there was little prospect of her life improving unless she took a risk and tried to understand and change the day-to-day difficulties that had come to constrain her life so much.

Over the weeks of meetings with an IPT therapist, Janine discussed her difficulties and started to understand the patterns at work in her life and how they blocked almost all opportunities for relationships, even those with her immediate family. As a result of these conversations Janine started to make small but manageable changes in her daily routine, including gradually reducing the amount of time she spent in her bedroom and spending more time with her family in the shared spaces of her home. By the end of therapy Janine had a much clearer idea of the specific difficulties that had occurred in past relationships, often leaving her feeling on the outside and unwanted, and that were being repeated in a more extreme way in the patterns that played out now. By the end of sixteen weeks of therapy her depression had lifted sufficiently to allow her to join support groups, which would provide training in assertiveness skills and developing more self-confidence.

Given that this is such a broad area of difficulty, simply deciding where to start can feel a daunting prospect. It can sometimes be easier to tackle general difficulties by referring to a specific example. If something has happened which has contributed to making relationships more difficult recently, e.g. a change in role, a conflict with someone, or a bereavement, you could use the ideas in this chapter to supplement whichever of the other chapters is relevant to your situation (chapter 14 for role change; chapter 16 for conflict; chapter 18 for bereavement). If your difficulty does not relate to any specific event, this chapter will serve as your main guide, but you can still use the ideas from the other focal areas if they overlap with the patterns of difficulty you identify when you look at your current and past relationships in more detail.

Passing and pervasive loneliness

In the previous chapters we have seen many examples of loneliness. Paul (chapter 15) felt lonely when his work relationships broke down and he found himself outside a team he'd once felt part of. Suzanna (chapter 17) felt lonely in her relationship when she and her partner silently retreated from each other, separated by their different expectations. Jean (chapter 19) felt lonely when her husband died and she could not imagine life without him, so stopped being part of the life around her. In each case, depression compounded the emotional distance between the main person in the story and the other people in their lives.

However, for Paul, Suzanna and Jean, as for most people, this isolation was reduced as their depression lifted. In each of the stories you have looked at here, the person had options and could make a choice to take up the support offered by other people. Paul was supported by his wife and his cycling club friends; Suzanna was supported by work colleagues and girlfriends; and Jean was supported by her daughter, sister and sister-in-law. When they turned to these relationships for assistance their depression diminished and they became part of a working, supportive network again. So loneliness was a temporary part of these stories, but not the driving force behind them.

The challenge of recovery from depression is very different when you do not have a network of relationships to turn to.

The same choices are not immediately available. If you typically find relationships difficult to develop or to keep going, even when there are no particular problems in your life, you will have less of a safety net to fall back on when problems develop. What might be generally unsatisfactory becomes obviously insufficient when more is asked of it. Even without additional specific problems, persistent loneliness and lack of support can be enough to fuel depression. Having no one to share the ups and downs of life with can itself become the problem. When that is the case, isolation and loneliness can become *a driving force* behind depression, as well as *a consequence* of it.

Background or foreground difficulty?

For some people, the prospect of being in a relationship of any kind is at the heart of the problem, while for others, relationship difficulties are among a number of contributing factors. The ease people feel in their relationships varies from person to person. Some people can easily strike up a conversation with a complete stranger, while for others the very idea is terrifying. Most people are somewhere between these two positions. The greater the difficulty you generally experience in dealings with other people, the more likely it is to complicate your efforts to resolve particular difficulties.

Let's take another look at the previous examples. Before the redundancy that triggered his episode of depression, Paul had, for the most part, avoided loneliness by actively involving himself in a range of work and professional relationships. He was skilled at engaging people and could work successfully as a member of a team. At times of stress, however, he tended to rely less on these interpersonal skills and worked longer hours on his own or drank alcohol to numb feelings of tension and anxiety. Opting for more individual strategies and distancing himself from the people around him increased his vulnerability to depression at difficult times.

Jean had always been part of a family group and played her part in keeping the group together with considerable devotion. Doing so, however, had meant her giving up some of the family relationships that had been important to her and accepting less satisfying alternatives in their place. This was generally enough to keep her going, but making do in this way with an enforced network of relationships she hadn't chosen did not help Jean to develop skills in meeting her own needs; consequently, she had little back-up when she faced significant problems.

Suzanna demonstrated the clearest pattern of keeping her distance from other people. Relationships were almost always temporary for her, and she rarely developed a broad and secure base of support that could accommodate her changing needs. When she tried to make a more permanent commitment to someone else she did so in a blunt and demanding way, and experienced greater loneliness when she faced the possibility that she would not succeed. She held other relationships at a distance and came close to removing herself completely and being alone again, as she had done in the past.

Each of these people had an area of vulnerability related to their interpersonal skills and relationships. Paul backed away from the people around him when he had a problem; Jean made do with relationships she did not really enjoy and didn't push for what she really wanted; and Suzanna generally held people at a distance and left relationships behind as soon as something changed. They each managed relationships well enough when things were going well, but their vulnerabilities were revealed when problems developed. These vulnerabilities determined how successful they were in addressing their problems. This is important to hold in mind when you try to set realistic goals for yourself.

In trying to understand the impact of recurring relationship difficulties in your life, it is useful to think about how often being around other people creates difficulty for you. If we imagine a spectrum of difficulty (see the diagram below), which stretches from no difficulty at all to significant difficulty in all relationships, we have a line on which everyone will find a place. This can be used to pinpoint your default position – that is, the level of difficulty you generally experience with relationships – and how this position changes when depression or specific life events are added to the story. Towards the left-hand side of the spectrum, occasional interpersonal difficulties crop up but only in specific situations, so they don't have much impact on life generally. This might include feeling anxious when speaking in public but generally coping well with relationships. As you move further along the spectrum the difficulty is experienced more frequently and in more relationships. Feeling embarrassed and awkward in conversations with new people might be a difficulty that is evident more often, but happens only at random intervals. As you move further still along the spectrum, the difficulties become more frequent and have more impact. If it is difficult to let yourself get close to anyone else, and as a result most relationships break down quickly, this would be a repeated general difficulty, which would sit to the right of the spectrum. Each of these problems is likely to be amplified when you feel depressed.

Occasional specific difficulties	Regular specific difficulties	Repeated general difficulties	Regular serious difficulties

To help illustrate this scheme, let's see where the four people we have been thinking about would be on the spectrum.

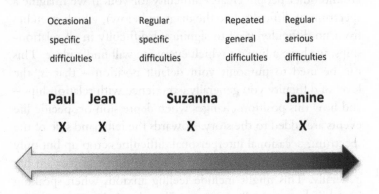

Occasional specific difficulties	Regular specific difficulties	Repeated general difficulties	Regular serious difficulties
Paul Jean		**Suzanna**	**Janine**
X X		X	X

Paul, Jean and Suzanna had all been able to develop and sustain relationships. Paul and Jean had been able to do this quite consistently and so are towards the left-hand side of the spectrum. Suzanna had a more on-and-off pattern in her relationships that had repeated through her life, so she is positioned closer to the middle of the spectrum. Janine found almost all relationships and even the prospect of relationships difficult most of the time, so she appears towards the right-hand side of the spectrum.

As Paul, Jean and Suzanna had relationships that they at least sometimes found enjoyable and supportive, it was useful for them to focus on the individual issues in their stories and to hold in mind the background interpersonal sensitivities or vulnerabilities which contributed to their problems continuing. Janine had few specific events to focus on, other than her cousin moving for work, and faced interpersonal difficulties every day, so her isolation was the central issue for her to address.

Building up your story of relationship difficulty

Think about the ways in which you find relationships difficult. For example, are there specific problems that frequently trouble you, such as not knowing what to say when you meet someone for the first time, or do you find relationships difficult in a variety of different ways that regularly interferes with day-to-day life?

Exercise 20.1: Isolation and depression: how closely are they connected?

- Copy the diagram below into your notebook and mark on the line how often you found relationships difficult *before you became depressed.*
- Then mark on the line how difficult you find relationships *now.*

Occasional specific difficulties	Regular specific difficulties	Repeated general difficulties	Regular serious difficulties

The gap between the two marks will give you a measure of how much more difficult depression has made making and holding on to relationships. A bigger gap reveals a greater impact. If your pre-depression mark already sits towards the right-hand side of the line, this suggests a sensitivity around relationships that cannot be entirely explained by depression, and which will benefit from specific and focused attention. If your pre-depression mark sits towards the left-hand side of the line, it will be useful to combine ideas from the chapters on other focal areas (chapters 14, 16 and 18) with the information that follows.

It is important to continue to monitor the links between your depression and feeling isolated. Rate your depressive symptoms each week (using the table in appendix 1) and think about whether any change in your symptoms is related to being isolated (using the table in appendix 3). Try to find two or three examples each week when symptoms and feelings of isolation overlap to think about in more detail.

There are, of course, many types of relationships, including those with family, friends, romantic partners, work colleagues, customers, casual social companions, etc. It is helpful to clarify whether all types of relationship are equally challenging for you, or if some have been easier to manage than others. Focusing on isolation doesn't mean assuming that all relationships are equally problematic, and it can be very useful to highlight the pockets of success where you do manage better that exist alongside the recurrent difficulties.

Exercise 20.2: Which relationships are easier than others?

Use the information collected in your interpersonal inventory (chapter 9) to answer the following questions. If you have an IPT team to support you, tell them about the relationships you find most difficult and those that are easier. If you do not have a team yet, write your answers in your notebook so that you can come back to them later as the support around you builds up.

- Which types of relationship do you find difficult to manage?
- Which types of relationships have you managed more successfully?

Judith

Judith worked as a care assistant for young people with profound learning disabilities. Many of the young people she worked with had limited control over their behaviour and it was a physically and emotionally challenging environment for everyone involved. Judith felt very empathic towards the young people in her care and understood how frustrated and isolated they felt. Her own experience of isolation and feeling like an outsider helped her to be understanding and respectful of other people who were facing similar types of difficulty. When Judith had an appraisal at work she was given an excellent review because her gentle approach was recognized as a considerable asset to the unit in which she worked.

Looking back over your relationships

In order to develop a clearer picture of your relationships, it is useful to develop an expanded story of the significant relationships you have been involved in during your life. This story will include both your successful and unsuccessful relationships, and we will look for clues in it about both the strengths you bring to developing relationships and the areas that need more careful attention because they repeatedly prove difficult to manage.

This process is similar to the interpersonal inventory you have already completed (see page 148), but is different in an important way: it is not limited to your current relationships, and includes important relationships from your past. By looking over the history of these relationships, you can start to identify patterns that repeat themselves and interfere with relationships starting and developing. The story of the past can help you to chart out a map for the future.

We have already seen several times that each person in a relationship makes his or her own contribution to how well it works. You may have started to think about your own patterns, or those of the people around you, and the ways in which they don't serve you as well as you would like. It will be useful to look at these difficulties more closely in order to understand the 'push and pull' of your relationships – that is, the things that draw you closer to other people and the things that tend to prevent closeness developing. The success of a relationship can be as much about the fit between two people as about the individual contributions of each person. It is just as important to think about how you select the people to be in relationship with, and how they select you, as it is to look at what happens once you have decided to build a relationship with each other.

It is quite likely that some of the difficulties you identify will overlap with the examples and themes we have looked at in the other chapters. Managing change, conflict or loss, and struggling to acknowledge and express your emotional experience and needs, account for a great deal of what happens in relationships, especially when they become difficult to manage. If you find that these themes repeatedly come up when you look at your relationship history, go back to the relevant chapter (12 for communication, 13 for emotions, 14 for change, 16 for conflict, 18 for loss) and think about how the ideas and techniques in that chapter might help you to understand what has happened in your relationships and how you might try to change this in the future.

Try to find a companion who will work through this task

with you. This might be one of your family, a friend or your IPT therapist. Thinking about relationships that have been troublesome or hurtful can be difficult, and it will be very helpful to talk about your experiences, because it will help you to see them from different points of view. This is not meant to make you feel bad about yourself or to create a long list of failings, but rather to help you to step back and start to see things from a different perspective, and to think about the ways in which you can help relationships to get started and to last.

This task might seem overwhelming at first, so let's break it down into more manageable steps. You are not trying to review every relationship you have had in your life, but rather the relationships that stand out in your mind and tell us something about your relationship style.

Each of these relationships will have its own narrative. They will have beginnings, middles and perhaps ends. It might initially seem that they have all been the same, especially if there are strongly repeating patterns, but the best clues may lie in some of the subtle differences. That is exactly what you want to find out – what happened at each stage of the relationship, which patterns repeat themselves and where they might change. By looking carefully at each step, you will develop a much better-informed picture of what happens between you and other people. It is important to try to suspend what you think you 'know' about this and to look at the evidence afresh. Deciding that other people do not like you or are not interested in you is a *conclusion* and conceals the steps that led you there. This exercise is much more about the process than the outcome.

SUCCESSFUL RELATIONSHIPS

Start with the relationships that have gone well. They do not have to have been perfect – few relationships are – and you can include short as well as longer relationships. Think about the people you have enjoyed meeting or knowing and who have made a positive impact on your life, however briefly. Try to be creative in thinking about who these people might be and think across the course of your life, from your schooldays right up to the present. The people you include might have been your family, your first friend at school, maybe a favourite teacher or helper at school, work colleagues, professionals you come into contact with, like a sympathetic doctor, and anyone else you found helpful or enjoyable company. Write them down in your notebook. These relationships might have been significant for you for a number of reasons – because you felt emotionally close, because the other person interested or inspired you, because you felt understood or that you understood the other person, because you had a common interest, because the other person was useful to know, or for any other reasons that are important to you.

Given that you have become used to relationships being problematic or disappointing, it will not be surprising if you find this task a little difficult. Depression can do a good job in persuading you how few good relationships there are to look back on and making you want to give up before you get started. However, you don't need to produce a long list. Starting with just one or two people with whom you have been able to share something will be a very good start. If more people come to mind later, you can come back and add them to your list.

If there is anyone in your life who can help you to think over your relationships it will be useful to include them in this process. Perhaps you have begun to work with an IPT therapist or team on the ideas in previous chapters. This suggestion might seem to be missing the point: if you had someone to help you, you might think, you wouldn't have chosen 'isolation' as your main focus. However, not everyone who feels isolated actually has no one to ask. Sometimes you may feel isolated because you have not imagined asking the people who could help. This might be a possibility that is revealed as you complete the exercise. Try to keep an open mind as more options become clear.

Exercise 20.3: Reviewing your good relationships

When you have a list of people to think about, start to build a timeline for each relationship. For each one, think about the questions below and write your thoughts down in your notebook or discuss them with your IPT therapist or team.

- When did the relationship start? What age were you?
- How did you meet? Did you do something to start the relationships or did the other person?
- Was it mainly a one-to-one relationship or were you part of a bigger group?
- How well did that suit you?
- What did you do together? How well did that suit you?
- What did you like most about that relationship?
- What do you think was successful about that relationship?
- What did you do that contributed to the success of the relationship?
- What impact did being in that relationships have on your depressive symptoms?
- Are you still in that relationship?
- If not, why did it end and how did that happen?

If you have added people who were not included in your original interpersonal inventory (see chapter 9), go back to the questions you answered in that chapter about your current relationships and ask the same kinds of questions about these good relationships in the past. Use the table here to note down your answers – or you can copy it into your notebook.

Name of the person					
Relationship with the person					
How much time did you spend together?					
Did the person know about your depression?					
Could you speak to the person about your feelings?					
Did you see each other socially?					

Could you ask the person for practical help and advice?				
Was it a flexible relationship?				
How would you describe the give and take in this relationship?				
Were you satisfied with this relationship?				
Did this relationship change when you became depressed?				

Thinking about each of your successful relationships in this way will produce a series of rich stories for you to draw on. Start by looking for repeating themes. Make a note of any similarities you notice across these successful relationships – for example, you chose the relationship and took the initiative to get it started; or you shared common interests, which gave you something to talk about; or you were part a bigger group, which kept the momentum going. Most people find certain social situations easier than others, and this is an opportunity to focus carefully on what has helped you to be in relationships with other people.

Martin

Martin taught English as a second language. He was an energetic teacher and enjoyed watching his students learn and use their new language skills. Martin felt confident in the classroom because he could plan ahead and could include lots of activities and exercises in his time with his students. He found it much easier to interact with other people when they were in groups and occupied on a task, and he did not feel that he was the centre of attention. All Martin's confidence seemed to drain away when he walked into the teachers' common room. He found small talk and one-to-one conversations unpredictable and anxiety-provoking, and he constantly criticized himself for not being spontaneous and quick enough in the discussions that circled around him.

Martin had found his experience of one-to-one interactions so off-putting that he had stopped going out socially and had become increasingly lonely and depressed. When he looked over his successful relationships in the past, he saw how often being in a group and having a shared activity had helped him. He held this in mind when trying to find ways of reducing his isolation. He decided to join a local choir. He enjoyed music and found that focusing on the pieces the choir was learning made it much easier for him to cope with being in company. The routine of weekly practice suited him well, and his mood and confidence gradually improved.

Exercise 20.4: Looking for the patterns in good relationships

Now, let's summarize what your review has revealed. For each relationship you have listed in the left-hand column, mark a tick in the table below to indicate what you found manageable and an X to signify what you found difficult. If you have noticed any features of your relationships not included in the table, add more columns with brief descriptions of the additional features. If you see a cluster of ticks or Xs under a particular column heading, this suggests a repeating pattern. Clusters of ticks highlight your strengths. Clusters of Xs highlight areas where you might want to focus your attention to develop more skills.

NAME	Starting the relationship	Keeping in touch	Managing difficulties	Asking for what I want	Feeling close

When you have reviewed these relationships from your point of view, switch the focus – imagine yourself as a movie director, turning the camera around to face the other person – and imagine how the other person would have described the relationship.

- What do you imagine the other person liked about their relationship with you?
- What do you think they thought went well in this relationship?
- What would they say you contributed to the relationship?
- If the relationship ended, why would they say it did?

This is, of course, more difficult to do. Some of these things may have been discussed, but often we are left to guess what other people think. Your IPT companion or therapist might be able to help you think about what other people value in their contact with you.

If you found any helpful routines or features in these relationships, especially any that are repeated, think about how they feature in your relationships today. Sometimes repeating routines and arrangements that have worked in the past can be one of the simplest and most straightforward ways of making small changes now.

- How could you reintroduce these helpful routines if they have been set aside for a while?

LEARNING FROM WHAT HAS BEEN DIFFICULT

Now repeat the same exercises for the relationships that have been more difficult. This list might include relationships that ended more quickly than you wanted or where disagreements were difficult to work out, or relationships that did not fully develop. You might have been deeply hurt or disappointed by some of these relationships. If that is the case, pace yourself gently as you go through these exercises. Take a break after you think through a significant relationship and do not force yourself to complete the whole list at once if you start to feel sad or upset. Remember that there is a positive reason for looking at past difficulties, and that is to learn more about the patterns which have caused you difficulties in the past so that you can think about how to change them in the future.

Again, if you have an IPT therapist or partner who can help you with these exercises, do involve them. This will help you to stand back and look at the relationship patterns rather than being drawn into the painful feelings that may come with these memories. Once again, try to see yourself as if you were making a documentary on your past experience, standing back to observe the whole scene and understand how it works.

Exercise 20.5: Reviewing less successful relationships

Again, build a timeline for each of the relationships you have listed to help you to understand more about the problematic patterns that have repeated in the past. Use the questions below to help you.

- When did the relationship start? What age were you?
- How did you meet? Was starting the relationship your choice or the other person's?
- How did you organize your time together and what did you do?
- Were there things you liked about that relationship?

- What were the difficulties in that relationship?
- Can you see any ways in which you contributed to the difficulties in the relationship? What are they?
- In what ways did the other person contribute to the difficulties in the relationship?
- What impact did being in that relationship have on your depressive symptoms?
- Are you still in that relationship?
- If not, why and how did it come to an end?
- What impact did ending the relationship have on your depressive symptoms?
- What are the things about the relationship that you are glad to have given up?

If your list includes people who did not feature in your original interpersonal inventory, again ask the same kinds of questions that you considered in chapter 9 about these additional relationships. Another blank table is provided here to help you.

Name of the person					
Relationship with the person					
How much time did you spend together?					

Did the person know about your depression?					
Could you speak to the person about your feelings?					
Did you see each other socially?					
Could you ask the person for practical help and advice?					
Was it a flexible relationship?					
How would you describe the give and take in this relationship?					
Were you ever satisfied with this relationship?					
Did this relationship change when you became depressed?					

Matt

Matt wanted to find a romantic partner, but quickly lost interest in each new woman he met. He had dated several women in the past, but each relationship came to an abrupt end within weeks of starting, leaving him feeling increasingly hopeless and lonely. He often could not face telling the women he dated that he didn't want to see them again, because he feared they would be angry with him, so he had ended several relationships by text message or simply by no longer getting in touch or replying to messages. When he looked back over his past partners he recognized that he rushed into each relationship almost immediately after meeting a woman he was attracted to, hoping she would solve his loneliness. He offered immediate declarations of love, hoping each time that he had found the partner he was looking for. However, he found it difficult to sustain this hope and as the relationship became more routine or demanded more of him, he lost interest and backed away. His partners' anxious or irritated responses convinced him they were not right for him and so he ended each relationship, leaving him feeling disappointed and all the more desperate to find a connection in the next person he met.

When he looked back over each of these relationships in detail, Matt realized that he had taken very little time to get to know the people he dated before trying to fit them into the role of partner. His enthusiasm was difficult to sustain because he expected so much so quickly and then was disappointed when the relationship did not keep up with his high expectations. He realized that the routine, day-to-day parts of a relationship caused him a great deal of anxiety and he expected to be judged and found wanting by his partners. His sudden exit protected him from this criticism but also prevented him from finding out what most of his girlfriends were really like. Matt, in fact, had many positive characteristics to bring to a relationship, but undermined his own objectives by not taking time to establish a more realistic view of what common ground he and his potential partner shared in terms of interests, values and hopes for the future. Learning to contain his feelings and take a more gradual approach to the early stages of his relationships became an important goal for Matt in his efforts to protect himself against future disappointment and depression.

Exercise 20.6: Looking for the patterns in less successful relationships

Now see if you can find any repeating patterns in your troublesome or disappointing relationships. Ask yourself, as you look over your table:

- Can you see any patterns that undermined the relationship?
- Do difficulties tend to start at the beginning of relationships or after you have known each other for a while?
- As you look back, can you imagine any ways in which the problematic pattern could have been changed?
- What would have been necessary for the pattern to change e.g. extra skills or knowledge, or a change of setting?

Once again, for each relationship you have listed in the left-hand column put a tick in the table below to indicate what you found manageable and an X to mark what you found difficult. If any clusters of Xs appear across a number of relationships, these will suggest particular areas you can concentrate on to learn new skills that will help you. If ticks appear across a number of relationships, they will highlight strengths that persist even when relationships are more challenging or vulnerable.

Name	Starting the rela-tionship	Keeping in touch	Managing difficulties	Asking for what I want	Feeling close	

Now, just as you did before, try to think about each relationship from the other person's point of view. Does this switch of viewpoint reveal anything new?

• What do you imagine the other person found difficult in this relationship?

- How would they describe their contribution to the difficulties in the relationship?
- What would they say you contributed to the relationship?
- If the relationship ended, why would they say it did?

A word of caution here. When you are feeling depressed, it can be tempting to rush to blame yourself for difficulties. While it is important to understand how you contribute to problems, because it will guide you in making changes, it is just as important to recognize the contribution other people make. It will be particularly useful to involve someone else in this part of the exercise to help you fully consider a different point of view.

REPEATING PATTERNS

You might have been thinking over a range of relationships as you completed these exercises and come up with some ideas about what happens to help and hinder them. Try to summarize the main things you have discovered in carrying out this review. Also, ask your IPT companion or therapist to pick out the main themes that he or she notices. This can give you another perspective on your difficulties.

Common patterns that reinforce isolation include:

- Feeling shy and not being able to approach people and start relationships.
- Not being able to ask for what you want in a relationship and being taken for granted or ignored.
- Being critical or intolerant of other people and having minor disagreements across many of your relationships.
- Not being able to tolerate any kind of conflict and leaving the relationship rather than sorting out difficulties.

- Not being able to get close to other people and holding them at an emotional distance.
- Rushing into relationships quickly and making a significant emotional investment before establishing if there is potential for the person to meet your expectations.

Exercise 20.7: Recognizing repeating patterns of difficulty in your relationships

What are the main difficulties or patterns you have noticed in your past relationships? List them in your notebook and discuss with your IPT therapist or team.

- Are any of the same patterns or difficulties happening in your relationships now?
- What effect does your depression have on these patterns?
- Can you apply any of the ideas you had about changing these patterns (in exercise 20.6) to your current relationships?

What are the main successes and strengths you can see in your past relationships? List them in your notebook and discuss with your IPT therapist or team.

- Are you repeating successful patterns and ideas in your current relationships?
- What effect does this have on your depression?
- What could you do to bring these strengths more into your current relationships?

At this point you can make use of one of the skills you have already been developing. When this process began, you started to develop an expertise in your experience of depression. In chapter 6 you learned about it as an illness and identified the various symptoms that make up the whole experience of that illness. You learned how your symptoms interact with each other and one can lead to another, creating a vicious circle. For example, when you do not sleep well you feel much more tired as you face a new day. Feeling physically drained makes it more difficult to feel motivated and enthusiastic about getting involved in anything, so you tend to hang back or withdraw. Having withdrawn from people and activities which might have been enjoyable, you experience less pleasure and your mood drops. The same kind of cycle can develop in relationship patterns – and you can learn to become expert in them in the same way.

Use what you discovered when you thought about your more successful relationships to uncover opportunities for similar successes now. Making random attempts to build up social contact or change problematic routines is unlikely to feel safe. However, if you make plans based on what has worked in the past, taking risks may feel less daunting. This can also help you to avoid repeating the same mistakes. Look for opportunities to make your routine less isolating and more sociable. This might involve making small changes, like going to the check-out rather than the self-service till in the supermarket, or going to a class rather than exercising on your own at the gym. Think of change in terms of stepping stones rather than a single great leap. Sometimes the stepping stones will still involve a stretch, and having someone at hand to steady you, like your therapist or IPT team, can be very useful.

- What opportunities can you identify in your day to increase the amount of time you spend with other people?

Once you have narrowed the gap between yourself and other people, you can start to practise the non-verbal and basic communication skills discussed in chapter 12 as part of your daily routine. For example, practise making eye contact with the people who feature in your day, such as family, flatmates, shop assistants or work colleagues. This may feel uncomfortable at first if it is not your usual style, but it will become easier with practice. You might have to start with a glance and then build up to looking long enough to be able to offer someone a smile. Practise this every day and gradually build up to the next step, such as saying 'Good morning' or 'Thank you' or wishing the person a nice day. As you become more confident you can start to introduce more open communication, such as asking them a simple question. The aim is to develop confidence in small, limited interactions, which can be stepping stones to more substantial communication. Use chapter 12 for ideas on how to develop this interaction.

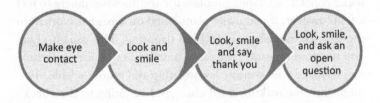

Look at what other people do

Alongside these daily exercises it is useful to watch what other people do. Some of the things that will help you to be more confident and engaged in relationships might be new to you; so, in order to generate some new ideas, put yourself in the role of movie director again and turn the camera away from yourself and on to other people. Watch how people talk to each other, behave around each other, recover from mistakes or respond to unexpected opportunities. Each meeting or conversation you observe can be broken down into smaller components, some of which you are already practising each day.

Exercise 20.8: Watching how other people behave

Find a place where you can spend a little time watching people unobtrusively from a short distance away – say at the bus stop, or in a coffee shop. The people you observe do not need to be people you know. As you watch them, try to notice examples of good and not so good ways of behaving towards other people. It is best not to stare at someone so much that they become aware that they are being watched; there is plenty of information that you can pick up from a less intense scrutiny or even a quick glance.

Do not worry about tuning in to what people are saying, as this will distract you from watching their behaviour. Actively try to find examples of people who use non-verbal communication well. These examples might look quite different from each other, as there are many different ways to do this well. For example, you might see a friendly shop assistant who has a brief chat with each customer, or a group of friends who are having a coffee together and giving each other their full attention. Take note of what you think each person does well.

Now consider the following questions:

- Do you do *any* of the things that you see in the good examples?
- How could you build some of these ideas into your daily practice, perhaps breaking them down into a series of smaller steps if necessary?

Discuss these ideas with your IPT therapist or IPT
team.

This exercise gives you an opportunity to think about what
your most comfortable social style might be. You might discover that you have been holding unrealistic expectations of
what your socially comfortable self will be like and have overlooked a more viable and achievable option. It is unlikely that
someone who is very shy is going to become a social butterfly
who enjoys being the centre of attention. The leap would be
too great. However, you might feel comfortable with a gentle,
encouraging style that quietly attends to one other person at
a time. Both are successful styles, and it is good to aim for
something that you will feel comfortable with.

Moira

Moira felt irritable and intolerant around other people
and could seem abrupt and unapproachable. In contrast,
she loved her dog and gave him a lot of attention and
very good care. She found her relationship with her dog
more rewarding than her relationships with most people,
but she admitted that she did feel lonely and that all her
needs were not being met by being a pet owner. When
she was feeling very depressed, Moira would walk her
dog around routes that she knew would be quiet, and
deliberately stayed away from other people. When she
decided to try to make her routine more sociable, she
adapted the thing she enjoyed most, time with her dog,
to include other people. Moira changed her route to walk
in the local park, where many other people walked their
dogs. She practised using more open non-verbal signals,

such as smiling at people as they walked past instead of looking at the ground. Given the common interest she shared with other pet owners, Moira found it relatively easy to move from offering a nod when someone passed to stopping to speak about their respective pets for a couple of minutes. As Moira's confidence grew, she started going for a coffee at the park café before going home. Over time she began to recognize people's faces, and would sometimes continue the initially brief conversations over coffee. As more time passed, it became easier to slowly introduce more details about other parts of her life into the discussion. The other pet owners remained friendly companions for just a small part of Moira's day, but this opportunity had been developed to make the most of its potential.

Exercise 20.9: Looking for poor use of non-verbal communication

Continue watching how other people behave to find three examples of people who use non-verbal skills poorly. This might be someone who is rude to a shop assistant and upsets other people, or someone who does not speak up and is passed over when they reach the front of the queue because no one notices them. Try to pick out what is happening in these exchanges that makes them work less well.

- Describe what went wrong in each example. Try to identify what contributed to the problem.
- Imagine ways in which this could be avoided.
- Do *you* do any of the things you see in the unsuccessful examples?

- Do the people around you do any of the things you see in unsuccessful examples?
- Do these things have the same effect when you do them?
- How could this change?

The point of this exercise is not to criticize other people but to become more practised in thinking your way out of difficult situations. By starting one step removed, that is, as a watcher of other people, you have more time to think and consider other options. As you develop this skill you will have more ideas available to you to manage difficulties that present themselves when you come across other people in your daily routines.

As with all the other exercises, it is really helpful if you can involve someone else in doing this, either directly, by asking them to observe, assess and problem-solve with you, or by discussing your observations with them afterwards. Again, this can provide you with another point of view and may pick up on details that you initially overlooked.

Recent examples of relationship difficulties

Identifying the problematic patterns in your relationships is particularly important because these difficulties and your symptoms of depression are likely to be keeping each other going. Understanding what has been happening will help you to work out how this can change, and how you can develop healthier habits that will protect you against depression. It is therefore useful to examine carefully some recent exchanges with other people in more detail, in order to understand how communication, expectations and repeating patterns influence how well you get on.

Exercise 20.10: Looking at what actually happened

Think back over the last week to an occasion when you felt isolated or uncomfortable in a social situation and this made your depression symptoms worse. Try to reconstruct what happened in as much detail as you can, writing each stage down in your notebook.

- Start by outlining the sequence of events from beginning to end.
- Pay particular attention to the communication involved, including verbal and non-verbal communication. Try to remember what was said and how it was said in as much detail as you can.
- Add a further layer by including all that you can remember about how you felt at the time, including your depressive symptoms before, during and after the episode, and what you understood the other person was feeling.
- Redirect your mental camera and describe the incident from the other person's point of view.
- Bring the example into the present moment and add how you feel about the incident now and note if this is different from how you felt at the time.
- Pick out any repeating patterns that were evident in this example.
- What are the main problems you can see in the way this exchange went?

You have spent a lot of time learning about communication, expressing feelings, recognizing your own interpersonal patterns and thinking about ways to change those patterns. Bring these ideas together now to help you to see how you could have changed the direction of the exchange you have just described in order to arrive at a different outcome, which would not make your depression worse. This will give you the basis of a new pattern which you can put into practice in your day-to-day meetings with other people from now on.

- How could the setting have been changed to improve the outcome?
- How could your communication have changed to improve the outcome?
- How could the other person's communication have changed to improve the outcome?
- How could your feelings, or how you expressed them, have been changed to improve the outcome?
- What did the other person need to know or understand more clearly to improve the outcome?
- What could you do to improve their understanding?
- What could you do or say now to change the way the pattern plays out?

Working through examples, as in the exercise above, is even more effective when you involve another person. Patterns often repeat themselves because they are difficult to resist and you feel pressure to behave in certain ways. This can be difficult to stop on your own, and with another person adding their perspective you may be able to spot opportunities to change the pattern that you haven't been able to see on your own.

Throughout this chapter, you have been working towards change and have developed a more detailed understanding of the relationship patterns that contribute to your depression now. This is a picture that you will need to update regularly.

Remember to rate your symptoms of depression each week, using the table in appendix 1. Think about how feeling isolated or dissatisfied with your relationships influences your symptoms, and each week identify two or three examples when symptoms and difficulties related to your relationships overlaps to think about in more detail (you can use the table in appendix 3 for this). Talk to your IPT team about these difficulties, and use the suggestions in this chapter to help you to manage the difficulties more effectively.

New options for developing new or better relationships will emerge with each stepping stone you cross. These may include taking part in more formal therapy or joining a group to help you to develop specific skills, such as assertiveness. You might have identified an IPT companion or therapist who can support you as you continue to take risks and step out of your isolation and into the spaces between people where relationships are created.

Summary

- Feeling lonely can happen both when you have too few relationships and when you are in relationships that don't meet your needs.
- Feeling isolated does not mean that all of your relationships are a problem; it is important to remember the areas, however small, where things do work well in your interpersonal world.
- Repeating routines that have worked in the past can be one of the simplest ways to make small changes now.

- Understanding how problems have developed in the past can help you to change those patterns in the future.
- Change involves crossing stepping stones rather than making a single great leap.

Chapter 21

Miranda's story

Miranda was a 28-year-old single woman who had experienced depression several times, occasionally quite severely, since her teens. Her current period of depression had developed gradually over three years, and she had difficulty identifying exactly when it had begun. She said that some symptoms of depression had been a constant feature in her life, especially feeling bad about herself and feeling tired and unmotivated, and this made it difficult to identify a time when she had last felt entirely well. She was concerned that the gaps between clear episodes of depression appeared to be shortening, and she was worried that if severe depression took over again it might never leave her.

Miranda described symptoms of mild to moderate depression, which interfered with her ability to function from day to day, but had not stopped her from working. She found concentration difficulties particularly problematic, because of the nature of her work, which involved long periods of paying close attention to written material. Miranda said she felt sad at least half of the time and became tearful easily. She had lost interest in most of her activities and felt tired and lethargic every day. Her eating habits had deteriorated quite badly, and she often comfort ate when her mood was low. This had resulted in noticeable weight gain over the last eighteen months, during which she had put on 7 kg. This contributed to her low self-confidence, and she was reluctant to go out because she did not want to be seen and thought people would be critical of her appearance. She often felt irritable with other people, although she mostly tried to hide this. At times she found this too difficult and she could be snappy and short-tempered. She described always feeling bad about herself and feeling hopeless about the future.

Miranda was a freelance translator, which involved long hours working on her own. She worked from home, much of her contact with clients taking place by email, and days could pass without her leaving the flat or speaking to another person. When Miranda had graduated with a language degree she had hoped to become a language teacher, but had been unable to cope with the practical demands of teacher training and left the course before completing it. Miranda was good at her job but had never had a permanent contract. She had been employed on a number of short-term contracts, but found the noise and activity in an office environment stressful, and so eventually opted to leave when the latest contract ran out. She found it difficult to make good working relationships with colleagues, and felt that this had worked against her in her attempt to secure a permanent contract. Miranda found working independently very stressful, partly because she worried about making enough money, and partly because she had become bored with the repetitive nature of the work she was doing. She felt trapped between equally unsatisfactory options and didn't know how to improve her situation.

Two years earlier one of the companies Miranda occasionally worked for had been taken over. The company moved to new open-plan offices, which Miranda found very stressful, and as it now stipulated that all work be completed on their premises she started to turn down short-term contract work with this firm. This increased Miranda's financial worries and she was very critical of her own decision, but she did not feel able to work in an environment where she felt exposed and under the scrutiny of new managers.

In the months that followed this decision, Miranda's depressive symptoms gradually got worse and she started to take anti-depressant medication. This did not last long, however: Miranda did not like taking medication, believing that it confirmed she was weak, and so she stopped taking it after four weeks. Her symptoms had begun to improve in the meantime, but this improvement did not last when she gave up the medication.

Around this time Miranda became unwell with appendicitis and required emergency surgery. She recovered well physically, but was unable to work for almost a month. She felt very alone during her recovery period, and noticing how few people came to visit her only emphasized her loneliness. Once she was able to start working again Miranda's mood improved a little, but she was constantly aware of depression in the background.

Miranda lived in a shared flat with two other people. She was not close to either of them, but tolerated other people being around and would occasionally chat or have a meal with them. Both her flatmates were students, and at the end of the term they gave up their rooms and two new people moved into the flat. Miranda made little effort to get to know them and spent more time alone in her bedroom. When the only friend she had made through work, Gina, moved to Spain a couple of months later, Miranda felt she had lost her last connection to life outside the four walls of her bedroom. With Gina no longer around to encourage her and include her in her plans, she retreated even further into herself. Miranda said this had been the final straw, and she ran out of energy and determination to stay ahead of her depression. At this point her symptoms became worse and she sought help.

Miranda's IPT therapist suggested she draw up a timeline to provide an overview of the difficulties she had been facing and to start to put her recurrent depression into an interpersonal context. (For a reminder of how the timeline is constructed, take a look back at chapter 8.)

Miranda's timeline

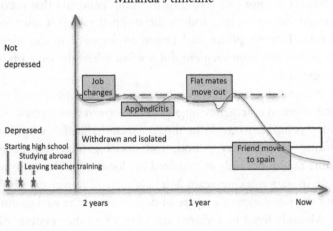

Miranda then expanded on her depression story by describing the times she had felt depressed in the past. She repeated that she couldn't clearly remember times when she had been happy, and said that she generally felt lonely and awkward around other people. She had made one close friend at primary school, with whom she was still in occasional touch by email. But they had attended different secondary schools and Miranda didn't find anyone to replace her now-absent friend. She described feeling very lonely and spending most of her time alone or in the library; it was at this time that she first became depressed. Her parents divorced in her second year at secondary school, and she said there was so much else going on and everyone was so unhappy that no one noticed that she was struggling to keep her head above water.

Miranda went on to study languages and spent a period of time abroad as part of her course requirements. She found this very difficult, as she didn't know how to make new friends when she was entirely on her own in an unfamiliar place. She returned home earlier than planned because she found it so difficult to cope, and this was the first time depression was formally diagnosed. She was prescribed anti-depressant medication, which she took for a few weeks, but then stopped. Her symptoms had improved a bit, and she did not go back to her GP or seek any further treatment.

Miranda had hoped to be a language teacher and started a teacher-training course. She found school placements very difficult, and in particular struggled to manage in the classroom and to build relationships either with the permanent staff or with her fellow student teachers. She felt overwhelmed and unsupported, and left college before completing the course, repeating a pattern from her earlier studies. Miranda was diagnosed with depression again at this point and was prescribed anti-depressant medication and brief counselling sessions. She found both helpful, but again stopped her medication after a few weeks when her symptoms started to improve.

By the time she began to see her IPT therapist, who agreed that she was depressed and had been for some months, Miranda knew the symptoms of depression very well. Yet despite this familiarity, it was new for Miranda to think of herself as ill rather than weak and a failure. She found it useful to think again about the repetitive nature of her depression and the treatment options available, although she felt pessimistic about her chances of being able to do anything to control the repeating pattern of depression in her life. Her therapist reminded her that she had come out of depression in the past, but Miranda focused more on the fact that the depression had come back. They discussed in detail the way anti-depressant medication is designed to be used, and the additional vulnerability that is caused by starting and stopping was explained fully. This helped Miranda to understand why it was important to use medication regularly and consistently, especially after several past episodes of depression, and how this could potentially help her to manage her depression more effectively in the future. She was encouraged to speak to her GP about restarting anti-depressant medication, and she and her therapist agreed to monitor each week how regularly she was taking it.

Miranda and her therapist noted that her persistent sense of loneliness lay behind much of her depression and also amplified the impact of individual changes in her life. They decided to look at this more closely through her interpersonal inventory.

Miranda found the inventory difficult to fill out, and she described feeling embarrassed by how little she had to show for her life. She started by adding her friend Gina, who had moved to Spain, and with whom she still had some contact, though she said that this relationship felt very different since Gina had moved away. Miranda said that she had relied on Gina for most of her social routine. She described Gina as more sociable than herself and said that she would often invite Miranda to join her when she went out with other friends. They both enjoyed books and theatre, and would sometimes queue together to buy on-the-day discount tickets for theatre shows. Gina would often chat to people in the queue, some of whom she would recognize from previous shows, but Miranda did not feel confident enough to talk to people in the same way. Miranda was reluctant to add the people she had met through Gina to her inventory because she did not think they were really her friends and thought they just agreed to her tagging along because she knew Gina. She had not seen them since Gina left.

Miranda described her new flatmates as friendly and pleasant but said she had not spoken to them other than when she had to, so she did not consider them friends. She had not maintained contact with her former flatmates.

Miranda occasionally exchanged emails with her friend from primary school, Pamela, but they had not seen each other in several years. Miranda remembered that they had been close but had hardly seen each other after they had gone to different secondary schools, and Miranda thought that this had contributed a lot to how lonely she felt at that time. She said her friend did most of the work to keep in touch, but she did generally respond when she received a message from Pamela and was pleased to hear from her.

Miranda's parents, who divorced when she was in secondary school, had both remarried. Both lived over three hours away by train and she rarely saw them. She spoke to her mother every couple of weeks and her father about once a month. She had two stepsisters, but had always felt as though she was inferior to them – less attractive and less intelligent – and they had not developed close relationships. She only saw them if they happened to visit her mother at the same time as Miranda did, and that did not happen often.

When encouraged, Miranda mentioned two other people, Julie and Helen, who worked in the translation firm Gina had worked for and with whom she had been out on a couple of occasions when Gina had still been in the country. She again described them as acquaintances rather than friends.

Miranda said that although she would like to have a family she did not think it would happen, and that she had never had a serious intimate relationship.

It became clear from this discussion that Miranda had very limited regular contact with other people, and that her social life either relied on someone else initiating a plan or required considerable effort on her part – an effort she rarely felt able to make when she was depressed. She never spoke about her depression or other feelings with anyone else, and so was very isolated in her emotional life. She had less support than she needed in almost all areas of her life, and was hampered in this by her closest friends all living a considerable distance away and so being unavailable for the day-to-day encouragement and companionship that she would have liked and that could have helped her to reverse the patterns created by depression.

Miranda and her therapist discussed how central her loneliness appeared to be to her depression, and agreed that it would not be helpful to rule out any potential relationships until the nature of her relationships and the surrounding difficulties were more clearly understood. So, in order to help her see all her possible as well as established relationships together, Miranda was encouraged to add all of the people who had come up in discussion to her inventory. Miranda said she could not see how to make more of the people around her, but agreed to think about this in more detail if it might help her feel better.

It became clear that several events had contributed to Miranda's depression, many of which had increased her isolation in both her work and her personal life. Her feelings of loneliness and lack of support were central to her experience, and so Miranda and her therapist agreed to focus on this issue for the rest of her therapy.

Miranda found it difficult to identify her goals. She said it felt like trying to shoot blindfolded and that she did not know what she was aiming at because her life now was much as it had always been.

Miranda's interpersonal inventory

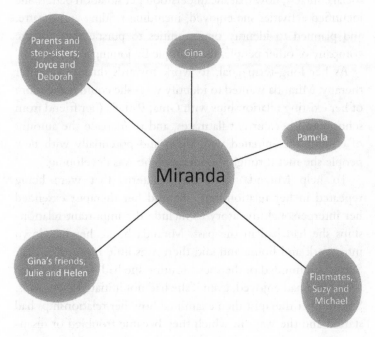

Her therapist suggested that it would be useful to understand how certain patterns repeated themselves to keep Miranda feeling depressed and stranded on the outside of relationships. In particular, they agreed to look carefully at how these patterns applied in the relationships she had now or had been involved in recently.

As a short-term goal, Miranda agreed to monitor how her non-verbal communication influenced the contacts she had with other people, particularly when she avoided greeting or acknowledging people and became snappy when she felt uncomfortable.

She set a medium-term goal to try to gradually increase her social contacts, now that she understood her situation better. She identified activities she enjoyed, including reading and theatre, and planned to identify opportunities to pursue these in the company of other people, for example by joining a book club.

As her long-term goal, to work towards during and after therapy, Miranda wanted to identify ways she could make more of her existing relationships with Gina, Pamela (her friend from school) and her current flatmates, and to increase the amount of contact she initiated with them and potentially with new people she met through the interests she was developing.

To help Miranda to identify patterns that were being repeated in her relationships, she and her therapist extended her interpersonal inventory to include the important relationships she had had in the past. Miranda broke her life down into work and home and said there was little more than that. She was reminded of the social routine she had had with Gina, which she had enjoyed, even if she had not initiated their plans. She and her therapist then examined how her relationships had started and the ways in which they became troubled or disappointing over time.

Miranda said that she often felt shy when she was introduced to new people and would criticize herself when she couldn't think of anything to say. Sometimes her irritation at herself would spill over, causing her to speak abruptly to other people. She thought they must think she was boring or rude.

She described her experience of working in an office environment in mixed terms. On the one hand, she enjoyed the work she did and sometimes found it helpful to have colleagues around to discuss difficult documents or unfamiliar technical language. On the other hand, she found it very difficult to establish good working relationships and rarely made friendships with work colleagues. Feeling shy around people she didn't know, she tended to arrive at and leave the office without speaking to anyone. Because she so often worked on short-term contracts and so was not in an office regularly for more than a few weeks at a time, she rarely had the chance to get to know people well enough to feel more relaxed with them.

She believed that the other staff in the offices she visited did not like her and excluded her from their discussions and plans. She felt left out and agitated, and couldn't imagine how to be anything other than an onlooker to other people's lives. This feeling of exclusion also made her irritable with groups who would chat and spend time at each other's desks. Miranda found it difficult to concentrate when there was a lot of noise, and would sigh loudly or ask people abruptly to be quiet because she was trying to work. As she described doing this, she realized that sometimes this was the first thing she had said to another person, and that this might make them reluctant to approach her or include her in more social routines around work. Her therapist suggested that her irritability appeared to be worse when she was depressed, but that other people who did not know her were unlikely to understand how much effort it took her simply to get through each working day.

Miranda's response to this pattern had been to stop looking for work through agencies and to do small pieces of translation work on her own at home. This reduced the chance of having socially awkward moments but created several other problems, such as making her much more isolated, reducing her income and narrowing the range and types of work she did, so that she became easily bored and lost the pleasure she normally took in her job. She recognized that avoiding other people was one of her main strategies for coping, but that this fed directly into her depression because it made her feel lonely and isolated.

When Miranda and her therapist looked at her home and social routines, they noticed similar patterns. She had not maintained contact with people Gina had introduced her to because she assumed they would not be interested in seeing her. She admitted that she had avoided Gina's leaving party because she felt nervous about facing so many people at once. She had received a couple of text messages from Julie and Helen in the weeks following, asking how she was, but Miranda said she thought they were just being polite and did not respond. She had believed they did not get in touch again because they did not want to see her, but she could see in hindsight that they might have thought her silence meant that she did not want to see them.

There was one recent occasion which she discussed with her therapist in detail. One evening Miranda had been to the theatre with her flatmate Suzy, who had asked her along when the friend she'd been planning to go with dropped out at the last minute. Miranda was nervous but pleased to take up the invitation. While they were waiting to go into the theatre, someone Miranda had worked with occasionally arrived on his own. He acknowledged Miranda and when she smiled in return he came and sat with them. Miranda introduced him to Suzy and was very embarrassed when she mispronounced his name and he corrected her. Miranda ran over this mistake in her head several times and criticized herself so much she found it difficult to follow the subsequent conversation and fell quiet. In the meantime Suzy and their new companion struck up a conversation. Miranda did not know anything about the subject they were discussing and didn't think that Suzy knew anything about it either, but noticed this did not seem to prevent their chatting to each other. As the conversation went on, Miranda felt excluded and withdrew further into herself. She began to feel angry that she was being left out, as she thought people did so often, and decided not to speak to either of them again.

As the time approached for the performance to begin, Miranda felt increasingly agitated when the other two did not stop talking, even when she stood up and put her coat on and stood over them as they spoke. After several minutes she could not bear to wait any longer and walked away. She intended not to go to the play but simply to leave and go home. Just as she got to the foyer door Suzy caught up with her and guided her back towards the auditorium. Miranda did not want to cause a scene by saying she wanted to go home, so followed her into the theatre, still feeling very angry. Suzy made a passing comment that she had not noticed Miranda leave as she had been enjoying talking so much and commented that Miranda knew some very interesting people. Miranda thought she was being sarcastic and did not respond. They sat through the rest of the evening in silence. Miranda left as soon as the play was over and felt the evening had been a disaster.

This incident illustrated many of the repeating patterns that Miranda had discussed with her therapist. Having described it in detail, Miranda managed to stand back and think through the different ways she could have responded and behaved in the situation, e.g. to laugh at her mistake about the name rather than criticize herself; to say she did not know much about the subject they were discussing and ask them to explain a little; and to accept Suzy's compliment as genuine and continue with the evening they had planned.

As a next step, Miranda and her therapist agreed that she would pay particular attention to how she behaved when she first met someone during the day. Doing this highlighted to her how seldom she looked at other people and how she almost never spoke first when she saw someone she knew, even in her own home. Miranda described how awkward she felt on these occasions, and how she felt panicky and unable to think what to say. She and her therapist discussed how often her internal distress was hidden from other people, who might therefore make the mistake of thinking she was not interested in them or rude. Miranda was appalled that she might be thought of that way, as she had not previously looked at these situations from a different point of view.

Armed with this information, she agreed to try to make small changes in the way she responded when she met someone. She practised this with her therapist several times before trying it on her own. She started by deliberately making eye contact, then added a smile and, after some practice, made a point of being the first to speak, saying 'Good morning' or 'Hello'. Miranda initially found this difficult but was very pleased with how often people responded well to her greeting and how much more relaxed she felt when she had a simple plan for the initial moments of a meeting, many of which lasted no more than a few seconds.

Miranda also started to observe other people more closely, watching the way people greeted and spoke to each other and what effect this had. She deliberately broke the pattern of staying in for days at a time by going out each day for coffee. She took a book as camouflage as she sat in the café and watched how people behaved towards each other. As she started to recognize the range of different ways people act when they are talking to each other, she rated what she thought were the more and less successful ways, noticing if there was give and take, if people appeared interested or bored, and if tensions were raised or avoided. Through these observations Miranda gathered more information to use in reading her own exchanges with other people. This helped her to avoid her recurrent pattern of retreating into an internal critical conversation and to stay involved in conversations with other people.

When Miranda looked back over her successful and unsuccessful relationships to identify which patterns had applied to them, she described the way in which Gina had approached her when they first met. Gina had introduced herself to Miranda on the first day they worked together and invited her for coffee when Gina took a break. Miranda was initially hesitant, but Gina was friendly and persistent and Miranda eventually accepted. She said Gina had been friendly and inclusive, often inviting people she did not know very well to join in on her plans because she enjoyed getting to know people. Miranda greatly admired Gina's ability to do this and gradually found it easier to say yes to the invitations that came her way. She and her therapist noted the contrasting patterns, and how Gina's open and friendly style had encouraged Miranda and had not come across as pushy, as Miranda worried she might appear if she made suggestions or spoke up.

She also recognized a similarity between Gina's friendliness and Pamela's persistence, which had helped them to stay in contact since primary school. This insight was used to reinforce Miranda's plan to make more of these positive relationships, and she wrote to both Gina and Pamela to tell them about what she was doing to try to address her depression. Both responded quickly and with encouragement. Gina suggested they should start to use Skype rather than emailing, which Miranda agreed to and enjoyed. Encouraged by this success, Miranda made a similar suggestion to Pamela, who was pleased to take up the opportunity to see Miranda more often. Being able to see her friends when she spoke to them boosted Miranda's confidence in their conversations and encouraged her to speak to them more frequently.

Soon after these discussions, Miranda had a chance to use some of her new skills in practice. On a visit to her local library she found details of a book club that met there and was open to everyone. The format was somewhere between a talk and a discussion, and so she felt reassured that she wouldn't be under pressure to speak if she didn't want to. Miranda mentioned this to her flatmate Suzy and asked if she would like to go along with her, which Suzy agreed to. At the group Miranda made a point of smiling at the people who were sitting nearby and returned the compliment when one of the women she spoke to said she hoped to see her at the next group. Miranda planned to attend again, and to invite Suzy as well, though she felt confident she could manage to go on her own even if Suzy was not available.

By the end of her therapy sessions Miranda had made slow but steady progress in improving her interpersonal world. She had taken steps towards achieving several of her goals, including having a better understanding of her communication style and an awareness of repeating patterns in her relationships. She was making better and more regular use of two positive relationships, and for the first time had let someone else know about the impact of depression in her life. This support was still quite limited, as both of her close friends lived far away, but she was in more regular contact with them and she had been talking about visiting Pamela when she next went to see her mother. Miranda had also started to build things she enjoyed back into her life, and was using the organized book group to help her to keep that going. After looking in detail at individual examples of exchanges with other people, she felt more confident about managing initial meetings and felt more relaxed in her day-to-day contacts.

These changes in her interpersonal life, combined with taking her anti-depressant medication, reduced Miranda's symptoms of depression to the mild level. Miranda said this allowed her to feel more satisfied with what she had, and more able to work on her remaining difficulties. She planned to continue on her medication and agreed to discuss any future change with her GP. Gina and Pamela said that they would talk to her if they felt her symptoms were getting worse – they had agreed that a withdrawal from them and a lack of response to phone calls and texts would all be signs to pick up on. Miranda recognized that irritability and lack of interest were significant signs and she thought that she would recognize these signs and talk to her friends if they became worse in the future.

The process you have been involved in over recent weeks has
been about change: change in your symptoms and change in
your relationships.

Chapter 22

Reviewing your progress and planning for the future

Counter-argument: Yes it can.

IAN HAMILTON FINLAY,
SCOTTISH WRITER AND ARTIST

The process you have been involved in over recent weeks has
been about *change*: change in your symptoms and change in
your relationships.

Depression is a painful and difficult illness to live with and
it will have had a considerable impact on you and the people
around you, possibly damaging relationships, blocking progress, and undermining your self-esteem and self-confidence.
It has therefore been important to try to challenge and reverse
this process as directly and quickly as possible.

Over recent weeks you will have become an expert not only
in your own experience of depression but also in what is known
more widely about this illness. You have used this knowledge
to guide your attempts to change the course of your experience
of the illness and to manage its impact in your life. You have
also shared this information with the people in your life, so
that they can help your recovery and avoid creating obstacles
to your feeling better.

Exercise 22.1: What have you learned about depression?

Look back over the time you have been using this book and think about what you have learned. Write the main points in your notebook and discuss them with your IPT team.

- What have you learned about depression, both generally and in your own life?
- Who has it been useful to tell about your depression?
- What impact has sharing this information had?

As you come to the end of this process, it is useful to review the progress you have made and to start to plan carefully for the future. Hopefully, you have been monitoring your symptoms of depression every week, using the chart introduced in exercise 6.1 and reproduced in appendix 1. This regular review will have helped you to track the changes in your symptoms and given you the information you now need to review your progress overall.

When we looked at what is known about depression, in chapter 6, we went through many of the symptoms and the kinds of impact they can have on your life. You used this information to guide your decision as to whether to use IPT alone, with a therapist, or as part of a combined approach with therapy and medication.

We noted that the number of symptoms that troubled you when you started using IPT would help you to distinguish between mild, moderate and severe depression, with more symptoms suggesting greater severity (see page 85). Before you do the next review exercise, it's worth recapping the main symptoms and how they relate to the various degrees of depression.

- Core symptoms are:
  - ° Sadness or low mood, most or all of the time.
  - ° General loss of interest or pleasure in activities, even for activities that you normally enjoy.
- Other common symptoms are:
  - ° Disturbed sleep compared with your usual pattern. This may be difficulty in getting off to sleep, waking repeatedly through the night, or waking early in the morning and not being able to get back to sleep. Sometimes the problem is sleeping too much.
  - ° Change in appetite. This often involves poor appetite and losing weight, but a pattern of comfort eating and weight gain can also develop.
  - ° Fatigue (tiredness) or loss of energy.
  - ° Agitation or, on the contrary, slowing down, sluggishness.
  - ° Poor concentration, forgetfulness and indecisiveness. For example, you may find it difficult to read, work, etc.
  - ° Feelings of worthlessness, or excessive or inappropriate guilt.
  - ° Frequent thoughts of death. For many people thoughts such as 'Life's not worth living' or 'I don't care if I don't wake up' are common. For a smaller number of people, this may develop into thoughts and even plans of suicide.

Back in exercise 6.1 you were encouraged to use red, yellow and green highlighter pens on the chart to indicate the symptoms that trouble you most or all of the time (red), those that bother you some of the time (yellow), and those that you don't experience at all (green). The same colour scheme is used in the summary below of the different degrees of depression:

- Severe depression involves most or all of the nine key symptoms and greatly interferes with most areas of life. If you are severely depressed, your rating form will be mostly red.
- Moderate depression involves more than five symptoms and has a noticeable impact on how we manage day to day. If you are moderately depressed, your rating form will be a mix of red and yellow.
- Mild depression involves five of the symptoms and usually does not stop us functioning normally most of the time. If you are mildly depressed, your rating form will be a mix of yellow and green.
- Sub-threshold depression involves fewer than five symptoms but may still be troublesome at times. If you have this kind of depression, your rating form will be mostly green.
- If you are not depressed, you have no symptoms of depression that have a noticeable impact on how you manage your normal routine, and your rating form will be mostly or entirely green.

Exercise 22.2: Comparing your depression symptoms before and after IPT

How does your experience of depression at the start of this process compare to how it feels now? Look carefully at the weekly rating forms you have completed and then circle the description that best describes your first (in column 1) and most recent (in column 2) depression rating forms.

Severity of symptoms before starting IPT	Severity of symptoms now
Mostly red	Mostly red
Mostly yellow	Mostly yellow
Mostly green	Mostly green

If there is less red and more yellow, or less yellow and more green, this is very good news: this means that at least some of your symptoms have improved. Well done! When you are in the midst of depression you can feel very stuck and as if nothing can change. But the difference in the colour of your charts shows at a glance that your efforts and those of your IPT team have helped you to become unstuck and to redirect your life towards the way you want it to be. This is a significant achievement and something to congratulate yourself on.

It is also useful to think in more detail about what has happened to your symptoms. It may be that all or most of your symptoms have improved, or you might have noticed that some symptoms are less bothersome while others remain difficult. Some symptoms might have changed more quickly than others. You might feel particular relief at the improvement in some of your symptoms, for example, being able to sleep at night, or no longer feeling life is not worth living. You might also have noticed that you manage better in some areas of your life, such as your home life, even if you still need some extra support to achieve the same improvement in other areas, for example at work.

Self-help can be very effective, but for some people it may be only the first step towards recovery. There are many treatments for depression, of various degrees of intensity, depending on your particular needs. If self-help has not provided everything you need to overcome your depression, looking at what has helped and what remains to be done can help you to plan your next steps in this journey.

Exercise 22.3: Assessing your overall progress towards overcoming depression

- How would you describe your depression and its impact on your life now?
- Which of your symptoms have improved?
- Have the symptoms that troubled you the most improved at all?
- Which symptoms have stayed the same?
- Have any of your symptoms become worse? Which?
- Have your symptoms improved enough to allow you to manage well at home, at work and socially?
- What problems remain, if any?

Recovery is very often not a simple and straightforward process. It doesn't simply follow a straight line from illness to wellness:

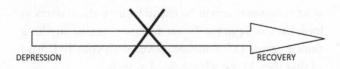

DEPRESSION   RECOVERY

Instead, it typically follows a more changeable course, with progress sometimes being interrupted by setbacks before following on the course towards recovery again:

RECOVERY

DEPRESSION

Over the past weeks, as you have worked through this book, you may have noticed progress towards your goals falter from time to time. Understanding setbacks when they happen and working out ways to recover from them and carry on can be among the most valuable skills learned in the recovery process.

Exercise 22.4: Dealing with setbacks in progress

Take some time to think through any setbacks you faced and, importantly, what helped you to overcome the obstacles life has a way of throwing in our path. These might have been times when your symptoms ratings increased, perhaps showing more red or yellow ratings than in the weeks before. Think about the following questions and write down your thoughts in your notebook. It will be useful to have these notes to look back over in the future in case you face anything similar again. Talk your ideas over with your IPT team so that they know what helped as well.

- What setbacks have you experienced during your recovery?
- How did you recover from those setbacks and continue to make progress?
- Who helped you to pick up after a setback and carry on?
- What did you learn from your setback and recovery?

But perhaps some or even all of your symptoms remain despite the work you have been doing. If you find this to be the case, remember: *it is not your fault*. There are several reasons why this might happen.

One relates to the intensity of the approach you have been using. Self-help approaches are most useful for treating mild depression. If you have been using this approach on your own, rather than with an IPT therapist, and your symptoms are still troublesome, this might indicate that this self-help approach has not been powerful enough to treat your depression. For example, you may have found the ideas relevant to your situation but perhaps found some of the exercises difficult to complete on your own. You have been encouraged throughout this process to work with an IPT companion or team; perhaps you might have found this very difficult to do, or perhaps your team has only been available for some of the time you needed them. If this approach has seemed to match your problems but you need a more actively supported version, speak to your GP and ask to see an IPT therapist in your area who can work with you.

If this approach has seemed relevant to your situation and you have not felt a lack of support, but still the self-help guidance has not seemed powerful enough to help you with all of your difficulties, using IPT in combination with anti-depressant medication might work for you. Try talking to your GP about this possibility. Many studies have shown the benefits of this approach, and this may help you to achieve more than the self-help approach could do on its own.

During the process of working through this book, you have often been encouraged to work with other people, whether your IPT team or your IPT therapist. Involving other people does not take away from your achievement – indeed, it shows how much *more* you can achieve when you combine your efforts with the support of other people. Trying to change how you felt and managed relationship problems was proving difficult to do on your own. Other people might have wanted to take away your problems; some might even have tried to 'sort you out' and told you what to do. They probably didn't get very far. By working together, however, you tapped into the potential to achieve genuine progress.

Exercise 22.5: The role of involving other people in your recovery

These are particularly important questions to talk over with your IPT team, who can continue to support you in the future. Write your answers down in your note-book to remind you to go on involving other people in the future.

- How has involving other people contributed to your recovery?
- What difference has this collaborative approach made to how you manage depression and address relationship problems?

At the start of this process you set a number of goals to work towards: 'smart' goals that were specific, measurable, achievable, relevant and timely. Go back to these goals now and review the progress you have made towards achieving them – especially the short-term goals and medium-term goals which were designed to be reached by the end of your journey through this book.

Exercise 22.6: Reviewing progress towards your goals

- Which of your goals have been achieved?
- What effect has achieving these goals had on you?
- What effect has it had on the people around you?

It is very important to include these details in your story of this period of depression. When you started to develop this story, you knew something about how it started but then found yourself circling around the middle. It was probably very difficult to imagine how the story would end. You are now in a much better position to describe how this part of your story has worked out. Your story does not stop here, but it may be possible to leave behind a number of the issues which have dominated your life for some time and to make new decisions about where to focus your attention.

It is helpful now to go back to the diagrams you created at the beginning of your IPT, your timeline and interpersonal inventory, and to update them. Has the 'depression line' on your timeline curved back up into the 'not depressed' area? Are there key events to add that have contributed to your feeling more optimistic about the future? Have you added people to your inventory, or perhaps moved them closer to you as your depression has lifted? These diagrams are only ever as complete as the last time you updated them. Keep the story up to date and use them to highlight your successes and the ways out of depression and relationship problems that have worked for you.

You may have found that some of your goals changed along the way or were more difficult to achieve than you originally anticipated. This is not unusual and does not take away from the success you have achieved. Depression can make us focus on problems and disregard our successes. This may still be happening now. Give yourself the credit you are due and allow for the setbacks, which are a normal part of the process.

Exercise 22.7: Looking at goals that have been hard to reach

First ask yourself:

- Have any of the goals been more difficult to reach than you anticipated? Which ones?

For those goals that *were* more difficult to complete, consider:

- Would a more clearly defined goal have served as a better guide?
- Was the goal realistic in the time you gave yourself?
- Might you get closer to achieving your goal if you had more time or support?
- Have new obstacles arisen that you could not have foreseen?
- Were any of the individual steps particularly difficult and, if so, in what way?
- Is this something you still want to achieve or is it no longer relevant?

- Have you achieved something else you did not expect?

It may be possible to use your experience of IPT to revisit some of these goals or the timescale in which you try to work towards them. Discuss your options for adapting your goals with your IPT team or therapist, and consider ways to continue to work towards those that remain meaningful for you. Studies of IPT have regularly shown that people continue to make positive changes after they finish treatment, especially in their relationships. This progress has been shown to go on for some time after the end of treatment, with significantly more progress reported when people have rated their relationships a year or more later. You have started a process of change, and that does not stop just because you have reached the final chapter of this book. All of the ideas and strategies remain available to you as you continue with the task of recovering and remaining well.

You have been through an emotionally challenging and inquisitive process. You have been asked on many occasions to reflect on your feelings and to share them with other people. The final part of the process is no different. This marks another stage of moving on, as you shift your attention from your medium-term goals to your long-term goals, while also perhaps revisiting some of your earlier goals if everything you hoped for has not yet been achieved.

Take some time to think about how well the IPT approach has worked for you, and how effective it has been in helping you to address your recent difficulties. There are many different approaches to treating depression and this approach gives particular emphasis to resolving difficulties or problems in your current relationships.

Exercise 22.8: A look back over the whole IPT process

- What has been the most helpful aspect of this process?
- What has worked well for you?
- What has not been helpful?
- Has anything been positively *un*helpful?
- Are there any outstanding difficulties that this approach has not helped you to address?

So far, you have focused on one area of interpersonal difficulty. However, many people face several challenges in their life at the same time. It's worth pausing now to ask yourself:

- Has the work you have done had a positive impact on any other areas of your life?
- Have any of the other focal areas become more relevant to your current situation?

If so, it may seem inviting to start work straight away on trying to tackle these. It's a good idea, though, not to be in too much of a rush. After you have worked hard to achieve a particular set of goals, it is important to allow some time for changes to settle in. Positive changes can become more routine and reliable with further practice. If one of the other focal areas has become significant for you, it is likely that the skills and knowledge you have developed will continue to serve you well if you decide to repeat this process using the self-help IPT guidelines and examine your story from another angle.

If you think a different therapeutic approach might be useful to build on what you have already achieved, such as looking at your past or at your style of thinking, it is helpful to wait at least three months before starting a new therapy. There is often a lot to take in when you start work with a new approach, and if you start to introduce new information too soon it can be difficult to hold on to any other ideas and skills you have recently acquired. Many of the ideas you have investigated in IPT are also likely to be useful in your work with any new approach, and so taking time to consolidate the work you have just done will continue to serve you well if you decide to try another psychological therapy. Details of other well-researched treatments for depression can be found in the last section of appendix 7.

Whichever path you take, it is important to look ahead to the future. You're entering a new phase where your focus will be on consolidating what you have learned and on maintaining the progress you have made. Throughout this process there has been repeated focus on working with your IPT companion or team. They are no less relevant at this stage.

Exercise 22.9: Reviewing your team for the future

- What do the people in your life need to know about what you are doing in order to help you to maintain your progress?
- What do they need to know about your longer-term goals to help you to achieve them?
- Do new people need to be added to your original IPT team to help you in this new phase? Who are they?
- What positive routines will be important to maintain in the future?
- What do they need to know about the possibility of depression returning in the future in order to help you most effectively? See appendix 4 for information about depression for friends and family.

For many people the prospect of becoming depressed again is very frightening. This might mean you become wary of any strong emotions you feel, especially those that are reminiscent of being depressed, such as feeling sad. This can be quite confusing when you are coming to the end of a process that you have found useful. We have been in a form of dialogue while you have been using this book, and so have formed a remote relationship. This, of course, will always be here for you to come back to in the future, but will not feature with the same regularity as it has in recent weeks. You have also been talking in detail with your IPT team or therapist, and these routines might also change now. If you have been working with a therapist, your sessions will eventually come to an end. The change might not be so dramatic with the people in your life with whom you have been developing closer and more open relationships, but the intensity of the support you are offered may change as you continue to feel better.

- How do you feel about the changing routine with your IPT therapist or team?
- How do you feel about moving on to the next phase of managing your depression?

It is very important to be able to distinguish any emotional reaction to change, including sadness, from depression. In chapter 6 we looked at all of the symptoms of depression. This highlighted the wide-ranging impacts of the illness – physical, emotional, cognitive and social. These symptoms have a much greater impact than passing low mood and last for much longer. In chapter 13 we also looked at the many emotions that are part of life and worked on developing an awareness of them which can help your own understanding and also help you to tell other people about what you are going through. As you move on, it is important to be able to tolerate and talk about the range of emotions that feature in your daily life as well as to identify early signals that depression may be returning.

One of the things we know about depression is that it can be a recurrent illness. Half of all those who experience depression will face it again at some point in the future. It is understandable, as you move out of a period of depression, that you won't want to think about the possibility of becoming depressed again. However, this is a very useful piece of information and can help you to plan and prepare for the future in a way that will serve to minimize the impact of any future depression. You may not be able to control whether or not depression features in your life again, but you *can* influence the impact it will have.

In planning for the future, it is very important that you and the people close to you are familiar with the early warning signs of depression returning. Think back over your most recent period of depression and think about what the earliest signs were that depression was developing. As you look back, you might notice changes and signs that you did not realize at the time were indications of developing depression. For some people, disturbed sleep is the first warning; or it may be a low mood that does not shift, or losing interest in what's happening around you so that you don't take phone calls or accept invitations. If you are forewarned by your early warning signs, you are forearmed against the insidious effects of depression and can protect yourself before it takes over all areas of your life.

Alongside your own observations, it is very useful to ask the people close to you to tell you what they noticed when you started to become depressed. The people around you might respond to changes that you are less aware of or that happen at a different point in the sequence. Your early warning list is more useful if you write it together with the people you are close to.

Share your list of early warning signs with the people you are close to and make a plan together on how to respond if these difficulties and symptoms become apparent again. This creates an opportunity to interrupt depression early and to limit its impact by actively using anti-depressant strategies, such as talking to people about how you feel and prioritizing doing the things that will help lift your mood. The recurrent nature of depression means that is likely that you will face periods of at least mild depression again in the future. This plan will provide you and the people around you with strategies that can effectively interrupt the predictable sequence at an early stage. If depression is well developed by the time these strategies are used, the uphill struggle to recovery is tougher.

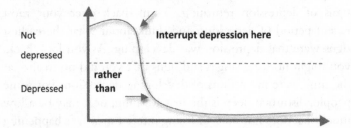

Each person has their own ways of responding to difficulties and loss, and you have already recognized that feeling depressed and withdrawing is part of how you respond, just as worrying or drinking more might form part of someone else's pattern. This vulnerability is difficult to change, but the way that you and the people around you respond to it is within your control. This is where your knowledge and expertise become power.

When you created your timeline of this and previous episodes of depression, you identified the types of life event that had overlapped with periods of depression in your life. You may have noticed that some themes repeated themselves, such as becoming depressed following a significant life change or when relationship problems become set in unhelpful repeating patterns. Are you likely to face any similar events which could destabilize your recovery in the coming weeks and months, acting as triggers for depression? These are the times when it will be most important to maintain clear and open communication with the people who are close to you and to use their support to help you through predictably difficult times.

When you have identified your early symptom patterns and triggers, make a plan about how you will respond to them, and think about what other people can do to help you at that point. It may feel tempting to put this off because you don't want to think about depression happening again, but this will not serve you as well as planning now. Relying on the plans you can make when you feel depressed places much greater pressure on you at a time when you are likely to feel unmotivated, confused and at your least imaginative. Making clear plans ahead of time about who you will talk to, who you will ask for help and support, who you will spend time with and what routines you will use to keep going will be a great advantage to you in the future. Think back to the start of this episode of depression and imagine the difference having such a plan in place would have made.

Exercise 22.10: Planning to cope with a possible return of depression

Use the questions below as a framework for your own plan. Involve your IPT team or therapist in creating the plan and then write it down (you can use the table in appendix 5 for this). Share it with the people who are likely to be involved. Make sure that each person has a copy, knows what is required of them and is able to meet this responsibility.

- What are the current sources of stress in your life that could trigger depression in the future?
- What can you or other people do to reduce these stresses?
- What are your early warning signs of depression returning? Identify at least three symptoms.
- What do other people notice when you become depressed? Identify at least three changes.
- What can you do to interrupt the onset of depression at an early stage? Identify at least three activities.
- What can other people do to help you to interrupt this sequence? Identify at least three ways in which someone else can support you.
- Who are the people who can help? Identify at least three people and discuss your plan with them.
- What anti-depressant activities and routines must be maintained as a priority? Identify at least three positive and enjoyable activities to maintain in your routine.
- How will you access professional assistance, such as your GP or a therapist, and who will support you to do that? Identify the route into support services before you need to refer yourself to these services. Plan to do this at the earliest point at which depression has become clear to you or other people.

If you have been using anti-depressant medication it is important to continue to take it, even if you no longer have symptoms of depression. This is how anti-depressant medication is designed to be used and does not mean you are now dependent on it. Research recommends that you continue to use medication for at least nine to twelve months the first time you become more than mildly depressed, continuing for at least six months after your symptoms have eased. If you have been depressed in the past, it is recommended that you continue to use medication for longer: for at least two years after your second episode of depression and at least five years after your third episode. Stopping medication too soon has been shown to increase the likelihood of depression returning more quickly. It is very important that you discuss this with your GP, and make sure that your response to medication continues to be monitored. If you feel your medication is not helping enough, even if it has helped in the past or if you have been taking it for a long time, ask your GP to discuss with you the options for changing the dose or type of anti-depressant medication you are prescribed. Clear information about using anti-depressant medication is available through the link provided in appendix 7.

As you finish this chapter and move on to the next stage of your story, be sure to take the key messages of this approach with you. Depression is a treatable illness and there are many ways in which you and the people around you can influence its course. Communicating clearly, sharing how you feel, and clarifying your expectations and options can greatly improve a situation in which you feel stuck and hopeless. You have been working very hard to improve your own understanding and that of the people in your life. You have shared vital information with a companion or team and now have the opportunity to take your story forward, embracing new relationships and opportunities with an awareness and confidence in what you have to offer to and need from the people in your life story. Good luck!

Summary

- Depression is a treatable disorder and you and the people in your life can influence its course.
- Recovery is often punctuated with setbacks, which can be among the most useful opportunities to learn resilience.
- Involving other people does not diminish your achievements but will demonstrate how much can be accomplished when your combine your efforts.
- Keeping your story up to date illustrates the way out of depression and relationships problems.
- Planning ahead with the people who are close to you and knowing your early warning signs and response will strengthen your position if you face depression in the future.

References

Barnes, M., 'Reactions to the Death of a Mother', *Psychoanalytic Study of the Child*, 19 (1964), 334–57.

Barnton Evans III, F., *Harry Stack Sullivan: Interpersonal Theory and Psychotherapy* (London, Routledge, 1996).

Blom, M. B., K. Jonker et al., 'Combination Treatment for Acute Depression is Superior only when Psychotherapy is Added to Medication', *Psychotherapy and Psychometrics*, 76: 5 (2007), 289–97.

Bowlby, J., *The Making and Breaking of Affectional Bonds* (London, Tavistock, 1979).

Burroway, J., *Writing Fiction: A Guide to Narrative Craft* (Glenview, Ill., and London, Scott, Foresman and Co., 1987).

Clark, H. (ed.), *Depression and Narrative: Telling the Dark* (Albany, NY, University of New York Press, 2008).

Cline, S. and C. Angler, *The Arvon Book of Life Writing: Writing Biography, Autobiography and Memoir* (London, A. & C. Black, 2010).

Cuijpers, P., A. van Straten et al., 'Psychotherapy for Depression in Adults: A Meta-analysis of Comparative Outcome Studies', *Journal of Consulting and Clinical Psychology*, 76: 6 (2008), 909–22.

DiMascio, A., M. Weissman et al., 'Differential Symptom Reduction by Drug and Psychotherapy in Acute Depression', *Archives of General Psychiatry*, 36 (1979), 1450–6.

Ekman, P. (ed)., *Darwin and Facial Expression: A Century of Research in Review* (Los Angeles, Malor Books, 2006).

Elkin, I. M. T., J. T. Shea et al., 'National Institute of Mental Health Treatment of Depression Collaborative Research Programme: General Effectiveness of Treatments', *Archives of General Psychiatry*, 46 (1989), 971–82.

Frank, A., *The Wounded Storyteller: Body, Illness and Ethics* (London, University of Chicago Press, 1995).

Frank, E. and V. J. Grochocinski, 'Interpersonal Psychotherapy and Anti-depressant Medication: Evaluation of a Sequential Treatment Strategy in Women with Recurrent Major Depression', *Journal of Clinical Psychiatry*, 61: 1 (2000), 51–7.

Frank, E., D. J. Kupfer et al. 'Early Recurrence in Unipolar Depression', *Archives of General Psychiatry*, 46 (1989), 397–400.

Frank, E., D. J. Kupfer et al., 'Three Year Outcomes for Maintenance Therapies in Recurrent Depression', *Archives of General Psychiatry*, 47 (1990), 1093–9.

Frank, E., D. J. Kupfer et al., 'Randomized Trial of Weekly, Twice-monthly, and Monthly Interpersonal Psychotherapy as Maintenance Treatment for Women with Recurrent Depression', *American Journal of Psychiatry*, 164: 5 (2007), 761–7.

Frank, E. and J. C. Levenson, *Interpersonal Psychotherapy* (Washington DC, American Psychological Association, 2011).

Grote, N. K., H. A. Swartz et al., 'A Randomized Controlled Trial of Culturally Relevant, Brief Interpersonal Psychotherapy for Perinatal Depression', *Psychiatric Services*, 60: 3 (2009), 313–21.

Hall, E. T., *The Hidden Dimension* (New York, Anchor Books, 1966).

Hansenne, M. and J. Bianchi, 'Emotional Intelligence and Personality in Major Depression: Trait versus State Effects', *Psychiatry Research*, 166: 1 (2009), 63–8.

Hart, J., *Storycraft: The Complete Guide to Writing Narrative Nonfiction* (Chicago and London, University of Chicago Press, 2011).

Hasson, G., *Brilliant Communication Skills* (London, Pearson Education, 2012).

Klerman, G. L., M. M. Weissman, B. J. Rounsaville and E. S.

Chevron, *Interpersonal Psychotherapy of Depression* (New York, Basic Books, 1984).

Lancaster, S. L. and S. E. Melka, 'An Examination of the Differential Effects of the Experience of DSM-IV Defined Traumatic Events and Life Stressors', *Journal of Anxiety Disorders*, 23: 5 (2009), 711–17.

Layard, R., *Happiness: Lessons from a New Science* (London, Penguin, 2005).

Leiper, R. and R. Kent, *Working through Setbacks in Psychotherapy: Crisis, Impasse and Relapse* (London, Sage, 2001).

Levenson, L. C., E. Frank et al., 'Comparative Outcomes among the Problem Areas of Interpersonal Psychotherapy for Depression', *Depression and Anxiety*, 7 (2010), 434–40.

Luty, S. E., J. D. Carter et al., 'Randomised Controlled Trial of Interpersonal Psychotherapy and Cognitive-Behavioural Therapy for Depression', *British Journal of Psychiatry*, 190 (2007), 496–502.

Maguire, J., *The Power of Personal Storytelling: Spinning Tales to Connect with Others* (New York, Penguin Putnam, 1998).

Markowitz, J. C. and M. M. Weissman (eds), *Casebook of Interpersonal Psychotherapy* (New York, Oxford University Press, 2012).

Mulcahy, R., R. E. Reay et al., 'A Randomised Control Trial for the Effectiveness of Group Interpersonal Psychotherapy for Postnatal Depression', *Archives of Women's Mental Health*, 13: 2 (2010), 125–39.

Mynors-Wallis, L., *Problem-solving Treatment for Anxiety and Depression* (Oxford, Oxford University Press, 2005).

Otto, M. W. and J. A. J. Smits, *Exercise for Mood and Anxiety: Proven Strategies for Overcoming Depression and Enhancing Well-being* (New York, Oxford University Press, 2011).

Pintor, L., C. Gastó et al., 'Relapse of Major Depression after Complete and Partial Remission during 2-year Follow Up', *Journal of Affective Disorders*, 73: 3 (2003), 237–44.

Reynolds III, C. F., E. Frank et al., 'Nortriptyline and Interpersonal Psychotherapy as Maintenance Therapies for Recurrent Major Depression: A Randomized Controlled Trial in Patients Older than Fifty-nine Years', *Journal of the American Medical Association* 281 (1999), 39–45.

Saxena, P., A. Dubey et al. 'Role of Emotion Regulation Difficulties in Predicting Mental Health and Well-being', *Journal of Projective Psychology and Mental Health*, 18: 2 (2011), 147–55.

Singh, S. and R. C. Mishra, 'Emotion Regulation Strategies and their Implications for Well-being', *Social Science International*, 27: 2 (2011), 179–98.

Stuart, S. and M. Robertson, *Interpersonal Psychotherapy: A Clinician's Guide* (London, Arnold, 2003).

Swartz, H. A., E. Frank et al., 'Brief Interpersonal Psychotherapy for Depressed Mothers Whose Children Are Receiving Psychiatric Treatment', *American Journal of Psychiatry*, 165: 9 (2008), 1155–62.

Van Londen, L., R. P. G. Molenaar et al. 'Three to Five Year Prospective Follow Up of Outcome in Major Depression', *Psychological Medicine*, 28 (1998), 731–5.

Weissman, M. M., J. C. Markowitz and G. L. Klerman, *Comprehensive Guide to Interpersonal Psychotherapy* (New York, Basic Books, 2000).

Williams, J. M. G and J. Scott, 'Autobiographical Memory in Depression', *Psychological Medicine*, 18 (1988), 689–95.

Wollburg, E. and C. Braukhaus, 'Goal Setting in Psychotherapy: The Relevance of Approach and Avoidance Goals for Treatment Outcome', *Journal of the Society for Psychotherapy Research*, 20: 4 (2010), 488–94.

Worchel, D. and R. E. Gearing, *Suicide Assessment and Treatment* (New York, Springer, 2010).

Zlotnick, C. and I. W. Miller, 'A Preventive Intervention for Pregnant Women on Public Assistance at Risk for Postpartum Depression', *American Journal of Psychiatry*, 163: 8 (2006), 1443–5.

Appendix 1

Symptoms of depression: your weekly rating form

Week: _____

Which symptoms have you noticed this week?

Use a red highlighter pen to mark the symptoms that bother you most or all of the time, a yellow pen to mark those that bother you some of the time and a green pen to identify those that do not bother you. If you don't have coloured highlighter pens, draw a circle around the symptoms your experience most regularly, underline those that you experience sometimes and leave the symptoms that don't bother you unmarked.

Describe the main events and people that relieved symptoms this week:

Describe the main events and relationships that triggered symptoms this week:

Sadness	Little interest	No enjoyment	Poor motivation
Waking up during the night	Cannot get to sleep	Do not want to see other people	Cannot concentrate
Hopelessness	Forgetful	Overeating	Cannot make decisions
No appetite	Lost weight	Waking early	Feeling life is not worth living
Always tired	Feeling slowed down	Want to die	Difficulty at work
Feeling guilty	Feeling agitated or on edge	Blame myself for everything	Easily confused
Feeling irritable	Feeling bad about myself	Feel I have let others down	Sleep too much

Appendix 2

Interpersonal inventory diagrams

(a) Concentric circles diagram

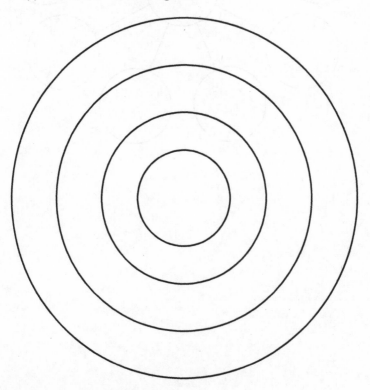

(b) Spider diagram

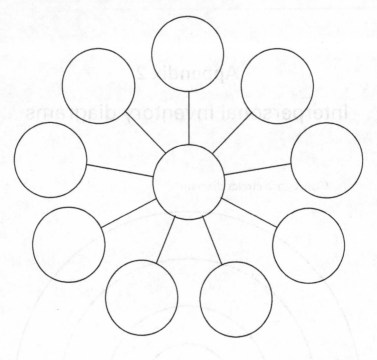

Appendix 3

Monitoring links between symptoms and relationships

For each day:

- Name the symptoms of depression you notice changing each day (under 'Depression').
- Name the person or interpersonal situation associated with a change in your symptoms (under 'Relationships').
- Draw a line between the symptoms and incidents when you can see a link.

	Depression . . . . Relationships
Monday	
Tuesday	
Wednesday	
Thursday	
Friday	
Saturday	
Sunday	

Appendix 4

Information for family and friends

Relationships can be complicated, especially when one person becomes depressed. Watching changes in someone you care about might leave you feeling frightened, frustrated and confused. It can be difficult to understand what they are going through.

It is helpful for families and friends of someone who is depressed to have good, clear information about depression. Knowing about this illness will help you to support the person and deal with your own feelings, so that you can work together to improve the situation.

The first step in tackling depression is to know what you are dealing with. Without understanding, you might undermine each other rather than depression.

What does it feel like to be depressed?

Depression is more than a change in mood. It affects how someone feels physically, behaves in relationships, thinks and manages daily routines. You may have noticed that the person:

- is unhappy most of the time
- has lost interest in things and people they used to enjoy

- talks about feeling guilty, ashamed or worthless
- looks anxious and agitated
- has lost confidence in themselves
- has problems concentrating and making decisions
- is irritable and perhaps angry
- isn't looking after themselves as well as usual
- is tearful and easily upset
- talks about life not being worth living or wanting to die
- has lost their appetite, or eats more than usual
- is forgetful
- sleeps more than usual, often during the day
- is not coping with things that used to be manageable
- is extremely tired
- has difficulty getting to sleep.

All these symptoms are difficult to live with and can be upsetting to see in someone you care about. These symptoms make it difficult to be in company, and people with depression often struggle to keep their normal routines going. It is important to be patient, and to understand that this kind of change is a common effect of depression and not a deliberate attack on your relationship.

Why do people get depressed?

The reasons why someone gets depressed are not always obvious. Some people are more vulnerable to depression if they have been depressed before or if they are physically unwell, and the illness can run in families. This vulnerability can be triggered if they face major changes or losses, such as relationship problems, job loss, becoming a parent or bereavement. Feeling lonely is also strongly linked to depression.

What is useful to know about depression?

Depression is a very common mental health problem – it affects one in four people at some point in their lifetime, twice as many women as men. It differs from the low mood we all experience at times because it is more unpleasant, lasts longer and interferes with day-to-day life and relationships. Mild depression involves at least five of the symptoms described above and it will have some impact on how the person manages day to day. Moderate or severe depression involves more symptoms and has a greater impact on work, family and social life, which become very difficult to manage.

It isn't possible to just 'snap out of' depression, but it is possible to help people to recover from this illness.

People typically become depressed for a period of time – usually about four to six months – and then recover, but an episode of depression can last much longer than this. Depression also comes back for about half of the people who have had it before, and for many people it is more helpful to think about managing their depression rather than curing it.

What treatments are available?

Depression is treatable. Treatments include self-help, talking therapies and medication. These different approaches can be used individually or together. Self-help is most useful when the person has mild depression. If depression is moderate or severe, talking therapy and medication have been shown to be helpful for many people.

The ideas behind Interpersonal Psychotherapy (IPT) can be used to guide self-help because most of the work takes place within the person's current relationships. In IPT, depression is treated by tackling the difficulties in current relationships, focusing on the difficulties that are commonly experienced when someone faces significant change, conflict or loss, or becomes isolated. Breaking down the connections between depression and what is happening in the person's relationships makes improvements in both more likely. Family and friends can make a very important contribution in this approach to the person's recovery.

Anti-depressants can be effective if the depression is moderate or severe or goes on for a long time without change. They can help to reduce symptoms and to make it easier to join in with other people and to cope better, so that the person can start to enjoy life and deal with their problems effectively again. Anti-depressant medications are not addictive – it isn't necessary to take more over time to have the same effect. However, it might be necessary for the person to try more than one medication to find the type and dose that will be most effective for them. Anti-depressant medications are designed to be taken over months and sometimes years, and the person should continue to take them for some time after their symptoms have improved to help protect against future risk. It can be very helpful for the person to have the support of the people around them to persevere with treatment so that they get as much benefit from it as possible.

Many people will recover from depression without active treatment, but this route to recovery can take much longer and is less likely to end in success if the depression is moderate or severe. It is in everyone's interests for depression to be treated as quickly and effectively as possible.

How can you help someone who is depressed?

Try to be a good listener – even if you hear the same thing

several times. Try not to judge or rush to solve problems. It may be too soon to talk about solutions. Encourage the person to tell you how they feel. Give advice, but only if you are asked to, and if you have thoughts about the problem that is behind the depression, offer to work with the person to find a solution.

Spend time with them and support them in doing things they might enjoy. Encourage them to keep going with helpful routines, such as taking regular exercise, eating well, avoiding alcohol and spending relaxing time with friends (and be patient even if they have to build this up gradually).

If the person with depression is quiet and withdrawn, let them know that you are available when they want to talk but also that you recognize this isn't easy for them. Lots of questions can feel overwhelming, especially when they don't have the answers you are both looking for.

Stay focused on one subject at a time. It may be difficult for them to concentrate.

Recognize that your ways of relating to each other might change while your friend or relative is depressed. They are likely to need more from the people around them than they can give back for a while. This will change again when the depression lifts. You can help by being flexible around these changes.

Remind the person that depression is treatable and that it's not their fault that they are depressed.

If they are irritable, it is helpful to slow down, remain neutral and try not to react. Listen for opportunities to acknowledge their feelings and comments. At these times, conversations about important decisions or issues are unlikely to be productive. Plan to discuss important issues some other (specific) time, and make sure to return to the discussion at the time you've agreed.

Take the person seriously if they talk about feeling hopeless or wanting to harm themselves. About 80 per cent of people with depression think about dying. A much smaller proportion of people plan to act on these thoughts, but even if they don't, the thoughts themselves are frightening and can make people feel very isolated. Talking about them does not put ideas into the person's head and it can be reassuring to know that someone will listen and give support when it is most needed.

IPT will provide several opportunities for you to help your friend or relative to recover from their depression. They will be developing their own personal story of depression. This will help you both to understand their experience as well as to talk about it in a way that you will both find useful. They may ask you to help in developing this story, perhaps by providing information or by talking about your relationship.

Some of the exercises in this book will be about using support more effectively; others can be used in sorting out difficulties between you and your friend or relative, if your relationship has suffered while they have been depressed. Neither of you is being blamed. Sorting out relationship difficulties can make an important contribution to helping someone recover from depression, and you can make a valuable contribution to this process.

Be ready for a relapse

It is tempting to try to forget depression as soon as it lifts. However, this is an illness many people will have to face more than once. The best way to handle the risk of it coming back is to know what to do before it happens.

As your friend or relative recovers and is able to think and plan more clearly, the self-help guidance will prompt them to plan what to do if depression returns in the future. They will be asked to create a list of early warning signs. They and you have different points of view, so together you can create a more comprehensive list than either of you could do on your own.

This will serve as a safety net for your friend or relative and for your relationship. The list should also include what you will each do in response to these signs to interrupt the depression as quickly as possible next time. Follow this plan if the need arises. (Appendix 5 on the next page will help you to structure your plan.)

Create extra support systems that include family, friends, and others who the person who has been depressed feels confident to include. When depression is kept secret, it is made stronger. Reverse the process by making sure the necessary people are well informed and ready to act when required, and you will help to protect your friend or relative in the future.

Appendix 5

Early warning signs and response plan

EARLY WARNING SIGNS

What are the current sources of stress in your life that could trigger depression in the future?
Which symptoms signal to you that depression is coming back? Identify at least three symptoms and describe them in as much detail as you can.
Which symptoms or changes signal to the people close to you that depression is coming back? Identify at least three symptoms or changes and describe any signs that are not already named above.

WHAT TO DO

What can you or other people do to reduce the sources of stress that could trigger depression?

What can you do to interrupt the early symptoms of depression that you have described above? Try to identify at least three activities e.g. talking about how you feel, exercise, speaking to your GP etc.

What can other people do to help you to manage the early warning signs of depression? Identify at least three ways in which someone else can support you e.g. spending more time with you, joining you when you do anti-depressant activities, sharing some of your responsibilities for a while etc. Try to identify at least three things other people can do to help.

SHARE THIS PLAN WITH THE PEOPLE WHO
CAN HELP YOU TO STAY WELL.

Who are the people who can help? Name the people who can help and what they can do. Discuss your plan with them.

What anti-depressant activities and routines will be a priority to keep going e.g. talking to the people close to you, regular exercise, time for your interests or hobbies? Identify at least three positive and enjoyable activities to keep going to help you stay well.

When should you ask for professional help, such as from your GP or a therapist? Plan to do this at the earliest point at which depression has become clear to you or other people.

How will you access these services and who will support you to do that? Identify the route into support services before you need to refer yourself to these services. Write down important telephone numbers.

Who are the people who can help? Name the people who can help and what they can do. Discuss your plan with them.

What are the important activities and routines will be a priority to keep doing e.g. linking to the ones close to you, regular exercise, time for your interests or hobbies? Identify at least three routines and enjoyable activities as you plan to help you stay well.

When should you ask for professional help, such as from your GP or a therapist? Plan to do this at the earliest point at which depression has become clear to you or other people.

How will you access these services and what will support you to do some? Identify the route into support services before you need to find yourself in these services. Write down important telephone numbers.

Appendix 6

What the research says

IPT has been very well researched for over forty years, and is one of the most widely recognized evidence-based therapies for depression. 'Evidence-based therapy' means that the therapy has been closely examined in research settings and has been shown to produce better results than no treatment and the same results as or better results than other well-researched treatments. As a result IPT is one of the recommended treatments for depression in the UK, USA, Australia and New Zealand, and across Europe.

IPT was first developed and evaluated in a research setting, and since then several hundred scientific papers have been written about it. It has been studied across continents with many different age groups and for a range of different problems. A brief summary of the main research findings for IPT as a treatment for depression is provided below.

Recovering from depression

In the first test of IPT as a treatment for depression over eighty people were offered IPT, anti-depressant medication (A/D), both treatments together (IPT & A/D) or general support from a psychiatrist. All of the active treatments (IPT, A/D, IPT &

A/D) were more helpful than simple support, and the combination of IPT and medication was more effective in reducing depression than either IPT or medication alone.

Treatment with IPT or medication alone produced similar results to each other, although their respective effects became obvious at different times during treatment, with medication producing earlier changes in sleep and feeling slowed down, while IPT produced improvements in low mood, hopelessness, motivation and suicidal thoughts later in treatment. When the treatments were combined the effects complemented each other, so that the people who received both treatments experienced the widest range of benefits.

A further interesting outcome was revealed one year after the treatment ended, when the people who had received IPT reported significantly better relationships. This improvement in the quality of relationships was greater than they had described at the end of treatment, and was not shared by the people who had been treated with medication alone.

In one of the largest studies to look at IPT as a treatment for depression over 250 people suffering from depression were offered either IPT, cognitive behavioural therapy (CBT), anti-depressant medication, or inactive medication (placebo) and general support. Most of the people who took part in the study reported fewer symptoms of depression after treatment and there were few differences in outcome between the active treatments (IPT, CBT, anti-depressant medication). When the people who entered the studies with most depressive symptoms were looked at separately, IPT and anti-depressant medication were shown to be the most helpful treatments.

Placebo   IPT   A/D
Support   CBT   medication

This comparison of IPT and CBT for depression was repeated with almost 180 people in Australia who were receiving treatment for depression, and again both treatments were found to be helpful in reducing depressive symptoms, with few differences apparent between them. Interestingly, in this study CBT seemed more effective when only the people who were more depressed at the start of the study were considered. This is in contrast to the results of the study described above, and suggests that the relative benefits of one type of therapy over the other for more severe depression are not yet clear; nevertheless, both talking therapies have been repeatedly shown to be equivalent when they are used to treat mild or moderate depression.

Staying well

When the people who had been treated in the first big comparison between IPT, CBT and medication were interviewed eighteen months after treatment ended, it became clear that the individual packages of treatment alone were not enough to keep most people well. Many people remained well for most of the eighteen months, but only 25–30 per cent of those who received one of the talking therapies, and only 20 per cent of those who had received medication for the few months of the study, remained well for the whole time.

Researchers therefore began to look at ways to make the benefits of treatment last longer. This in fact turned the clock back to the very first study of IPT, which had looked at how to keep people well after they had responded to medication. In the first research study of IPT, which tested its usefulness as a means of maintaining well-being, the therapy was offered over eight months, either alone or with medication. Long-term medication proved to be the most effective treatment to keep people well, but weekly IPT alone was shown to be almost as effective. The combination of medication and IPT was shown to have the best overall effect, as it both prevented a return of depression and improved relationships.

Later studies built on this finding. Almost 130 people who had had depression many times before received combined treatment of IPT and anti-depressant medication. Those people who responded to treatment, and whose depression did not come back within four months, were then offered one of five possible treatments which included medication alone, IPT alone or IPT and support combined with medication or placebo. The study ran for three years and IPT was offered monthly throughout. The people who received combined treatment of IPT and anti-depressant medication remained well longest, on average over two years; the next most successful treatments were medication alone and then IPT alone. Both active treatments (IPT and medication) were more effective than inactive treatments (placebo).

A similar study with over 230 women who had experienced depression more than once supported the original finding that IPT offered monthly is helpful in preventing or delaying further depression, and also revealed the importance of finding the right package of treatment for each individual. Three-quarters of the women who had recovered from depression with IPT alone were helped to stay well for at least two years with monthly sessions of IPT. However, those women who had needed IPT plus medication to recover from depression did not fare so well when IPT alone was used to try to keep them well. Half of these women became depressed again within two years, and it appeared that those who needed combined treatment to get well also needed combined treatment to stay well.

Another study looked not simply at whether or not the treatments were combined but also at when they were combined. In this study, 180 women received combined treatment of IPT and anti-depressant medication from the outset. A further 159 women received IPT, initially alone and with the addition of medication if they had not responded by halfway through treatment. Two-thirds of those women who received combined treatment throughout recovered, while almost 80 per cent recovered when the combination treatment had followed later, that is, with medication started about halfway through treatment. This finding is particularly important to remember if you are concerned about using medication, or perhaps think that if you haven't taken it from the start of treatment it is no good beginning later. Clearly some people require a combined approach to recover from depression, and carefully monitoring your own response to treatment may reveal a further opportunity for even greater gains if treatments are combined only when it becomes clear that an individual therapy is not sufficient.

It is very important to find the right package of treatment to tackle your difficulties. Research suggests that when people have mild depression a single form of therapy is likely to help recovery, while many people with moderate or severe depression will benefit more, and more quickly, if a combination of IPT and anti-depressant medication is used, at least some of the time. It is important to monitor your symptoms and relationship difficulties and to consider combining talking therapy and medication if significant change is not evident by halfway through the course of treatment. It is also very important to

remember that the same combination of therapies that is necessary to get you well will help to keep you well for longer.

Depression in mothers

As we have already noted, the time following childbirth is one
when women are particularly vulnerable to depression. Several
different research groups have tested IPT as a treatment for
new or expectant mothers.

In one study, almost 100 pregnant women were offered
either standard ante-natal care or standard care plus a short version of IPT. Three months after their babies were born, only
two of the new mums who had had IPT became depressed,
while four times as many new mums who had received standard care developed depression.

A second study provided brief IPT or standard care to
almost sixty pregnant women and found that the women who
received IPT had significantly fewer symptoms of depression
both before giving birth and six months after having their
babies compared to the mothers who received usual care. The
IPT mums also showed significant improvements in how they
managed their relationships compared to the other mums.

IPT was offered as a group treatment for new mothers in
Australia and the outcome was compared to standard care.
Mothers who received IPT had far fewer symptoms of depression after treatment and were continuing to improve three
months after the therapy ended. The women who had IPT also
described more improvement in their relationships with their
partners and their newborns compared to the other mothers.

Fifty depressed mothers who were facing additional problems, such as poverty or mental health issues in their children,
were offered eight sessions of IPT or usual care. The mothers
who received IPT reported significantly fewer symptoms of

depression and were managing significantly more effectively nine months after treatment ended than the mothers who received usual care. The children of the mums who received IPT also reported fewer symptoms of depression nine months after the IPT ended than the children of the 'usual care' mothers.

Does focus make a difference?

IPT offers a choice between four interpersonal themes in treating depression. While the individual problem areas share techniques and ideas, it is natural to wonder whether the problem area you focus on is more or less likely to lead to a good outcome. This question was addressed with over 180 people who used IPT to treat their depression. The outcomes for each of the four focal areas were tracked and success was found to be just as likely and just as rapid in each focal area. Choosing a problem area to focus on is less about getting that choice right and more about starting to understand how relevant the different techniques might be to the problems you are facing. Understanding how your symptoms of depression and relationship problems are influenced by each other can help you to target your efforts more specifically, but there are many features of IPT that will apply across each of the types of relationship difficulties that you try to sort out.

Summary

- IPT has been the subject of research for over forty years.
- IPT is recommended as an evidence-based treatment for depression in the UK, USA, Australia and New Zealand, and across Europe.
- IPT has repeatedly been shown to be as effective as other

talking therapies for depression and in some studies has been shown to be more effective.

- IPT combined with anti-depressant medication can produce quicker and better results in treating moderate to severe depression than either treatment alone.

- IPT has repeatedly been shown to improve the quality of our relationships and the way we manage them day to day, often with the improvements increasing in the months following the end of therapy.

- Staying well after IPT ends relies on the same combination of strategies and medication as was necessary to recover from depression.

- Each of the four problem areas is equally likely to be helpful in treating depression and improving relationship difficulties, and all take the same amount of time to achieve success.

Appendix 7

Useful links and contact details

Information about depression

National Institute of Clinical Excellence (NICE)

www.nice.org.uk

NICE guidance supports healthcare professionals and others to make sure that the care they provide is of the best possible quality and offers the best value for money. The website provides information for the public on a range of disorders, including depression, and details on opportunities for patient, carer and public involvement.

MIND

www.mind.org.uk

infoline: 0300 123 3393

A mental health charity that offers advice and support for those experiencing mental health problems. Their website and helpline offer advice and information and they also run local support groups.

The Black Dog Institute

www.blackdoginstitute.org.au/index.cfm

Based in Australia, the Black Dog Institute provides a wealth of information and advice on its website, covering depression and bipolar disorder, treatment options, support groups and advice on seeking help.

Help and support

Samaritans

www.samaritans.org

24-hour helplines:

UK: 08457 90 90 90 (open 24 hours a day)

Republic of Ireland: 1850 60 90 (open 24 hours a day)

Email support: jo@samaritans.org

This charity aims to provide emotional support to people who are experiencing feelings of distress or despair, including those which may lead to suicide. Volunteers offer support by responding to phone calls twenty-four hours a day as well as emails and letters. Alternatively, you can drop into a branch to have a face-to-face meeting. The website provides easily accessible information about how to find your local branch.

Exercise

www.nhs.uk/livewell/fitness/Pages/Fitnesshome.aspx

This NHS website provides a lot of information on health and fitness, including advice about nutrition and diet, exercise and stopping smoking.

www.nhs.uk/Change4Life/Pages/why-change-for-life. aspx

This site provides tips on a wide range of fitness-promoting activities, including getting more active and eating healthily, and includes links to activities in your local area.

www.patient.co.uk/directory/exercise-physical-activity-fitness-advice

This website offers lots of information about exercise and physical activity and links to a range of local and national resources across the UK.

Anti-depressant medication

www.rcpsych.ac.uk/mentalhealthinformation/mental healthproblems/depression/anti-depressants.aspx

This website contains up-to-date information from the Royal College of Psychiatrists about anti-depressant medication.

Information on evidence-based treatments for depression

http://guidance.nice.org.uk/CG90/PublicInfo/doc/ English

This website contains information on recommended treatment options for depression from the National Institute for Health and Clinical Excellence (NICE), the British government body which recommends treatments for physical and mental illnesses to medical professionals working in the NHS.

Self-help

www.moodscope.com

Moodscope is a social networking tool that helps treat depression by giving sufferers a way of getting help from their friends.

www.llttf.com/

The Living Life to the Full website offers a course in life skills that aims to provide access to high-quality, practical and user-friendly training. The course uses the principles of cognitive behavioural therapy (CBT), which has been shown to be very helpful for people with depression.

https://moodgym.anu.edu.au/welcome

This Australian website offers a free self-help programme to teach CBT skills to people vulnerable to depression and anxiety.

http://www.beatingtheblues.co.uk

This website is based on CBT and offers a course of eight online sessions to help you to understand the link between how you think and how this influences your feelings and behaviour. The programme teaches strategies to help you cope better in the short term and workable skills for life so that you can face the future with confidence.

www.apa.org/helpcenter/road-resilience.aspx

This brochure provides information on resilience, factors that affect how people deal with difficulties and how to develop more effective strategies.

Index

Aeschylus 359
agitation 85, 86, 88, 200, 224, 279, 280, 288, 322, 328, 459, 461, 468, 492, 498
alcohol/drug misuse 85, 321, 415, 501
American Psychological Association 24
anger 93, 234, 277, 278, 295, 354
   grief and 360, 380, 384, 386, 404
anti-depressant activities 2–3, 116–17, 188, 249, 290–1, 484, 506, 507
   see also under individual activity name
anti-depressant medication 85, 92, 98–100, 102, 103, 110, 114, 146, 290, 299, 345, 346, 385, 451, 453, 454, 464, 467, 473, 484–5, 499, 500, 509–13, 516, 519
appendices 491–520
appetite, losing 26, 84, 88, 290, 468, 492, 498
attachment:
   'crippling' 362
   dismissing 23
   disorganized 23
   patterns of 22, 23, 262, 294, 363
   preoccupied 23, 262, 294, 363
   relationships as 21
   secure 23

Balzac, Honoré de 409
behavioural activation 101
Bennett, Alan 65
bipolar disorder 1, 103, 518
Black Dog Institute, The 518
blame 26, 88, 111, 121, 203, 231, 244, 246, 249, 274, 292, 310, 314, 333, 353, 354, 379, 384, 386, 437, 492, 502

boss, relationship with 31, 32, 68, 80, 265, 274, 275, 277, 278, 281, 304, 342
Bowlby, John 21, 23
Brilliant Communication (Hasson) 221
bullying communication 220
Burroway, Janet 148

cancer 25, 365, 396, 404
childbirth 93, 102, 514
childhood:
   learning relationship 'dance' in 21–2, 45
   loss in 136, 374, 402, 403, 404, 405
closed questions 217
coffee, problems with sleep and 2, 3, 288
cognitive behavioural therapy (CBT) 96, 101, 510, 511, 520
communication, the process of 197–229
   a helpful and effective style of communication 221–2
   anticipating a hostile or uninterested audience 199
   as a process rather than an event 200
   assertive 221–2
   attacking or aggressive 219
   based on interpreting behavior rather than direct discussion 198
   bullying 220
   clarifying 216
   closed questions 217
   communication style 218–19
   confidence and 221
   depression and 198–9
   empathy 222
   eye contact 205–6
   facial expression 206–7

gesture and touch 211–12
how do we communicate? 201–12
how meaning changes with emphasis
    (Exercise 12.1) 203–4
identifying strengths and weaknesses
    in communication (Exercise 12.2)
    205
interpreting facial expression
    (Exercise 12.4) 207
IPT team and 228–9
leading by example 200
listening deliberately 213–14, 218,
    306
movement and position 208–9
non-verbal communication 201,
    204–5, 214
observing style of communication
    (Exercise 12.9) 220–1
open questions 216–17
paraverbal communication 201,
    202–3
passive 220
passive aggressive 220
perceived worth of what you have to
    say 198
personal space 208–10
posture 210–11
practising deliberate listening
    (Exercise 12.8) 218
practising helpful communication
    habits (Exercise 12.10) 223
practising use of posture and
    movement in communication
    (Exercise 12.6) 210–11
preaching 219
principle one: start with your purpose
    – what you want the other person
    to know 226
principle two: think about how you
    say it 227
principle three: understanding the
    other person's perspective will
    help you to communicate more
    effectively 227–8
principle four: make sure there is
    time for questions 228
principles of good communication
    226–9
the reasoning brain and the
    emotional brain 199–200
reflecting feelings 215–16
reflecting what is said 214–15

reviewing communication styles and
    skills 222–4
storyteller, the good 197–8
successful and unsuccessful
    conversations – what works?
    (Exercise 12.11) 223–4
summarizing 217–18
thinking about personal space
    (Exercise 12.5) 209–10
thinking about touch (Exercise 12.7)
    212
timing 20
two-way process 197
understanding the other person's
    perspective will help you to
    communicate more effectively
    227–8
unhelpful styles of communication
    219–20
using eye contact (Exercise 12.3) 206
verbal communication 201, 202
the whole message: clarity and
    communication 212
complicated grief 102
concentration, difficulties with 26, 38,
    85, 88, 89, 90–1, 247, 264, 288,
    346, 449, 459, 468, 492, 498, 501
conflict:
  goals and 189
  interpersonal role see interpersonal
    role conflict
  IPT theme 5, 11, 14, 20, 32, 37, 42,
    43, 48, 65, 66, 81, 132, 134–6,
    142, 147, 149, 157, 162, 163, 167,
    171, 174, 175, 176, 181, 186
  managing role 70–1
couples therapy 101

Darwin, Charles 207
Davis, Donald 51
death:
  beliefs about death (Exercise 18.9)
    387–8
  grief, loss and 17, 41–2, 72–3, 80–1,
    102, 137, 359–93, 394–408 see
    also grief and loss
  Jean's story 394–408
  remembering the time around the
    85–7, 383–7
  thinking about the time of death
    (Exercise 18.8) 85–7
  thoughts of 85–7, 90, 91, 289, 468

deliberate listening, practising 218
depression:
  anti-depressant activities 2–3, 116–17, 188, 249, 290–1, 484, 506, 507 *see also under individual activity name*
  anti-depressant medication 85, 92, 98–100, 102, 103, 110, 114, 146, 290, 299, 345, 346, 385, 451, 453, 454, 464, 467, 473, 484–5, 499, 500, 509–13, 516, 519
  conditions related to 101–3
  diagnosis of 18, 26, 27, 85, 86, 87, 111, 113–14, 115, 121, 290, 348, 360, 396, 401
  episodic disorder 91
  family history of 94
  how can you help someone who is depressed? 500–2
  in context 103–10
  IPT and *see* Interpersonal Psychotherapy
  knock-on effect for people around you 111, 126, 283, 288
  mild 86, 91, 95–8, 110, 469, 473, 482, 499, 513
  moderate or severe 85, 86, 90, 95, 98–101, 102, 110, 449, 467, 469, 499, 500, 511, 513, 516
  past 145–7
  post-natal 101–2
  recurring problem 92
  relapse of 483–5, 502–3
  responding early to signs of 91
  risk factors 93–4
  symptoms *see* symptoms of depression
  term 35, 82
  treatable illness 92
  understanding the story of your 122–47
  understanding your 82–110
  unnoticed 90
  vulnerability to 18–19, 23, 24, 44–5, 66, 126, 138, 146, 179, 180, 181, 198, 256, 258, 260, 288, 348, 411, 416, 498, 514, 520
  what are you feeling? 11–12
  what are you saying or not saying? 11
  what do we know about? 90–1
  what does it feel like to be depressed? 497–8
  what is useful to know about? 499
  what is? 82–4

  what treatments are available? 499–500
  who gets? 93–4
  why do people get depressed? 498
  women, more common in 93
Dickens, Charles 207
direction and purpose, sense of 33, 34–5, 50, 52, 54, 55
dismissing attachment 23
disorganized attachment 23
Dynamic Interpersonal Therapy (DIT) 101
dysthymia 86, 103

early warning signs 243, 246, 481, 482, 484, 486, 402
  and response plan 505–7
emotions, understanding 230–50
  emotional vocabulary 236–41
  feelings and communication: keeping the airwaves open 230–1
  gaps in our emotional awareness 233
  how emotional skills can help you 231–3
  how well developed is your emotional vocabulary? (Exercise 13.1) 238–41
  interpersonal awareness 244–7
  new or unacknowledged feelings 247–8
  recognizing and naming your feelings 232
  self-awareness 232, 233
  sensations, thoughts and feelings 234–6
  standing back from your feelings 242
  withdraw, resisting urge to automatically 232
empathy 221, 222, 290, 347, 421
exercise, physical 96–7, 114, 119, 146, 178, 180–1, 290, 501, 507, 518–19
exercises:
  1.1: Identifying the cycle of depression and relationship difficulties 4
  1.2: Thinking about putting your team together 8
  3.1: Thinking about your own story 42
  3.2: Sketching out the timeline of your story 45

6.1: Identifying your symptoms of depression 87–90, 127, 468

6.2: Thinking about the links between symptoms and relationships 104–6

6.3: Exploring the links between your symptoms and your relationships 109–10

7.1: Thinking about the effects of depression on you and others 112

7.2: Thinking about the consequences of accepting your diagnosis 115

7.3: Giving yourself a break and asking for help 115–16

7.4: What can you do straight away to start making opportunities for improvement 118

7.5: Choosing your IPT team 120–1

9.1: Creating your inventory 153–5

9.2: Beginning to explore your relationships 155–7

9.3: Reviewing your inventory (1): contact and routines 157–8

9.4: Reviewing your inventory (2): help and support 158–62

9.5: Reviewing your inventory (3): interpersonal themes 163–4

9.6: Reviewing your inventory (4): overview 168

10.1: Organizing your story 173–8

10.2: Distinguishing between focus and context 178–81

10.3: Telling your story 181–3

11.1: Setting your goals 195–6

12.1: How meaning changes with emphasis 203–4

12.2: Identifying strengths and weaknesses in communication 205

12.3: Using eye contact 206

12.4: Interpreting facial expression 207

12.5: Thinking about personal space 209–10

12.6: Practising use of posture and movement in communication 210–11

12.7: Thinking about touch 212

12.8: Practising deliberate listening 218

12.9: Observing style of communication 220–1

12.10: Practising helpful communication habits 223

12.11: Successful and unsuccessful conversations – what works? 223–4

13.1: How well developed is your emotional vocabulary? 238–41

14.1: What support is available to you in facing change? 257

14.2: The wider context of change 260

14.3: Getting help to fill out the story of the old role 266

14.4: Thinking over the old role 266–7

14.5: Creating a timeline for your old role 268

14.6: Looking for continuity 269–70

14.7: Focusing on the change itself 272–3

14.8: Examining your support at a time of change 273

14.9: Examining the nature of the change and your use of support 274–6

14.10: Feelings at the moment of change 277–9

14.11: How do you feel about your new role? 281–2

14.12: Looking at new routines 282

14.13: Looking at new skills 283–4

14.14: Looking at the benefits of role change 284

16.1: Observing the relationship 305–6

16.2: Beginning to involve the other person 315

16.3: Starting to observe your relationship 315–17

16.4: Your relationship timeline 318–19

16.5: Setting the scene 320–1

16.6: Filling out the scene 321–2

16.7: Watching an argument unfold 325–6

16.8: How your own conversations unfold 326–7

16.9: Gathering information about non-verbal communication 328–9

16.10: Assessing non-verbal communication 329

16.11: The take-home message 330–2

16.12: Pinpointing the main issues of disagreement 333

18.1: Thinking about your memories 371
18.2: Sketching out the story of your relationship 373–5
18.3: Working out what you have lost 376
18.4: Beginning to develop other relationships 378
18.5: Remembering the bad times as well as the good 379
18.6: Remembering difficulties in the relationship 381
18.7: Thinking about new opportunities 383
18.8: Thinking about the time of death 385–7
18.9: Beliefs about death 387–8
18.10: Doing things and seeing people again 390
20.1: Isolation and depression: how closely are they connected? 419
20.2: Which relationships are easier than others 420–1
20.3: Reviewing your good relationships 425–8
20.4: Looking for the patterns in good relationships 429–30
20.5: Reviewing less successful relationships 431–3
20.6: Looking for the patterns in less successful relationships 435
20.7: Recognizing repeating patterns of difficulty in your relationships 438–40
20.8: Watching how other people behave 441–2
20.9: Looking for poor use of non-verbal communication 443–4
20.10: Looking at what actually happened 445–7
22.1: What have you learned about depression? 467
22.2: Comparing your depression symptoms before and after IPT 469–71
22.3: Assessing your overall progress towards overcoming depression 471–2
22.4: Dealing with setbacks in progress 472–4
22.5: The role of involving other people in your recovery 474–5

22.6: Reviewing progress towards your goals 475–6
22.7: Looking at goals that have been hard to reach 476–7
22.8: A look back over the whole IPT process 478–9
22.9: Reviewing your team for the future 479–83
22.10: Planning to cope with a possible return of depression 483–5
eye contact, using 201, 204, 205–6, 210, 223, 440, 462

facial expression, interpreting 204, 206–7
family and friends, information for 497–503
    be ready for a relapse 502–3
    how can you help someone who is depressed? 500–2
    what does it feel like to be depressed? 497–8
    what is useful to know about depression? 499
    what treatments are available? 499–500
    why do people get depressed? 498
family history of depression 94
fatigue 84, 93, 248, 468
finding your story and selecting a focus 170–86
    distinguishing between focus and context (Exercise 10.2) 178–81
    focusing on a single central theme 170
    I have poor/adequate/good social support available 182, 185
    I use my social support 182, 185
    maximum change by manageable means 170
    organizing your story (Exercise 10.1) 173–8
    telling your story (Exercise 10.3) 181–3
Finlay, Ian Hamilton 280, 466
focal areas 5, 65–7, 75–81
    case studies 80–1
    questions and concerns about 75–81
    why choose just one focus when there is so much going on? 75–7
    why if I choose the wrong focal area? 78–9

focus, does it make a difference? 515
Forster, E. M. 30, 251
four themes of ITP: change, conflict,
    loss, isolation 4–8, 11, 14, 37,
    65–7, 170, 251–465 *see also under*
    individual theme

Galbraith, John Kenneth 111
gesture and touch 211–12
goals:
    act of setting a goal as anti-depressant
        188
    being 'stuck' and 188
    change of role and 190
    general goals and personal goals
        189–93
    'goal buddies' 192
    hitting the target 193–5
    involving other people in 191–3
    long-term 190, 191, 195
    medium-term 190, 191, 192–3, 195,
        292, 293
    setting achievable 187–96
    setting your (Exercise 11.1) 195–6
    short-term 190–1, 195, 292
    simplifying 13
    SMART 193, 194
General Practitioner (GP) 90, 91, 98, 99,
        100, 146, 345, 408, 413, 453, 454,
        464, 473–4, 484, 485, 506, 507
Greer, Germaine 300
Grief and Loss, dealing with (theme
        three) 17, 41–2, 72–3, 80–1, 102,
        136–7, 359–93
    beginning to develop other
        relationships (Exercise 18.4) 378
    beliefs about death (Exercise 18.9)
        387–8
    bereavement, depression and IPT
        359, 361–2
    developing existing and new
        relationships 388–92
    doing things and seeing people again
        (Exercise 18.10) 390
    following your memories and
        tracking the link to depression
        370–2
    grief and mourning 359–60
    Jean's story 17, 37, 41–2, 72–3, 137,
        363–4, 394–408
    managing memories and emotions
        379–81

remembering difficulties in the
        relationship (Exercise 18.6) 381
remembering the bad times as well as
        the good (Exercise 18.5) 379
remembering the time around the
        death 383–5
remembering your relationship 368–9
sketching out the story of your
        relationship (Exercise 18.2) 373–5
thinking about new opportunities
        (Exercise 18.7) 383
thinking about the time of death
        (Exercise 18.8) 385–7
thinking about your memories
        (Exercise 18.1) 371
understanding responses to
        bereavement 360–1
using your timeline 363
what have you lost? 376–7
working out what you have lost
        (Exercise 18.3) 376
your grief story 366–8
guilty, feeling 26, 85, 88, 93, 104, 107,
        234, 238, 239, 240, 243, 244, 248,
        249, 288, 292, 310, 314, 340, 345,
        353, 361, 362, 366, 371, 372, 380,
        382, 389, 403, 404, 405, 406, 468,
        492, 498

Hardy, Barbara 29
Havan, Cindy 22
help someone who is depressed, how
        can you? 500–2
Hemingway, Ernest 170

interpersonal awareness 232, 244–7
interpersonal inventory 147, 148–69,
        176, 291, 292, 293
    beginning to explore your
        relationships (Exercise 9.2) 155–7
    chart for summary notes 160–2,
        165–7
    concentric circles diagram 150–1,
        209, 493
    creating your inventory (Exercise
        9.1) 153–5
    getting an overview of your
        relationship world/creating an
        inventory 150–5
    helpful and unhelpful categories 149
    reviewing your inventory (1): contact
        and routines (Exercise 9.3) 157–8

reviewing your inventory (2): help and support (Exercise 9.4) 158–62
reviewing your inventory (3): interpersonal themes (Exercise 9.5) 163–4
reviewing your inventory (4): overview (Exercise 9.6) 168
spider diagram 152, 494
taking a closer look 155
the characters in your story 148–50
Interpersonal Psychotherapy (IPT) xi, 1, 2
basic aim of 2, 13
best-researched therapies, one of the 27
communication and see communication
exercises see exercises
focal areas 5, 6, 12, 65–7, 72, 75–81, 132, 189, 302, 410, 414, 420, 478, 515
four themes 4–8, 11, 14, 37, 65–7, 170, 251–465
goals see goals
how IPT developed 15–28
importance of interpersonal over the intrapersonal 19, 65
importance of relationships in 16–20
IPT and diagnosis 18
'no blame' approach to diagnosis 111
phases 4–7, 14, 33, 43, 318, 479, 480
pragmatism and 17–18, 27
redirects attention from the unconscious and invisible to the observable and known 18
step by step 9–13
stories and see story and storytelling
team see IPT team
therapy sessions 290–9
time-limited therapy 6–7
what can IPT do for you? 1–14
your interpersonal world 10–11
Role Conflict (theme two) 300–58
active renegotiation 312–13
assessing non-verbal communication (Exercise 16.10) 329
beginning to involve the other person (Exercise 16.2) 315
the big and the small picture 317–18
content 334
context and background 334
ending the relationship 312

filling out the scene (Exercise 16.6) 321–2
gathering information about non-verbal communication (Exercise 16.9) 328–9
getting to the point 330
give and take: negotiating expectations 335–7
how your own conversations unfold (Exercise 16.8) 326–7
identifying non-reciprocal expectations 338
impasse 311–12
incomplete negotiation 310–11
involving the other person 313–15
IPT and interpersonal conflict 302–3
issues and key difficulties 333
making a choice 307
manner 334–5
monitoring your progress 315–17
observing the relationship (Exercise 16.1) 305–6
ongoing process 335
options 338–40
pinpointing the main issues of disagreement (Exercise 16.12) 333
remembering your objectives 307
repeating patterns across relationships 341–3
responding rather than reacting 307–8
the role of communication 319
seeing the big as well as the little picture 307
selecting a relationship to focus on 303–4
setting the scene (Exercise 16.5) 320–1
setting the scene 320–2
starting to observe your relationship (Exercise 16.3) 315–17
Suzanna's story 17, 44–5, 71, 107, 108–9, 136, 235–6, 345–58
the take-home message (Exercise 16.11) 330–2
taking time to observe 304–6
using your network as a resource 340
watching an argument unfold (Exercise 16.7) 325–6
what stage is the dispute at? 309–13
what was said? 323–4
your relationship timeline (Exercise 16.4) 318–19

Isolation, dealing with (theme four)
    73–5, 138–9, 259, 292
  background or foreground difficulty
    415–18
  building up your story of relationship
    difficulty 419–20
  isolation and depression: how closely
    are they connected? (Exercise
    20.1) 419
  learning from what has been difficult
    430–1
  look at what other people do 440–1
  looking at what actually happened
    (Exercise 20.10) 445–7
  looking back over your relationships
    421–3
  looking for poor use of non-verbal
    communication (Exercise 20.9)
    443–4
  looking for the patterns in good
    relationships (Exercise 20.4) 429–30
  looking for the patterns in less
    successful relationships (Exercise
    20.6) 435
  Miranda's story 17, 75, 139, 449–65
  passing and pervasive loneliness
    414–15
  recent examples of relationship
    difficulties 444
  recognizing repeating patterns of
    difficulty in your relationships
    (Exercise 20.7) 438–40
  recurrent relationship difficulties
    410–14
  repeating patterns 437–8
  reviewing less successful relationships
    (Exercise 20.5) 431–3
  reviewing your good relationships
    (Exercise 20.3) 425–8
  successful relationships 423–5
  watching how other people behave
    (Exercise 20.8) 441–2
  when solitude becomes loneliness
    409–10
  which relationships are easier than
    others (Exercise 20.2) 420–1

job:
  changing role in 259
  changing your 171, 409
  leaving 123, 124, 126, 265, 273,
    396–7

  losing 16–17, 40, 68–9, 80, 133, 134,
    140, 141, 174, 179, 181, 183, 184,
    255, 257, 266, 267, 283, 284–5,
    287–99, 498
  redundancy 34, 37, 66, 69–70, 133,
    178, 179, 180, 183, 187, 287–99,
    415
  starting a new 123, 137, 138, 254,
    282, 298, 394, 412

keeping it going 12–13
Klerman, Gerry 15, 362

leading by example 200
life not worth living, thinking 26, 85,
    88, 468, 470, 492
listening deliberately 213–14, 218, 306
Living Life to the Full website 520
loneliness 19, 67, 76, 93, 94, 110, 212,
    278, 300
  passive and pervasive 414–15
  when solitude becomes 409–10
low mood 1, 25, 82–3, 84, 98, 103, 299,
    345, 353, 468, 480, 481, 499, 510

medication 85, 92, 98–100, 102, 103,
    110, 114, 146, 290, 299, 345, 346,
    385, 451, 453, 454, 464, 467,
    473, 484–5, 499, 500, 509–13,
    516, 519
memory 38–9, 83, 85, 89–90, 129, 199,
    262, 264, 268, 324, 359, 368,
    370–2, 381, 392, 405
Meyer, Adolf 16, 17, 18–19, 23
mild depression 86, 91, 95–8, 110, 469,
    473, 482, 499, 513
MIND 517
moderate or severe depression 85, 86,
    90, 95, 98–101, 102, 110, 449,
    467, 469, 499, 500, 511, 513, 516
moodgym 520
moodscope 520
mothers, depression in 514–15
motivation, poor 2, 3, 7, 25, 26, 41,
    70, 75, 83, 88, 96, 106, 120, 189,
    192, 198, 244, 246–7, 285, 288,
    298, 302, 303, 311, 315, 345, 346,
    347, 353, 356, 366, 389, 397, 402,
    405, 439, 449, 483, 492, 510
moving home 123, 126, 412, 418

naps, daytime 2, 3, 88, 395, 399

National Institute of Clinical Excellence (NICE) 517, 519
Nevill, Dorothy 197
NHS 518–19
non-verbal communication 201, 204–5, 212, 214, 220, 221, 222, 223, 328, 329, 439, 441, 442–4, 445, 457

open questions 216–17
overeating 26, 88, 93, 102, 492

paraverbal communication 201, 202–3, 212, 213, 220
Parsons, Talcott 112, 113
passive communication 220
passive aggressive communication 220
past depressions 145–7
patterns:
    attachment 22, 23, 262, 294, 363
    looking for the patterns in good relationships (Exercise 20.4) 429–30
    looking for the patterns in less successful relationships (Exercise 20.6) 435
    recognizing repeating patterns of difficulty in your relationships (Exercise 20.7) 438–40
    repeating relationship 4, 17, 20–5, 74, 92, 101, 102, 109, 157, 171, 210, 301, 302, 303, 304, 307, 310, 311, 314, 316, 334, 340, 341–3, 422, 423, 429–31, 435, 437–40, 444, 445, 446, 447, 448, 453, 454, 456, 457, 458, 459, 461, 462, 463, 464, 468, 482, 483
    sleep 3, 83, 84
peer support 97–8
personal space 208–10, 211
post-natal depression 101–2
post-traumatic stress disorder (PTSD) 102
posture and movement in communication 210–11
pragmatism 2, 17–18
preaching 219
preoccupied attachment 23, 262, 294, 363

Radner, Gilda 122
reasoning brain and the emotional brain 199–201, 205

recovery, your role in your 9–10, 111–21, 509–11
    accepting responsibility to work towards your recovery 116–18
    acknowledging and accepting diagnosis 113–15
    deliberately seeking out anti-depressant activities and 116–17
    diagnosis 18
    giving yourself a break and asking for help (Exercise 7.3) 115–16
    IPT team and 116
    less interest in people and activities 116–17
    negotiating around illness: using your story 112–13
    thinking about the consequences of accepting your (Exercise 7.2) 115
    thinking about the effects of depression on you and others (Exercise 7.1) 112
    what can you do straight away to start making opportunities for improvement? (Exercise 7.4) 118
    you and your IPT team 118–21
redundancy 34, 37, 66, 69–70, 133, 178, 179, 180, 183, 187, 287–99, 415
relapse of depression 483–5, 502–3
relationships:
    break-ups 21, 123, 136, 190, 193, 259, 267–8, 279–80, 345–58
    'dance' 21–2
    difficulty in making 17
    patterns in 20–5, 74, 431, 439, 447
    uncertainty in 17, 44, 136
relaxation exercises 146
research, what it says 509–16
resilience 24, 25, 28, 242, 361, 486, 520
retirement 1, 41, 66, 80, 81, 263, 270–1, 274, 275, 277, 311, 396, 400
reviewing your progress and planning for the future 466–86
    a look back over the whole IPT process (Exercise 22.8) 478–9
    assessing your overall progress towards overcoming depression (Exercise 22.3) 471–2
    comparing your depression symptoms before and after IPT (Exercise 22.2) 469–71
    dealing with setbacks in progress (Exercise 22.4) 472–4

looking at goals that have been hard to reach (Exercise 22.7) 476–7

planning to cope with a possible return of depression (Exercise 22.10) 483–5

reviewing progress towards your goals (Exercise 22.6) 475–6

reviewing your team for the future (Exercise 22.9) 479–83

the role of involving other people in your recovery (Exercise 22.5) 474–5

what have you learned about depression? (Exercise 22.1) 467

Role Change, managing (theme one) 68–70, 251–86

are there any ways you can change this picture now? 261

building a balanced story of the past 264–5

building bridges between past and present 269

change as a process not an event 285–6

change brought about by someone else 257

creating a timeline for your old role (Exercise 14.5) 268

the destabilizing effect of the change on other relationships and supports 256–7

examining the nature of the change and your use of support (Exercise 14.9) 274–6

examining your support at a time of change (Exercise 14.8) 273

feelings at the moment of change (Exercise 14.10) 277–9

focusing on the change itself (Exercise 14.7) 272–3

general stability and competing demands 257–60

getting help to fill out the story of the old role (Exercise 14.3) 266

how did the change happen? 271–2

how do you feel about your new role? (Exercise 14.11) 281–2

how you felt then and how you feel now 276–7

looking at new routines (Exercise 14.12) 282

looking at new skills (Exercise 14.13) 283–4

looking at the benefits of role change (Exercise 14.14) 284

looking for continuity (Exercise 14.6) 269–70

monitoring your progress 261

Paul's story 16–17, 37, 69–70, 132, 134, 141, 142, 143, 145, 174, 175, 176, 177, 180–1, 183–5, 287–99

role 251–3

the significance of the role you lost 255–6

thinking over the old role (Exercise 14.4) 266–7

transition 251, 253–5

what support is available to you in facing changes? (Exercise 14.1) 257

where are you stuck? 261–4

the wider context of change (Exercise 14.2) 260

Roosevelt, Theodore 187

Royal College of Psychiatrists 519

Russell, Bertrand 1

Rutter, Michael 23–4

sadness 82, 84, 86, 88, 107, 230, 236, 248, 267, 277, 296, 345, 360, 361, 384, 390, 468, 480, 492

Samaritans 91, 518

seasonal affective disorder (SAD) 102

secure attachment 23

self-confidence, low 26, 450, 466

self-esteem 26, 88, 189, 466

self-help 47, 87, 95, 96, 97, 110, 411, 471, 473, 478, 499, 502, 520

severe depression 85, 86, 92, 95, 98–101, 102, 110, 449, 467, 469, 499, 500, 511, 513, 516

sex, interest in 26, 88

Shaver, Phil 22

sleep, difficulties with 2–3, 18, 26, 83, 84, 86, 88, 89, 93, 98, 102, 106, 130, 183, 288, 298, 299, 305, 321, 322, 346, 360, 395, 397, 407, 439, 468, 470, 481, 492, 498, 510

social life 75, 85, 164, 259, 291–2, 293, 383, 456, 499

staying on track 12

staying well 511–14, 516

stories:
    anti-plot and 32
    basics of 40–9

characters 47–8
dealing with grief and loss 72–3
dealing with isolation 73–5
difficulties in telling your 37–9
drawing others into 36–7
focal areas, questions and concerns about 75–81
how do stories help us to remember and understand? 34–6
key words 36
language we use in 35–6
managing role change 68–70
managing role conflict 70–1
memory and 38–9, 83, 85, 89–90, 128
objectives and strategies 68–75
point of view 46–7
recovering from depression by narrative 29–30
scene 48–9
sense of direction and 34–5
storyboard 43–4, 45
storytelling and the brain: a dance for two 33–4
structure 42–5
themes 36, 40–2
thinking about your own story 42
types of story 35
understanding the story of your depression 122–47
what is your story about? 10, 65–81
why do I need a story at all? 31
why they are so important? 29–50
you cannot imagine anyone would want to hear your story 39, 52
you cannot remember your story 38–9, 52
you do not know how to tell your story 38, 52
you do not want to tell your story 38, 52
storytelling, practicing 51–64
step one: choosing your story 53–4
step two: putting the pieces together 54–8
step three: telling your story 58–63
step four: reviewing the exercise 63–4
think of a brief story about yourself 52–3
Storycraft (Hart) 40
sub-threshold depression 86, 95, 103, 469

suicide 85, 91, 93, 362, 384, 468, 518
Sullivan, Harry Stack 15, 16, 19, 20, 23, 230, 249
symptoms of depression:
biology and 25–7
clustering of 26, 83, 86
comparing your depression symptoms before and after IPT (Exercise 22.2) 469–71
core symptoms 84, 468
exploring the links between your relationships and (Exercise 6.3) 109–10
how symptoms can become intertwined in a self-perpetuating sequence 4
identifying your (Exercise 6.1) 87–90
interpersonal inventory and 148, 149, 168
links between relationships and 2, 4, 5, 6, 13, 18, 48, 104–10, 495–6
list of 26, 84–90, 468
monitoring links between relationships and 495–6
monitoring your progress and 261, 315, 343, 495–6
organizing your story and 173, 174
rating your 89
recognizing 9
thinking about the links between relationships and (Exercise 6.2) 104–9
timeline and 125, 127, 129, 130, 135, 137, 142, 143
why bother monitoring? 94–5
your weekly rating form 491–2
see also under individual symptom description or name

talking therapy 27, 100–1, 102, 103, 110, 499, 511, 513, 516
talking to friends and family, not 280, 290
team, your IPT xi–xii, 8–9, 51, 118–21, 182–3, 185
building up the picture 120
choosing your 120–1
communication and 228–9
companionship and 119
examining your support at a time of change and 273
goal setting and 192–3

monitoring progress 120
practical help 120
practising communication with 228–9
self-help and 96
symptoms 105, 107, 109
talking through responses with 3, 105, 109, 154, 205, 229, 265, 270, 273, 278, 286, 318, 320, 322, 326, 327, 329, 331, 333, 338, 342, 343, 366, 369, 372, 373, 377, 379, 383, 385, 387, 388, 390, 392, 420, 425, 438, 439, 442, 447, 467, 470, 472, 473, 474, 477, 479, 480, 483
telling them about your experience of depression 89
thinking about putting your team together 8–9
watching an argument unfold and 326
you and your 118–19
timelines 174, 288, 289
change or 'role transition' and 133–4
conflict and 134–6
context and 126
creating 10, 16, 27, 43, 44, 45, 268
creating a timeline for your old role (Exercise 14.5) 268
depression in the past and 145–7
drawing your own 129–34
how do timelines work? 122–4
isolation and 138–9
loss and grief 136–7
memories and 379
preparing to make your own 125–6
reviewing relationships 425, 426

sketching out the timeline of your story (Exercise 3.2) 45
story of symptoms and 125
the three stages of 126–7
using 363–4
who can help you construct your? 129
your relationship timeline (Exercise 16.4) 318–19
tiredness 26, 84, 468 see also fatigue
touch, communication and 211–12
treatments:
    IPT see Interpersonal Psychotherapy
    IPT compared with other 509–14
    options 95–101, 499–500
    see also under individual treatment name

unnoticed depression 90
useful links and contact details 517–20
using support from the people around you 8–9

vulnerability to depression 18–19, 23, 24, 44–5, 66, 126, 138, 146, 179, 180, 181, 198, 256, 258, 260, 288, 348, 411, 416, 498, 514, 520

'The Whole Story' (workshop) 51
withdrawal 2, 71, 100, 136, 165, 179, 198, 232, 293, 294–5, 351, 356, 365, 389, 399, 408, 439, 465, 482
working long hours 69–70, 134, 142, 287–99, 450
Wounded Storyteller, The (Frank) 34

Zen and the Art of Motorcycle Maintenance (Pirsig) 188